Longevity

Books by Kenneth R. Pelletier, Ph.D.

Mind as Healer, Mind as Slayer/
A Holistic Approach to Preventing Stress Disorders

Toward a Science of Consciousness

Holistic Medicine/
From Stress to Optimum Health

Longevity/
Fulfilling Our Biological Potential

Longevity

Fulfilling Our Biological Potential

Kenneth R. Pelletier, Ph.D.

A Merloyd Lawrence Book
Delta / Seymour Lawrence

A MERLOYD LAWRENCE BOOK
A Delta/Seymour Lawrence Edition
Published by
Dell Publishing Co., Inc.
1 Dag Hammarskjold Plaza
New York, New York 10017

ACKNOWLEDGMENTS

Excerpts adapted from Henrik L. Blum, "Proposal to National Advisory Council on Economic Opportunity," 1978. Used by permission of the author.

Excerpts from Ng, L.K.Y., Davis, D. L. and Manderscheid, R. W.: The Health Promotion Organization: A Practical Intervention Designed to Promote Healthy Living Public Health Reports, Vol. 93, No. 5, September–October 1978, pp. 446–455. Used by permission.

Excerpt from "The Mechanics of Aging" by B. L. Strehler, March 1979, pp. 34–35. Reprinted by permission of Body Forum Magazine.

Excerpt from DOCTOR ZHIVAGO by Boris Pasternak, translated by Max Hayward and Manya Harara, revised translation by Bernard Guilbert Guerney. Copyright © 1958 by Pantheon Books, Inc. Reprinted by permission of Pantheon Books, a Division of Random House, Inc., and Collins Publishers.

Excerpt from "Informed Consent May Be Hazardous to Your Health" by E. F. Loftus and J. F. Fries, Center for Advanced Study in Behavioral Sciences, Stanford, California 94305, Science, Vol. 204, p. 11, 6 April 1979. Copyright 1979 by the American Association for the Advancement of Science. Used by permission of the American Association for the Advancement of Science and the authors.

Excerpts from "Boosting Our Healing Potential" adapted from Science Year, The World Book Science Annual. © 1974 Field Enterprises Educational Corporation. Used by permission.

Excerpt from "Why Do Women Live Longer Than Men?" reprinted by permission from Social Science & Medicine, July–August 1976, 10 (7–8), 349–362. Copyright 1976, Pergamon Press, Ltd.

Excerpt from "The Potential Impact of Sexual Equality on Health" by C. E. Lewis and M. A. Lewis reprinted by permission of The New England Journal of Medicine, 207 (16), 863–869, 1977.

Excerpt from "The Mortality of Swedish and U.S. White Males: A comparison of experience" by R. D. Tomasson. Reprinted by permission from American Journal of Public Health, October 1976, 66 (10), 968–974.

Excerpt from "Logical Bases for Action in Nutrition and Aging" by Donald Watkin reprinted by permission of the American Geriatrics Society from American Geriatrics Society Journal, May 1978, 26 (5), pp. 193–202.

Excerpt from "The Relationship of Physical Activity to Coronary Heart Disease and Life Expectancy" by A. S. Leon and H. Blackburn reprinted by permission from Annals of the New York Academy of Sciences, 1977, 301, 561–578.

Excerpt from "Non-Medical Intervention in Life and Death" by R. A. Kalish reprinted by permission from Social Science & Medicine, December 1970, 4 (6), 655–665. Copyright 1970, Pergamon Press, Ltd.

Delta ® TM 755118, Dell Publishing Co., Inc.

ISBN: 0-440-55016-5

Reprinted by arrangement with Delacorte Press/Seymour Lawrence

Printed in the United States of America

First Delta printing—November 1982

To R. James Yandell, M.D., Ph.D.
A friend of genuine humility and quiet wisdom

Published by arrangement with
Robert Briggs Associates, San Francisco

ACKNOWLEDGMENTS

Longevity represents one aspect of the biological potential of the human species which is now being helped toward fulfillment in the many forms of planetary ecology, state and national government programs emphasizing health maintenance, equal rights for women, programs in major corporations to enhance the health of their employees, and the empowerment of individuals to assume greater responsibility for their lives as well as their collective social and biological evolution. Each of these many forms of the transformation of humankind is embodied by the many friends and colleagues who have inspired and guided this present work. Most of all, the inspiration for *Longevity* grew from the love and concern of Elizabeth Anne Berryhill to understand this precious gift of life. Throughout the last five years Robert Briggs, Seymour Lawrence, and Merloyd Lawrence have given so generously of their support and encouragement to make this quest a reality. Rather than relegating the profound transformations of humankind to the realm of abstractions, a group of clinicians including R. James Yandell, M.D., Ph.D., Norman S. Tresser, M.D., and Sadja Greenwood, M.D., have formed a clinic where we have sought to manifest these ideals in our practices and daily lives. Ultimately it is the lives of those we love the most which demonstrate to us the highest ideals of human life. My parents, Roger N. Pelletier and Lucy B. Pelletier, and my oldest friends, Arthur M. Young and Ruth Forbes Young, have been special companions through these many lifetimes. For this I am most thankful.

During this period of transformation we are fortunate that there are visionary individuals who can see beyond the present flux to map the unexplored terrain of the future, and it has been a great inspiration to work with and learn from the insights of Gregory Bateson, Governor Jerry Brown, Norman Cousins, and Hans Selye, M.D., Ph.D., in many ways and many times. Out of the shared altruism which is the basis for these transformations of every aspect of human life in individual, social, spiritual, corporate, political, economic, and planetary dimensions, there are numerous friends and colleagues who have undertaken the formidable task of translating these visionary ideals into pragmatic form. I am most grateful for the friendship of Bruce Africa, M.D., Ph.D., Robert O. Becker, M.D., Arthur Blaustein, Doug Boyd, David E. Bresler, Ph.D., James R. Brown, M.D., Fritjof Capra, Ph.D., Rick Carlson, J.D., Cosme and Clara Castanieto, Leonard J. Duhl, M.D., Ken Dychtwald, Ph.D., Tom Ferguson, M.D., Dan Goleman, Ph.D., James S. Gordon, M.D., Joseph B. Helms, M.D., Joe Kamiya, Ph.D., Peter M. Litchfield, Ph.D., Sheldon Margen, M.D., John R. O'Neil, Mike Samuels, M.D., C. Norman Shealy, M.D., Ph.D., O. Carl Simonton, M.D., and David S. Sobel, M.D., who have worked with compassion in this period of great transformation. Finally, the research and preparation of this manuscript was possible only through the efforts of Natale Heiffetz, Lee Peake, and the loving encouragement of Frances Wilcox and her wonderful smile.

A world view based on Newtonian mechanics, separate and isolatable parts, hierarchies of power and authority, ecological and economic exploitation, and lack of respect for future generations is undergoing a profound transformation with effects on every aspect of planetary institutions and evolution. Out of this metamorphosis is emerging a planetary culture based on a view of the human species and environment as a unity of interacting and inseparable components, emphasis on voluntary simplicity, movement toward alternative energy sources independent of petrochemical subjugation, restoration of a balance between material and spiritual values, and relationships based on mutual trust and compassion. These are not philosophical speculations but represent a fundamental undercurrent of change that is frequently misunderstood or underestimated and yet is evident in individual lifestyle changes, corporate health programs, national and state government programs on health promotion, emphasis on environmental protection from petrochemical and radiation hazards, and a thousand other manifestations of the emergence of a new age-consciousness. We are in a period of metamorphosis, a period of shedding old forms in order to manifest the highest biological and visionary ideals of the human species. That is the vocation for us all at the turn of the twenty-first century.

Kenneth R. Pelletier
San Francisco, California
April 1980

CONTENTS

Longevity

ONE

Our Psychobiological Potential

Sumerian legend proclaims that the god-king Larke lived to be 28,800 years old. Chronicled in the Bible are such lesser records of longevity as Methuselah, who lived to be 969, Noah, who died at 950, and Abraham, who was a virtual adolescent when he took Sarah as his wife at the age of 90 and fathered Isaac at 100. Among more recent records is the unauthenticated report of an Englishman named Thomas Parr who was reputed to have died in 1635 at the age of 152 and been buried in Westminster Abbey. From the postmortem examination the English physician William Harvey, author of *Exercitatio de Motu Cordis,* concluded that Parr had died following a major dietary change in interaction with the foul London air when he was brought from Shropshire County to be presented to Charles I. Parr had been brought to London by Thomas, Earl of Arundel, who then made Parr a domestic to his family. During this employment Parr was "fed high and drank plentifully of the best wines, by which, after a constant plain, and homely diet, the natural functions of the parts of his body were overcharged, his lungs obstructed, and the habit of the whole body quite disordered; in consequence, there could not but speedily ensue a dissolution. If he had not changed his diet, he might possibly have lived many years longer" (Easton, 1799). Easton's conclusions were based upon his book *Human Longevity,* which contained published anecdotes of 1,712 individuals who had lived at least one hundred years between A.D. 66 and 1799. Although the volume is laden with Puritanical admonishments, Easton did enumerate factors contributing to the longevity of these people as well as point out the interaction between specific habits and practices and extended life expectancy. Other unauthenticated claims include 145 years of age for Norway's Christian Drakenberg and 256 years for China's Li Ching-yun. Authenticated reports include those of Ramazan Alikishiev, Soviet Master of Medicine and author of more than sixty papers on gerontology. He reported in 1972 that the oldest man in Russia as of 1970 was Shirali Mislimov at 165 years and the oldest woman, Ashura Omarova at 195 years (Novosti Press Agency, 1970). Alikishiev also pointed out that the oldest individuals whose ages could be authenticated were Said Musavi of Iran at 190 and a 203-year-old woman, Makarnajo, who still worked in her native Bolivia.

Among the records of long life in the *Guinness Book of World Records* (McWhirter, 1978) are those of a French-Canadian bootmaker named Pierre Joubert, who died at age 113, and an American named John Sailing, who died in 1959 at age 113. Most recently, a former slave named Charlie Smith, who was verified as the oldest person in the United States, died on October 7, 1979, at age 137. Aside from these isolated instances there is extensive documentation from certain geographic regions of the planet of ethnic groups whose members have been reported to live to great age at optimum levels of health. This is an area of great complexity due to incomplete and conflicting evidence and is considered in detail in Chapter VIII. Evidence of extreme longevity is not a phenomenon limited to rural and inaccessible regions of the planet. According to the evidence garnered by Representative Claude Pepper in congressional hearings, the number of centenarians in the United States has risen from under 3,000 in 1969 to over 10,000, according to the most recent census (Pepper, 1979). Since longevity has been in evidence throughout recorded history, and in diverse cultures, this is an indication that it is a latent biological potential of the human species. While longevity may be more evident in certain regions than others, the fact that it is clearly not limited to such areas is a confirmation of its potential occurrence anywhere. Among the centenarian locales are the small kingdom of Hunza in northwestern Kashmir, the Vilcabamba in the Andes region of Ecuador, and the Abkhazian Republic lying between the Black Sea and the Caucasus in the Soviet Union (Leaf, 1977). Such observations and research usually have been relegated to the status of idle curiosities, but in fact they are of great significance for the future of the human species.

The Search for Longevity

Throughout recorded history issues of longevity have been the central concern of virtually all social orders, and this concern extends into the present age with a renewed interest focused upon the rapidly growing elderly populations. From the *Egyptian Book of the Dead* (Evans-Wentz, Jr., 1960) to the epic film, *2001: A Space Odyssey,* the horizon of immortality has intrigued humankind as much as the distant galaxies. Every history primer recounts the quest of Ponce de León, who devoted a major portion of his life to a search for the Fountain of Youth. Postrevolutionary American newspapers and magazines carried abundant anecdotes about extreme longevity. Increased life extension in the new world was generally equated with health, solid morals, and the ease of earning a living (Estes, 1976). Books concerning various means of attaining great age were in great demand in the late eighteenth century, and Luigi Cornaro's classic *Probable Way of Attaining a Long and Healthful Life,* published in the 1500s, was in wide circulation after being reprinted in Portsmouth, Rhode Island, in 1788. Another early attempt in 1788 to conduct an objective inquiry into this phenomenon was conducted by Brissot de Warville, who noted the greater life expectancy for graduates of Harvard University no matter what their geographic location. From this he concluded, "one can logically induce the causes of longevity: regularity of morals, an enlightened mind, independence of spirit, and freedom from want" (Brissot de Warville, 1964). Although his observations were more poetic than predictive, researchers are conducting similar lines of inquiry with essentially similar conclusions at the present time. Faust and Dorian Gray were variants of the same theme, and in Aldous Huxley's *After Many a Summer Dies the Swan* the physician protagonist succeeds in reversing the aging process with tragic consequences. The limits to longevity, however, have always been evident: "The days of our years are threescore years and ten; and if by reason of strength they be fourscore years, yet is their strength labour and sorrow" (Psalm 90). Two thousand years later the United States Public Health Service echoes this limit by noting that an American born in 1974 will live to be 71.9 years old. Life expectancy has been dramatically shorter at various periods of history, with the average life expectancy in ancient Greece being 22 and, for an American born in 1800, only 48 (Greenblatt, 1977). Some researchers have concluded that the biological limit of longevity has been attained by the human species at "threescore and ten." To others it is increasingly evident that 70 years of age is not a limit and that the biological potential of the human species is considerably longer.

Despite this intense interest in the subject for thousands of years, over every continent and among all peoples, there has been little progress in unraveling the eternal mystery of longevity until quite recently. Perhaps the first attempt to address longevity as a physiological concern rather than a purely philosophical conundrum was undertaken in the last century by the pioneering French neurologist Jean Martin Charcot, who declared, "Life is a vital force of limited duration." This thesis gradually evolved to become the basis for the study of the physiological processes of aging. It is important to note here a distinction between longevity and aging. Although the two realms of inquiry obviously overlap to a considerable degree, the focus is somewhat different. Aging research has tended to stress the biological and psychosocial causes of aging within the prescribed limit of "threescore and ten." Such research generally falls into four main areas: genetic endowment, cellular processes, nutrition, and environmental influences. Traditionally, the processes investigated have concentrated on the progressive decline in structure and function of the adult; the nature of the senile state as differentiated from other disease states; and the processes whereby progressive loss of structure and function become incompatible with continued life and lead to death.

By contrast, longevity research focuses on the biological and psychosocial potential of the human species to achieve an extended life expectancy and to remain in optimum health. This distinction is extremely important throughout this entire book, which addresses three separate but related areas: (1) aging, which is concerned with the degenerative processes of aging as well as any biological or psychosocial rejuvenation programs initiated late in life (Luce, 1979); (2) the attempt to attain the present maximum life expectancy in sound health, which is the orientation of holistic medicine; and (3) longevity, which includes the previous two areas but explores the variables which extend the quantity of life beyond a century.

According to gerontologist Alex Comfort, "We do know that biological interference with the life-span is already practicable in rodents using relatively simple dietary and chemical means. It seems likely that similar means would increase the human life-span by 10–20 percent" (Comfort, 1970). While these percentages might appear to be small, the fact that they represent seven to fourteen years of human life lends great significance. Also of consequence is the timetable for such progress: "It seems justified to assume that by 1990 we shall know of an experimentally efficacious way to prolong vigorous life by about 20 percent; that the agents involved will be simple and cheap and will not depend on elaborate intensive-care units, large physical apparatus, or transplant of major organs" (Comfort, 1970). These two statements suggest that we may achieve a long-lived, healthy population prior to the end of this century without reliance upon the present ubiquitous and cost-effective system of biomedical technology. They raise the possibility of individual, institutional, social, and economic transformations of a major magnitude. Conservative estimates of the capacity to extend life expectancy range between 10 and 20 percent; more speculative but equally well-founded projections result in even more extraordinary implications. Bear in mind that the figure of 10 to 20 percent is based upon the immediate application of the now commonplace results of laboratory and clinical research of ten to forty years ago. Given any further discoveries, which are more likely than not, the projections of the biological potential range from 110, as noted in the regular "Cobb's [S. Cobb of *JAMA*] Column" (1977) of the *Journal of the American Medical Association,* to 120, according to physician Walter Bortz of the Stanford University School of Medicine (Bortz, 1978). While some of the interventions needed to produce such a pronounced life extension must be introduced at a specific critical stage in the development of an organism, others can be introduced at any stage of life with considerable efficacy.

In a youth- and material-fixated culture, the quest for longevity can readily be reduced to sensationalism and exploitation, already unfortunately evident. If extension of the next biomedical industry is not to become cloning, cryogenics, and revitalization centers, then some fundamental issues need to be considered. The excesses and abuses of such an approach have been documented in *Who Should Play God?* by Ted Howard and Jeremy Rifkin (1977). These dramatic and expensive developments tend to make us overlook the fact that there are relatively simple procedures by which extended longevity can become a reality for anyone who is now reading these words.

Quality of Life

Perhaps more pertinent than the quest for physical immortality is the very real possibility of vanquishing the physical toll of passing time. The means by which to maintain vigor and health into a late age remain an enormous frontier to be explored. Today it is certain, according to Joel Kurtzman and Philip Gordon in *No More Dying,* that "we are without doubt—for good or bad—at the gate of a new era, when *Homo sapiens* will be medically transformed into *Homo longevus.* . . . If this is so, it demands an entirely new perception of life" (1977). There are no miraculous elixirs to prevent aging or to revitalize prematurely aging individuals, but there are definite means to slow down the process. The principles defined in *Holistic Medicine: From Stress to Optimum Health* (Pelletier, 1979) that determine the quality of life are the very same ones, with relatively minor but important modifications, that play the most significant role in achieving our biological potential. Essentially this is an ecological model of longevity where the focus is on interacting systems rather than a pharmaceutical, biomedical, or surgical panacea. Virtually every aspect of contemporary life is concerned with choices between conservation of resources versus continued consumption with the promise of technological breakthroughs to avoid dire consequences. That attitude also characterizes the predominant orientation toward longevity which ignores the need to adopt certain measures immediately after birth and continue them throughout adult development. Pharmaceuticals and technological innovations will undoubtedly play a role, but their capacity to extend life is no greater than their capacity, acknowledged to be quite limited, to achieve and sustain health in a given population. Noted aging researcher Zhores A. Medvedev of the National Institute for Medical Research in London has clearly stated that "neither a single unified theory of aging nor a simple method to control the rate of aging and longevity is considered possible . . . increasing the human life-span in the future can be envisaged, but not a longevity revolution connected with some kind of simple biochemical or environmental interference" (Medvedev, 1973). Holistic medicine has emerged as a powerful social force. Its realms of application are expressed cogently by Aaron Wildavsky, Dean of Public Policy at the University of California, Berkeley:

> According to the Great Equation, medical care equals health. But the Great Equation is wrong. More available medical care does not equal better health. The best estimates are that the medical system (doctors, drugs, hospitals) affects about 10% of the usual indices for measuring health: whether you live at all (infant mortality), how well you live (days lost due to sickness), how long you live (adult mortality). The remaining 90% are determined by factors over which doctors have little or no control, from individual lifestyle (smoking, exercise, worry) to social conditions (income, eating habits, physiological inheritance), to the physical environment (air and water quality). Most of the bad things that happen to people are at present beyond the reach of medicine [Wildavsky, 1977].

Increasingly there is a recognition that morbidity and mortality relate more to psychosocial and environmental factors than to the quality of the medical care system per se. Those same factors appear to have as profound an impact upon the quantity of life as upon the quality. This is not to deny or denigrate current research concerning recombinant DNA or reversing the cellular processes related to aging but rather to emphasize the importance of applying available knowledge until the messianic pharmaceutical does emerge from the laboratory. One of the greatest psychological impediments to a comprehensive system of health care focused on optimum health and longevity is the search for a magical external agent which would resolve complex diseases and conditions with nothing more than passive compliance on the part of the individual. Heroic measures to prolong life after catastrophic illness has already occurred will create only an ever more infirm and growing elderly population. What is needed is not more crisis care facilities but a systematic and sustained program of prevention to insure both the quantity and quality of life. Recognizing this pressing need is physician Lorenz K. Y. Ng of the National Institute of Drug Abuse: "Even beyond the elderly, the prospect of having increasing numbers of individuals who may be prematurely chronically ill and impaired but nevertheless will have many years of life before them, raises questions about the quality of life which our concepts of health must begin to take into account . . . . Prevention, too, represents only one side of the total health equation. The prevention of disease must be linked also to the promotion of positive health strategies" (Ng et al., 1979). Concern for longevity cannot start at an advanced age. A fundamental revision of health care is called for, from pathology management to health promotion.

Speculations concerning longevity would be relegated to philosophical speculation or the annals of science fiction if it were not for their eminently pragmatic implications. There is virtually unanimous agreement among researchers that if both cardiovascular disease and cancer, the two leading causes of morbidity and mortality, were completely eliminated today, the overall life expectancy as a whole would increase by less than seven years. For those individuals over 70, the expectation would increase much less . . . at one and a half to two years. According to Leonard Hayflick, one of the most outstanding researchers in longevity, this startling conclusion is due to the fact that

> The common impression that modern medicine has lengthened the human life-span is not supported by either vital statistics or

biological evidence . . . accomplishments in medicine and public health, however, have merely extended the *average* [emphasis in original] life expectancy by allowing more people to reach the upper limit, which for the general run of mankind still seems to be approximately the Biblical fourscore years [Hayflick, June 1978].

Before truly extended longevity can be attained, we need a deeper understanding of the biological and psychosocial processes related to aging.

Aging and Disease

Every major disease is age-dependent. In the case of the human species, after the age of 30 there is a steady and inexorable increase in the probability of morbidity and mortality from one disease or another. This probability doubles about every eight years as a person grows older. Both the phenomenon of aging and of the development of disease appear to be related to more fundamental disruption occurring at the cellular level. Although it is not possible to make definitive statements about causation, it is increasingly evident that the progressive degeneration of aging is a precursor to the development of increasingly severe disorders. Once a disorder is manifest, it places increased strain upon the organism, thus accelerating the degenerative process in a downward spiral.

In attempting to stem this decline an ironic situation has developed which has been termed "the failures of success" by Ernest M. Gruenberg of the Johns Hopkins University School of Hygiene and Public Health. Gruenberg and other analysts noted that a major innovation in medicine occurred in 1936. In that year a group of investigators with a small grant from the Rockefeller Foundation were searching for a cure for puerperal fever and discovered sulfanilamide. Sulfa drugs with their antibacterial potency had a remarkable effect in curtailing pneumonia, which had been the most frequent terminal infectious disease. At the same time, the clinical trials methodology was developed in 1937 by Professor A. Bradford

Hill, and together the sulfas plus improved clinical trials accelerated the elimination of certain terminal disorders. However, "these new techniques did not cure the chronic diseases, nor did they prevent them in the next patient" (Gruenberg, 1977). As the bacterial diseases were curtailed the incidence of the "afflictions of civilization" were both more evident and actually increasing due to increased stress, inappropriate nutrition, inadequate physical activity, and environmental deterioration. But faith in biomedical approaches was undaunted. If in its infancy such an approach could cure pneumonia, diphtheria, and smallpox, then in its maturity it should certainly be able to cure cardiovascular disease and cancer.

Despite the myriad fallacies in this assumption, it has become the rationalization for the predominance of the biomedical model until recent years, as well as the justification for enormous research and technological investments by individuals and government alike. Among the most articulate analysts of these erroneous assumptions is Thomas McKeown, Professor of Social Medicine at the University of Birmingham in England and author of *The Role of Medicine* (1979). In this revised edition of his earlier book, McKeown clearly demonstrates that in the instances of tuberculosis, pneumonia, tetanus, measles, scarlet fever, and pertussis or whooping cough, all had declined to within 10 percent or less of their high incidence prior to any medical intervention. According to McKeown, "The improvement of health during the past three centuries was due essentially to provision of food, protection from hazards, and limitation of numbers." In a more recent article McKeown goes on to say, "If health is determined essentially by nutrition, personal behavior and the quality of the environment, then it is clearly desirable to reconsider the role and responsibilities of medicine in relation to such influences" (McKeown, 1980). By their very nature the chronic, degenerative "afflictions of civilization," "the modern plagues," or "diseases of affluence" are often too extensive or advanced to be reversed by the time they are detectable. As the elderly over 65 increase, both the percentage and absolute numbers of individuals manifesting these disorders increases. Moreover, "the net effect of successful technical innovations used in disease control has been to raise the prevalence of certain diseases and disabilities by prolonging their average duration" (Gruenberg, 1977).

All of the major causes of death and disability appear to be secondary to the progressive degeneration of aging. This situation was foreseen by pioneering physician Sir William Osler, who termed pneumonia "the old man's friend." Nowadays many individuals who would have died survive, but with extremely impaired functions. Again, Osler observed in his classic 1904 textbook, *The Principles and Practice of Medicine,* that "There is truth in the paradoxical statement that persons rarely die of the disease with which they suffer. Secondary *terminal* [emphasis in original] infections carry off many patients with incurable disease" (Osler, 1935). Only one pathway seems to lead out of this cruel dilemma of protracted suffering due to the success of certain medical interventions and that is to turn attention toward the processes underlying both the "afflictions of civilization" and longevity.

To stem these modern plagues and extend human life both preventive measures and the establishment of optimum health practices are necessary. This point is succinctly stated by Ernest M. Gruenberg:

> Now that we recognize that our life-saving technology of the past four decades has outstripped our health-preserving technology and that the net effect has been to worsen the people's health, we must begin the search for preventable causes of the chronic illnesses which we have been extending. . . . We will not move forward in enhancing health until we make the prevention of nonfatal chronic illness our top research priority [Gruenberg, 1977].

Although this statement is addressed to chronic, degenerative disease, it also holds true for the underlying dimension of these disorders, which is the aging process itself.

It is interesting to note that in terms of etymology the Greek and Anglo-Saxon roots for health are both totally unrelated to all the words for disease, disorder, illness, or sickness. The same clear distinction must hold between holistic medicine and the many techniques for pathology management. There is a plethora of ostensibly "holistic" approaches to health care which actually conform to older models, including assessments of malabsorption, diagnostic analysis of hair specimens, or intravenous chelation. A vast range of such technical innovations was noted in a survey published in the first issue of *American Holistic Medicine,* the official journal of the American Holistic Medical Association (1979). Although these approaches may be commendable, they tend to place holistic medicine back into the realm of diagnosis and treatment of pathology rather than the promotion of optimum health and longevity. Health is not a subspecialty of medicine. The next chapter will address these issues, but the main point here is that any pathology-oriented approach to longevity will ultimately fail due to its inherent limitations.

The fallacies of this approach have been pointed out by Johan Bjorksten, a leading theoretician in the area of longevity and an industrial chemist with the Bjorksten Research Foundation in Madison, Wisconsin. As a chemist his approach to longevity is pragmatic, his goal clear-cut: "To give as many people as possible as many more healthy vigorous years of life as possible" (1971). By reducing the incidence of the afflictions of civilization to a series of charts, Bjorksten concludes, "We see here that every one of the major diseases tabulated is age-dependent. To attack the problems of these diseases separately, as is now the preponderant course of action, is akin to trying to stop a hemorrhage by closing all of the capillary vessels separately rather than ligating the main artery" (1971). Directing research, whether it is purely biomedical or nominally holistic, toward specific disorders rather than toward the underlying cause or causes is a shortsighted and archaic orientation. Echoing this important point is Richard G. Cutler of the Institute for Molecular Biology at the University of Texas in Dallas: "There are only a few major disease processes that are now identified as being the major causes of death in man. . . . Much medical research has been focused on obtaining an understanding of these disease processes. However, the importance of these diseases to the overall health and longevity of the general population is frequently overemphasized and the importance of the general aging process ignored" (Cutler, 1976). Or as Bjorksten concludes, "The old fields have been plowed over and over" (1971) and there is a definite tendency to repeat old, dysfunctional patterns with only the semantics being changed. This point cannot be overemphasized, because critical choices are being made and will continue to be made regarding the future directions of medical research. With limited resources available, the resulting decisions are not medical as much as they are ethical and economic.

The Fastest Growing Minority

Virtually no one is opposed to the humanitarian ideal of improving the health and longevity of humankind, although there is bitter disagreement on how that is to be achieved. A consequence of emphasizing prevention and improving the quality of life is to increase further the number of elderly people in the United States. Since 1950 the population of the United States has doubled while the number of people over 60 has grown eight times. Shortly after the turn of the twenty-first century almost one third of the entire population of the United States will be over the age of 60. If the present low birthrates continue, this means that there will be almost 29 million older individuals over 65, or every ninth person. Even if our society does not concern itself with the quality of life, it does react to the social and economic pressures of the sheer quantity of people represented by a large minority. As the postwar baby boom has moved through the American culture, it has had a disproportionate influence, and soon that same large and vocal minority will be growing old with the potential for considerable political and economic influence. Whether or not they exert that influence is open to question. Herman B. Brotman, Assistant to the Commissioner for Statistics and Analysis, Administration on Aging, Department of Health, Education, and Welfare, states:

> It is particularly frustrating irony that progress in man's search for a longer life should produce the "problems" of aging. In fact, the very successes in economic, medical, and industrial "progress" that now permit such a large proportion of our population to reach old age also have produced the changes that make the elderly a generally dependent group and have robbed them of their most important and traditional functions, roles and statuses [Brotman, 1974].

Other interesting facts emerge from a more detailed analysis of population trends. While the over-65 population has grown much more quickly than the rest of the population, the over-75 segment has grown even faster. Furthermore, longevity has increased most markedly for elderly white females, resulting in a large number of widows in this population—and this sex differential has been widening. This trend holds true for males of all ages including prenatal (*Statistical Bulletin,* 1977). There is a great deal to be learned from the male/female differential in mortality, particularly regarding lifestyle, a point which is discussed more fully in Chapter V.

At this point in history the increase in the number and proportion of the older population results primarily from the fact that a much larger proportion of the younger population reaches advanced age rather than from any increase in the upper limit of life expectancy. Actually, "the major part of the gains in life expectancy result from improvements during infancy, childhood, and young adulthood death rates and the control of contagious diseases" (Brotman, 1977). In fact, most of the trend is due to the continuing decline in infant mortality. However, graphs of life expectancy at birth from 1900 to 1970 indicate that biomedical research has already reached a point of diminishing return even in this strong area (Bjorksten, 1971). When epidemiologists search for the factors underlying the decline in infant mortality, it is clear where the predominant influences have come from: "Improvements in health care, nutrition, sanitation, and other aspects of daily life over the three quarters of a century since 1900 have added almost 24 years to life expectancy at birth" (Brotman, 1977).

New Priorities

Statistical analyses and projections of life expectancy can be extremely misleading. As one example, Weldon J. Walker of the editorial board of the *Journal of the American Medical Association* has noted that there is great confusion over whether or not mortality from coronary artery and heart disease is increasing or decreasing. It appears that while the actual number of deaths has increased, the number per age group has decreased in "age-adjusted" statistics. According to Walker, "This increase will continue so long as gains in life expectancy result in bigger populations in the older ages, even though there may be a decrease in mortality for every individual age group" (Walker, 1974). Overall it does appear that there have been significant decreases in coronary mortality, including ischemic heart disease, cerebrovascular disease, and strokes, since 1970 in groups up to the age of 85 (*Statistical Bulletin,* 1977). These statistics apply to virtually all other population data concerning the elderly. Another area of confusion is the statistics circulated by the National Cancer Institute regarding mortality due to cancer. In an open letter to *The New York Times,* physician Richard Burack pinpointed statistical fallacies which are being recognized by an increasing number of researchers. Burack objected to an NCI graph entitled "Time Trends in Cancer Incidence" which indicated an "explosive epidemic" of cancer from 1937 to the present. The graphs fail to note that the United States population has increased nearly 100 million since 1933 and that the proportion of the population over 65 in 1979 far exceeds that of 1933. Since cancer is more frequent in occurrence in advanced years, the result is naturally a greater total number of cancer deaths per year. When "age-adjusted" statistics are applied, there is evidence of an actual decrease in incidence. From his observations, Richard Burack concludes that there is "no epidemic of cancer" and further that "there is a disproportionate number of cancer deaths due to cigarette smoking. Given our current economic problems, provision of more tax money to the NCI for more 'research' should be low on the list of our national priorities. Tax money should be substantially diverted from the cancer establishment and be channeled into a nationwide action program about the dangers of cigarettes, a program which ought to start in kindergarten" (Burack, 1979). When deciding priorities in health expenditures, it is imperative to bear in mind that early-life decreases in disease and death have been due predominantly to psychosocial, educational, and preventive measures. Furthermore, the increasing number of elderly people suffering from the modern plagues late in life is not a justification for increased pharmaceutical or technological expenditures, since such measures do nothing to alter the basic process of aging which underlies the specific disorders. In terms of improving the quality of life for a rapidly growing elderly population, the most meaningful and effective programs have been demonstrated to be and probably will continue to be preventive in orientation.

The emphasis throughout this book will be on the causes of aging and preventive methods which permit "not just an extension of the maximum human life-span, but also—and more importantly—prevention of the declining vigor that accompanies increasing years" (Marx, 1974). Writing in *Science*, Jean Marx rendered an extensive overview of the major biochemical theories and research projects bearing on longevity. It is clear that there is great value to such research, and positive results are likely, given the margin for improvement. As was noted earlier, the United States ranks seventh in life expectancy behind Sweden, Norway, Iceland, Denmark, Japan, and Canada. Men in Sweden have a life expectancy of 72 years as compared to 68.7 in the United States. Women of Sweden live an average of 77.4 years as compared to 76.5 in this country. In two of the least industrialized nations of the world, Greece and Iceland, a man's life expectancy at 65 in Greece is 79.3 and in Iceland is 80.3, as compared to 77.8 in the United States and most Western European countries (Popov et al., 1976). As surprising as these data might seem, they support the observation that while medicine has resolved many diseases, it has not dealt well with the nonspecific disorders induced by the stress of contemporary society. Given the undercurrent of psychosocial stress compounding and interacting with the natural process of aging, the traditional, fragmented approach of eliminating or altering specific aspects of disease or aging is only minimally productive. Molecular biologist Richard G. Cutler has pinpointed the fallacy of such an approach:

> The elimination of one disease process would immediately uncover another disease process, and so forth. It is therefore apparent that the elimination of these specific diseases, even if successful, will not result in a uniform maintenance of health, which is necessary for a more useful and enjoyable lifespan. A more general approach to the maintenance of health is necessary. This goal is a primary objective of some of the investigation now being carried out in gerontological research in the biological sciences [Cutler, 1976].

Much scientific inquiry in the realm of health and longevity is governed by the politics of grantsmanship and an outdated medical model rather than a goal of improving the human condition. All too often the development of research programs has "been controlled by professional specialists . . . responding to a series of unrelated demands or relying upon . . . the technologic imperative . . . tend[ing] to insist upon a universal application of their own assumptions, approaches or technology" (Lewis, 1970). This situation predominates in much of the research and clinical efforts in the area of longevity. If real progress is to be achieved then it is necessary to examine these assumptions and redirect priorities toward more productive ends.

Attitudes Toward the Elderly

A recent front-page article of *Clinical Psychiatry News* (1978) was entitled "Geriatrics Now Popular, but the Elderly Are Not." While gerontology is enjoying popular interest and governmental support including the formation of the National Institute of Aging, the elderly, said the article, are still "unpopular and viewed in rigid stereotypes such as senile." If the elderly are not to become the occasion to justify increased expenditures for biomedical technology, pharmaceuticals oriented toward rejuvenation, or dehumanizing convalescent homes, we must not lose sight of the real needs of elderly people. The onset of old age is often seen as a biological threshold, at age 65, but the reality is closer to Bob Dylan's lyrics, "Those not busy being born are busy dying." In order to work toward optimum health in later years it is necessary for every individual to see himself or herself as involved in the process rather than seeing the aged as separate, isolated groups, i.e., "them." In the words of Francis J. Braceland, senior consulting psychiatrist at the Institute of Living, we are a " 'gerontophobic' or old-age-fearing culture which is fixated upon youth. We have been prodigal of manpower, wisdom, and experience, and it is time that we resurveyed the situation. If our belief in the dignity of man is to be anything but a catchword, we are going to have to find some workable solution to the present-day wastage of human resources . . . aging is not a reason for despair but a basis for hope, not a slow decaying but a gradual maturing, not a fate to be undergone but a chance to be embraced" (*CPN,* 1978). It is precisely this subtle reorientation of priorities which is dependent upon increased professional and public awareness rather than upon a technological panacea.

Longevity Research in Context

It is far easier to grasp the import and details of longevity research, no matter how complex it might be, than to see clearly the equally if not more important psychological issues and context of this inquiry and its far-reaching impact. Foremost among those individuals recognizing context as the critical but subtle element in all systems of inquiry is Gregory Bateson in his excellent book *Mind and Nature: A Necessary Unity* (1978), where he states, "Children in school . . . are taught at a tender age that the way to define something is by what it supposedly *is* [emphasis in original]. . . . Without context there is no meaning" (Bateson, 1978). Virtually all research and clinical applications of longevity research have overlooked the larger context and have focused narrowly on the biochemical DNA-RNA level of reality. While this has unquestionably been productive, it has also resulted in a blindness to practical realities and philosophical and ethical issues.

However, it is becoming increasingly clear that a holistic, integrated approach is both possible and cost-effective. Even a conservative estimate of the efficacy of establishing programs of optimum health and longevity is extraordinary. Looking at the matter from a cost-effective standpoint is Johan Bjorksten, who notes, "A near 100% success is not unknown in medicine—diseases have all but disappeared—smallpox, plague, most recently, perhaps, polio. But let us be conservative. Few will argue with the notion that a 10% success is a reasonable expectation where systematic, well-directed research is brought to bear. A 10% success in control of aging might be expected. . . . This would lead to a far more tangible result than if all of the research were directed to all of the specific diseases"

(1971). This is also true with regard to organ transplantations, bionic or electronic implants, and new antibiotics or other pharmaceuticals, since none of these methods can achieve their full potential until the progressive loss of human resistance due to aging is brought under regulation. To many professionals the relationship between holistic medicine and longevity is not evident. The primary connection resides in two basic facts: (1) longevity is dependent upon the same factors conducive to optimum health, and (2) an increasingly elderly population potentially places a greater demand upon already overextended medical services, making the approaches of holistic medicine more appealing.

In a recent *Science* editorial, Philip H. Abelson touches upon one of the major underlying problems:

> Studies seem to show that longevity depends on a combination of factors. Prominent among them are good nutrition, weight control, abstention from excessive drinking of alcohol and from cigarettes, and getting enough exercise and sleep. Faced with the prospect of giving up smoking and engaging in vigorous exercise, many people would just as soon take their chances. However, others would like to pursue a more prudent course. They would be encouraged to do so if they had specific information about the effort required to increase their life span [Abelson, 1976].

The single greatest impediment to a health care system devoted to optimum health and longevity is the resistance on the part of individuals and institutions to reorienting their personal habits and economic priorities. In 1978 physician Steven Jonas noted in his book *Medical Mystery: The Training of Doctors in the United States* that the major shortcoming of contemporary medicine resides in its very structure with its disproportionate emphasis on specialization and pathology management rather than primary care and prevention. Jonas also emphasizes the personal commitment necessary by citing the Hippocratic maxim, "It [is] impossible for a man to remain in perfect health unless he organize[s] his entire life for such a purpose." While that might be both extreme and unnecessary, it does underscore the effort which such an orientation will require. Predictably, the book was chastised by physician Michael J. Halberstam (1978): " . . . there are other estimable professions devoted to issues in preventive medicine, whereas the medical profession is the only one charged with treating individuals one at a time." Not only is that statement inaccurate, it demonstrates the common fallacy of restricting health care to the diagnosis and treatment of pathology. Since that biomedical model has dominated health care for at least the last fifty years, the resulting conflict over territorial rights has left a vacuum of individual responsibility and institutional direction. Fortunately, such a limited outlook is being criticized by physicians such as Samuel J. Hessel of Harvard Medical School. "The allocation of medical resources depends not only on objective cost considerations but is also based in part on less easily quantifiable factors . . . emotional factors . . . and political considerations are some of the influences which affect these decisions. . . . It is likely that the two primary disease processes in the adult population, cancer and atherosclerotic disease, will not be eradicated by earlier and better diagnosis . . . in a nation of over 200,000,000 people. There is no purpose in uncritically extolling the virtues of examination without quantitative data . . . we must be cognizant of the underlying assumptions, limitations, and problems inherent in these analyses" (Hessel, 1977). The search for longevity brings these concerns into sharp focus. Aging brings with it more susceptibility to illness, which means more medical care for both chronic and terminal conditions which require more hospital care, more health care professionals, health administrators, escalating costs and insurance reimbursements, or, in brief, more of the same. This is the fundamental fallacy of our present health care system.

The present crisis in health care is not merely a problem of temporary shortages but the result of moving in a dead-end direction. Biomedical solutions to the health problems of the elderly include technological advances such as prosthetic limbs, renal dialysis, and "an unending stream of new, wanted, and potentially available services, needing only money to carry them out." Henrik L. Blum of the University of California at Berkeley, who made the above observation, underscored the necessity of a comprehensive approach to aging rather than pursuing present strategies: "This particular set of forces for new services unleashed by aging cannot easily be turned aside so that the problem will get infinitely worse if not intelligently handled now. Just hip replacements in California will cost $35 million annually at current prices based on an estimated 160 replacements per 100,000 elderly persons" (Blum, 1978). These issues define the context for any consideration of longevity. Many others have pointed out that technological advances in artificial systems and organ transplants do prolong life but do not necessarily improve the quality or "meaning" of these added years (Frolkis, 1968). The rehabilitation of "chronic physically ill patients" requires that the restored functions be integrated into the patient's life through innovations in psychotherapy (Lohmann, 1967). This importance of context in any consideration of longevity, from molecular biology to economic imperatives, cannot be overemphasized.

Developments in the field of longevity are further hampered by an extraordinary degree of specialization. Such compartmentalization seems to be much more of an artifact of professionalism and competition for funding than anything to do with the phenomenon of aging itself. Before any understanding of longevity and its social implications can be reached, it is necessary to relate these divergent and antagonistic aspects to each other. Robert N. Butler, the first director of the National Institute on Aging of the National Institute of Health, has clearly recognized the necessity of such an integrated approach in his Pulitzer prize book *Why Survive? Being Old in America* (1976). According to Butler, "The old are submitted to enormous emotional stresses and low social position. Preventive medicine and recognizing the complex interplay among physical, emotional, and social factors is set aside in favor of simplistic diagnoses of 'senility' and prognoses of 'chronic' or 'irreversible.' " Later he notes, "Healthy as well as sick older people should be studied from many perspectives. Disease must be distinguished from the effects of the aging process itself." Although most of Butler's excellent and insightful book focuses upon the larger issues of public health policy and institutions, he has a clear vision of the type of individual practitioner who must evolve to assist the elderly toward optimum health and extended longevity:

[H]ealth education and prevention of illness should be emphasized in late life. The doctor should function as teacher (the original meaning of the word "doctor"), by educating older people regarding the maintenance of health through diet, exercise, relaxation, early detection and treatment of illness and other aspects of preventive medicine. Older people require knowledge about their bodies as they change through time and in the presence of diseases. Myths, ignorance and misinformation abound [Butler, 1976].

Such issues are psychosocial, ethical, and moral rather than biomedical. Ultimately it is aggregates of individuals through personal, economic, and political initiative rather than vested professionals who must decide the priorities.

Holistic Principles—Yet to Be Practiced

Thanks to the popular media, holistic medicine has become a very familiar term to many people. It may even seem that the issues have been resolved and that the main impact of this innovative approach has passed. This is hardly the case. Just reflect for a moment and ask how much has really changed in the nature and structure of our contemporary health care system. While there has been a great deal of rhetoric, there has been relatively little effective action. Some resistance has taken the form of waiting for the evidence to come in, to support what are viewed as unsubstantiated claims. Such an attitude is woefully ignorant of nearly fifty years of solid basic research which has yielded limited but effective clinical results. Research articles too numerous to cite fill the annual compendiums of *Biofeedback and Self-Control,* excellent anthologies such as *Ways of Health,* edited by physician David S. Sobel (1979), and *Doing Better and Feeling Worse,* edited by the late John H. Knowles (1977), as well as books citing from this body of evidence such as *The Stress of Life* by Hans Selye (1956), *The End of Medicine* by attorney Rick J. Carlson (1975), *Mind as Healer, Mind as Slayer* (Pelletier, 1977) and *Holistic Medicine* (Pelletier, 1979), and *The American Way of Life Need Not Be Hazardous to Your Health* by cardiologist John W. Farquhar (1978). In short, the statement that there is a lack of empirical evidence to support practices oriented toward holistic medicine and optimum health is irresponsible. John W. Farquhar chastised the excesses of "scientific conservatism" in noting, "We should continue to support basic research while *simultaneously* implementing our best efforts for appropriate preventive measures, rather than sit passively and wait for the basic research to yield conclusive findings on *all* facets of the complex puzzle" (1978). We have yet to see a "major restructuring of the financing and basic organization of our health sector so as to create the incentives needed to control cost, make services equitably accessible, and move us in the direction of equalizing the opportunities to be healthy" (Blum, 1978). Chapter III is an extensive consideration of these pressing issues of public policy and funding priorities.

Our present approach to health care has in fact not changed significantly. There is a marked ability in a media-saturated culture to comprehend a problem such as the health care crisis intellectually and then to dismiss it as resolved once it has ostensibly been understood. However, the energy crisis of the last several years has clearly demonstrated the enormous chasm between recognizing and resolving a crisis. The issues surrounding longevity provide a focus for exposing the fallacies inherent in our current thinking about health care. The elderly are the result or, more accurately, the debris of the current approach. Just as anthropologists examine waste disposal sites to determine the lifestyle and consumption patterns of a population, a long hard look at our nursing homes and chronic hospitals tells us how we all have been living. Efforts to enhance longevity must by definition be holistic in nature.

> Sound health practices cannot begin in adult life, since by then much damage may already be done. Prevention should begin with prenatal and infant care, followed by good health education for the nation's 55 million school children. The physical and emotional environment, sanitation, level of stress, diet, rest, exercise and self-conscious control of harmful habits are elements of preventive care [Butler, 1975].

Denial of old age, however, creates a state of apathy that permits the links between prevention and longevity to remain unexamined. One of the earliest researchers to recognize this dilemma is physician Joseph W. Still, who wrote extensively about his concept of "personal preventive medicine" in the 1960s. Throughout his extensive publications (1959, 1969), Still has clearly recognized the critical link between prevention and longevity in such observations as:

> We still do not have as much knowledge as we would like about the causes of arteriosclerosis, coronary attacks, strokes, cancer, arthritis, aging and other degenerative diseases and conditions. However, we have learned how to treat their precursors—obesity, hypertension, excessive smoking and drinking—as well as how to teach people to cope with excessive stresses and tensions in their environment. The difficulty is that too few people and too few physicians are interested in treating these conditions [Still, 1968].

That was the case in 1968 and that situation remains essentially unchanged. Unquestionably there have been modifications in health care, but the "major restructuring" cited by Henrik L. Blum and other medical care analysts has not occurred. Clearly this restructuring cannot occur within the traditional limits imposed by a strictly biomedical approach. The results of such an attempt would terminate in a dilemma well known to computer analysts as "GIGO," or "garbage in, garbage out." These issues are considered at length in the next chapter, but the essential point here is that the search for longevity depends on principles of holistic medicine which, despite the plethora of rhetoric, remains more in the realm of potential than practice.

A Comprehensive Approach

Longevity is a phenomenon which involves an inextricable interaction between biochemical, psychosocial, and socioeconomic influences. Researchers in fields ranging from molecular biology to medical anthropology consistently cite the overwhelming importance of psychosocial influences in the determination of an individual's longevity. In a lengthy article entitled "Optimizing Adult Development," James L. Fozard and Samuel J. Popkin of the Veterans Administration Hospital in Boston have specified several major areas of normal, adult development where specific interventions could optimize both psychological and physical health. Among the areas are "vision," "memory and learning," and "health, leisure, and work." In each instance, the two researchers note a vast gap between the abundant data available from laboratory and clinical assessments and the limited applications of these findings to the realm of longevity and health for the elderly:

> Our present knowledge about the relationship between disease and aging suggests that we have a fair degree of control over some factors that increase the likelihood of our reaching an old age—for example, diet, exercise, weight control, styles of reacting to stressful situations, and habits relative to the use of tobacco, alcohol, and drugs.
>
> At present, the possibilities for early medical detection and intervention for many diseases associated with aging are limited . . . . While the value of some public health interventions is well established, their implementation is not easy. For example, public education efforts relative to choices about the use of alcohol, tobacco, drugs, and "fast food" have met with limited success. On the positive side, it is evident from the increasing interest in jogging and exercise programs that given the proper opportunities many will select health-related activities [Fozard and Popkin, 1978].

As the percentage of elderly people in the population continues to rise and the life expectancy is extended, it becomes increasingly important to avoid lifestyles which lead to an institutionalized, incapacitated old age. It is clearly possible to redesign environments and the psychosocial milieu to accommodate the lifestyle changes which must occur during the life-span between 30 and 100 years of age in order to maintain a high degree of health and fulfillment.

Among the factors which must be considered in any such comprehensive approach are: (1) basic research concerning the parameters of optimum health, longevity, the aging process itself, and the psychosomatic etiology of chronic illness (Benson, 1979); (2) systematic exploration of phenomena such as placebo response, spontaneous remission, autonomic regulation, and the role of increasing personal responsibility in health care (Bresler and Trubo, 1979); (3) creation of networks of individuals with family, social, and institutional communities (Duhl, 1980); (4) increased awareness of preventive health translated into positive public action. This would involve a decreasing focus upon biomedical technology and a maximizing of software and self-care education (Farquhar, 1978; Blum, 1978); (5) a health care system based upon prepayment rather than fee-for-service. Such a system of prepaid health service offers incentive for all health professionals to keep the public healthy and out of expensive hospitals (Blaustein, 1979; Wildavsky, 1977); (6) ecological programs intended to optimize environmental influences upon health (Becker, 1979, 1980); and (7) a major shift in philosophical attitude. In *The Yellow Emperor,* Huang Ti (2697–2597 B.C.) states: "Hence the sages did not treat those who were already ill; they instructed those who were not yet ill. . . . To administer medicines to diseases which have already developed and to suppress revolts which have already developed is comparable to the behavior of those persons who begin to dig a well after they have become thirsty, and of those who begin to cast weapons after they have already engaged in battle." While this enumeration could be extended ad infinitum, these points suffice to suggest the multiple levels of health which require restructuring if we are to move from pathology management to optimizing health and longevity.

The Psychobiological Frontier

While this book does address, in a limited manner, the research concerning aging, it is not limited to that data but goes beyond it to ask what is possible. To examine human life expectancy is to inquire into the psychobiological potential of the human species. During the 1940s and 1950s there were isolated case histories appearing in medical research journals of the purported ability of certain adept meditators to regulate autonomic functions such as heart rate, blood pressure, and the electrical activity of the brain (Brosse, 1978). However, it was not until the late 1960s and early 1970s that extensive laboratory assessment verified this phenomenon and clinical biofeedback began to emerge as a potent means of restoring and maintaining optimum health. Recently the first large-scale research project to compile such occurrences was funded by Laurance Rockefeller and several other private individuals and foundations, under the title of the "Transformation Project." It is headed by Michael Murphy, Esalen founder and author. According to Murphy, "We are looking at recurrent phenomena, the personality characteristics of people who manifest such changes and the circumstances in which they take place" (Murphy, 1979). Among the phenomena under study are hypnotically induced blisters, traumatic body memory, stigmata, and extraordinary physical capacities exhibited by athletes and individuals under extremely trying circumstances. Through a systematic compiling and analyzing of these research reports and anecdotal accounts, the project intends to create a "field of inquiry" concerning "extraordinary physical capacities mediated by consciousness." Clearly the phenomenon of longevity is just such an occurrence, a biological capacity developed in certain individuals and isolated centenarian communities but not yet manifest in the species as a whole. Determining why some individuals age less rapidly or live considerably longer than others is the first step toward creating the internal and external conditions which will enable more people to live as long as those who live longest today.

Despite advances in molecular biology, the behavioral and psychological dimensions of aging have remained essentially unaltered since Oedipus solved the riddle of the Sphinx: "What has one voice and yet becomes four-footed and two-footed and three-footed?" It is man, who first crawls on all fours as a baby, then walks upright, to end in old age assisted by a third leg, a cane. Shakespeare's description of the later ages of man still applies to most of us:

> All the world's a stage,
> And all the men and women merely players.
> They have their exits and their entrances;
> And one man in his time plays many parts,
> His acts being seven ages. At first the infant,

Mewling and puking in the nurse's arms.
And then the whining school-boy, with his satchel
And shining morning face, creeping like snail
Unwillingly to school. And then the lover,
Sighing like furnace, with a woful ballad
Made to his mistress' eyebrow. Then a soldier,
Full of strange oaths and bearded like the pard;
Jealous in honour, sudden and quick in quarrel,
Seeking the bubble reputation
Even in the cannon's mouth. And then the justice,
In fair round belly with good capon lined,
With eyes severe and beard of formal cut,
Full of wise saws and modern instances;
And so he plays his part. The sixth age shifts
Into the lean and slipper'd pantaloon,
With spectacles on nose and pouch on side;
His youthful hose, well saved, a world too wide
For his shrunk shank; and his big manly voice,
Turning again toward childish treble, pipes
And whistles in his sound. Last scene of all,
That ends this strange eventful history,
Is second childishness and mere oblivion,
Sans teeth, sans eyes, sans taste, sans everything.

[*As You Like It,* II, vii]

By contrast, an advertisement in the popular science journal *OMNI* boldly announced, "In the future, incredibly expensive technology could enable a few people to live for 200 years or more. Who will be chosen? And, who will choose? . . . Within the next four decades a lifespan of 100, 200, 400 years and up may become a part of *Homo sapiens'* on-going evolutionary destiny" (*OMNI,* September 1979). While that is certainly inspiring, it does raise the specter of increasingly specialized technology for the benefit of a few at a monumental cost to many. Among the present research approaches to longevity, the advertisement cites transplantation of organs, cellular and organ regeneration, the elimination of lipofuscin accumulation in cells, restriction of diet, prosthetics and cyborgs, and lowering body temperature. Will these be the products and services of an external youth industry?

Several extensive literature reviews of the field of aging and longevity clearly indicate that psychosocial variables are more accurate predictors of longevity than are any biological variables. Among the psychosocial factors predictive of longevity are higher income, occupational status, more education, greater social activity, and greater life and work satisfaction (Palmore, 1969; Reynolds and Kalish, 1974; Greenberg, 1978). Furthermore, according to Erdman Palmore from the Center for the Study of Aging and Human Development at Duke University Medical Center, "There is considerable evidence that environmental factors such as nutrition, disease, stress, psychologic attitudes, social roles, and lifestyle probably outweigh the hereditary factors influencing the actual lifespan of given persons" (1971). Palmore has carefully researched this assertion by deriving a "longevity quotient (LQ)" derived from entering 20 predictors of longevity into a stepwise, multiple regression analysis, a statistical procedure which gives an indication of the relative importance of each of the 20 predictors. With data from 271 volunteers over 60 and by controlling for the effects of sex, age, and race, Palmore found "cardiovascular disease, work satisfaction, cigarette smoking, physical function, and happiness ratings" (Palmore, 1976) were the most significant predictors of longevity. Happily these factors are ones which an individual can influence. These data confirmed an earlier study of 268 people aged 60 to 94 (Palmore, 1969) and both studies have since been replicated and confirmed.

The purpose of this book is not to delve into the phenomenon of aging per se, nor to reify longevity, but rather to explore the possibility that optimum health and zeal are more natural to advanced age than the present disability, senility, and excessively high incidence of suicide.

An Overview of This Book

Longevity is a biological potential which focuses all of the issues in our evolving system of health care like a laser. Chapter II treats the public policy issues and the nature of the alterations which must be made if we are to move from a pathology management industry to a true health care system. Many of the issues central to holistic medicine and the ensuing public policy decisions are brought into sharp focus. A key element in both optimum health and longevity is individual participation as addressed by Thomas McKeown: "the role of medicine is essentially sinister: for many reasons, but particularly because it usurps the right of the individual to face and deal with his own health problems" (1979).

This is an important issue since several socialist critics of holistic medicine have pointed out that it tends to "blame the victim" (Berliner and Salmon, 1979, 1980) and neglect issues of economics, political interest groups, and other variables outside the immediate control of the individual. Because that perception is not without merit, policy issues were considered in *Holistic Medicine* (Pelletier, 1979) and are discussed in the next chapter.

Moving from the public policy and delivery system issues, Chapter III is an in-depth analysis of the major biochemical and neurophysiological approaches to aging, their dominant models, and the experimental evidence. Virtually all of the present research has focused on the genetic and biochemical aspects of aging, and any discussion of aging requires an understanding of these approaches. At present the excellent book *Pro-longevity* (1977) by Albert Rosenfeld, former Science Editor of the *Saturday Review,* provides an overview of the research concerning the biochemistry of aging accompanied by interviews with many of the most innovative researchers in this area. It is important to bear in mind that Chapter III is concerned with aging, that is, the biologically degenerative process of advancing age, rather than the longevity potential.

Building upon the information in Chapter III, Chapter IV focuses on the latent regenerative capacity of the human organism. Rather than perceiving individuals as passive victims of an inevitable aging process, innovative researchers have shown that both slowing the aging process and biological regeneration are a reality. Central to this chapter is a consideration of the research of orthopedic surgeon Robert O. Becker and his work with the "electromagnetic induction of limb regeneration" (1978). Furthermore there is now considerable evidence that individuals can alter basic biochemical functions in the body in a manner analogous to biofeedback. Drawing upon this research, it is possible to explore the positive aspects of "placebo response" (Benson and McCallie, 1979), the research demonstrating an individual's capacity to regulate the body's endogenous opiates or endorphins for regulation of pain, and the implications of naturally occurring substances such as interferon in the body. Each of these approaches demonstrates a subtle biochemical energy system in the body which can be regulated through human consciousness. Psychological factors are important as initiators and mediators of neurophysiological and biochemical processes conducive to degeneration or regeneration. Voluntary regulation of the central nervous system and internal biochemistry may prove to be an important step toward optimum health and longevity.

Moving from the purely biological realm to the psychosocial level of analysis, Chapter V considers the behavioral and environmental determinants of longevity. Even with respect to the infectious plagues, these factors were of major influence on mortality, as noted by Ernest M. Gruenberg: "While the universal fear of the great plagues might leave us with the impression that they were no respecters of persons, in fact, all of the great killers have discriminated, more readily taking those who were half dead or half grown than those who were healthy and in their prime" (1977). These influences also affect an individual's chances of achieving the average life expectancy. Issues considered in Chapter V are the universally lower mortality rate of women, psychological factors conducive to longevity, and research with subgroups, such as Seventh-Day Adventists, Mormons, and Amish, who experience significantly less disease and a greater average life expectancy than the United States population as a whole. As a further indication of the potency of psychophysiological factors in attaining the average life expectancy is recent research on the effects of retirement. "Retirement has been linked with coronary death in a case-controlled study. . . . Retirement . . . is associated with an 80% increase in the risk of coronary mortality . . . . Financial concerns, loneliness, boredom and other consequences of retirement may result in anxiety and depression" (*Medical Tribune,* 1980). Retirement contains in microcosm all the biological, psychosocial, financial, and public policy issues involved in the study of longevity.

Essential to any consideration of lifestyle and longevity is diet and nutrition. Building upon the basic biochemical evidence in Chapters

III and IV, Chapter VI describes the dietary practices which in over fifty years of research have been demonstrated approximately to double the life expectancy of laboratory animals (McCay, 1939). This is one of the most significant areas of longevity research since it demonstrates that specific procedures are required at critical developmental stages, continuing through adult development. Furthermore, it is an instance where laboratory experimentation is proving applicable to the human condition. There are specific, beneficial measures which can be adopted now, but adequate dissemination of that information will depend upon politics and lobbying influence. Following the release of the findings of the McGovern Committee (1977), a heated debate ensued, as noted in the *New England Journal of Medicine:*

> But what's disturbing is to notice some of the differences—more of tone and perspective than anything else—between the Agriculture-dominated *Guidelines* and the nutrition-related passages in the Surgeon General's *Healthy People*. The *Guidelines,* as Secretary Bergland acknowledged, isn't going to offend any agricultural producers. To the extent there are lobbyists for "too much" fat, sugar, or sodium, they're keeping quiet. *Healthy People,* with the admitted advantage of book length rather than pamphlet space, does not confine itself to those nutritional matters that are likely to draw no counterfire [Greenberg, 1980].

Again we see the interaction between public policy and health promotion practices.

Following this discussion is a consideration of physical activity in Chapter VII, since it is also an essential factor in optimum health and longevity. In experimental as well as observational research, particular forms of sustained physical activity have been clearly demonstrated to be conducive to an extended life expectancy. The chapter also looks at instances of cardiovascular fitness which far exceed the standard parameters, as in the case of the Tarahumara Indians of Mexico. For purposes of developing positive models of health and longevity, the study of such prototypic populations both abroad and within the United States is essential.

Chapter VIII examines instances of advanced longevity throughout the world. This chapter is a detailed analysis of the conflicting information regarding "centenarian communities" (Leaf, 1975), an area of controversy for the last decade. However, the olympian age records are not the significant issue. Of greater importance are the questions raised by clinicians such as Alexander Leaf:

> Arteriosclerosis, arthritis, and other degenerative diseases are common among elderly Americans. But are such diseases an essential part of the aging process? Are there not places in the world where a significant proportion of the people live to a ripe old age and yet somehow remain in vigorous health, retaining their mental capacities even to age 100 or more? . . . I am now convinced that when the social environment encourages one to feel socially useful and needed in the economy, and to be looked up to and revered as a wise figure, the extremely elderly keep their mental faculties and physical abilities so that they can respond appropriately. This is quite contrary to prevailing trends in modern industrialized societies, which tend to emphasize youth and to regard old people as useless and standing in the way of progress [Leaf, 1973c].

More important than the incidence of longevity in isolated geographic regions is its incidence throughout history in all regions and, increasingly, in the United States at the present time. This pervasive incidence indicates a biological potential of the human species. Centenarian individuals represent a living prototype which is both predicted and supported by laboratory and observational research.

In the final chapter the implications and future directions of longevity research and programs are discussed. If a Methuselah Project were to become a national priority, a psychobiological approach to longevity would yield dramatic results in the immediate future. It is hoped that such an endeavor would include the requisite wisdom and compassion, the insight, experienced during Bach's "Magnificat," Gounod's "Cäcilienmesse," or Strauss's "Death and Transfiguration." In studying longevity we must acknowledge a dimension of humankind that transcends the questions of how future generations will exceed threescore and ten.

TWO

From Pathology Management to Longevity Promotion

An Idea Whose Time Has Come

Former Secretary of Health, Education, and Welfare Joseph A. Califano, Jr.'s final official act in office made most speculations concerning preventive health care obsolete. HEW issued a report entitled *Healthy People: The Surgeon General's Report on Health Promotion and Disease Prevention* (1979) that was a rallying directive for "a second public health revolution." According to Califano's foreword to the two-and-a-half-year study, "Let us make no mistake about the significance of this document. It represents an emerging consensus among scientists and the health community that the nation's health strategy must be dramatically recast to emphasize the prevention of disease." Going even further, Califano reiterates some of the basic postulates of holistic medicine:

> I can compress what we have learned about the causes of these modern killers in three summarizing sentences: We are killing ourselves by our own careless habits. We are killing ourselves by carelessly polluting the environment. We are killing our-

selves by permitting harmful social conditions to persist—conditions like poverty, hunger and ignorance—which destroy health, especially for infants and children.

By "modern killers" Califano was referring to the afflictions of civilization, which include all of the chronic degenerative diseases such as cardiovascular disease and cancer. Although the report acknowledges the fact that "The health of the American people has never been better," this has been due primarily to the marked reductions in deaths from communicable diseases and a decrease in infant mortality. By contrast, the incidence of the modern killers has increased sharply and they are now estimated to account for 75 percent of all deaths in the United States. There is widespread consensus that these afflictions of civilization are not and cannot be adequately decreased through more concerted efforts of the present medical care system (Knowles, 1977; Engel, 1977; Kristein et al., 1977; McKeown, 1971, 1978; Cousins, 1979; Vayda, 1978). Recent reports indicate a rise in the incidence of these disorders as the Soviet Union becomes increasingly westernized (Davis and Feshbach, 1978). As a result of these observations the report states unequivocally that "Prevention is an idea whose time has come." Statements such as these are no surprise, but the novelty of the report lies in the fact that it was issued from such a high office of the United States government.

Ironically, the report was also a swan song for Califano. The very concepts he espoused in his report are among the controversial issues which led to his dismissal from office. Observers of health care politics noted that the 1979 Surgeon General's report parallels the previous 1964 report, which focused public attention on the dangers of cigarette smoking. That 1964 report lay fallow for many years and gained impetus with Califano's more concerted campaign against smoking, and it was precisely because of his "anti-tobacco campaign" (*APA Monitor,* 1979) that he came to be considered a political liability. Among the specific issues cited in the report is once again smoking, with Califano's unrelenting message that "We can see certain signs that millions of Americans are taking this message to heart . . . signs that cigarette smoking is declining, as more people recognize smoking for what it really is: slow-motion suicide." Actually the report notes that cigarette smoking, through its contributing effects to both cardiovascular disease and cancer, is the single most preventable cause of death after forty (accidents of all types being the leading cause of death from age one until the early forties). In addition, three recent studies of the supposed interaction between oral contraceptives and cardiovascular disease now indicate that cigarette smoking, not the oral contraceptives per se, is responsible for subsequent cardiovascular disorders (*Science News,* 1979a). Among the other observations of the report: (1) "Personal lifestyles are responsible for a large share of unnecessary disease and disability in the United States"; (2) alcohol abuse is a factor in more than 10 percent of all deaths; (3) individuals consume excessive amounts of sugar, salt, red meat, fat, and cholesterol while consuming too little whole grains, cereals, fruits, vegetables, fish, poultry, and legumes; (4) "adults should be encouraged to exercise vigorously, if possible at least three times a week for about 15 to 30 minutes each time"; and (5) up to 20 percent of all cancer deaths may be linked to exposure to chemicals and other hazards on the job. Again, each of these observations is based upon the extensive research and publication of many clinicians and researchers over the last fifty years and these conclusions will be of no surprise to them.

Practitioners in the field of holistic medicine have already addressed themselves to specific means of rectifying these appalling conditions. Among the books defining specific programs are *90 Days to Self-Health* (1977) by former neurosurgeon C. Norman Shealy; *Mind as Healer, Mind as Slayer* (Pelletier, 1977); *Holistic Medicine: From Stress to Optimum Health* (Pelletier, 1979), which details specific health promotion practices in stress management, nutrition, and physical exercise for individuals and institutions while also considering the economics of such approaches; *The American Way of Life Need Not Be Hazardous to Your Health* (1978) by cardiologist John W. Farquhar; *Free Yourself from Pain* (1979) by David E. Bresler (and R. Trubo), Director of the UCLA School of Medicine Pain Control Unit; and a comprehensive report by National Institute of Mental Health physician James S. Gordon in the form of his *Final Report to the President's Commission on Mental Health of the Special Study on Alternative Mental Health Services* (1978). Collectively these documents and many other articles and books move away from the present pathology-fixated system of care, toward prevention, optimum health, and extended longevity.

A third major area of the current Surgeon General's report concerns the actual implementation of such programs. There is no reason to enumerate the plethora of practices which call themselves holistic medicine. For an exhaustive and somewhat exhausting list of such practices, a brief overview has been compiled by Clement Bezold, Director of the Institute for Alternative Futures (Bezold, 1979). Already there is a glut of methods, many of which are no more integrated, comprehensive, or effective than the purely biomedical approach they seek to supplant. Vested interests, professional myopia, and self-aggrandizement affects "holistic" practitioners as much as any other group. Nevertheless there already exists considerable consensus that a finite set of practices, applied in conjunction with allopathic medicine, can have a significant positive effect on health and longevity. The major issue now at hand is to identify the approaches, which are well-documented in the previously cited publications and others, and to integrate them into individual lifestyles and health programs of major corporations, as well as the priorities of state and local government. These are the significant issues and these are the ones addressed in this chapter.

Obstacles to Change

Among the looming impediments to such a redirection of resources are powerful vested interests by medical, pharmaceutical, food processing, and hospital lobbyists. The greatest potential for positive change, as well as the greatest obstacle to change, are the attitudes of individuals in the United States. The Surgeon General's report observes that many Americans are "apathetic and unmotivated" toward better health and often view illness as "a matter of random choice, not to be averted but to be tolerated and accepted." Such a stoic attitude, while admirable in some respects, has become excessive. Individuals assume a posture of "helplessness and hopelessness" (Seligman, 1975) long before all or any efforts to initiate individual health practices have been exhausted. In looking over the range of viable alternatives proposed under holistic medicine, Califano has noted, "To know these things gives hope that we can devise new strategies for health. . . . What is in doubt is whether we have the personal discipline and political will to solve these problems." This essential point is echoed by virtually every practitioner of preventive health care.

Although the report itself is less impassioned than Califano's foreword, it does consistently emphasize a necessary union between personal health behaviors and public policy. This link of personal and institutional responsibility in developing a true rather than nominal "health" care system is perhaps the single most important implication of the report. All too often the very potent concept of individual responsibility is perversely employed in a maneuver known as "blaming the victim" (Duhl, 1980). Essentially the ploy involves placing responsibility for these conditions upon the very people who suffer most. State and national government, professional organizations, biomedical and pharmaceutical corporations, and other large aggregates thus abdicate their collective responsibility. However, the disturbances of our global ecology, rampant inflation, and the spectre of modern plagues have demonstrated that everyone, regardless of social position, is directly affected. There are no isolated self-interests which can be satisfied without considering the consequences and impact upon society as a whole.

Given the scope of the report, including breast-feeding, firearm control, and youth employment programs, the document was inevitably controversial. Again Califano anticipated this reaction:

> There will be controversy—about what role government should play, if any, in urging citizens to give up their pleasurable but damaging habits. But there can be no denying the public consequences of those private habits. . . . And of course there will be controversy about welfare, income maintenance programs, food stamps and other efforts to alleviate poverty. But we simply cannot avoid the fact that if we are to mount a successful second public health revolution we must deal effectively with deep social problems that destroy health.

While the observations and conclusions of the report are hardly new, the fact that it sets five public health goals to be achieved by 1990 gives it more power and credence. Those five goals are: (1) a 35 percent reduction in infant mortality; (2) a 20 percent decrease in deaths of children aged 1 to 14; (3) a 20 percent reduction in deaths of adolescents and young adults to age 24; (4) a 25 percent cut in deaths in the 25 to 64 age group; and, most striking, (5) a 20 percent reduction in the average number of days that older people are ill each year. Virtually all of the measures cited to achieve these ends fall within the realm of holistic health care, with a clear de-emphasis of biomedical and pharmaceutical intervention. Finally, the Surgeon General's report recognizes the inextricable interactions between mind, body, and psychosocial systems with "It is important to emphasize that physical health and mental health are often linked. Both are enhanced through the maintenance of strong family ties, the assistance of supportive friends, and the use of community support systems."

The prevention of alcohol and drug abuse, the report says, "depends in many ways more on our skills in mobilizing individuals and groups working together in the schools and communities, than on the efforts of the health care system."

The Pathology Management Industry

As a future vision of health care, such a document portends major restructuring of what has become the "second largest and fastest growing industry in the United States" (*Business Week,* 1978), the pathology management industry. Over the last five years there have been innumerable proposals, most notably the Carter versus Kennedy versions of National Health Insurance, which attempted to outline an implementation procedure for an efficient, cost-effective health care system (Saward, 1973). For most individuals, even those directly involved in the proposals and those professionals serving as consultants, the result is often a bewildering array of acronyms and shopworn rhetoric. However, there are specific criteria by which one can evaluate a given proposal. Inherent to any specific plan are a set of explicit assumptions that govern which facts are garnered to support a particular course of action. As an example one could examine the 11th report of the National Advisory Council on Economic Opportunity, released in June 1979. Together with the Surgeon General's report, these two unusually clear documents mark a hopeful direction in removing the deliberate obscurity characteristic of many government reports. A major theme throughout the report, written under the direction of its Chairman, Arthur I. Blaustein, was the direct connection between economic affairs and health. There were four major headings in it: Food, Energy, Medical Care, and Housing. Under Medical Care the report noted several significant factors affecting the economics of health care:

> A growing body of literature has pointed out that three major factors are the basis for the rising cost of health care. . . . First is the "fee-for-service" nature of payment. . . . Providers of these services have a built-in incentive to increase the number of items consumed. . . . The second factor is the technical nature of medical knowledge and the relative inability of people to comparison-shop for less costly services. . . . Further, as many services performed on a fee-for-service basis are paid for by a third party—a private insurance company or the government— the full cost is not borne directly by the consumer but is spread out in the form of higher taxes and insurance premiums, still further incentive to schedule unnecessary services. These factors are most noticeable in regard to rising hospital costs [Blaustein, 1979].

Even more striking is the committee's conclusion that "Because the problem of inflation in health care costs is primarily one of the structure of incentives within the industry, it cannot be solved without altering those incentives." This last point is extremely important because any program of national health insurance or local health plan structured upon the same vested incentives would generate even greater utilization and commensurately greater expenses with no improvement in the overall health status of individuals in the United States.

Other instances further illustrate the basic assumptions of Blaustein's report. Among the many issues contributing to impaired health, the report focused on both the short-term and long-term effects of unemployment. The links included: ". . . rises in the official unemployment rate and the rate of deaths from severe illnesses

.... This suggests that the 1.4 percent rise in the unemployment rate in 1970 was responsible for over 25,000 deaths. . . . But the effects of unemployment run even deeper, for they strike not only the jobless themselves but also, in one way or another, their children. The first and most drastic effect is in increased infant mortality" (Blaustein, 1979). Given this situation the unemployed individual is in the double bind of needing increased care with costs of care being driven upward by many of the same forces which gave rise to the unemployment.

One physician who had substantial input into the report of the National Advisory Council was Henrik L. Blum of the School of Public Health of the University of California, Berkeley. In the preparation of a proposal for National Health Insurance and a subsequent health care delivery system, Blum was even more outspoken concerning the fundamental flaws underlying the present approach. Of highest priority to Blum is

> a major restructuring of the financing and basic organization of our health care sector so as to create the incentives needed to control cost, make services equitably accessible, and move us in the direction of equalizing the opportunities to be healthy . . . . The proposal creates a set of objectives which are operationalized in a way that consumer and provider alike find it totally in their own interest to control costs, promote health, and make health care available equitably [Blum, 1978].

His lengthy critique and proposal is quoted at length here because it pinpoints specific practices which result from present approaches and defines significant areas which require change. In analyzing the present state of mutual concern over health care costs by professionals and patients alike, Blum cites the following factors as contributing to the present plight: (1) "The daily press routine of reporting on medical 'miracles' and even potential miracles revealed at scientific conferences adds fuel to the fire of potential demand. . . . Bad education such as the lay and public health sponsored 'see your physician' campaigns, even when they have little or nothing to offer as in the routine physical exam, needs definite counteracting with useful information"; (2) "There will be an increasing capacity of technology to care for many old things better, and to care for many heretofore untreatable conditions. . . . This could easily lead to a doubling of the services every decade"; (3) "Dangerous lifestyles or living habits . . . provoke a constant stream of potentially avoidable demands for care"; (4) "Fee-for-service remuneration is a major key to excessive prescribing of services and institutional creation of services. . . . Whether it is medical tradition, problems of professionals, maintaining income, or whatever, the differences indicate just how much needless work is done." This point has been emphasized by two Congressional reports by John E. Moss based on records from 1974 and 1977 stating that "unnecessary surgery remains a major national problem which requires urgent and accelerated attention" (*AMA News,* 1979b) and a dramatic drop in death rate during a physicians' strike in the Los Angeles area with the decline attributed to a decrease in elective surgery; (5) "Needless services generated by insufficiently busy practitioners. . . . The ratio of doctors to population is now rising significantly, and particularly for those specialties least needed. This suggests that income enhancement will be an increasingly grave force"; (6) "Competition based on attractiveness but not on price is used particularly by hospitals to draw in doctors and patients. This involves hotel-type luxuries . . . massive investments in special equipment. . . . The result can be and commonly is atrociously high prices and shifting of burdens or cross-subsidization by other hospital services able to charge less conspicuously." (Recognition of this factor has already been acted upon by both the Blue Cross and Blue Shield associations, which revoked their routine reimbursement of the "admission batteries" of medical tests for virtually all hospital admissions. Stating the position was Blue Cross President Walter J. McNerney, who intended the plan "to encourage medical professionals to think about the cost of procedures routinely performed." Under the plan, twenty-six diagnostic laboratory procedures now considered "unnecessary, unreliable, or of no established value" will be phased out [*Modern Medicine,* 1979].) (7) "The changing medical practitioner outlook about trying to live like others, enjoy a family and free time, has made after-hours and weekends a hard time to get care. When combined with relatively high earnings, the private practitioner more and more encourages people to seek emergency room care, the vast majority of which is therefore not at all emergency in nature"; and finally (8) "Pseudo-scientific beliefs about what affects health . . . find doctors treating symptoms, often by surgery, while overlooking major underlying stress provoking situations which go on to involve other bodily systems which in turn need more medical care. Thus a parade of needless and often mutilating procedures are done all for lack of concern about basic survival problems that will not go away with traditional medical therapy." If this critique seems harsh or unwarranted, bear in mind that these conclusions and others have been pointed out in many ways by many spokesmen largely drawn from within the health care profession itself. Also, unless this representative list be construed as a condemnation, which it is not, it is important to note one of Blum's general conclusions: "It is possible to conclude that medical care directed to prevention or amelioration of specific conditions is increasingly effective, spectacularly so in some situations. What cannot be said is that increasing amounts of medical care beyond some basic minimum is correlatable with any evidence of generally improved well-being." These points serve to counterbalance the persistent tendency of national health proposals to approach the problem with plans to pour more and more federal funds into the purchase of medical services. Very little attention or allocation of resources are directed toward prevention of illness and the optimization of health and longevity.

A Shift of Priorities

Fortunately, complex issues do not have to engender complex solutions. "Major restructuring" is clearly the treatment of choice. Nothing short of this restructuring can fully resolve the present impasse. As a starting point the National Advisory Council report recommended: (1) ". . . that Congress support the President's proposal and enact hospital cost-containment legislation"; (2) ". . . that Congress appropriate more funds for Health Maintenance Organizations and specify that they be used to expand the number that operate in low-income and medically underserved areas"; and (3) ". . . that Congress increase its appropriations for nutrition education and other preventive health-care programs." Although the mandate for such actions has been voiced from Washington, the changes actually imply an elimination of many government programs and regulation of the resulting organizations and services. To date, the most promising models for such an organization are the Health Maintenance Organizations (HMO) which have been discussed at length in *Holistic Medicine* (Pelletier, 1979) and fully explicated in the pioneering work of Ernest W. Saward (1972, 1975, 1976, 1978). For details concerning HMO history, structure, and benefits as well as liabilities, an excellent article by Saward is entitled "The Organization of Medical Care" (1973) and is readily accessible in a special issue of *Scientific American* devoted to "Life, Death, and Medicine."

Our present pathology management industry employs 6 percent of the nation's workers, requires 9 percent of the gross national product, and while it is billing 1,500 percent more than it did in 1950, it is serving only 43 percent more people (*Business Week*, 1978). Trends such as these are worsening in a degenerative spiral. There is a clear interaction between the successful interventions and cures of a pathology management industry and longevity. Paradoxically, these improvements lead to still larger expenditures because the aged require 2.5 to 3 times as much care as others and that proportion of the general population is rapidly rising. While that population enjoys an extended life-span, it is all too frequently encumbered by chronic degenerative diseases. If individuals and government officials are not sufficiently conscious of this interaction, the vested interests of the pathology management industry will be unlikely to undergo a "major restructuring" but will simply shift their emphasis to the new territory of the growing elderly population.

Certain increasingly common chronic conditions represent ". . . the failure of success. Their growing prevalence and longer duration are a product of progress in health technology" (Gruenberg, 1977). An insightful article by Ernest M. Gruenberg of the Johns Hopkins School of Public Health has noted the increase of certain chronic conditions, including mongolism, senile brain disease, arteriosclerosis, hypertension, schizophrenia, diabetes, and spina bifida, a congenital anomaly of the spine. Success in preventing death from these conditions has led to prolongation of chronically impaired lives. Based upon his observations Gruenberg concludes, "We cannot avoid the successes. We must learn to overcome the ensuing failures . . . . We haven't failed in our efforts to find preventable causes of these conditions—we have hardly made any effort at all! . . . Our life-saving technology of the past four decades has outstripped our health-preserving technology and the net effect has been to worsen the people's health" (1977). To avoid this impasse, a true health care system must meet the formidable task of curtailing the incidence of the modern plagues with the result being an improved quality of longevity. That this seems unlikely at the present time is due far more to the fact that it has not been attempted than to whether it is difficult or impossible. There is a lack of evidence for the efficacy of prevention, public education, health care facilities, and related programs because government and the pathology management industry have invested the money elsewhere. Dramatic changes have occurred in the lifestyle and the health problems of the people of the postindustrial nations, and yet the traditional methods of coping with these problems have remained essentially unchanged. This has resulted in a major disparity between the factors known to have the greater impact on health and the resources devoted to them.

One significant departure from this trend has been the concept of the "Health Field" used by the Canadian Ministry of Health. Marc Lalonde, former Minister of National Health and Welfare, authored the landmark study *A New Perspective on the Health of Canadians* (1975), which has had a significant impact on many subsequent health proposals, including the 1979 Surgeon General's report. Details of the applications and limitations of this document, which now serves as the guiding principle of the Canadian health care system, are discussed in *Holistic Medicine* (Pelletier, 1979) and in an excellent article by Canadian physician Eugene Vayda, which states, "Public health requires collective as well as individual action and a government sensitive to the needs of its people should not attempt to skirt this responsibility. . . . Careful evaluation is essential; otherwise we will only exchange one wasteful program for another" (Vayda, 1978). In the Health Field model, health status is influenced by four major components: (1) human biology—all inherited, genetic factors; (2) environment—those aspects of the physical, psychosocial, and economic environment which are external to the individual; (3) lifestyle—which is the health care system as it is presently structured; (4) health care organization. In Lalonde's words, this model permits a system of analysis in which any question can be examined under the four elements in order to assess their relative significance and interaction. For example, the underlying causes of death from traffic accidents can be found to be mainly due to risks taken by individuals with lesser importance given to the design of cars and roads, and to the availability of emergency treatment; human biology has little or no significance in this area. In order of importance, therefore, Lifestyle, Environment and Health Care Organization contribute to traffic deaths in the proportions of something like 74%, 20%, and 5%, respectively. This analysis permits program planners to focus their attention on the most important contributing factors [Lalonde, 1975].

Even if these four factors were considered to be equally important, the allocation of funding and human resources to each category would be grossly distorted in the United States. In an analysis of the $29.2 billion 1974 health budget of the United States government, G. Alan Dever noted that 90.6 percent was allocated to health care organizations, 6.9 percent to human biology, 1.2 percent to environment, and 1.5 percent to lifestyle. In effect, 90.6 percent of resources are allocated to the one segment of the Health Field which has been estimated to affect 19 percent of the usual indices for measuring health (Wildavsky, 1977). Approximately 90 percent of health issues are related to factors outside of and beyond the control of health care organizations (Ng et al., 1978). From these data Dever's conclusion was quoted by physician Eugene W. Fowinkle, Public Health Commissioner in Tennessee:

The conclusion is obvious. Based on current procedures for reducing mortality and morbidity, it is clear that unless we dramatically shift our health policy, we will see little or no change in our present disease patterns. In fact, with our aging population we might very well see dramatic increases in mortality and morbidity [Fowinkle, 1977].

These findings are essentially unchanged as of this year, and predictions are that this will remain the case "until the proposed shifting of training opportunities takes effect (at least 10 years before any effects will be felt)" (Blum, 1979). Even if these assertions seem overstated, the present state of crisis and the substantial lead time required for any degree of resolution call for prompt action.

Aldous Huxley, in his visionary classic *Island,* summed up our present system vividly:

> So you think our medicine's pretty primitive? That's the wrong word. It isn't primitive. It's fifty percent terrific and fifty percent non-existent. Marvellous antibiotics—but absolutely no methods for increasing resistance, so that antibiotics won't be necessary. Fantastic operations—but when it comes to teaching people the way of going through life without having to be chopped up, absolutely nothing. And it's the same all along the line. Alpha Plus for patching you up when you've started to fall apart; but Delta Minus for keeping you healthy. Apart from sewage systems and synthetic vitamins, you don't seem to do anything at all about prevention. And yet you've got a proverb: prevention is better than cure.

Health Promotion Organizations

On a more positive note, there are several trends which indicate that health care organizations and certain United States corporations are moving in constructive directions. One individual who has developed a promising alternative delivery model in contrast to Huxley's vision is physician Lorenz K. Y. Ng of the National Institute on Drug Abuse. In conjunction with his colleagues, Devra L. Davis and Ronald W. Manderscheid, he has proposed a plan for a Health Promotion Organization (HPO) which would promote healthy life-styles and yet be part of existing medical care facilities rather than requiring the creation of another equally untenable bureaucracy. According to Ng:

> We propose the establishment of voluntary, community-based health promotion organizations (HPOs) that will (a) reward

healthy lifestyles by teaching people to take greater responsibility for their own health, and (b) create incentives for health promotion and disease prevention by stimulating a closer working relationship among government, business, labor, and the health care system.

His model is based upon the following premises:

1. All people can strive to improve their health, relative to their own individual capacities and restrictions.
2. Achieving physical and mental well-being is a learning process for people. Individuals can develop and maintain behaviors consistent with good health if they are given appropriate incentives and rewards and shown how to do it.
3. Involving and teaching people about self-help and self-control practices in disease prevention and health promotion is possible only if the public and private sectors are willing to make major intermediate and long-range investments in the restructuring of economic and social incentives that will encourage change in the behavior of both consumers and providers [Ng et al., 1978].

Ng proposes a specific structure for an HPO. It is one that is strikingly parallel to the one which has evolved for the Psychosomatic Medicine Clinic in Berkeley (Schleicher, 1980) as well as in other facilities throughout the United States. The HMO structure of the Kaiser-Permanente Medical Group in California, while sharing some of these premises, differs from the proposed HPO model in that it remains essentially a pathology management institution (Garfield, 1970). With the exception of the Kaiser-Permanente approach, virtually all of the present trials to create an HPO format are still based upon a fee-for-service structure, and even though those fees are substantially reduced, there are still no incentives to provide quality care with minimal utilization. That drawback is a thorny issue which is unlikely to be resolved except at the national level.

Funding is emphatically not the impediment. There are several potential sources of funds when prevention is a priority. Among these are funds from the federal government as part of a comprehensive program of national health insurance. Another source is health insurance companies through programs oriented to maintain health and reduce claims; and lastly, from corporations and business as part of the fringe benefits provided to employees. In each of these three instances the institution stands to gain economically and functionally from a healthier population. The myriad specific issues involved in such programs cannot be addressed here, but one proposal by Henrik L. Blum, Arthur I. Blaustein, and other health care economists deserves mention. Essentially they propose that health care be returned to local control to account for local variations in consumer groups through the establishment of prepaid health plans on a smaller scale than systems such as Kaiser-Permanente. Each facility will serve a limited geographic area with individuals within that area still being free to choose care at another facility outside of their immediate locale. Health Promotion Organizations would be dependent upon and therefore sensitive to consumer demands since they would literally need to compete for prepaid membership. While that smacks of "survival of the fittest," it is not far removed from the reality of present private and group practice where professional expertise and quality determines a successful practice. According to Henrik L. Blum:

> Each [HMO] receives a total fixed quarterly pool of resources based on its membership roster, with which it must provide all of the specified services to the designated population of subscribers. This puts tremendous pressure on consumer and producer alike to eliminate unneeded procedures and costly hospitalization, provide earlier care, encourage better health promoting habits, consumer education and involvement in their own well-being, promote workplace, home and recreational safety, and so on [Blum, 1978a].

Within such a system are cost-containment measures, incentives for health promotion, and consumer influence, since an individual is free to move to a competing HMO with a resulting loss in allocations to the first HMO. It is very important to bear in mind that the Canadian health care system, Health Maintenance Organizations, and the proposed Health Promotion Organizations are not panaceas and the deficits and faults of each have been researched and are apparent

(Harrington, 1977; Saward, 1973). However, their flaws are not ir-remediable and the advantages are considerable. Certainly as a potential strategy for containing health care costs while improving the quality of health care and health promotion, these approaches merit a serious and concerted trial.

Most importantly such models introduce the element of real competition between health care providers. While that might seem to be the case under the present system, it is not. After an extensive analysis of health care fees, Zachary Y. Dyckman of the Council on Wage and Price Stability has confronted this widespread misconception. Contained in a "Special Report" to *Business Week* are a few conclusions of Dyckman's study:

> Nor does competition appear to affect fees. Indeed, in those areas where doctors are concentrated, fees are invariably higher. In Alabama, for instance, where there are only 86 practicing doctors per 100,000 people, a surgeon's average fee for a gall bladder operation is $450; in Washington, D.C., where there are 343 doctors per 100,000, that same procedure brings $552, while in New York City, home of three major medical schools and 10 major hospitals, the average fee is $900. . . . Neither physicians' expenses, the cost and length of their training, lack of competition, nor their added productivity account for the untoward rise in fees [Dyckman 1978].

Health Promotion Organizations would create services likely to lower the incidence of lifestyle-related disorders. Also, such a system would be amenable to public scrutiny of its procedures, and all taxpayers would reap the benefits of a system that is both efficient and effective. Health care professionals would also benefit in many ways. At the end point of the current trend of the pathology management industry, the most likely scenario involves even greater government regulation of the overall health sector and particularly of the medical profession itself. Neither the medical profession nor the public would benefit from feeding an even larger, more inefficient federal government bureaucracy.

In the near future we may see the Federal Trade Commission, state, and private groups engaged in antitrust suits against organized medicine. Kenneth R. Reed of the FTC predicted, "State antitrust prosecutions will concentrate on fee schedules, third-party-reimbursement arrangements, and licensing restrictions that create unnecessary barriers to entry" (*Medical World News,* 1979a). Movements such as these are not new and represent such a level of dissatisfaction with current health care delivery systems that litigation seems to be the only, and very unfortunate, solution. Health Promotion Organizations help to reverse this trend while meeting high standards of health care. By their very nature HPOs must provide community education services which can be conducted by paraprofessionals (Stead, 1967; Ostergard et al., 1971) and thus free physician time to be devoted to the "diagnosis and treatment of pathology" (Chow and Chen, 1977) and away from treating the "worried well" (Garfield, 1970) who do not actually require medical care. Unquestionably the key person in the pathology correction aspect of an HPO would remain the physician. There are many excellent medical practitioners who advocate such an approach and welcome the opportunity to apply their extraordinary skills with patients who require such attention and to be freed of the draining responsibility of attempting to treat the worried well, who have been estimated to comprise upward of 40 percent of any given patient population. For these individuals it would be possible to conduct counseling and health education courses in self-care, nutrition, physical exercise, stress management, as well as family planning and a wide range of services conducted at low cost. Such an experimental project has been under way since 1974 and is still continuing at the Kaiser-Permanente facility in San Jose under the direction of physician Robert L. Harrington. Details of the 1977 interim report of that program and its considerable success, as well as its shortcomings, were discussed in *Holistic Medicine* (Pelletier, 1979).

Another direct benefit to medical practitioners is that they can negotiate contracts with the HPOs to promote flexibility in work schedules and remuneration. Through a more diversified, health-team approach to medical resources in a prepaid health plan, the processing of endless reams of paperwork and overhead would be minimized. It is undeniable that cost-control measures must be and will be applied to the health care industry. If that is not to result in costly, frustrating, and even humiliating surveillance, as well as sanctions and controls by government over the providers of health care, then an alternative model must be perfected. It is likely that cooperative efforts between health care practitioners and the consumers they serve would provide a very viable alternative. Any HPO approach to optimum health and longevity is inherently holistic since it requires an individual's active participation and motivation. Finally, an extremely important point is made by Lorenz K. Y. Ng of the National Institute of Drug Abuse:

> It is important to point out that it is not necessary to achieve perfect results to justify an HPO. What may be critical is the potential social utility of such a prevention-oriented endeavor compared with the cost of conventional ameliorative treatment. By promoting healthier lifestyles and environment, through the involvement of individuals, business and labor, and government, HPOs might be expected to reduce national health costs and indirectly stimulate the economy. Such considerations indicate solely the potential economic value of establishing HPO-like organizations across the nation. Yet, if the HPOs did nothing but increase longevity and decrease morbidity, they would be worthwhile [Ng et al., 1978].

Certainly the proposal presented here is more a vision than a reality at present, but there are specific, operating models containing functioning elements of HPOs, and these did not exist in any substantial number until a few short years ago. As a growing trend, HPOs mark a significant direction away from a strictly pathology management industry toward a health care system.

Although this discussion has focused on an HPO within the health care system per se, its greatest potential resides in the fact that many of its approaches and its very structure can be applied elsewhere in society in elementary schools, universities, corporations, and community organizations. As long as the consumer is the focus rather than the application of a particular expertise, then such measures have much in common no matter what the context. That common ground applies to all health care practitioners, who need to recognize an important principle formulated by Henrik L. Blum:

Until the inseparable whole person is at the center of their attention, these one-sided healers will continue to do lots of ineffective, expensive and even dangerous therapy. They have to be drawn together, particularly in the primary setting where, without issues of eligibility and professional territorialism, each healer is given incentives to get and keep his client well whether it involves sharing him with or shifting him to other modalities of therapy until the one most relevant to the client's well-being is tapped [Blum, 1978b].

The HPO philosophy clearly extends far beyond the narrow confines of the present medical care system and even beyond extended parameters where HPOs would be limited to a traditional health care facility.

A brief outline of how an HPO actually functions can also serve to clarify which elements can be used in other contexts. Aspects of the HPO overview which follows are drawn from several sources, including the Harrington Study (1977), the Prospective Medicine Program of the Methodist Hospital of Indiana (Robbins and Hall, 1970), an excellent analytic report by Lorenz K. Y. Ng and his colleagues (1978), and an NIMH-funded study of the Psychosomatic Medicine Clinic in Berkeley (Schleicher, 1980). Structurally an HPO would be organized in the following manner: (1) A prepaid subscriber to a local HPO would request an intake and evaluation session which would usually be conducted by a physician for the first contact. During the intake session the patient's previous medical records and current psychological and physical status would be evaluated according to medical assessments and clinical self-report histories; (2) based upon that session, a number of further services might be required. Whatever the next stage is to be, the rationale, sequence, and timing of the individual's program is reached by a mutual understanding and decision. During this interview it is of utmost importance that the patients' expectations be explored in order to insure that they are realistic and can be met by the services offered within the HPO. Depending upon the outcome of the interview, the two individuals would decide the first step, which could involve medical procedures such as a general physical examination, further laboratory or medical diagnostic assessment which would need to be conservatively applied within the context of a prepaid health plan, a medication evaluation and update, or a referral to another HPO or individual practitioner for services not offered within the local HPO. This is an important stage because it acknowledges that not all services can or should be offered within one HPO and encourages cooperative referrals with competition limited to quality of care rather than quantity of patients. Additionally, the limited services offered within the HPO would encourage the practitioners to establish an effective referral system to other specialists in the community from whom the HPO would also receive referrals in a symbiotic relationship. For operational purposes, patients could be classified according to Sidney Garfield's (1976) typology of sick, asymptomatic sick, worried well, and well. From this point on, the doctor conducting the intake would be responsible for that patient's care and would be available for periodic assessments and consultations as the patient progresses through the determined program. Those patients who require medical care would be referred on to the appropriate medical specialist, either within the HPO or to another agency or individual practitioner with provision for a follow-up to be returned to the originating HPO.

Even within the context of traditional medical care, a holistic model remains applicable, as noted by Naomi I. Rae-Grant of the Canadian Department of Health in Toronto: "The psychiatric complications of open-heart surgery, of cardiac transplantation, of chronic hemodialysis, and of renal transplantations have emphasized clearly the need for adequate pre-operative and post-operative psychological preparation and care, both for the patient and for his family" (Rae-Grant, 1972). It is very important to note that this physician contact is one of the most powerful aspects of the HPO. It is clearly evident in a recent poll of 1,510 adults by *Medical World News* that "For a large number of sedentary Americans, a doctor's advice would be the single factor most likely to motivate them to take up exercise" (1979) as well as other health-promoting behaviors. A similar poll by Pacific Mutual Life clearly indicated that there must be greater involvement of physicians if the health promotion movement is to succeed. Specifically, 57 percent of the respondents thought they would be greatly helped in achieving a healthy lifestyle if advised by their doctors, while only 47 percent said they received "a great deal" (*AMA News,* 1979a) of advice from them about health and medical care. Going a step further than the Pacific Mutual Survey, the poll by *Medical World News* also noted, "The saddest part is that the public by and large is going it alone. They aren't getting much help from the medical profession, or much encouragement in changing to healthier lifestyles." This situation can be and is being dramatically altered through the intake assessments and consultations offered by HPOs.

During the initial HPO consultation it might be determined that the individual utilize several nonmedical lifestyle assessments which may involve: (3) The completion of a computer-based lifestyle appraisal known as the Health Hazard Appraisal (HHA), which can be used to depict graphically the number of years a person can increase his or her longevity by modifying identifiable and hazardous behaviors. These aspects of lifestyle directly related to longevity are covered later in this book in Chapters V through VII. Another related and frequently useful assessment is a "Nutrition Profile," which also utilizes computer assessment procedures to suggest specific modifications of an individual's diet and nutritional status to promote optimum health. Both of these assessments are described in *Holistic Medicine,* and those aspects of nutrition most relevant to longevity are discussed in Chapter VI of this book. Experiences of the Kaiser-Permanente Group (Garfield, 1976) suggest that a health profile assessment could be accomplished in volume for as inexpensively as $10 per person, which is infinitesimal considering the potential benefits. Other assessments may involve an exercise assessment which was detailed in Chapter 7 of *Holistic Medicine.* Its applications to promoting longevity are discussed in Chapter VII later in this book. In addition to these health assessments the array of counseling and educational services noted earlier would be conducted by paraprofessionals at greatly reduced expense to the consumer.

Another aspect of the HPO involves tracking and periodic monitoring of the individuals engaged in an HPO program, whether it is for medical care or health education. For this, the services of the HPO must be well integrated in fact rather than by virtue of proximity. Consumers and staff would need to familiarize themselves with how any individual can take advantage of as many or as few of the HPO services as is necessary but not excessive. One means of achieving integrated services occurs in the initial intake where the patient has the procedures and steps clearly outlined and the option of returning to the intake physician for periodic assessment. In addition, the staff of a local HPO would be relatively small in number and would engage in regular group supervision so that the entire staff, as well as the patients, would benefit from collective input and expertise. It is essential that a patient not be overwhelmed by so many alternatives, choices, and decisions that more stress is produced than resolved. Under an HPO it is absolutely necessary that the health care professional assume the responsibility for the patient concerning the course of care. All too often the invaluable concept of shared responsibility has been abused and has resulted in an abdication of any responsibility or even in indifference on the part of a few health care practitioners. Approaches to optimum health and longevity require a reeducation of professionals and public alike if they are to move from principles to practice.

Incentives for Health

Underlying both the philosophical and economic viability of Health Promotion Organizations is the fact that it is less expensive and more effective to stem the afflictions of civilization by maintaining and enhancing health than to treat disease and disability after it has occurred. However, it is painfully evident from the limited success of present health education programs that simply providing information to a population does not result in positive behavioral changes. Implementation of HPOs will require:

> A concerted enterprise . . . that engages the collaboration of the public, government at all levels, the health professions, the insurance industry, and the whole range of consumer related industries, for example, recreation, nutrition, fashion, media, and communications in order to give people and institutions the motivation, incentives, and techniques for altering their health-aversive lifestyles and for promoting behaviors that will increase their well-being [Ng et al., 1978].

In the move away from "sick care" incentives, described by Marvin M. Kristein and his colleagues in "Health Economics and Preventive Care" (1977), incentives must be developed to help individuals maintain optimum health and thus longevity. Psychotherapists acknowledge the difficulty involved in helping a patient give up even extremely painful disorders because the "secondary gains" outweigh the discomfort. Successful therapy occurs when a more positive method can be devised for the patient to obtain the secondary gain, such as privacy, without the disorder, such as migraine. On a much larger scale the dilemma confronts all HPOs since they must consider health care incentives which are more attractive than either the present disease-oriented incentives or the questionable rewards of a high-risk lifestyle.

At present the health care system "provides economic incentives for sickness rather than health. . . . people receive financial rewards from most health care plans only when they are ill. . . . Such practices not only fail to reward those who are healthy or make an effort to stay healthy, but also implicitly penalize them" (Ng et al., 1978). Many, if not all, of the risks pinpointed with the Health Hazard Appraisal are directly attributed to excessive and misplaced affluence. It is truly ironic that few other countries could afford to repair the damages created by such hazardous lifestyles. Among these hazards are excessive intake of animal protein and fat, consumption of excessive prescribed drugs such as minor tranquilizers, which *Time* magazine dubbed "Valium Abuse: The Yellow Peril" (1979), and the overprescription of sleep medications (Smith, 1979), indulgence in proscribed or self-administered social drugs such as alcohol and tobacco, dangerous recreational sports and high-speed driving, to name but a few. All of these behaviors are possible only under conditions of affluence. It is no longer possible to support such hazardous lifestyles and their consequences; excessive affluence is no longer the order of the day.

Central to any HPO would be the development of specific means to motivate individuals to curtail self-destructive behaviors and to engage in alternative activities that encourage optimum health and longevity. Most importantly such approaches must be engaging and interesting, because too many fitness programs have been characterized as dour, restrictive regimens administered by new-age missionaries driven by their neurotic zeal to convert the savages. That is not and cannot be the case in an effective HPO system. Among the incentives suggested by Lorenz K. Y. Ng and his colleagues are:

> The incentive system would include courses in self-care and stress management (relaxation training, yoga, biofeedback, transcendental meditation); consumer discounts on material goods and services; and recreational facilities and activities (gymnasiums, tennis, swimming, and other athletic clubs) . . . . Accumulation of [health] stamps would allow people to choose among certain rewards such as running shoes, athletic club membership, discounts on certain foods, and health educational courses in self-care, things which themselves encourage healthy lifestyles. . . . In addition sociocultural incentives giving healthy behavior a coveted status symbol should be developed [Ng et al., 1978].

While these health incentives might seem exotic or even manipulative, they are actually quite mundane and direct by comparison with the barrage of contrived, often subliminal incentives toward unhealthy consumption offered incessantly by media and an economy based upon unchecked consumption. At the present time there are a limited number of health incentives such as reductions in life insurance premiums for not smoking or automobile insurance premiums for an accident-free record, the use of "well leave" in addition to vacation time for employees who demonstrate low absenteeism, and health education programs within existing HMO systems and corporations.

Within the health care sector itself, Hawaii's Blue Shield program provides subscribers with preventive screening and health promotion, and Blue Cross of Rhode Island has a program for its members in self-care (Ng et al., 1978). Future developments might lead to a profession of health care advocates whose duties would range from assisting individuals in situations of hazardous lifestyle in an extended Alcoholics Anonymous model to lobbying for sound housing, safe employment practices as in instances of herbicide and asbestos manufacturing, overseeing efficient, low energy consumption public transportation, and working toward a nontoxic physical and psychosocial environment. Actually the current trend to publicize individuals who participate in amateur marathons, bicycling, and other recreational events is a very positive indication of the development of social incentives conducive to optimum health and extended longevity. When the scope of the transition from pathology management to health promotion is considered with all of its ramifications, it is evident that powerful vested interests will resist such change. Undoubtedly there will be many indignant rebuttals, assurances that not only have "things never been better" but that a major breakthrough is "just around the corner," as well as the totally unfounded and irresponsible assertion that no scientific or economic evidence exists to support such approaches.

Such resistance is actually quite overt, as evidenced by a recent article in the widely disseminated *Medical Economics* entitled "Don't Swallow All Those Scare Stories About Health Reforms" (1979). Written by noted economist Eli Ginzberg, the article is an excellent comprehensive overview of the likelihood of such reforms when measured against certain economic restraints and vested interests. Ginzberg astutely perceives the influences contributing to the necessity of a holistic approach in noting "the simplified belief in the curative powers of modern medicine appears to be eroding." Despite numerous observations such as these and an apparent sympathy for such a movement on his part, Ginzberg concludes that major progress over the foreseeable future is likely to be slow at best. Resistance is also evident in conflicts over automotive safety, carcinogenic pharmaceuticals, environmental contaminants. These issues are of major significance, and neither party is in possession of a complete resolution. Disagreement is inevitable and constructive but the orientation toward health is supported by humanitarian ideals and economic imperatives.

Corporate Health Programs

Again moving beyond the health care system per se, the preeminent institution for the implementation of optimum health and longevity programs will be the corporation. The corporation reigns as the institution which most directly affects and influences the lives of individuals in the United States. While it has been both praised and castigated, its influences have been largely assessed in terms of profit, which still remains the undisputed barometer of corporate activities. However, more recent values such as social responsibility and the preservation of employee health have emerged. Private business has acknowledged a substantial responsibility in health promotion, and the number of corporations with innovative health programs is increasing. Actually, corporations have been more responsive and innovative than the health care industry itself. A front-page article of *The Wall Street Journal* noted:

> Some companies are helping employees to stay healthy through medical screening and on-the-job exercise regimens. Many employers, in conjunction with insurers, are requiring a second opinion before surgery or are cracking down on what they consider excessive doctor fees and unnecessary hospital stays. A few are even using corporate muscle to block controversial hospital expansion and construction. And there is increased business interest in health maintenance organizations, or HMOs, prepaid group-practice plans that emphasize preventive and outpatient care over hospitalization [Lublin, 1978].

Many companies of the *Fortune* 500 such as IBM, Johns-Manville, Alcoa, and Xerox provide a wide variety of health services for all employees.

Corporate institutions and private individuals share much the same disenchantment with the pathology management industry. Bearing an estimated one-third of all health care costs, they are beginning to look for ways to keep healthy people off the sick rolls. According to a special report in *Business Week,* "At the top of their lists are physical fitness and screening programs. Even though the results will not be in for five or ten years, the health care burden is so heavy, and its projected costs so awesome, that companies are willing to invest right now in what seem likely solutions" (1978). This forward-looking approach is much more evident in corporations than in the health care system per se. Furthermore, the necessary concern for cost-containment and cost-effectiveness is inherent in business enterprise and cuts through many of the superfluous issues raised by vested interests within health care itself. Freed of such interests and their subsequent resistances, certain corporations have moved aggressively and effectively in the promotion of optimum health.

One important reservation needs to be noted at this point. While certain corporations have worked toward health, prompted both by humane and economic considerations, others such as the petrochemical and pharmaceutical industries have ignored corporate responsibility and have created products degrading to both environment and individuals. Both the petrochemical and pharmaceutical industries have produced many products which have enhanced certain aspects of the quality of life, and no one could argue with that point. However, it is equally accurate that excessive production and promotion of over-the-counter and prescription drugs, unchecked application of herbicides and insecticides, and the proliferation of carcinogenic agents by those same companies is irresponsible to the extreme. Effects of these measures are so great that they cannot be assessed in terms of the usual parameters of economic analysis. There is no need to press this point further since there are penetrating analyses by Barry Commoner (1975, 1976) and other ecology-minded individuals.

Among the corporations which are increasingly sensitive to both internal and public effects generated by their activities, there are some positive innovations under way. One successful and conservative format has been for a company to establish its own Health Maintenance Organization in the fashion of industrialist Henry J. Kaiser, who began the HMO concept in the early 1940s when he retained a physician to provide prepaid health care for employees of his shipbuilding empire. As of this year Kaiser-Permanente and approximately 160 similar plans now exist nationwide, and that number is increasing. According to estimates by Joseph A. Califano, Jr., "Big business could have saved up to $150 million last year if just 5% of the employees of Fortune 500 companies belonged to HMOs" (Lublin, 1978). For corporations and health professionals interested in such a system, the United States Chamber of Commerce will provide a 250-page guide. This guide is the product of a committee of twenty-two leaders from business, labor, insurance, and health care. Through the use of charts and references the report details:

> . . . how to set up health-promotion programs; steps businesses can take to get the local Chamber of Commerce involved in health care; ways in which companies can make more demands on their insurance carriers; methods for emphasizing economy, quality, and accessibility of care; and procedures for becoming involved in health planning [*Medical World News,* 1978a].

Another useful overview of the structural elements and functions of an HMO is a brief article entitled "Feasibility of Simulation of Health Maintenance Organizations" by A. Taher Moustafa and David W. Sears (1974) of the University of Massachusetts. Three major corporations, Goodyear, Firestone, and B. F. Goodrich, who have adopted such programs under the industry's rubric of "self-insurance" (*Business Week,* 1976), have reported substantial reductions in health care costs.

Other corporate giants involved in such programs are General Motors, Deere and Company, and Ford Motor Company, which noted that health care was the single most expensive fringe benefit, costing the company "an estimated $520 million this year and $600 million next year, up from $450 million in 1977 despite no increase in coverage" (Lublin, 1978). For the consumer Ford estimates that this results in an increase of $120 per automobile produced in 1977, with General Motors citing $160 for the same period. With such figures at stake the provision of more cost-efficient health care is a point of agreement between labor unions and management. A 1979 Report of the President's Council on Wage and Price Stability described 126 HMO programs developed in cooperative efforts between employers and unions since 1973. At the present time "Ford is saving $2 million a year from HMO participation by 10,000 employees, or just 4% of its U.S. work force" (Lublin, 1978).

Virtually all of the corporations which have adopted voluntary HMO systems have noted additional benefits common to this approach, such as: (1) an increased ability to pinpoint irregularities or excessive fees for services; (2) without using an outside insurance carrier, the saving of taxes on premium reserves and insurance company profits; and (3) reductions of 3 to 5 percent of their previous health benefit expenditures. One major impediment to the further effectiveness of an HMO approach is not the corporation's willingness but "acceptance by employees." As one instance, Charles S. Ryan, who is Director of Health and Safety at Sun Company, has noted that his company began its own HMO in Pennsylvania several years ago. Since that time "only 433 of Sun's more than 32,000 employees have so far enrolled" in the voluntary program (*Business Week,* 1978). This observation holds true of every existing HMO facility and points up the absolute necessity of providing both types of facilities simultaneously as well as individual education and incentives.

An even more striking departure from traditional pathology management is the number of corporate programs offering an HMO approach plus programs and physical fitness facilities as a means of promoting optimum health. Corporations have recognized a clear link between prevention, optimum health, and longevity, since the premature loss of key executives is costly. *The Wall Street Journal* described a jogging program at Kimberly-Clark. This corporation has invested $2.5 million in a health-screening and fitness center. It is staffed by twenty-three people including physicians, exercise specialists, and technicians and is open from 5:00 A.M. to 9:00 P.M., Monday through Saturday, at a cost of $600,000 annually. Assessments are currently under way to compare the incidence and subsequent cost of illness of those employees in the program and those of a control group. Results of such experiments will have a major influence upon the future of all aspects of health care in the United States. One participant is Steven Samu, a 44-year-old research scientist, who runs three miles per day after undergoing open-heart surgery and quips, "Instead of saying goodbye at 48, I may say goodbye at 68. It's a good deal all around—for me and for the company" (Lublin, 1978). That sentiment is echoed many times over throughout corporations which have recognized that the health and longevity of key personnel are synonymous with corporate well-being. According to one corporation, "Xerox spends more than $58 million annually on insurance and medical premiums. It estimates the loss of an executive who suffers a fatal heart attack at age 41 costs the company $600,000" (Dillman, 1979). While many of the corporate programs have been utilized by those executives of middle management and up, there is an expanding trend to make such opportunities open to all personnel. Many corporations such as Olin, Exxon, and Union Carbide have long had screening and prevention programs which were traditionally medical in orientation. Now these programs are being extended for even earlier prevention through fitness programs.

One of the most extensive health programs is offered at Brunswick Corporation, the highly diversified billion-dollar-a-year leisure products company. At its Skokie, Illinois, branch it has initiated a series of programs at several of its largest facilities. According to Rial O. Herreman, Vice-President for Human Resources, "We are more sensitive to health care needs because we are in the recreation and health care business" (*Business Week,* 1978). Among the services offered for voluntary participation are weight reduction and dietary counseling as well as the more traditional screening for cancer and hypertension. Recently Brunswick constructed an exercise course at a plant in Tulsa, Oklahoma.

Xerox announced its program called the "Xerox Health Management Program" under the direction of George Pfeiffer, Manager of Corporate Fitness of the company's headquarters in Stamford, Connecticut. From Xerox's description it is "a preventive-maintenance approach to fitness through regular aerobic exercises and common-sense lifestyle. It does not offer any new exercises, diets, gimmicks, mail-order gadgets or shortcuts to fitness and health. . . . We view the . . . Program as a way to keep both our employees and our company in top shape" (Pfeiffer, 1980). There are now eight fitness centers in the United States and one abroad. Also the program has been systematically introduced with reduced facilities at twenty Xerox facilities. At present the largest facility is a $3.5 million complex in Leesburg, Virginia. Another active program of Xerox is in

Rochester, New York, under direction of Jim Post, who is the Program Director of their Executive Fitness Program. In an open letter Post described the program as "one major step on behalf of our employees and their families toward the holistic concept to better health" (1980). As a model of future corporation-based Health Promotion Organizations, the Xerox undertaking is an excellent prototype.

Under the Xerox health program the voluntary participants are given three booklets: *Take Charge of Your Life; The Road to Better Health and Happier Lifestyles;* and *Fitbook.* Although there is overlap in the content of each booklet, each of them emphasizes one aspect of optimum health. *Take Charge of Your Life* (Xerox, 1980) introduces the program and provides specific assessments and forms for anyone to evaluate their current health status, particularly cardiovascular risk factors. Included are an excellent self-administered series of evaluations including: (1) a cardiovascular disease risk-factor estimate based on numerical values for certain answers to a series of fifteen questions resembling a credit card application form; (2) a "step test" modeled after the aerobic approach of Kenneth Cooper (1977); (3) a self-administered body composition test to determine the percentage of body weight which is fat; and (4) a joint flexibility exercise and evaluation. Each is clearly described, with illustrative photographs, and practical record-keeping forms. Such a clear approach is undoubtedly the result of a great deal of research and organization, and the results are most impressive. Also, the simplicity and lack of gimmicks is a refreshing departure from the plethora of "how to" books currently being marketed. All of the necessary information is known; what remains is its unequivocal presentation and implementation, and that is precisely what the Xerox program accomplishes. *The Road to Better Health and Happier Lifestyles* (Xerox, 1980) emphasizes warm-up exercises with illustrations for seven basic stretching exercises. Additionally, the brochure provides practical information concerning heart-rate protocols for endurance training, instructions for cool-down periods, a list of "Six Do's and Don'ts of a Good Workout," and information regarding personal athletic equipment. Again each potentially complex topic is covered clearly and with understatement. *Fitbook* (Xerox, 1980) is the most comprehensive booklet and includes a sequence of four "modules."

Module one concerns the warm-up exercises previously noted in *The Road to Better Health and Happier Lifestyles.* Module two focuses on the "target pulse protocol" and the basic principles of aerobic exercise. In module two are specific instructions for the safe development of an aerobic exercise program in jogging, cycling, swimming, and rope skipping. Module three contains "developmental exercises" which are designed to develop strength, flexibility, and endurance for major muscle groups. Module four contains illustrations of exercises appropriate for a five-minute cool-down period as well as seven exercises specific to strengthening and preserving the integrity of the back. Among the other topics addressed in the booklet are smoking, drugs and alcohol, caffeine consumption, nutrition and weight control, and relaxation exercises. The section on stress and relaxation is quite comprehensive and is similar to the relaxation procedures detailed in *Mind as Healer, Mind as Slayer* (Pelletier, 1977). Overall, the program is comprehensive and presented with extraordinary clarity. Many elements of the program are drawn from the Canadian *Fit Kit* (1980), which is a 33 1/3 rpm record and exercise charts illustrating an aerobic exercise program. Variations of the Xerox program are conducted at various facilities and there is an overview of the Rochester-based program of Jim Post in *Executive Fitness Program* (Xerox, 1980). Included in this program are many of the above exercise programs plus an emphasis on the use of biofeedback. There are many reasons why this Xerox program warrants significant attention. It is of great importance that a major corporation has invested considerable economic and human resources to develop and implement a program conducive to optimum health and longevity. That is an important and highly noteworthy step.

From this brief overview of the Xerox program it is clear that there is an emphasis on cardiovascular conditioning through regular aerobic exercise. To a certain degree this emphasis is warranted, based on preliminary observations from studies indicating the major importance of physical activity in health maintenance. One four-year study of 100 individuals who engaged in jogging for one and a half hours three times per week was conducted by A. H. Ismai of Purdue University to determine if it would reduce their health care costs. Participants were free to eat and smoke without restriction. One surprising result was that the people who remained in the program had as many medical claims as those who dropped out, but the relative expenditure was $3,695 for participants and $7,698 among dropouts. From these findings it appears, "The physically fit people went to the doctor right away about their problems, but the sedentary ones went only when a condition became aggravated—and therefore more expensive to treat" (*Medical World News,* 1978b). Preliminary findings such as these and others indicate an important role for physical exercise, but it too has limitations which need to be acknowledged. There are effective but very limited references and programs noted in the *Fitbook* (Xerox, 1980) to other areas of health care, such as stress management, prescription and proscription drugs, and nutritional factors. One potential shortcoming of a program similar to the series conducted at Xerox is this very emphasis on physical exercise.

Any approach to optimum health which adopts a holistic orientation needs to be more comprehensive. In developing such a program it is important to include educational programs concerning hazardous lifestyles, health profiles such as the Health Hazard Appraisal, computer-based dietary assessments, and a stress management technique through biofeedback or a related deep-relaxation method, all highly effective components for any preventive care program. Additionally, each of these components is much less hazardous to administer and much less costly than a predominantly exercise-focused approach because it requires no special facilities. The computer assessment procedures themselves are very low cost, especially in quantity, and the number of personnel required to administer such a program is greatly reduced. When corporate health programs either grow predominantly out of the medical departments or fall under their jurisdiction, the results are likely to result in highly technological, instrumentation-laden programs tending to emphasize physical and visible approaches to preventing specific disorders such as cardiovascular disease. While such efforts are commendable, they narrow the scope of health promotion to pathology prevention. Diversified programs of health promotion for corporations can be greatly enhanced, and overhead greatly reduced, by placing physical exercise in its proper perspective alongside the other components of a comprehensive approach.

Future developments might include a health status accounting as an integral part of the corporation's fiscal statement. These "health accounts" (White, 1977) would:

> . . . specify how much each firm is paying for health benefits, what the corporation spends on occupational health and safety programs, on physical fitness activities and on employee and community health education and what the corporation does about smoking on the job and about vending machines with junk food, cigarettes, or soft drinks [Ng et al., 1978].

Such an accounting system would serve to keep the goal of health promotion in clear view because it is all too easy to regress to the familiar model of attempting to prevent specific pathologies. Most importantly, it is increasingly and unnecessarily expensive and ineffective to isolate even a comprehensive program of health care to the health department of a corporation. That oversight abounds in virtually all of the existing programs which are relatively isolated from the entire context of the corporation. Ubiquitous "coffee breaks" and the deleterious effects of excessive caffeine upon the central nervous system and cardiopulmonary functions exist side by side with jogging programs; difficult and stress-provoking working conditions and faulty interpersonal communications compete with stress management programs; corporate dining rooms and vending machines supplied with excessive amounts of refined carbohydrates undercut both dietary and exercise programs. This listing could be extended much further.

Several forward-looking corporations are reaching out into community organizations, becoming involved in "regional health planning agencies" (*Business Week,* 1976), and scrutinizing federal actions in an approach which links their individual, corporate, and community actions and responsibilities. Inherent in a health promotion program is an ecological model where all components of the system remain in inextricable interaction. To the extent that a corporate health program ignores this imperative, it will fail; to the extent it is acknowledged, it will succeed.

All of the measures discussed here are within the scope of the Surgeon General's report *Healthy People* (1979). Recently an editorial in *Science* by Bruce Stokes of the Worldwatch Institute in Washington, D.C., cited numerous examples of the efficacy of "self-care" in promoting optimum health. Measures directed toward optimum health have been criticized as "middle class preoccupations with health" (Duhl, 1980), and that would be the case if it were not for the fact that every preventive care program would free services to treat the seriously ill with the best medical expertise, technology, and pharmaceuticals at reduced cost. That point is made abundantly clear in Stokes's discussion of building in health incentives to any program of national health insurance: "Such a national health plan could help create a public awareness that runaway health care costs are, in part, a social problem arising from overreliance on the medical system for treatment of even the simplest illnesses and that cost containment is a joint government and individual responsibility" (Stokes, 1979).

Health and Longevity Promotion

Throughout this chapter the link between the promotion of optimum health and longevity has been implied and in some instances made explicit. At the present time the United States ranks an appalling seventeenth in terms of comparative studies of worldwide longevity. Not only are hazardous lifestyle practices not conducive to extended longevity, they curtail the fulfillment of even the current average life expectancy. Preliminary data from the Human Population Laboratory of the California State Department of Health in Alameda County clearly underscore this observation. By reviewing data from the populations studied by the laboratory, Lester Breslow determined the relationship between seven common health habits and longevity. These common practices were: eating breakfast; eating regularly, that is, not snacking between meals; eating moderately, that is, maintaining normal weight for height; not smoking cigarettes; drinking alcohol moderately, if at all; exercising at least moderately; and sleeping regularly seven to eight hours per night.

There was an impressive relationship between these health habits and subsequent mortality. By way of example, the life expectancy of a 45-year-old male could be extended by eleven years depending upon the extent to which he practiced these lifestyle characteristics; life expectancy for a 45-year-old female, already higher, could be extended seven years. That conservative measures such as these can have a profound effect upon both optimum health and longevity is hardly debatable. What is yet to be evidenced is a national commitment toward that goal. Again, Lester Breslow, Dean of Public Health at the UCLA School of Medicine, has formulated the critical question:

> Now we have reached the point where, already in America and soon generally in the world, we have the industrial machinery and have converted the people into a work force capable of producing what we actually need. Waste and failures in equitable distribution of the products are obviously still problems. Still, the productive capacity is there. Shall we continue to use it mainly guided by the former ethic, namely enhancing production for economic interest as the highest priority, or shall we now harness our productive capacity primarily in the interest of promoting health and well-being? [Breslow, 1977].

That fundamental question remains unresolved. Limited progress is evident in the present conflict over the production and sale of unequivocally destructive cigarettes, regulation of carcinogenic food additives, corporate health promotion programs, the Stanford Heart Disease Prevention Program of John W. Farquhar and his colleagues (Farquhar et al., 1977), organized self-care programs with hemophiliacs at Tufts Medical Center and with diabetics at the University of Southern California (Stokes, 1979), and the overall heightened awareness evident in media and publications of at least public interest in optimum health and longevity. All of these experiments and their outcomes as well as many others will compel concerned individuals in the United States to make clear choices in the allocation of limited human and economic resources in the pursuit of health.

Finally, the quest for optimum health and longevity will challenge a precious illusion of all humankind with even greater consequences than the issues of economics, public policy, and individual responsibility discussed so far. That fundamental challenge is to the illusion of immortality. In 1846, Emily Dickinson commented in a letter to her friend Abiah that: "I don't know why it is but it does not seem to me that I shall ever cease to live on earth—I cannot imagine with the farthest stretch of my imagination my own death scene" (Johnson, 1958). Poetically, Dickinson expressed a pervasive psychological stance which may very well account for the persistence of self-destructive lifestyles. In the all too familiar litany of such behaviors —ignoring genetic counseling, failure to comply with medical instructions, seat belts not used, and cigarette smoking—there is an irrational defiance of logic and education. In an article entitled "The High Cost of Self-Deception," Robert L. Berg of the American Health Foundation in New York City has traced the illusion of immortality to several roots. According to his analysis, this self-deception and denial has three components: ". . . the probability of incurring a disorder, the low value placed on life in later years, and the discount rate applied to gains long delayed. In addition, fanciful thoughts about immortality or being lucky and not falling ill may well play a substantial role" (Berg, 1976). Of all of these components, the sense that advanced age is clearly devalued lends a great weight to the denial of its inexorable progression. Virtually every individual overlooks this progression and in doing so does not recognize the specific potentials in each developmental stage of life.

Ironically, concern over longevity is often relegated to advanced years when even extreme measures have no detectable influence. Of particular note in this regard is a study by Kunimitsu Moriya, who compared the attitudes toward their own future of 663 college students between 18 and 20 years old with those of 101 nursing-home residents between 64 and 98 years old. Each individual was asked if they wanted to live 100 years or more, how long they wished to live, and what death meant to them. There were numerous analyses performed on the subsequent data, with one clear outcome being ". . . that with age the desire for relative immortality (100 years or more) tends to increase" (Moriya, 1975). While certain limited measures can be adopted late in life, most life extension measures need to be initiated from birth. Clearly a fundamental challenge is to enhance the awareness of the potential of longevity at earlier developmental stages. To a great extent the resistance to adopting a lifestyle conducive to optimum health and longevity derives from the unwillingness to acknowledge that such a choice even exists. The choice is greater than we think. To this point in time efforts to achieve longevity have been limited to the present life expectancy. That potential can be achieved with the application of current knowledge and collective effort. Beyond that horizon lies the unrealized psychobiological potential for unprecedented longevity in the human species.

THREE

Through a Microscope Darkly

The plethora of theories purported to explicate the process of aging has a bewildering, *Alice in Wonderland* quality. The field is highly fragmented. On one level there are descriptions of the physical and mental characteristics of the aged, on another a variety of attempts to identify the cellular and biochemical mechanisms which underlie those characteristics, with few direct links between these two kinds of analysis. Even within the biochemical area, longevity research is highly specialized and fragmented, with key researchers not citing the findings of colleagues working along closely related lines (Marx, 1974a, 1974b). Biochemical approaches have received the predominance of attention, as detailed in Albert Rosenfeld's excellent overview *Pro-longevity* (1976). This inordinate emphasis is a reflection of the predominant scientific paradigm which dictates that the ultimate nature of reality resides in the microscopic realms of biochemical interaction. This chapter is intended to review the research into the biochemical mechanisms underlying the processes of aging and longevity, since no inquiry into human longevity would be complete without such an excursion. This review will provide background for later chapters on the psychosocial, nutritional, and physical activity aspects of longevity.

While physical and biochemical laws have considerable influence upon longevity, the operation of these laws is inextricably linked to higher orders of organization in the human organism and its psychosocial context. Cellular aging is an unquestionable reality, but it is increasingly evident that "we kill ourselves more often than we die" (Knowles, 1977).

Theories of Aging

Attempts to define aging are as varied as are the research efforts to determine its causes. Esoteric efforts to resolve this riddle have included: (1) mathematical computations based upon a finite number of breaths and heartbeats in a lifetime—*"Homo sapiens* is a markedly deviant mammal in more ways than braininess alone. We live about three times as long as mammals of our body size 'should,' but we breathe at the 'right' rate and thus live to breathe about three times as much as an average mammal of our body size" (Gould, 1977)— *Homo sapiens* and the bottlenosed dolphin apparently demonstrate the greatest deviance from predicted end points; (2) an elaborate multivariate analysis relating brain weight, body weight, resting metabolic rate, and body temperature (Sacher, 1978); (3) systems theory approaches where a system's "increase in noise level represents the phenomenon of aging" (Goldman, 1968); and also (4) measuring the "life line" on the palm of the hand. The palms of fifty-one cadavers were examined to predict life expectancy, in a study published in the *Journal of the American Medical Association* which turned out to be ". . . blessedly free of scientific worthiness or usefulness to life insurers" (Wilson and Mather, 1974). These are among the more reputable studies, and innumerable others have strained credulity to its limit.

Central to each definition of aging is the concept that for all living organisms, "aging and senescence are considered to be essentially a matter of increasing vulnerability that results in a progressive reduction of functional effectiveness culminating in death" (Greenberg and Yunis, 1978). Aging occurs primarily because the cells of the human body that cannot replace themselves either die or lose a small part of their function with every passing year. From that common observation the predominant theories concerning the aging process divide into the two main categories, those which focus on intrinsic factors and those which focus on extrinsic factors. Intrinsic factors are processes within cells and extrinsic factors are those occurring at higher levels of hormonal and even environmental organization. While each group of researchers is attempting to arrive at a unified theory of longevity, a recent article in *Science* noted that, ". . . a one researcher–one theory portrayal of aging research would be a more accurate approximation of the current situation" (Marx, 1974a). Each theory contributes understanding of one aspect of aging. By clarifying these major theories it is possible to determine the applications and limitations of each in the quest for longevity.

Nearly two thousand years ago Virgil lamented that "time bears away all things, even our minds" (*Eclogues* IX, line 51). Despite all the vaccination and antibiotic advances of biomedical technology plus the limited applications of more holistic approaches to prevention and health promotion, remarkably little has changed. This human condition mirrors Newton's second law of thermodynamics or the "increasing entropy" law which was thought to apply to all systems. According to the law of entropy, all systems tend to become more disorganized as time passes, unless energy is expended to generate order. Unless molecules are stored at absolute zero and shielded from all forms of radiation, they will gradually deteriorate to less ordered arrangements of their constituent atoms. Aging can be interpreted as a complex variant of this basic law. While the law of entropy remains invariant, except in the instance of subatomic particles, the duration of time over which order is maintained is highly variable. Our longevity is a measure of how long order can be maintained in the human species. For the present discussion, emphasis is essentially on the degenerative processes characteristic of aging, while the primary focus of the next chapter is on negative entropy, on the regenerative capacities of the organism striving toward longevity. More individuals attain the average life expectancy now than in the first century B.C., but the maximum life expectancy has not increased significantly since Virgil. Furthermore the mental and physical deterioration accompanying extended old age might actually be increasing and nullifying the minimal increase.

Many theories and research attempts have focused on this fundamental issue, but current knowledge remains in a state described by Leonard J. Greenberg of the University of Minnesota Medical School, ". . . relatively little is known about the pathogenesis of senescence and little agreement exists regarding the true nature of the aging process" (Greenberg and Yunis, 1978). With that caveat in mind it appears there are seven major theories concerning the intrinsic, extrinsic, and interactive mechanisms underlying the process of aging. These major theories are: (1) limits to cellular longevity (Hayflick, 1973, 1974); (2) DNA or genetic approaches (Watson and Crick, 1953; Burnet, 1973; Strehler, 1977), an important subset of this approach being "error catastrophe theory" (Orgel, 1973); (3) free radical mechanisms (Harman, 1973; Packer, 1976, 1977); (4) cross-linkage theories (Bjorksten, 1963, 1968; Cutler, 1976); (5) lipofuscin accumulation interpretations (Sheldrake, 1974); (6) neurophysiological and immunological approaches which address a higher order of organization (Finch, 1975; Denckla, 1978; Makinodan, 1978); and finally (7) mechanisms mediated by stress and psychosocial variables which range beyond biochemistry and are considered at length in Chapter V. Aspects of each of these theories are superficially compatible and may ultimately prove to be mutually enhancing rather than mutually exclusive. That issue cannot be resolved here. Each major approach is briefly considered in order to show the spectrum of present approaches to longevity. In terms of presentation this chapter begins with cells, then the realm of DNA, and extends outward to neuroimmunology, and total organism levels of complexity and organization.

Limits to Cellular Longevity

One of the earliest attempts to explore longevity at the cellular level was undertaken by Nobel prize winner Alexis Carrel of the Rockefeller Institute. Near the beginning of this century Carrel placed a section of embryonic chicken heart tissue in a laboratory culture flask, or *in vitro.* For thirty-four years the cells continued to divide. The culture was voluntarily terminated with the conclusion that when cells were released from the living organism, or *in vivo,* they could divide and function normally in cultures for periods in excess of the life expectancy of the species. Two conclusions were drawn from these and related experiments: (1) aging per se was not the result of biochemical events in the cell itself and (2) *in vitro* cells were essentially immortal. By contrast to the progression of aging, these results raised the question "Can vertebrate cells, functioning and replicating under ideal conditions, escape from the inevitability of aging and death, which is universally characteristic of the whole animals from which they were derived?" (Hayflick, 1977). Further evidence from two other experiments appeared to support these conclusions. Cell cultures from mouse connective tissue initiated in 1943, and HeLa cells—an acronym for the first and last names of the woman whose cervical carcinoma was the origin of this strain of cells —which were begun in 1951, appeared to replicate indefinitely and still continue to flourish today in research laboratories throughout the world. While these data created a great deal of optimistic speculation, later experimentation refuted these results and marked a new era of longevity research.

In 1961 Stanford University's medical microbiologist Leonard Hayflick proved that the long-standing interpretation of Carrel's experiments were not accurate. Hayflick's experiments involved the placement of normal human embryonic fibroblasts, connective tissue cells, in tissue culture. From a sophisticated series of experiments it became evident that even under ideal conditions these human fibroblasts replicated only a limited number of times before they began to deteriorate, became senescent, lost their capacity to replicate, and eventually died. Under the most optimum conditions the outside limit for human embryo fibroblasts appears to be 50 replications (Hayflick and Moorehead, 1961). Fibroblasts removed from persons after birth demonstrate a doubling, or a twofold increase, in cell numbers that occurs during conditions of continuous growth, but less often, perhaps 20 to 30 times. This finite point has been termed the "Hayflick limit" by other researchers.

Normal human and animal cells have a finite capacity to divide both *in vitro* and *in vivo*. The number of population doublings that these cells are capable of undergoing is inversely related to the age of the donor and the life span of the species. Functional decrements that precede the loss of division potential are thought to produce the common manifestations of age changes seen *in vitro* [Hayflick, 1973a].

It appears that Carrel's cultures were inadvertently contaminated when the chick embryo medium was added to maintain the cultures since the medium probably contained a number of new cells which were then observed to undergo a seemingly infinite number of doublings. Contemporary attempts to replicate Carrel's findings indicate that chick cell fibroblasts cannot be maintained *in vitro* much beyond one year. Some cells do exhibit seemingly infinite replicability, but these are abnormal cells such as cancer cells (Stewart et al., 1959). Perhaps an exploration of the mechanisms of why normal cells are finite will provide a means of enhancing their capacity to replicate while providing the information necessary to terminate cancer cell doublings.

Significant interspecies differences have been found. "A fruit fly is ancient in 40 days, a mouse at 3 years, a horse at 30, a man at 100 and some tortoise species not until about 150 years" (Hayflick, 1973). The existence of such a range of life-spans for different animal species may indicate the evolution of a more perfect mechanism of repair and replication in the cells of the animals with an extended longevity. If that mechanism can be discovered, it may prove applicable to the human species. For the human species, it has been demonstrated that laboratory fibroblasts have been maintained for up to 60 doublings. If the entire human organism could function at that level, the human life expectancy would be extended to approximately 150 years. Reviewing the results of his research, Hayflick has pinpointed three mechanisms which appear to be responsible for this finite doubling:

> Normal cells may cease dividing or functioning *in vitro* as a result of the ultimate loss of genetic information either as a consequence of the "playing out" of the genetic program, the expression of "genes for aging," or of the accumulation of errors or misinformation in information containing molecules. . . . The cause could, in chain reaction fashion, involve progressively higher orders of cell, tissue and organ systems [Hayflick, 1973a].

Each of these functional changes within the cell are disruptive and cause the cell to terminate before it can reach its maximum division limit. Hayflick's model clearly indicates that the genetic program in a cell eventually accumulates errors and instability which results in errors in translation of the DNA messages into RNA and protein sequences. These errors are considered to be analogous to the serial photographing of a photograph. As each picture is made from a preceding picture, the image becomes increasingly blurred until it is unrecognizable at a certain point in time. Again this is essentially an expression of the second law of thermodynamics. For biological organisms, this sequence has been termed the "mean time to failure" (Hayflick, 1970), which is the end result of the "wear and tear" to which a single cell, tissue, organ, or the intact organism is subjected. While the average or "mean time to failure" is variable, its finite nature appears to be an absolute.

Longevity and the Genetic Code

Virtually every researcher in the field of longevity has echoed Hayflick's observation that, "Probably no other area of scientific inquiry abounds with as many untested or untestable theories as does the biology of aging" (Hayflick, 1974). Given this widespread acknowledgment, it is ironic that certain data concerning the possible interaction between cellular processes, higher orders of organization such as neuroendocrine mechanisms, and particularly any suggestion of psychosocial variables as in centenarian communities are categorically dismissed. Although there are flaws and problems with research concerning higher order and psychosocial factors, it is apparent that the present over-reliance upon cellular processes to explicate aging and longevity is not entirely warranted. Remaining at the cellular level for the present time, the question remains one of identifying the underlying mechanisms responsible for the built-in limits to cellular replication.

Whatever the process, it ultimately involves DNA or genetic coding. DNA is an abbreviation for deoxyribonucleic acid, which is a large biopolymeric molecule. Modern molecular biology was initiated on April 25, 1953, when John D. Watson and Francis H. C. Crick published their paper on the molecular structure of nucleic acids. That paper began with the now classic understatement, "We wish to suggest a structure for the salt of deoxyribonucleic acid (D.N.A.). This structure has novel features which are of considerable biological interest" (Watson and Crick, 1953). It is now nearly thirty years since that key discovery indicated that the genes of any given cell in an organism contain all of the information necessary for its moment-to-moment existence, including "extracting energy from molecules assimilated as food and for repairing itself as well as for replication" (Crick, 1966). Through a series of articles in *Scientific American,* Francis H. C. Crick detailed the complexity of DNA encoding, which is essential to any understanding of the genetics of longevity (Crick, 1962, 1966). DNA is the basic unit of genetic information for every species on earth. When organisms reproduce they transmit DNA, which serves to guide the manufacture of all the body's proteins and regulates their functions. DNA is a polymer molecule which is constructed of linked, repeating, smaller molecules. Watson and Crick discovered that the physical structure of the DNA molecule was a double helix with two exterior backbones of phosphate and a five-carbon sugar which are coiled around each other with a right-hand twist. Between these two backbones are suspension bridges, small repeating molecules composed of four chemicals termed "bases."

Visually the DNA structure looks like an elegant, suspended spiral staircase. There are four standard bases, which are each given a letter of the alphabet: ". . . adenine (A), guanine (G), thymine (T), and cytosine (C). They are the four 'letters' used to spell out the genetic message. The exact sequence of bases along a length of the DNA molecule determines the structure of a particular protein molecule" (Crick, 1966). Proteins, the fundamental element of all life, are made up of 20 different kinds of small molecules or amino acids which are strung together into long polypeptide chains. All proteins are derived from the same 20 amino acids obtained from food but not all proteins contain all the amino acids. These proteins often contain from 100 to 300 amino acid units linked together, with the links arranged in each protein according to a genetic program. In effect, a protein is a long sentence written in a language which has twenty letters.

As in any language the order of the letters determines the meaning, just as the letters A, R, T, form "art," "rat," "tar," or a meaningless "tra." From Crick's overview, "The genetic code is not the message itself but the 'dictionary' used by the cell to translate from the four-letter language of nucleic acid to the 20-letter language of protein" (Crick, 1966). Although this letter and alphabet analogy is universally applied, it is important to bear in mind the virtually infinite complexity of the language of life. Only recently has the genetic code for certain bacteria been resolved, and more complex life forms have very complicated DNA structures. Accordingly, "Man's DNA is fiercely complex, a molecular strand six feet long and 1/250,000,000th of an inch wide coiled up inside almost all the body's cells" (Rhodes, 1979). Also, DNA is uniquely capable of replicating itself. Replication of the DNA genetic code is the vital phase in the generation of life, and also vital to researchers seeking the mechanisms underlying the phenomenon of aging. Translating the message in DNA occurs in a prescribed sequence of steps. DNA is first transcribed into a similar molecule called "messenger ribonucleic acid" (Crick, 1966), or RNA. Approximately six proteins prepare the DNA double helix for replication. One protein pries the two strands apart, another stabilizes these strands, while others guide the stabilized protein to its replication site. Structurally, RNA is similar to DNA, but RNA is a single-stranded helix and cannot replicate itself. Like DNA, RNA has four kinds of bases as side groups, with three of them being identical to those found in DNA. However, the fourth base is uracil (U) instead of thymine. Usually genetic models use the RNA letters of U, C, A, G, to designate their structure (Crick, 1957). Also, RNA forms occur in three or four main varieties, with approximately sixty types of transfer RNA alone. RNA performs its functions both inside the cell nucleus and outside the cell nucleus in the cytoplasm. Of the many proteins within the cell, the proteins which function as enzymes are present in thousands of molecular structures with the common function of serving as catalysts for each stage of biochemical reaction in cells. At the most fundamental level, DNA directs RNA to construct proteins out of amino acids through the use of these enzymes.

After these basic findings the unraveling of the specific processes by which the genetic code is read and transcribed became extremely complex.

... experimental evidence (mainly indirect) suggested that the code was a triplet code: that the bases on the messenger RNA were read three at a time and that each group corresponded to a particular amino acid. Such a group is called a codon. Using four symbols in groups of three, one can form 64 distinct triplets. . . . Protein synthesis takes place on the comparatively large intracellular structures known as ribosomes. These bodies travel along the chain of messenger RNA, reading off its triplets one after another and synthesizing the polypeptide chain of the protein, starting at the amino ends [Crick, 1966].

Looking back to 1953, this degree of precision in the reading of the genetic code is a major development from Watson and Crick's second classic understatement, "It has not escaped our notice that the specific pairing we have postulated immediately suggests a possible copying mechanism for the genetic material" (Watson and Crick, 1953). Although a great deal of the genetic code has been deciphered, there are an infinite number of issues yet to be resolved. From numerous laboratories it is evident that the apparently fixed DNA structure noted above actually stretches, bends, shears into sections, and unwinds. Details of the actual process of replication remain enigmatic, and issues of how and when replication begins or how DNA strands are simultaneously formed on both of the parent strands are still unresolved. At the twenty-fifth anniversary party of the announcement of the structure of DNA, over 400 scientists converged on the Cold Spring Harbor Laboratory in Long Island, New York, where the model was introduced. In the years since that first pioneering announcement, numerous other researchers, such as Arthur Kornberg of Stanford University Medical School, have developed "purified enzymes"; Jerard Horwitz of the Albert Einstein College of Medicine has dissected the "primer enzymes" which link DNA nucleotides; and Robin Holliday of the National Institute for Medical Research in England has utilized the electron scanning microscope to reveal the "chi" structure which promotes recombination (Miller, 1978). Although some consensus is beginning to emerge regarding these vital questions, many aspects of DNA replication remain undiscovered.

This idealized sequence of DNA to RNA replication *in vitro* does not proceed with unerring accuracy *in vivo*. Damage from various sources impairs the DNA, and when that dysfunction is either too subtle for the DNA repair system to detect or when it occurs more rapidly than repairs can be achieved, the entire process begins to deteriorate. Control over the essential enzymes is lost and the cell eventually dies. By juxtaposing the optimum replication process with the observed deviations from that process, researchers have derived several major theories relating these transcription errors to the phenomenon of aging. Certain critical cells of the human organism are particularly susceptible to this degenerative process. The three basic cell types are the mitotic cells which replicate throughout the life of the organism, the postmitotic cells which cease replication after the organism reaches maturity, and a group of cells which appear to be postmitotic but will begin replication after maturity under certain circumstances. Mitotic cells are evidenced in the epithelial cells of the gastrointestinal tract and skin, postmitotic cells are those of the central nervous system and heart, with the borderline cells constituting the liver, which has a limited capacity for regeneration. These regenerative properties and the experimentation in deliberately inducing and enhancing these latent properties are discussed in the next chapter. Clearly, the cells most jeopardized by aberrant DNA replication are the postmitotic cells, which are not replaced after they have differentiated to their mature form. Cellular aging and eventual destruction has been generally described by Holger P. von Hahn of the Institute of Experimental Gerontology in Basel, Switzerland, as occurring at the ". . . level of transcription of genetic information from the DNA onto the intermediary messenger RNA . . . the bulk of the available experimental data seems to favor an 'error accumulation' type of hypothesis rather than an 'aging programme.' . . . Error accumulation . . . will not favor any type of cell, and only those organs retaining sufficiently high mitotic rates throughout life will be able to eliminate such damaged cells through selection at mitosis" (von Hahn, 1979). After that point of agreement the theories to account for this observation proliferate rapidly.

One of the most prominent theories is that of Bernard L. Strehler of the University of Southern California in Los Angeles. Aging is due primarily because cells that cannot replace themselves either die or lose a small part of their function every year. From the research of

Strehler and others, it appears that the length of life of a species is directly related to the ability the cell has to repair damage to DNA. Strehler has found that certain repetitive gene sequences, such as those coding for ribosomal RNA (rRNA), may be lost in the aging organism. His theory is extremely complex, but he has outlined it briefly in a recent article:

A. The primary event in aging is the arrest of cell division in certain important cell types, such as brain, heart, etc.

B. The loss of ability to divide is programmed within the genes a cell contains, specifically perhaps in the "sequence of languages" that is used to specify the proteins needed for cell division. When a cell loses its ability to decode some of these words, it also loses its ability to divide.

C. After cell division is stopped, the cell is at the mercy of its environment, and can only repair itself to a limited degree, a degree that depends on other genes' activities. A key defect that accumulates is the loss of a specific kind of gene, present in multiple copies and called rDNA. Dividing cells, however, can dilute out damage they have accumulated and defective cells are not replaced when they die, so the effect is that the cell population remains young.

D. Loss of rDNA causes a decreased production of rRNA, needed for *any* protein synthetic activity.

E. Decreased rRNA causes increased accumulation of damaged products such as low-activity enzymes and age pigments.

F. Cells that possess large amounts of age pigments and/or ineffectual enzymes cannot carry out their functions normally.

G. As normal function decreases at the cellular level, there are consequent decreases in the integration of the body, in the rate at which challenges can be overcome—and ultimately in the probability of death [Strehler, 1979].

Although Strehler's theory focuses upon the postmitotic cells, his hypotheses are consistent with Hayflick's findings since even the mitotic cells have a finite number of doublings which is related to the maximum life-span of that species. Starting with the assumption that almost all of the amino acids have more than one code word,

Strehler's theory proposes that only some of the code words are used at any given point in the lifetime of a cell. Additionally, protein synthesis is dependent upon the presence of the corresponding synthesizing agents. Throughout the life of the cell the genes for protein synthesis are switched on and off in a prescribed sequence. For postmitotic cells in particular, these mechanisms cease operating and the synthesizing process eventually deteriorates. Experimental evidence for Strehler's theory is cited by *Science* writer Jean L. Marx: ". . . DNA extracted from the brains of 10-year-old beagles found 30 percent less labeled rRNA than did DNA from young animals. This indicates that the former DNA contained fewer sequences complementary to the RNA than did the latter" (Marx, 1974a). When Strehler's theory is translated into terms of human life expectancy, he points out:

> The essence of these findings is that most functions decrease gradually, at a rate of 1 percent of the original capacity per year after age thirty. This means that the reserve ability to do all kinds of work will run out at about age 120. It is not surprising, therefore, that about 118 years is the greatest age attained by any human being for whom good records of birth and death are available [Strehler, 1973].

Although Strehler's concluding statement is refuted by reliable albeit limited data, his overall theory is among the most comprehensive attempts to decipher the genetic code of longevity.

As early as 1962 Strehler's research led to the publication of a classic in the field of aging entitled *Time, Cells, and Aging*. While his research has been on aging, it is clear in the most recent edition of that book that his underlying interest is in longevity. Concluding his second edition, he states:

> . . . *long-lived forms have* indeed *evolved from short-lived ancestors. . . . This fact has some* rather *startling implications . . .* the entire transition from shorter-lived ancestor to our present long-lived state took place in much less than 100,000,000 years and perhaps as recently as during the last few million years, or less . . . *it is difficult to imagine how a doubling or tripling of longevity*

. . . could have been possible unless a very small number of mutant genes produced this great retardation of the rate of aging [Strehler, 1977—emphasis in original].

It is Strehler's opinion, substantiated by some preliminary research, that a finite number of 10 to 200 basic cellular properties governing mutation are responsible for this outcome. Since this is a relatively small finite number in biochemical and genetic realms, Strehler notes that, *"The implications of this conclusion are startling, with respect to the further extension of the healthy human life-span in the future!"* (Strehler, 1977—emphasis in original).

Strehler does not limit the means by which this is to be achieved to genetic or biochemical cellular processes. He has considered the effects of reduced temperatures, restricted diet, and environmental considerations (Strehler and Mildvan, 1960). Strehler has stated a principle which is a key theme throughout this book: *". . . there is no inherent contradiction . . . no inherent property of cells or of metazoan organization which by itself precludes their organization into perpetually functioning and self-replenishing individuals"* (Strehler, 1977—emphasis in original). Hypotheses and details of the means to attain this biological potential are explicated in later chapters. When confronting the issue of potential immortality, Strehler is clear that the process involves both cells and psyche:

> To me, life is manifold. As an expression of a cold, chemical code there is the mathematical beauty of a Bach partita to it; as a personal experience of sinews, muscles, vessels, and myself, it is something quite different; and despite a prompting from pure rationality, there is a seductive quality to a synthesis of the self —and all in a modern mystical renaissance that I find quite tempting and cannot objectively reject [Strehler, 1968].

In the interaction between the discoveries of basic research and alterations of life-style and attitude resides the potential increase in longevity. Since long-lived life forms do evolve from short-lived ones, perhaps concerted efforts in the field of longevity will mark a major evolutionary step from *Homo sapiens* to *Homo longevus*.

Error Theory

Closely related to DNA replication theories of aging are other hypotheses which focus upon specific mechanisms by which errors occur in the replication process. Each theory can only account for and predict a limited range of the phenomena observed in the aging process, and it is likely that these theories emphasize one aspect of a more unified approach which is yet to be formulated. Most existing theories of biological aging can be divided into two basic concepts: ". . . one argues that age-dependent deterioration is the result of an active 'self-destruct' program, and one that it is the result of passive 'wearing out' processes" (Hayflick, 1975). Strehler's theory is essentially one of programmed cellular death where the operation of cellular activity results in a predetermined series of events which cause aging and the eventual death of the individual. Among the theories related to Strehler's "codon restriction" approach are the "redundant message theory" of Zhores A. Medvedev (1966, 1973), the "error catastrophe theory" of Leslie Orgel (1973) of the Salk Institute in La Jolla, California, and Sir F. MacFarlane Burnet (1973) of the University of Melbourne in Australia, and the "transcriptional event theory" proposed by Holger P. von Hahn (1979). Each of these approaches is compatible with Hayflick's basic observations and is in the realm of the "self-destruct" programs. Later in this chapter, consideration is given to the more "passive" theories. The distinction, of course, is not always clear-cut.

Medvedev, the main proponent of the "redundant message theory," has theorized that redundancy in genetic information due to repetition of genes may be the primary mechanism determining the life-span of a species. "If 1/500 of all genes are active and 499/500 are specifically repressed, and if mutagenic factors act equally on the repressed and active cistons, the mutation rate of repressed genes must yield more mutations than those occurring in active genes" (Hayflick, 1975). From this observation it follows that as errors accumulate in the functioning genes the "redundant" or reserve sequences containing the same information would take over. When the redundancy in the system is depleted, the result is degenerative changes manifesting as aging. Thus, Medvedev concludes that ". . . different species' life-spans may be a function of the degree of repeated sequences. Long-lived species should then have more redundant messages than short-lived species" (Hayflick, 1975). Medvedev's theory is compatible with Strehler's theory, since one other means of exhausting genetic redundancy is through the progressive loss of genetic material proposed by Strehler.

Closely related to Medvedev's theory is the "error catastrophe theory" of Leslie Orgel. This theory is based upon a concept first postulated by Medvedev and first demonstrated by David and Harriet Gershon, of the Technion, Haifa, Israel, who noted inefficiency in some enzymes isolated from older animal cells. Orgel's approach does not view the DNA per se as either the source of programmed aging or as the target of mutations. According to Orgel, mistakes or "errors" could occur during transcription when the messenger RNA is synthesized to specify the amino acid sequences of various proteins. Also, these errors could occur during protein synthesis. However, in actual experimentation, ". . . distinguishing between errors in proteins caused by mutation and those arising during transcription or translation may be difficult, if not impossible" (Marx, 1974a). Under whatever circumstances the "errors" occur, the accumulation of errors, especially in specific enzymes required for protein synthesis, would result in further errors and this increasing error frequency would result in the "catastrophe" of cell deterioration and death.

More recently Orgel has revised his theory to suggest a feedback loop between inaccurate protein synthesis and inaccurate DNA synthesis where each potential source of error reinforces the other in a coupled phenomenon. Also, it now appears that the deterioration of enzyme function in older animal cells is not due to the fact that older cells manufacture defective enzymes. Rather, it is now hypothesized that older cells might manufacture enzymes at a slower rate than young cells and the enzymes have a longer time to deteriorate before they are replaced. Further extension of Orgel's research has indicated that extracellular as well as intracellular processes are involved and coupled. This research is indicative of the broadening scope of aging theories at the genetic and biochemical level of analysis. Experiments by Robin Holliday and his colleagues at the National Institute for Medical Research in London have supported Orgel's theories. Holliday (Holliday et al., 1974) shortened the life-span of adult fruit flies by feeding them amino acids, such as p-fluorophenylalanine and ethionine, in place of the normal amino acids, phenylalanine and methionine, since the former acids are incorporated into the proteins just like the normal ones but interfere with the function of the proteins. Earlier basic research by Holliday demonstrated this same phenomenon to be responsible in the aging process of fungi (Holliday, 1969). In a second experiment Holliday found that aging human fibroblasts contained abnormal forms of enzymes. Up to 25 percent of two key enzymes were more sensitive to heat destruction when isolated from old cells than from young cells where the enzymes remained stable under equal heat.

Despite these apparent affirmations of Orgel's "error catastrophe theory," there is also considerable evidence weighing against this interpretation of aging. John Holland of the University of California noted no differences in virus production in young and old cultured cells, and sophisticated research by Vincent Cristofalo of the Wister Institute in Philadelphia concludes that ". . . cells with errors serious enough to compromise their survival are overgrown by healthy cells so that the overall life-span of the population is not affected" (Marx, 1974a). Cristofalo has observed that disruptive amino acid analogs, such as those in Holliday's research, do not appear to impair the proliferative capacity of the cultured WI-38 cells used in the research laboratories of Hayflick and other researchers. Very high concentrations of the amino acid analogs did inhibit doubling, but when the cells were placed in a normal medium they achieved virtually the same number of population doublings as the controls. Inconclusive and often contradictory results such as these abound in aging research. These experiments seem to indicate that the accuracy of protein synthesis may be maintained in certain aged cells while not in others and that the errors predicted by Orgel's "error catastrophe theory" may be more important in cells that do not proliferate after maturity. These might be more subject to the form of aging he predicts than are the mitotic cells.

A third theory which is closely consistent with both Hayflick's and Strehler's observations is the "transcriptional event theory" of

Holger P. von Hahn, who was noted earlier in this chapter. Essentially von Hahn's contribution was refinement of the concept of "aging regulator genes" which supposedly assume dominance at a certain stage of cell mitosis. Aging is due to the fact that once these genes are activated, they affect the transcription of genetic information from DNA to the intermediary messenger RNA (Stein et al., 1975). With increasing age these deleterious alterations have most effect upon the postmitotic cells. Only those cells and organs which maintained high mitotic rates throughout life would be able to eliminate damaged cells through selection at each mitosis. According to von Hahn:

> Such "aging regulator genes" might, for instance, produce a repressor which cannot be inactivated ("de-repressed") by the normal inducer molecules. . . . The result for the cell is a loss of genetic information due to the blocking of the transcription step of protein synthesis. This is exactly the type of situation we are proposing here for an aging cell [von Hahn, 1979].

A basic assumption in von Hahn's theory is that there is a universal biochemical aging process due to negative alterations in the cell's nuclear chromatin and these deleterious events increase with age. This assumption is shared in Strehler's theory and in Hayflick's research. One of von Hahn's predictions is that detailed biochemical analysis of the chromatin and protein synthesis in Hayflick's "Phase III cells" will reveal a great deal of information about the primary aging process.

Von Hahn states that he favors an "error accumulation" theory rather than an "aging programme" approach, although his evidence lends some support to each theory. Errors in transcription in these theories are derived from two sources: one is genetically controlled and the other involves processes described by "error catastrophe theory." All of these theories describe progressive change in the structure and function of cells which causes the organism to deal less effectively with its environment. As noted earlier, there are certain germ plasm and some transplantable tumor cell populations which replicate indefinitely, but the mechanisms remain unknown. At the organismic level this results in a "progressive diminution in adaption to stress and in the capacity of the system to maintain the homeostatic equilibrium characteristic of the adult animal at the end of growth and full development" (Hayflick, 1975). From the perspective of geneticists and microbiologists, these genetically programmed alterations may appear to explain the phenomenon of aging. However, when these theories are considered in the context of neurophysiological and neuroimmunological approaches, it is clear that the entire organism is involved in a systemic interaction which manifests as aging or longevity.

Researchers are beginning to hypothesize that there may be important differences between the genes of higher organisms and those of bacteria and this may be found to account for some of the apparent diversity in basic research using these different genes. Recently (1979) Donald D. Brown of the Carnegie Institution of Washington reported on the gene "promoter site," which is the initial binding place for the polymerases enzymes which move along an active DNA to create the appropriate RNA molecule. It appears that the promoter site may be inside the structural gene of animals and outside in lower forms. This basic discovery helps to resolve some inconsistencies observed in previous genetic replication research involving truncated genes. In yet another area of DNA research, physicist Mark Abzel indicates (1978) that the "patterns" of DNA sequences may be an important element in the genetic alphabet in addition to the letters themselves. It is possible that these questions can be most effectively answered through a more systemic approach. Recent findings in biochemistry, immunology, and neurobiology involve a higher level of biological organization than the research which has been detailed up to this point. These later approaches also attempt to trace aging to cellular processes but do not focus upon DNA as the source of programmed aging or as the endpoint of organismic mutations.

Free Radical Theory

Moving from the DNA level of cellular organization, the next higher level of analysis in the field of aging involves those biochemical processes which occur outside DNA but which can have an effect upon it. One of the major theories in this area is the "free radical" theory proposed by key researchers such as Denham Harman of the University of Nebraska College of Medicine and Lester Packer of the University of California at Berkeley. "Free radicals" gain their name from their transient presence during the course of chemical reactions of highly volatile substances. High chemical reactivity of free radicals is due to the presence of a free electron, manifested as electron spin resonance (ESR), which makes them very reactive due to the number of electrons. In order to complete the molecular structure, the free radical attempts to attach to other molecules, resulting in a wide range of possible reactions. Among the common instances of free radical interactions are oxygen with gasoline in an automobile engine, the drying of oil-based paint, formation of many plastics, butter becoming rancid, and the unpleasant properties of smog. Most importantly, free radical interactions are common and "almost invariably irreversible" (Harman, 1973). One example is that it is extremely difficult to take the carbon dioxide and water emitted from an automobile exhaust and restore the original gasoline and oxygen.

Where these reactions are of most immediate concern is in living cells where oxygen reacts with polyunsaturated fats to form nonfunctional peroxide molecules (Fridovich, 1978). When this and other similar reactions occur in the cell, the resulting free radicals tend to attach themselves to any proximal molecule, which leads to disruption of enzyme activity, damage to cell membranes, and other deleterious effects. Free radicals can damage the DNA as well as these cell structures by acting ". . . either directly or indirectly by generating strong oxidizing agents. Free radicals may either be produced by cells as a result of their metabolic processes or they may come from the environment" (Marx, 1974a). There are many degenerative changes noted in aging which are consistent with the free radical hypothesis:

- cumulative oxidative alterations in the long-lived molecules of collagen, elastin, and chromosomal material
- breakdown of mucopolysaccharides through oxidative degradation
- changes in membrane characteristics caused by lipid peroxidation

- accumulation of metabolically inert material, such as ceroid and age pigment, through oxidative polymerization reactions
- arteriolocapillary fibrosis (Packer and Walton, 1977).

Among the environmental sources which interact within cells to produce free radicals are radiation, environmental pollutants, and carcinogenic agents. ". . . Many chemical carcinogens and/or their intermediates may either be free radicals themselves or else may be activated by free radicals. Harmful environmental agents such as fumes, gas, and smoke often can be detected by their electron spin resonance (ESR) signals" (Packer and Walton, 1977).

In the previous chapter the issue of longevity was placed in the context of political, economic, and environmental concerns. It should be evident here that even the most minute extension of aging research beyond the DNA level immediately involves these same larger issues. There is a substantial body of research indicating that the by-products of free radical interactions have a deleterious effect upon cellular functioning, which is evidenced as aging. Accumulating evidence has linked free radical formations in the pathogenesis of ". . . cancer, amyloidosis, senility, atherosclerosis and hypertension—all disorders associated with aging. Smog-related pulmonary disorders may also be due, at least in part, to free radical reactions" (Harman, 1973). The free radical theories of aging not only lead directly to environmental concerns, they also suggest possible action which can be taken to encourage health and longevity. Specific dietary and environmental factors such as antioxidants, including vitamin E, and reduced radiation exposure are discussed in Chapter IV with its focus upon the latent regenerative capacity of the human organism.

Cross-linkage Theories

Closely related to the free radical theory is the "molecular cross-linkage" theory. Foremost among the proponents of "cross-linkage" theory is Johan Bjorksten, Director of the Bjorksten Research Foundation in Madison, Wisconsin, who originally proposed his theory in the 1940s (Bjorksten, 1963). Cross-linkage occurs as one possible outcome of biochemical interactions of free radicals and occurs randomly when two large molecules, either intracellular or extracellular, link together. Perhaps the most familiar example of cross-linkage was Charles Goodyear's discovery that natural rubber could be cross-linked by means of sulfur to stabilize rubber in the process known as "vulcanized rubber." In a living organism, when the large molecules link, the enzymes of a young cell usually break the bond. However, irreversible cross-linkages occur more frequently as an organism ages. Eventually the increasing amount of inflexible, linked molecules disrupts the activity of the cell and degeneration, aging, and death ensue. Cross-linkage involving DNA molecules has been the subject of interesting research. "Protein DNA cross-linkage may partly account for reported decreases in the percentage of DNA transcribed with increasing age in mice and rats. DNA damage caused by cross-linkage agents is irreparable when it involves corresponding sites on both strands of the helix so that after excision, no template remains for DNA replication" (Packer and Walton, 1977). DNA molecules are particularly susceptible to cross-linkage because even a reversible linkage would disrupt replication if it occurred during mitosis. According to the theory, these linkages slowly immobilize the large molecules in all cells and tissues and destroy elasticity, a process believed to underlie certain degenerative disease. For a recent overview of cross-linkage theory, there is an excellent chapter by Richard G. Cutler of the Gerontology Research Center of the National Institute of Aging in Baltimore in the book *Aging, Carcinogenesis, and Radiation Biology* (1976).

Writing in 1968, Bjorksten summarized some of the ways aging could be affected by cross-linkage theory:

1. The life-shortening effect of overeating. With a low-calorie diet, oxidation proceeds rapidly to the innocuous end-products, carbon dioxide and water. In overeating, intermediate products accumulate at the metabolic "bottlenecks," and many of these are crosslinking agents.
2. The life-shortening effect of ionizing radiation and the aging effect of ultraviolet irradiation of the skin. The free radicals are known crosslinking agents. That ultraviolet induces for-

mation of tanning agents from unsaturated fatty acids present in all cell membranes is fully proved.

3. Crosslinkage changes the immunological behavior of proteins. This is a prelude to auto-immunity.

4. Crosslinkage causes changes of proteins from hydrophilic to oleophilic. This is a prelude to atherosclerosis. Another prelude is that crosslinkage destroys elasticity, thus causing microfractures in organs, including arterial endothelia [Bjorksten, 1968].

Many aspects of these observations have led Bjorksten and other researchers to hypothesize about the regenerative potential of "low caloric intake," "chelation," "antioxidants," and "physical exercise," and the ability of some soil bacteria to dissolve virtually all cross-linkages. Specific instances of these possibilities are discussed in the next chapter.

Among the numerous agents in the organism which can undergo cross-linkage are ". . . aldehydes, liquid oxidation products, sulfur, alkylating agents, quinones, free radicals induced by ionizing radiation, antibodies, polybasic acids, polyhalo derivatives and polyvalent metals" (Bjorksten, 1968). Diseases believed to be associated with cross-linkages are "atherosclerosis," "senile cataracts," "osteoporosis," "diabetes," "immunologic impairment," and "cancer" (Bjorksten, 1978). Critics of the theory are numerous. One major criticism holds that even with the impressive array of agents noted above, there are an insufficient number of cross-linking agents in the normal organism to account for the phenomena observed in aging (Sinex, 1964). While researchers agree that cross-linkage occurs and increases with age, the prevailing opinion appears to be that cross-linkage is a result rather than an underlying cause of aging. Virtually every theory of aging has been criticized on the same grounds, but they appear to be particularly applicable to cross-linkage theories, which have declined in importance recently. The whole field, in great innovation and flux, remains to be determined.

Lipofuscin Accumulation

Still in the realm of free radical theories is research concerning "lipofuscin," or age pigments. This approach is one of the earliest attempts to define the biology of senescence, since these pigments were observed as early as 1842. These decrements in cellular function are visible to the unaided eye in the form of dark areas of pigmentation which are evident as an individual grows older. Pigmentation within the cell appears to indicate that the aging cell has increasing difficulty in purging itself of waste products. These fatty pigments originate when subcellular organelles undergo peroxidation reactions (Packer and Walton, 1977; Comfort, 1976). The biochemistry of lipofuscin pigmentation resembles a mixture of "protein and varnish" derived from "the reaction of the free amino groups of proteins present in membranes with by-products of the oxidation of unsaturated fats" (Strehler, 1979). Organelles are the sub-structures of the cell; they include the nucleus and other structures in the cytoplasm, and also the cell membrane. Among the organelles are lysosomes, which are the focus of lipofuscin theories since lysosomes appear to serve the function of waste disposal for the cell. Lysosomes and their enzymes are structures in cells which can be programmed to release certain destructive enzymes. They were termed "suicide bags" by Christian DeDuve (1955), who received a Nobel prize for his discovery of the lysosome. According to Richard Hochschild of the Microwave Instrument Company, ". . . lipofuscin pigments may be the debris left over from free radical attacks on cell components, debris which lysosomes are unable fully to digest. The undigested material accumulates, polymerizes and stays locked inside the cell, a visible record of the damage sustained by the cell. . . . Over a period as long as a lifetime, many if not most of the cells in the body may lose some or all of their function in this manner" (Hochschild, 1973). Deposits of lipofuscin increase in a linear manner with age, and eventually might occupy as much as 50 percent of the cytoplasmic volume of some postmitotic cells. "It is thought that the excessive amounts of melanin pigment present in these degenerating cells directly causes their atrophy by the progressive reduction of protein synthesis levels, through membrane displacement and disruption, until insufficient protein is produced to meet the cell's metabolic demands" (Mann and Yates, 1974). These progressive disruptions are greatest with the postmitotic cells but also affect the mitotic cells, especially if the resulting lipofuscin accumulation limits the mitotic potential of these cells.

Despite the considerable evidence for lipofuscin accumulation and subsequent damage, the extent to which lipofuscin actually disrupts normal cell function remains unknown. An observation weighing against lipofuscin as a causative agent in senescence is that melanin granules, which are pigmentations similar in many respects to lipofuscin (Bagnara et al., 1979), are apparent in certain nerve cells at birth and again at 18 months in human infants (Hollander, 1970; Mann and Yates, 1974). These melanin levels increase in a linear manner until late middle age, approximately 60 years, and then actually appear to decrease due to a general loss of pigment from all cells. Since lipofuscin and melanin are present in the early stages of certain cells, it is possible that they serve a specialized function within cells up to a certain developmental stage but then excessive accumulation might be disruptive and become a causative agent of senescence at a later stage. One researcher, A. R. Sheldrake of the Department of Biochemistry at the University of Cambridge, has noted, "Lipofuscin granules do not seem to damage cells directly except when they accumulate, as they do in certain diseases, to such an extent that they mechanically interfere with the structure and functions of the cell. . . . So little attention has been paid to the ageing and death of cells during growth and development, both normal and abnormal, that detailed information about these processes is scarce" (Sheldrake, 1974). Lipofuscin apparently accumulates to a significant degree in the myocardial tissue of the heart as well as in the testes. However, it appears possible to prevent and reverse lipofuscin deposits through antioxidants such as vitamin E, other dietary influences, and physical exercise (Kritchevsky, 1979). Although the role of lipofuscin as a causative agent in aging remains ambiguous, the research to be discussed in the next chapter does indicate the possibility that efficient lipofuscin disposal enables an organism to attain its full genetic potential.

Neuroendocrinological Theories of Aging

The major theories of aging discussed so far have focused upon the genetic and cellular levels of analysis. Undoubtedly these processes are involved in senescence. But these factors alone cannot account for the totality of the phenomenon of aging. Among the recent approaches to aging are those that address organismic levels of organization and focus on endocrinology, immunology, and neurophysiology. Endocrine and nervous systems have increasingly been found to function together and appear to be the primary means by which an organism adapts to environmental stimuli and stressors. In this area are found the first clear links between the exogenous influences (environment and psychosocial factors) and endogenous biochemical processes.

One of the most perplexing problems in aging research is that ". . . old age is accompanied by increases in the incidence of a number of diseases. This makes it difficult to determine whether the changes associated with old age cause the diseases or whether the reverse is true" (Marx, 1974b). Issues such as those classic "chicken/egg" conundrums can only be resolved by recognizing the reciprocal interaction of both factors. Reciprocal interaction, as in biofeedback (Pelletier and Shealy, 1979), is a key concept underlying the research in neuroendocrinology. In the age-associated disorders, ranging from cardiovascular disease and cancer to Alzheimer's senile dementia and osteoporosis, the underlying mechanisms all involve complex interactions in the immunological and neurophysiological systems. In this perspective, aging and senescence are considered to be ". . . essentially a matter of increasing vulnerability that results in a progressive reduction of functional effectiveness culminating in death . . . there is a progressive decline of function associated with increased vulnerability" (Greenberg and Yunis, 1978). Susceptibility of older people to conditions such as cancer and autoimmune diseases is considered to be due to a decline in immune function which in turn predisposes an individual to increased morbidity and mortality. Much innovative and promising research into aging and longevity lies in this area.

As individuals age their ability to respond to environmental stimuli, especially stressful occurrences, is diminished. Their response may be slowed and decreased in magnitude or there may be a general "loss of sensory acuity and discrimination; impairment of postural reflexes" (Hebb, 1978). There are a wide variety of physical and psychological instances of diminished capacity which do not yet manifest themselves as a severe disorder. While these alterations are considered "normal" at the present time, they are simply average and certainly not inevitable. Although the emphasis here is upon the immune system and physiology, it is important to note that the responses of these systems are inextricably linked with psychosocial factors such as stress, lifestyle, and numerous other influences which will be discussed in Chapter V.

Connections between the brain and the endocrine system are now firmly established: "the brain helps to control hormone secretion and hormones in turn affect the brain's operation—that is not an overstatement" (Marx, 1979). From this basic observation has evolved the field of neuroendocrinology. Interactions between the brain and endocrine system are extremely complex, and the presentation here is limited to their effect upon aging and longevity. For an overview of the basic neuroendocrine systems, Hans Selye's classic *The Stress of Life* (1956) and chapter two of *Mind as Healer, Mind as Slayer* (Pelletier, 1977) provide a background. One basic distinction in the neuroendocrinology of aging is between "intrinsic" cell aging factors and "extrinsic" factors. Intrinsic influences are accounted for by theories such as those of Hayflick, Orgel, and Strehler, discussed earlier. Extrinsic influences include the hormonal and neural factors which are external to cells but which appear to govern cellular aging changes. These, of course, are not mutually exclusive. The extrinsic influences observed in neuroendocrinology are our concern here.

Paola Timiras of the University of California at Berkeley has noted that "Aging is not a disease or a sickness but a period in the life-span with its own physiological characteristics, which are still largely unknown" (Marx, 1979). The pivotal question is whether there is an unavoidable decrease in function with age, or is the observed deterioration an indirect effect of repeated stresses upon a person's health in the course of normal development. Of central concern in attempts to answer these questions are the effects of aging on the hormones and receptors of the pituitary, adrenal cortex, thyroid, pancreas, and the ovaries and testes. A leading researcher in this field is Caleb E. Finch of the University of Southern California, who has divided life-span into three epochs:

> Although mammals range in lifespan from 3 years (mice) to 100 years (humans), they share many physiological changes. . . . Mammals typically achieve their maximum physiological functions in the first third of life (maturation). During the second third (midlife), many physiological indexes begin a gradual decline to the end of life. . . . In the final third of life (senescence), there is a rapid increase in disease which precedes the rapid increase in mortality rate, the ultimate determinant of maximum longevity [Finch, 1975].

During the midlife epoch the neuroendocrine alterations are most clearly evidenced and appear to give rise to the incidence of certain diseases in the senescent phase.

A key decrement which occurs in midlife is a progressive decline in immune system function. Within the immune system, which consists of about a trillion cells termed lymphocytes and about 100 million trillion antibodies secreted by these cells, the two cell types which have received the most attention are the "B cells," or bone marrow–derived cells, and the "T cells," or thymus-derived cells. An excellent overview of this complex system and its parallels to central nervous system function is contained in a *Scientific American* article, "The Immune System" (1973), by Niels Kaj Jerne, who is director of the Basel Institute for Immunology in Switzerland. Generally, B cells differentiate into plasma cells which secrete antibodies and provide immunity against diseases caused by microorganisms. T cells are lymphocytes which serve a "killer" function of devouring foreign cells, including cancer cells (Solomon, 1969). Also the T cells promote B cell differentiation and act as suppressors of B cell activity. With age there is a decline in the competence of the immune system partly due to changes in the bodily environment of the T and B cells but mostly due to negative changes in the cells themselves. According to Takashi Makinodan of the National Institute of Aging, it is clear that about ". . . 90 percent of the total decline in immune function is due to changes in the cells of old animals" (Makinodan, 1978). To date, the research evidence indicates that the T cells appear to play the most important role in this observed decline. If they do, this suggests an important link between cellular and psychosocial influences on aging. T cells are derived from precursor cells in the bone marrow under the regulation of the thymus gland which, in turn, is partially governed by the brain's hypothalamus. The hypothalamus is the primary mediator between the central nervous system and the physical and emotional environment of the individual. This delicate and intricate balance must be at the core of any holistic model of aging and longevity.

The thymus gland is seen by many investigators as an important governor of the aging process. Sir F. MacFarlane Burnet of the University of Melbourne in Australia has indicated that the thymus might function as a biological clock or pacemaker which determines both the rate and critical stages of aging through its influence upon the T cells (1970). It is well known that the thymus begins to atrophy shortly after puberty in humans. According to Takashi Makinodan, ". . . age related involution and atrophy of the thymus could be the key to immunologic aging, for it is the first change manifested chronologically" (Makinodan, 1978). Accompanying the thymus atrophy are numerous endocrine changes which serve to explain the etiology of a wide range of aging disorders including the autoimmune diseases such as rheumatoid arthritis where the immune system actually destroys the body's own tissues. In autoimmune diseases the T cells' decline in activity may lead to a decline in the B cell differentiation to antibody producing cells or a loss of B cell suppressor control by the T cells which would result in the abnormal and unchecked B cell activity characteristic of these conditions (Marx, 1975a).

Writing in *Lancet,* Ian C. Roberts-Thompson and his colleagues of the Royal Melbourne Hospital in Australia reported their research on the impaired function of the immune system of humans of advanced age. They were particularly concerned with the "thymus-dependent cell mediated responses" which would be manifested as "delayed-type hypersensitivity (D.T.H.)" to injections of five antigens. For their research they selected 52 people over 80 years of age and noted the differences in the cell-mediated response as shown by DTH in this group as compared to younger patients. From their research they reported, ". . . cell mediated immune functions deteriorate greatly with age, and mortality is higher in old people with impaired DTH responses. The defects of cell-mediated immunity in aging could be explained by inadequate numbers of T cells or by a functional impairment of T cells. . . . We conclude that whilst the thymus may not necessarily be the 'life-span controller' the integrity of the thymus-derived component of the immune system could be an important determinant of longevity" (Roberts-Thompson et al., 1974). While these insights are promising, it should be noted that research concerning thymus function is in its rudimentary stages. On the one hand, some investigators question whether the thymus even qualifies as a member of the endocrine system (Goldstein and White, 1973; White and Goldstein, 1968). On the other hand, ". . . the thymus gland, once thought to be about as useful as the human appendix, may well be the master gland of the immune system" (Marx, 1975b).

Virtually all of the research concerning thymus function and its effects upon the immune system have dealt with pathology. However, there have been a few noteworthy experiments which have demonstrated that immune response can be rejuvenated. Among such experiments are a study in which the spleen, which is a reservoir of T cells, was removed from aging mice, leading to a doubling of their life-span. By contrast, injecting spleen cells of old mice into younger ones led to a decreased life-span (Favazza, 1977). While such research is in its infancy, it does indicate that thymus atrophy and subsequent stages of immunological compromise may not be inevitable. Preliminary evidence indicates that the immune function can be restored and sustained. Many of the earliest and most significant attempts at regeneration such as caloric restriction and lowered body temperature appear to be mediated by the neuroendocrine system.

There are several other areas of interaction between the central nervous system and the hormonal secretions of major organs which are pertinent to aging. As noted earlier, Caleb E. Finch has hypothesized that aging pacemakers might be located within selected groups of neurons in the brain. Finch places decreased importance upon certain aging processes emphasized by genetic theorists and notes,

". . . it seems very unlikely that random genetic damage or other intrinsic changes are major factors in causing the selective changes of hormones, receptors, and neural factors" (Finch, 1975). Central to Finch's research is the well-documented observation that the basic functions of major organs are maintained throughout life but the hormonal and neural mechanisms required to trigger those functions are deficient. This is an extremely important distinction because it lends support to the possibility that certain functions might be regenerated.

As was pointed out earlier, virtually all of the mechanisms in this field are based upon delicate balances governed by biofeedback principles. Concepts of causation and single-factor, cause-and-effect relationships are obsolete. Central to the operation of these biofeedback processes is the function of receptors. Within the central nervous system electrical impulses are transmitted to and from the brain. Between the cells of the nervous system are gaps, or synapses. At the synapse the electrical impulse changes into the biochemical carriers, or neurotransmitters, which fit into the receptor site in the next nerve to receive the impulses. When the neurotransmitter is received into the receptor site, it transforms back into an electrical impulse and this constitutes the essential activity of the central nervous system (Snyder, 1974).

Applying this receptor concept to the neuroendocrinology of aging, Caleb E. Finch states, "In order to regulate the endocrine glands, the brain must have mechanisms to detect their output . . . . the brain contains proteins (receptors) that bind specific . . . steroids and transport them to the cell nucleus. . . . Apparently the synthesis or degradation of . . . receptors may be regulated by the hormone they bind. . . . Hence, changes of one or more endocrine factors during aging could destabilize feedback relationships" (Finch, 1975). In particular Finch has focused on the concentrations of the monoamine neurotransmitters of serotonin, dopamine, and norepinephrine in the brain as well as on the steroid and enzyme receptors of the brain and major organs. His observations are consistent with previous studies indicating an important regulatory function of the hypothalamus which both regulates and is regulated by intricate feedback systems of these neurotransmitters and hormones. Not only does the hypothalamus interact with the thymus but it also has a direct interaction with the pituitary, ovarian hormones, gonadal hormones, and related systems. Disturbances in the delicate balances of these systems appear to underlie many of the disorders manifested in aging individuals.

Claude Bernard was the first researcher to state that an organism needed to sustain a state of internal equilibrium in order to attain a certain degree of freedom from fluctuations in the external environment. Taking that concept one step further, V. M. Dilman of the N. N. Petrov Research Institute of Oncology in Leningrad has emphasized the role of the hypothalamus in coordinating this internal balance. From his research he has noted that, "The elevation of the hypothalamic threshold and the resulting increase of the activity of a number of hypothalamic centres lead to a compensatory increase in the activity of several peripheral endocrine glands. . . . These alterations gradually result in permanent deviations from the law of constancy of the internal environment, ultimately producing the specific lesions of aging" (Dilman, 1971). In other words the insensitivity of the hypothalamus is compensated for by an increase in hormone levels which attempts to retain the feedback mechanism but at a higher level. As the hypothalamic regulatory process becomes less sensitive to levels of hormonal balance, many different diseases result. Among these "diseases of compensation" (Dilman, 1971) are the female climacteric, obesity, adult onset diabetes, atherosclerosis, some forms of malignancy, decreased resistance to infections, and numerous other aging disorders discussed later in this chapter.

Although in the words of Caleb E. Finch, "Causal relationships among the endocrine events of aging are almost unknown at present with the exception of consequences of the loss of ovarian estrogens after menopause" (Finch, 1975), there are several promising areas of research which link "hypothalamic-pituitary-peripheral endocrine system" and receptor theory to a wide range of aging phenomena. One of the foremost researchers in this area is W. Donner Denckla of the Harvard Medical School, who has concentrated on the function of the pituitary gland, governed by the hypothalamus, which controls the thyroid which in turn produces thyroxine, the hormone governing the rate at which cells and tissues perform such functions as oxygen consumption and basal metabolism. "The pituitary appears to secrete two classes of substances that influence the immune system. Certain substances are beneficial, such as growth hormone and thyroid stimulating hormone: the latter acts to produce thyroid hormones. However, with advancing age there is some evidence that the pituitary may also secrete a substance(s) that prevents these two beneficial hormones from having their full effects" (Denckla, 1978). This pituitary factor has an influence similar to that observed by V. M. Dilman since it appears to cause a loss of responsiveness in peripheral tissues to circulating thyroid hormones. Denckla has termed this pituitary secretion DECO, or "decreasing oxygen consumption hormone" which appears to prevent aging cells from properly utilizing the thyroxine which remains in abundant supply in the circulatory system. In this manner the pituitary slows down the body's metabolic rate by releasing DECO rather than failing to stimulate the thyroid. When critical levels of thyroxine drop within the cell, many of the destructive processes of aging would be triggered. Among these are increased oxidation with attendant increases in free radicals, also greater potential for cross-linkage, lipofuscin accumulation, and decreasing efficiency of the immune system. Thus Denckla shares Hayflick's concept of an underlying genetic program determining cellular longevity. It appears that the pituitary hormone ". . . would not have to *cause* [emphasis in original] the specific detailed changes; it would simply *trigger* [emphasis in original] the sequence of events already pre-programmed in the given cell" (Rosenfeld, 1976).

In the convergence of these two theories there appears to be a biological redundancy; the cellular limit is imposed to limit replication in the event of failure of the pituitary hormone. For the detection of subtle metabolic processes the basal metabolic rate (BMR) was refined by Denckla into a measure of minimum oxygen consumption rate (MOC) regulated by the brain and genetic metabolic rate (GMR) regulated by the cell's DNA. Through the use of these more sensitive measurements, Denckla has performed pioneering experimentation with laboratory mice which indicates ". . . the possibility of reversing the age-associated changes in the immune system" (Denckla, 1978). At this point the procedures involve surgical removal of the pituitary from adult rats followed by the administration of thyroid hormones which restore immune competence. While such research is not immediately applicable to the human condition, it does indicate the compatibility and interaction between various theories of aging and begins to provide a basic understanding of the elaborate principles involved in the neuroendocrinology of aging.

Disorders Associated with Aging

Among the great diversity of findings in the neuroendocrinology of aging remains a focus upon the totality of the organism. This observation is underscored by V. V. Frolkis of the Chebotarev Institute of Gerontology in Kiev, who has stated, "The aging of an organism is not a simple sum of aging of its individual cells. At each new level of biologic organization appear not only quantitative but qualitative features of the aging process. That's why the analysis of the neurohormonal regulation (brain, nerves, glands, hormones), adapting the activity of cells to the needs of the whole organism, is of primary importance for the purpose of understanding the essence of aging of a whole organism" (Frolkis, 1972). When this principle is coupled with the previous observation that major bodily organs and functions remain functional, although it appears that the neuroendocrine triggers do not operate properly, it is possible to elaborate the processes underlying many of the major disorders associated with aging.

Among the conditions associated with aging are: (1) menopause and sporadic increases in peripheral skin temperature referred to as "hot flashes"; (2) osteoporosis; (3) diabetes; (4) Parkinson's disease; (5) senile brain disease or Alzheimer's disease; and (6) the entire range of disorders termed the afflictions of civilization. Many of these age-related disorders are so ubiquitous that they are considered "normal" rather than "average." This is illustrated by a classic joke where a 100-year-old man sees his doctor for a pain in one of his knees. After an examination the physician assures him, "It is only your age." To which the man responds, "But my other knee is just as old and it doesn't hurt!" As research in longevity progresses it is evident that these afflictions are not inevitable or normal and that it is possible to alter or abolish the time and even the absolute incidence of these diseases which cloud the later years of life.

Perhaps the most common instance of an age-related disruption of both biological and psychosocial functioning is female menopause. Menopause appears to be an inevitable consequence of endocrine changes occurring at approximately 50 years of age. Following menopause, women have an increased risk of developing breast and uterine cancers which may be partly due to the activity of the female sex hormone estrogen when it is not counteracted by progesterone. Following menopause, the female ovaries no longer produce estrogen or progesterone. Researcher Barry Sherman and his colleagues at the University of Iowa Medical School have found that obese women have a higher than average incidence of breast cancer. Obese women are subject to greater than average levels of estrogen during their reproductive lives because they begin menstruating earlier, end later, and have shorter menstrual cycles than thinner women. These researchers have hypothesized that the increased estrogen exposure is a significant risk factor (Sherman and Wallace, 1979). Other researchers have demonstrated hormonal factors which are consistent with this hypothesis. From the work of Pentti Siiteri of the University of California School of Medicine in San Francisco, it is noted that adipose or fat tissue continues to produce estrogen even after menopause when the ovaries have ceased production of both estrogen and progesterone. Perhaps the continued stimulation of the breast and uterine cells by estrogen in the absence of progesterone is a factor in the increased cancer susceptibility at these sites following menopause (Siiteri, 1979).

Closely associated with menopause are the unpleasant symptoms of sporadic increases in peripheral circulation and skin temperature referred to as "hot flashes." These affect about 75 percent of women undergoing menopause. Estrogen supplements which have been used to counteract these phenomena have been linked to increased uterine cancer and are used less frequently as a treatment (Siiteri, 1979). In seeking alternative methods, Howard Judd of the UCLA School of Medicine has found that hot flashes coincide with increases in the circulatory system of luteinizing hormone (LH), which is a pituitary secretion. It is clear from several major research projects that certain pituitary hormones accelerate the aging process. From his research A. V. Everitt of the University of Sydney in Australia has concluded, "Almost all of the anterior pituitary hormones and their target hormones have been shown to have ageing effects in one organ or

another. . . . The pathological effects eventually shorten the lifespan
. . . . These ageing or pathological effects are probably due to prolonged stimulation by hormones and hence overuse of these organs.
According to the wear and tear theory of ageing, the more an organ
is used the faster it wears out. Each organ or function has a finite
lifespan and after being used a certain number of times, or after
having done a certain amount of work, it starts to break down"
(Everitt, 1973). Referring to earlier research, the pituitary is regulated by the hypothalamus and the LH release may be a secondary
result of a malfunction in certain neurons of the hypothalamus predicted in the theories of both Caleb E. Finch (1979) and W. Donner
Denckla. In fact, Finch has suggested that ". . . it is the cumulative
impact on the brain of the ovarian hormones that eventually signals
the brain to bring an end to a female's reproductive period" (Marx,
1979). Again this is evidence of an elaborate neuroendocrine biofeedback system, and it is highly debatable whether or not the onset of
menopause is due to an aberration of brain function or an inevitable
and normal process. Whatever the case, the research does suggest
that the negative consequences of the postmenopausal period can be
prevented if the research continues to yield knowledge of the underlying biochemical processes.

Another prominent researcher has focused on the interaction between the hypothalamus and the ovaries with respect to menopause.
Paola Timiras and her colleagues at the University of California at
Berkeley have demonstrated that the hypothalamus regulates not
only LH production but also the follicle-stimulating hormone of the
pituitary. Follicle-stimulating hormones induce the ovaries to produce mature egg follicles, which in turn produce estrogen. When
these researchers inject a serotonin inhibitor into the hypothalamus
of young rats, the result is a menopause-like condition. This suggests
that the ovaries stop producing their hormones because of changes
in hypothalamic regulation and triggers rather than an inherent
defect of the ovaries. ". . . a delicate balance between serotonin and
other neurotransmitters in the brain is needed to maintain the normal cycling activities of rat ovaries. Slight disturbances in this balance can greatly alter ovarian activity" (Marx, 1979). Findings such
as these are applicable to the human condition and provide a critical
distinction between neuroendocrine functions which are irreversibly

terminated as opposed to being dormant with a potential for regeneration.

Osteoporosis is a condition whereby the skeletal system loses calcium and becomes fragile to the point where relatively minor stresses create fractures and breaks. Both men and women tend to lose bone mineral beginning at approximately age 35, with the loss greatly accelerated in women at menopause. Since women have a smaller bone mass than men from birth, they are more susceptible to the effects of osteoporosis. Statistics indicate that osteoporosis and its complications account for approximately 190,000 hip fractures, 180,000 vertebral fractures, and 90,000 broken forearms every year. There have been attempts to demonstrate that lack of estrogen accelerates osteoporosis, but it is now considered to be one of ". . . ten or so agents, including hormones, vitamins, and other factors, [which] directly affect bone, causing either deposition or dissolution of bone mineral" (Marx, 1979). Estrogen may enhance or counteract the actions of any one of these factors or act directly upon absorption in the gastrointestinal tract or its excretion by the kidney. Among the more optimistic approaches to osteoporosis is that of Robert Heaney of Creighton University, who found that premenopausal women and postmenopausal women on estrogen supplements needed less calcium to maintain their relative calcium content. From his research Heaney has suggested that 800 milligrams of calcium per day is sufficient to prevent calcium depletion in premenopausal women or postmenopausal women taking estrogen supplements. Estrogen deprivation increases the requirement to 1,500 milligrams of calcium per day, which is equivalent to one and a half quarts of milk. Overall, Heaney's research indicates that ". . . osteoporosis is preventable by replacing the estrogens given to postmenopausal women . . . with calcium supplements" (Marx, 1979). Osteoporosis is one seemingly inevitable consequence of aging which might be prevented or alleviated through dietary and nutritional factors (see Chapter VI).

Adult onset diabetes is yet another condition which is so ubiquitous that it is virtually considered to be a normal aspect of the aging process. As an individual ages, the body loses its ability to utilize glucose, which is a major source of energy. Although this phenomenon is partially explained by hormonal imbalances, recent research by Mayer Davidson of the UCLA School of Medicine indicates that there is no apparent decrease in insulin, which is needed for glucose metabolism, with advanced age. Adult onset diabetes is not an inevitable consequence of a decreased ability to metabolize glucose. There are many psychosocial and other risk factors such as obesity, genetic predisposition, and stress reactivity which actually determine "whether diabetes is present or not" (Gruenberg, 1977). Going a step further, research by Ralph de Fronzo of Yale University Medical School indicates that the activity of insulin may be impaired or minimized. From his research de Fronzo has noted that "individuals who develop diabetes late in life also have normal or even elevated insulin production . . . reduced tissue sensitivity to the hormones . . . may be because their cells have fewer receptors for binding insulin than do normal cells" (Marx, 1979).

The importance of receptor site activity in diabetes has been studied by Richard Adelman of the Temple University School of Medicine. His research has investigated the induction of the enzyme glucokinase in the liver in response to glucose which acts indirectly by stimulating the pancreas to secrete insulin (Adelman and Britton, 1975). By observing male rats as they aged from 2 to 24 months, he noted that the time required for glucose to increase glucokinase activity in the liver increased. However, when young and old rats were injected with insulin and corticosterone, which act directly upon the liver, both groups of animals responded with equal speed. From these experiments, and related studies by Caleb E. Finch, it appears that ". . . aging does not . . . impair the capacity of [the] liver to respond to insulin. . . . The biological activity of insulin does not decrease with age. . . . Another possibility is a decrease in insulin binding to membrane receptors" (Marx, 1979).

Among other major disorders being investigated in light of such observations are: (1) Parkinson's disease, which has been associated with dopamine deficiency in certain brain areas, which might indicate an inability of the aging mammalian brain to maintain adequate dopamine levels (Finch, 1975); (2) alteration in serotonin binding sites in the brain associated with depression and sleep disturbances (Shih and Young, 1978); (3) diminished capacity of lymphocytes to differentiate between "self" and "non-self" leading to autoimmune disorders (Warr and Marchalonis, 1978; Hildemann, 1978; Jerne, 1973; Hayflick, 1978); (4) recent research clearly indicating that "endocrine systems, in particular the adrenal steroids, can directly induce brain changes of the type seen in aging"; (5) interactions between neuroendocrine and genetic factors which give rise to the "diseases of modern civilization"; (6) disruption of protein synthesis which affects polarity of cell membranes and eventually leads to alterations in cell function (Frolkis, 1973; Frolkis et al., 1970).

This brief listing is representative but far from exhaustive or even comprehensive in the complex and burgeoning field of the neuroendocrinology of longevity. Despite scientific sophistication and precision the ultimate resolution of the issues raised in this research is unlikely to be completely resolved within the boundaries of biochemistry per se. The neuroendocrine system functions not as a closed biofeedback system but rather as one that is open to input and influence from external influences at numerous points. Among the most potent and well-documented influences are physical environment factors, excessive stress, and a wide range of psychosocial variables. Neuroendocrine factors are necessary but not sufficient to explain some of the most fundamental aspects of aging and longevity.

Among the clearest instances of such interactions are disturbances of male testosterone levels and the presence or absence of senile dementia or Alzheimer's disease in an aged population. Research by Alex Vermeulen of the University of Ghent in Belgium has confirmed that testosterone concentrations in men decrease beginning as early as age 50. Decrements both in sexual activity and in the ease with which conception may be achieved due to diminished numbers of sperm per ejaculation may be accounted for by this drop in testosterone levels accompanied by increased estrogen production. A significant research project undertaken at the Gerontology Research Center in Baltimore has surprisingly illustrated the interaction between these changes and psychosocial factors. The long-term Baltimore Longitudinal Study on Aging follows certain individuals over many years to observe the aging process. In one study concerning testosterone production in older men, 69 of the 76 men selected for the research were taken from the Longitudinal Study group. When the results were analyzed, they indicated that the testosterone levels were not lower and were even slightly higher in these older men than in younger men. There is an important discrepancy between the Baltimore study and virtually every other finding regarding testosterone levels. In examining these data, S. Mitchell Harman of the Gerontology Center has observed major psychosocial differences between the Baltimore men and age-related populations from other studies. According to a report in *Science* by Jean L. Marx:

> . . . the men they studied are unusual in that they have more education and are more prosperous than the general population. People who are well educated and members of the higher socioeconomic classes tend to take better care of themselves and to receive better medical attention than those who are less fortunate. . . . The Baltimore results may also carry the encouraging message that a decline in testosterone production need not be inevitable, provided good health can be maintained [Marx, 1979].

Findings such as these have profound implications for longevity since they indicate an intimate connection between the factors which enhance both the quality and the quantity of life.

Of even greater significance and controversy are the factors governing the presence or absence of senile dementia in an aged population. "Even in a youth-oriented society, being old may not be a crime. But is it a disease? . . . Most concede that aging has been viewed historically as a sickness or something abnormal to the healthy condition" (Greenberg, 1979). The onset of senility is roughly equivalent to schizophrenia in terms of its unknown etiology, ambiguous diagnosis, and punitive connotation. Recent research has begun to clarify dementia, which involves such symptoms as failure in problem solving, difficulty in short-term memory as well as speaking, and an overall disorganization in personality until the elderly person is so changed that he or she no longer recognizes or is recognized by family and friends. At present it is estimated that one million people in the United States are diagnosed in various stages of senile dementia. However, the pivotal question is whether this condition is an organic or functional disorder. While both influences are involved, it is evident that neither set of conditions is sufficient for the diagnosis and its subsequent stigma.

There appear to be at least two types of senility with the condition of presenile dementia or Alzheimer's disease striking individuals as young as 40 or 50. Alzheimer's disease ". . . accounts for more than 50% of such cases and is a very common disorder as well as being very costly in emotional, economic, and medical terms. It carries a markedly shortened life expectancy" (Terry, 1978). By contrast to the presenile onset of Alzheimer's disease, clinicians have usually reserved the diagnosis of senile dementia to individuals older than age 65, although there is a trend toward consideration of Alzheimer's and senile dementia as one and the same, with Alzheimer's being the formal diagnosis for both categories. Issues such as these have filled psychopathology journals for years and are likely to continue. However, there is an emerging consensus concerning certain neurophysiological aspects of Alzheimer's disease. Based upon autopsies performed on senile patients and employing computerized axial tomography, or CAT scanner, techniques, there emerge certain similarities and striking differences between the normal aged brain and the senile brain. Overall these observations have indicated: (1) ". . . the senile brain contains numerous plaques and tangles whereas the normal, aged brain contains only a few . . . plaques and tangles [which] are common in the frontal and temporal lobes of the cerebral cortex—especially in the hippocampus, which is in the temporal lobe and . . . is known to be involved in memory storage"; (2) ". . . a greatly reduced number of neurons can also be found in the senile hippocampus . . . in contrast to a normal aged brain, [the senile brain] shows dramatically reduced blood flow in the cerebral cortex, and the decrease is proportional to the patient's psychological deficits" (Arehart-Treichel, 1977). In accounting for these observations there are numerous theories, including: (1) a genetic basis for senility linked to three haptoglobin proteins; (2) senility as an autoimmune disease where antibodies react against the neurons of the brain; (3) slow viruses which reproduce in the microtubules of cells and alter the configuration of the essential microtubules; and (4) buildup of the trace element of aluminum, found to be four times as high in the nuclei of senile brain neurons and especially prevalent in brain areas evidencing extensive tangles (Arehart-Treichel, 1977; Greenberg, 1979). At the present time there is preliminary evidence from the research of Robert D. Terry of the Albert Einstein College of Medicine of an "infectious etiology" (Terry, 1978) for Alzheimer's disease.

While all of these issues are extremely important and some offer promise of developing a means of preventing Alzheimer's disease, none address the devastating effects of this disease and its social stigma. The necessity of working with senile patients in a positive context has been pointed out by physician Frances A. Hellerbrandt, Professor Emeritus at the University of Wisconsin School of Medicine and a resident of a retirement community. She and many other spokeswomen such as Maggie Kuhn, founder of the Gray Panthers, have emphasized that the degree to which senility is manifest or not can be greatly modified by psychosocial factors. Hellerbrandt has observed that, "Not all custodial patients are classifiable as victims of organic brain syndrome. Confusion and dependency may be attributable to a combination of isolation, sensory deprivation, immobility, muscle weakness, visual, auditory and dental deficits rather than the patho-physiological changes of senile dementia" (Hellerbrandt, 1978). Even for the accurately diagnosed cases of Alzheimer's disease, the degree of manifest degeneration can be reduced by a "supportive and humane environment." These individuals ". . . may have changed from what they were before, but what remains is unique and individual and worthy of preservation as long as faculties remain which are capable of responding to the humanistic endeavors of concerned and caring people" (Hellerbrandt, 1978). Throughout her numerous and compassionate articles, Hellerbrandt offers specific constructive solutions to the potential dehumanization of institutional care of the aged.

While such measures may seem idealistic at best, they can and have been achieved. Gay Gaer Luce, founder of the SAGE project in Berkeley, has documented such an approach in her inspiring book *Your Second Life* (1979). Among other excellent works displaying this approach is an autobiographical essay by eminent psychologist Donald O. Hebb entitled "On Watching Myself Get Old" (1978), a photographic essay of the SAGE project entitled *Life Time* by Karen Preuss (1978), and a moving book with the wonderful title of *An Old Guy Who Feels Good* by Worden McDonald (1978), father of Country Joe McDonald. These books offer hope and clearly demonstrate the regenerative capacity inherent in every individual. The neuropathology of Alzheimer's disease, convalescent care reforms, and even programs of revitalization for the elderly deserve the highest possible priority in the future of holistic health care. However, they still deal with the phenomenon of aging as contrasted to longevity, which poses altogether different questions.

Evolution and Longevity

Homo sapiens demonstrates a marked deviance in longevity from the normal curve of life expectancy in other species. According to Stephen Jay Gould of Harvard University:

> We can provide some numerical precision to support the claim that all mammals, on average, live for the same amount of biological time. . . . *Homo sapiens* is a markedly deviant mammal in more ways than braininess alone. We live about three times as long as mammals of our body size "should," but we breathe at the "right" rate and thus live to breathe about three times as much as an average mammal of our body size [Gould, 1977].

The essential feature of this deviation is that all of the developmental stages from puberty to adulthood arise later than would be predicted. This is of particular importance since it reflects research findings concerning regeneration discussed in the next chapter and is a well-documented effect of dietary manipulation conducive to longevity, discussed in Chapter VI. Most interesting of all is that we share this deviance from the normal curve with the bottle-nosed dolphins, who at least equal if not surpass humankind in the evolution of highly intelligent and peaceful life forms estimated to have existed for approximately 30 million years (Lilly, 1978).

For the most part the evolution of the longevity of the hominid precursors of the present human beings has been attributed to genetic regulation. However, the research of George M. Martin and other individuals has noted certain surprising anomalies in the evolution of the human species. Looking back over the course of evolution, "The results revealed periods in which there were dramatic increases in the rates of evolution of longevities" (Martin, 1979). These periods of accelerated activity are not predictable from the steady evolutionary clock model of evolutionary geneticists. Due to this anomaly, Martin has concluded, "The rates at which maximum life spans have been increasing, especially among hominids, have probably been too rapid to be accounted for by changes in the amino acid sequences of proteins" (1979). One suggestion by Martin is that these periods of acceleration are due to or at least "consistent with" theories that ". . . alterations in gene regulation, presumptively resulting largely from chromosomal rearrangements, are major determinants of longevity among mammals" (1979).

While that theory is in keeping with the observations of the evolutionary evidence, it is limited to the genetic level of analysis and may not account for the other influences conducive to longevity, especially for the human species. Given the multiplicity of factors influencing longevity, it is equally likely that a confluence of genetic, cellular, neuroendocrine, and environmental triggers may have initiated periods of accelerated longevity. At this point in the evolution of scientific inquiry, the paradigm built around single factor causation has yielded to a paradigm characterized by interconnected and dynamic processes (Capra, 1975). Perhaps the clearest application of this principle is to biological systems which can be considered as interconnected systems subject to biofeedback principles, as illustrated throughout the discussion of neuroendocrinology. Systems such as these are open to new input at many points, making them capable of continually reacting and adapting to internal and environmental demands.

For the most part this process of progressive adaptation has been considered primarily in terms of pathology. P. W. Landfield and his colleagues have researched the influence of neuroendocrine influences of aging, particularly with regard to the hippocampus. Out of this research has emerged a view consistent with numerous other experiments that ". . . initial age-related alterations in brain synaptic function could lead to gradual changes in neural control of endocrine processes, which, in turn, could lead to 'cascading' physiological imbalances and age-correlated physical deterioration" (Landfield et al., 1978). In the "cascading" effect, any minute input is instantaneously amplified in the neuroendocrine system, resulting in a progressive adaptation and restoration of homeostasis at a higher level of functioning. From the extensive literature of biofeedback research and its clinical applications (Peper et al., 1979), it is unequivocal that this cascading effect can have a negative influence resulting in a wide range of disorders, *or* a positive influence resulting in biological regulation and optimum states of health. Furthermore, the resulting effect is frequently accelerated at a critical point, with an effect analogous to the sudden precipitation of a supersaturated solution. Perhaps the seemingly inexplicable accelerations in the hominid evolution of longevity are the result of a positive process occurring under a confluence of factors. Given that this is even a remote possibility, and evidence indicates that it is not so remote, it could indicate that an evolutionary transformation from *Homo sapiens* to *Homo longevus* could occur with unprecedented rapidity given conducive circumstances. That is a transformation predicted by Teilhard de Chardin's "Omega," Jonas Salk's "Epoch B," and Albert Rosenfeld's "Genesis II." Whether that vision becomes reality may be determined in the twenty-first century.

FOUR

Regeneration and Rejuvenation

Medieval alchemists revered the salamander's ability to regenerate its severed limbs. During the eighteenth century alchemy and chemistry parted to pursue separate lines of inquiry, but the motif of the *Serpens mercurii,* the dragon which creates and destroys itself, remained the *prima materia* and was often represented by the salamander (Holmyard, 1968). Alchemy would have disappeared into obscurity altogether if it were not for the extensive inquiries of C. G. Jung, who perceived the psychological dimensions of that arcane discipline. Stating this observation, Jung noted, "I am therefore inclined to assume that the real root of alchemy is to be sought less in philosophical doctrines than in the projections of individual investigators. . . . He experienced his projection as a property of matter; but what he was in reality experiencing was his own unconscious . . . . Such projections repeat themselves whenever man tries to explore an empty darkness and involuntarily fills it with living form" (Jung, 1977). Three hundred years later the enigmatic ability of the salamander to undergo profound regeneration remains the focus of speculation and scientific inquiry. There is a tendency to dismiss the quest for regeneration as the projection of unconscious fantasies and the preceding quotation of Jung is often cited as evidence of this phenomenon. Quite the contrary. It is evident from Jung's extensive writings that he saw the transformations of alchemy as anticipating and prefiguring the role of human consciousness in regeneration and longevity. Furthermore, his insights do lend an appropriate note of caution, for regeneration elicits strong effect and can be clouded by projection. Psychological influences on longevity are discussed in the next chapter.

Regeneration and restoration of psychological and physical functions which ebb with advanced age have been an abiding preoccupation of all humankind. Recent documented research has revealed measures which can retard the aging process as well as regenerate the organism subject to its ravages. Research into the biology of aging has provided a basis for experimentation governing regeneration and longevity. There is a vast range of approaches, which extend from speculative extremism to immediately applicable techniques, including: (1) deliberate reduction of the body temperature of warm-blooded mammals; (2) pharmacological agents such as RNA supplements and the ubiquitous procaine injections; (3) exploration of brain chemistry and psychological techniques of influencing internal biochemical processes and thus to induce the same effects now produced by many pharmacological agents; and (4) electromagnetic means to induce limb regeneration and boost the body's healing potential. Each of these four areas will be considered in this chapter.

Temperature reduction and pharmacological interventions have received the greatest amount of research to date, and yet psychophysiological and electromagnetic techniques are likely to yield the greatest benefits in the future. While the effects of temperature reduction and pharmaceuticals upon the aging process are most evident, the link between psychological and biological processes may provide the most promising leads in longevity research. The third major section of this chapter is an extensive discussion of these processes since psychological factors are essential as initiators and mediators of biochemical and electromagnetic processes of the body. Through these psychological influences it is possible for an individual to initiate voluntarily either the degenerative or regenerative processes of the body with the same degree of potency as externally induced temperature regulation or pharmaceutical effects. Today there is an emerging field concerned with not only exploration of brain chemistry but also psychologically mediated analgesia as well as "psychoimmunology" (Rogers et al., 1979). Among the inexplicable phenomena which can be addressed and understood by such an approach are self-induced pain control, acupuncture, regulation of the body's internal opiates or endorphins, and the positive and negative aspects of the placebo response. Each of these subjects are considered since they provide preliminary evidence that the supposedly irreversible degeneration of aging can be retarded and perhaps reversed through the influence of human consciousness upon biological processes. Finally, the chapter concludes with a consideration of the effects of electromagnetic fields upon healing and regeneration of the human organism. Perhaps more than any other area of longevity research, the evidence of the effects of electromagnetic fields upon regeneration ignites the imagination. These effects are more subtle than the preceding biochemical processes and may prove to be the vital and experimentally accessible link between the psychological, neurological, and biochemical processes underlying the whole life cycle.

One problem in studying longevity is that the rate of aging occurs slowly and often undetectably over a prolonged period of time. In order to evaluate experimentation and apply it to the human life, measurements are needed to determine the rate of aging for short-time intervals. Lack of such measurements has hampered much research in this area. Drawing upon studies designed to measure the rate of aging in 450 Japanese survivors of Hiroshima, Alex Comfort has outlined possible methods: "Available test-procedures fall into three groups—straightforward (anthropometry, clinical and chemical examination, sensory tests, psychometric tests), those requiring, for example, biopsy, and those depending on the fact that deaths will occur in the test samples" (Comfort, 1969). From this basic tenet Comfort selected 53 indices of aging with various subtests and formulated a test battery with items including "Hair-greying score," "Protein-bound Iodine," "Nail Calcium Content," and "Black Design" assessments (Comfort, 1969). In 1969, Comfort states that this "ageing assessment unit" would be a prerequisite for clinical trials for possible approaches to slowing the aging process if such tests were not to be confined to laboratory animals or patients in other countries. Unfortunately, the application of Comfort's battery or any similar comprehensive measure has still not been implemented, partially due to its complexity and high cost but also due to the relatively low priority of longevity research in the national funding hierarchy.

Lowered Body Temperature

One of the earliest interventions demonstrating the longevity potential of various species is lowered body temperature. There appear to be no exceptions to the rule that animals live longer at lower body temperatures. Actually this phenomenon was documented as early as 1917 in experiments by Jacques Loeb and John H. Northrop of the Rockefeller Institute. Their research indicated that reduced body temperatures in poikilotherms (cold-blooded animals), fluctuating with that of their environment, did appear to slow the aging process. These results have been replicated and confirmed through numerous experiments continuing at the present time. Among the researchers defining these processes are Roy L. Walford and R. K. Liu of the University of California at Los Angeles School of Medicine, who have noted,

> Within broad limits, lifespan varies inversely with temperature in poikilotherms. Thus, decreasing the environmental temperature may lead to significant prolongation of lifespan. . . . The rate of aging of poikilothermic vertebrates is not independent of temperature during any phase of their lifespan. A lower temperature during the latter half of life and a higher temperature during the first half may yield the longest lifespan. . . . Those which undergo periodic mild temperature depression, torpor, or hibernation appear to live much longer than comparably-sized species which do not [Liu and Walford, 1972].

Research by Charles H. Borrows of the Gerontology Research Center significantly extended the normal 18-day life expectancy of ratifers, a microscopic multicellular invertebrate. Through reduced temperature he induced 36-day lives, and reduced food intake resulted in 54-day survival. Writing in *Pro-longevity,* Albert Rosenfeld observed, "By combining temperature with diet control, then he was able to *triple* the life span, adding another whole lifetime, as it were, at each end of life" (Rosenfeld, 1977). Among the many instances of this phenomenon in poikilotherms were the South American fish *Cynolebias belattii* and the ubiquitous laboratory fly, *Drosophila.*

More recent research has concerned itself with these effects in homeotherms, or warm-blooded animals including man which normally maintain body temperature within a range differing only from one to one and a half degrees centigrade. It has consistently been observed that core body temperatures of homeotherms tend to be lowered by underfeeding and this could contribute to the observed extended life expectancy. Although the factors of temperature reduction are more complex in homeotherms, Barnett Rosenberg and his colleagues from the Biophysics Department of Michigan State University have conducted extensive experimentation and concluded that ". . . small decreases in core body temperatures of homeothermic mammals produce marked increases in life expectancy" (Rosenberg et al., 1973). Consistent with Walford's observations regarding temperature reduction in the later stages of life of poikilotherms is the finding of his colleague and coresearcher Richard H. Weindruch that, "Unlike dietary restriction, body temperature lowering displays maximal efficacy as a life-prolonging force when instituted late in life, suggesting that temperature suppression of age-induced autoimmunity may override the disadvantage of simultaneously accentuating the immunodeficiency of aging" (Weindruch et al., 1979). This necessity of temperature lowering later in the developmental stages of homeotherms has received considerable research attention since it has been found that exposure of homeotherms to chronic low temperature for prolonged periods of time does have negative effects. With poikilotherms, lowered environmental temperature tends to lower core body temperature. However, the lowering of environmental temperature for homeotherms without an actual lowering of core body temperature has no advantages and is observed to have definite negative effects. Exposing laboratory rats to prolonged low temperature results in early onset of age-related pathology as well as a shortening of the life-span (Everitt, 1973). This is in marked contrast to the effects of short-term, internally initiated lower body temperature, as in hibernating animals, which indicates increased resistance to infection parasites, and irradiation (Liu and Walford, 1972). A distinction between externally imposed versus internally regulated lower body temperature for homeotherms has major implications. With laboratory mice, reduced body temperature is only evidenced in those which were underfed since weaning and not those restricted later in life. This indicates that early-life underfeeding may be required as the precursor for the most advantageous effects of a further lowering of body temperature in later developmental stages.

Attempts to define the biochemical processes underlying these observations involve the effects of reduced core temperature on DNA repair and regulatory functions, immune system responses, and neuroendocrine mechanisms. At this point in time the most promising explanation appears to be that the effects of internally lowered body temperature in homeotherms is mediated through the neuroendocrine axis consisting of the hypothalamus, pituitary, and thyroid. From the research of Roy L. Walford it appears that the internal temperature regulation function of the hypothalamus is of considerable importance. Using marijuana derivatives known to influence the hypothalamus, Walford induced mild temperature depressions in male mice resulting in prolonged life expectancy with minimal side effects (Liu and Walford, 1972). There are now well over twenty pharmacological agents which have been claimed to prolong life expectancy in laboratory animals and in humans, and these are briefly considered later in this chapter. The involvement of the hypothalamic function would also account for the data that prolonged exposure to external low temperature has negative effects. According to A. V. Everitt of the University of Sydney in Australia, excess cold causes the hypothalamus to influence the thyroid to increase its hormone production, since "Heat production is increased by thyroid hormone, which stimulates metabolic processes in almost every organ of the body and probably accelerates aging generally. It is believed that the more work an organ does, the higher its metabolic rate and the shorter its life" (Everitt, 1973). Lowering body temperature through external means in homeotherms can have the effect of increasing the metabolic rate in a compensatory manner through this neuroendocrine axis.

In accounting for observation that the effects of lowered core temperature are more pronounced in later life, the hypothalamic influence on the body's immunological system may again be a key factor. R. K. Liu and Roy L. Walford hypothesize that "the rate of aging in vertebrates may operate through immunological mechanisms. That this action may be greatest during the last half of life is noteworthy in that it is precisely during this period that autoimmune processes postulated to be pathogenetic for aging are most easily demonstrable" (Liu and Walford, 1972). Clinical applications of these measures with humans is complicated by many known and as yet undiscovered factors. Within the homeotherm body there are marked temperature variations such as in the testes which are maintained 2°-8°C below core temperature in order for sperm to remain functional. For centuries transient periods of functional sterility in males has been induced by hot baths in Japan, loincloth padding in India, and most recently through the applications of clinical biofeedback to induce similar effect through scrotal warming (French et al., 1973). Perhaps such methods can evolve into a means of nonpharmaceutical male birth control, although the present stage of the art is not reliable.

In addition to biochemical research it would perhaps be fruitful to determine whether centenarian individuals evidence reduced core body temperature or if individuals evidencing episodic or chronic hypothermia show an increase in life expectancy. Among the researchers recognizing these implications is Barnett Rosenberg, who has compared the effects of such measures to the incidence of "vascular lesions, cancer and heart diseases." From his data he concludes, "We can state, therefore, that the survivorship curves due to decreasing the mean core body temperature by 2°C predict a longer survival time for humans than would result from total cures of all three of the major causes of death at the present time" (Rosenberg et al., 1973). Rosenberg's research has generated sophisticated mathematical predictions accounting for the death rates of poikilothermic animals at high temperatures due to "protein denaturation" (Rosenberg et al., 1971). This underscores the potential of temperature reduction. Despite this potential, the effects of internally induced hypothermia in homeotherms has not been, and is not being, fully explored.

Bernard L. Strehler has proposed an evolutionary interpretation of the present elevated core body temperatures for humans. He hypothesizes that low body temperatures would have had negative survival value since they would impair man's ability to engage in sustained work, hunting, combat, and would have made early ancestors a rather torpid, easy prey. As the species evolved and the nature of survival was radically altered, elevated body temperatures may have become anachronistic or even detrimental. Regarding this possibility, Strehler hypothesizes:

> Our thesis, then, is that a mammal such as man, in a modern technological milieu, is no longer dependent on his capacity for sustained muscular work, unless he is a football player, mountain climber, or exceptionally affectionate; and that one of the most promising ways of adding years to life without subtracting life from years may be to find a means to reset the hypothalamic thermostat without producing idiots or sleepwalkers [Strehler, 1967].

Speculations such as these are consistent with existing research data and suggest the possibility of an evolutionary metamorphosis of the human species.

Pharmacological Approaches

Gerontological pharmacology involves the application of chemical agents to decelerate physiological aging, including the decline of memory and intelligence. Among the approaches noted by Charles G. Kormendy of Bristol Laboratories and A. Douglas Bender of Smith, Kline & French Laboratories are "... antioxidants, lipofuscin and cross-link inhibitors, immunoregulators, hormones and learning enhancing agents" (Kormendy and Bender, 1971). This is a vast area of research which is limited only by the virtually unlimited resources of the pharmaceutical industry. Since every pharmaceutical "breakthrough" is hailed by the popular press as the ultimate panacea, that trend will undoubtedly continue in a culture fixated on miraculous elixirs since Ponce de León. *Alice's Adventures in Wonderland* is a cogent commentary on the present situation. " 'I know something interesting is sure to happen,' she said to herself, 'whenever I eat or drink anything: so I'll just see what this bottle does.' " Since pharmaceutical panaceas will continue to be dwelt upon by the popular media and the advertising-laden professional journals and since these developments are not a major focus of the present inquiry, they are only briefly considered.

While certain drugs appear to retard the rate or effects of aging at a biochemical and cellular level, they do not offer the potential for actual regeneration as do the electromagnetic techniques discussed at the conclusion of this chapter. Moreover, it is highly likely that the biochemical responses created by pharmaceuticals can be duplicated by psychological techniques now the subject of research, which can exert a profound influence on the biochemical and neurophysiological processes of the body.

An article in the science fiction magazine *OMNI* shows the high hopes the popular media holds out for miracle drugs: "If life extension becomes a national priority . . . if there were a $200 billion assault on aging and death . . . in five years we'd have a program that would put such a dent in death we might wipe it off the face of the earth" (Stein, 1978). While the goal is admirable, it is unlikely to be fulfilled through such bellicose directives. Unquestionably, pharmaceutical intervention in the aging process could yield results particularly in the areas of research isolating naturally occurring hormones of the body and central nervous system. Most notable among the present pharmaceutical armamentaria are:

> . . . ribonucleic acid (RNA), Isoprinosine vasopressin, Hydergine, Deaner lecithin chain phenylalanine, amphetamines and related compounds, magnesium pernicine, diphenythydantoin, Ritalin vitamin B_{12}, Nootropyl ACTH. 1-prolyll-leucyl glycine amide, caffeine, Metrazol, strychnine, marijuana derivatives, and innumerable other compounds [Stein, 1978].

While this list is not exhaustive by any means, it does give a sense of the range of development of such agents. Most recently, Sandy Shakocius and Durk Pearson reviewed many of these developments in an article entitled "Mind Food" (1979). That article provides an excellent overview of the available pharmaceuticals in addition to noting specific dosages, applications, and sources where they can be obtained. Briefly, the article discusses: (1) choline, a nutrient found in meat, eggs, and fish which can increase the acetylcholine level of the brain, resulting in "improved memory and serial learning," and lecithin, phosphatidyl choline, which has a similar effect; (2) the prescription drug Deaner, dimethylaminoethanol-p-acetamine benzoate, which "improves memory and learning in the aged and in hyperkinetic children"; (3) RNA supplementation, which "protects against oxidizing chemicals . . . a daily dose of 25 milligrams extended the average life span of laboratory mice by 16 percent"; (4) the pharmaceutical Isoprinosine, containing inosine, which passes "through the blood-brain barrier and . . . enhances learning efficiency, aids memory, improves behavioral organization, and increases organization and integration of perceptual information"; (5) norepinephrine, a neurotransmitter, which can be sustained between nerve synapses by the action of "amphetamines, Ritalin, and magnesium pemoline . . . thereby increasing the amount of neurotransmitter in the synapse"; (6) Diapid nasal spray, a synthetic version of vasopressin, which has restorative effects upon "motor rapidity and memory in men in their fifties and sixties"; (7) Nootropyl, 2-oxopyrrolidine acetamide, which seems to "promote the flow of information between the right and left hemispheres of the brain" (Shakocius and Pearson, 1979); and numerous other elements of gerontological pharmacology. Contained at the end of the article is an extensive bibliography citing the original articles from which many of the above quotations were excerpted.

Among the more judiciously researched and documented pharmaceuticals is apomorphine, which is a dopamine receptor stimulant, and L-dopa, a biosynthetic precursor of the neurotransmitter dopamine and used in the treatment of Parkinson's disease. In an excellent study John F. Marshall and Norberto Berrios of the University of California at Irvine watched the swimming capacity of young adult rats (3 to 4 months) with aged rats (24 to 27 months). The concern was to explore the movement disturbances and relative immobility and inflexibility of older humans. In observing the swimming behavior of the rats they noted that the older animals moved their limbs less vigorously and were less successful in keeping their heads above water. Then the older rats were injected with apomorphine in one instance and with L-dopa in another. In both experimental conditions, movement was "dramatically restored" in the older rats within fifteen minutes, as judged by observers in a double-blind procedure. Based upon these results, Marshall and Berrios have concluded,

> The dramatic rejuvenation of performance by compounds that enhance the activity of brain dopamine receptors holds potential significance for understanding the movement disturbances of aging . . . the results suggest a central nervous origin of the deficit, in particular, the poor performance of the aged animal seems linked to the age-related changes in neurotransmission of brain dopaminergic synapses [Marshall and Berrios, 1979].

These results have helped to clarify the possible involvement of the deterioration of dopamine neurotransmitters and receptors in movement disturbances of the elderly.

With just this brief overview it should be evident that there is a plethora of pharmaceuticals to dazzle and delight even the most avid consumer. While a few might prove to be both safe and beneficial, even a cursory glance at the *Physicians' Desk Reference* (1981) testifies to both the toxic effects and complications of virtually every pharmaceutical yet discovered, and that is most likely to be the case for the longevity pharmaceuticals as well. Even the term "side effects" (Graedon, 1976) has been challenged since these complications may actually outweigh the primary effects and benefits for a substantial number of patients. Pharmaceutical interventions in the aging and psychological impairment process are laudable but need to proceed with conservative caution. Aging and longevity are dependent on environmental and psychosocial influences beyond the realms of pharmacological sites of action. Systemic considerations are easily ignored or dismissed in the barrage of pharmacological panaceas for every conceivable human condition. When a holistic perspective is brought to bear upon these developments, it is clear that the greatest potential resides in the systematic enhancement of naturally occurring chemical compounds in the organism through the interaction between human consciousness and the central nervous system.

One further pharmaceutical requires consideration. In 1945 research began on a substance spanning the gap between dietary supplementation and pharmacological intervention, procaine. Pharmacologically, procaine, the primary agent in novocaine, is combined with benzoic acid, a preservative, and potassium metabisulfate, an antioxidant. When this substance is injected, it produces two agents, which are para-aminobenzoic acid (PABA) and diethylaminoethanol (DEAE). From this derives the highly controversial GH3, or "Gerovital," developed by physician Ana Aslan of the Bucharest Geriatric Institute in Romania. Over the last thirty-five years major political figures such as Mao Tse-tung and Nikita Khrushchev, and Hollywood luminaries have ostensibly benefited from GH3 injections. Its efficacy has been both challenged and supported by research which continues at the present time (Tyson, 1979). Unfortunately there is such an emotional furor over its clinical efficacy that it is difficult if not impossible to assess its merit. At a gerontological conference in 1974, Aslan herself indicated that " it . . . had tremendously beneficial effects in helping older people regain and maintain physical and mental health. But she admitted that so far she had been unable to demonstrate that Gerovital could prolong the lives of older people" (Kurtzman and Gordon, 1977). A brief chapter in John Langone's book *Long Life* (1978) offers an overview of the procaine controversy. More recently, orthomolecular physician Warren Levin (*Behavior Today*, 1979a) has indicated that a modified version of procaine may function as a monoamine oxidase, or MAO, inhibitor, which is the primary action of antidepressant medications. MAO inhibitors slow the elimination of neurotransmitters such as serotonin and norepinephrine from the body. Perhaps the rejuvenation effects noted for Gerovital are due in part or entirely to this antidepressant property. Several earlier studies, however, refuted the hypothesis that procaine exerted an antidepressant effect through MAO inhibition, showing that the doses of procaine needed to inhibit MAO are much larger than the usual clinical dosage. Without advocating or denying the efficacy of procaine, it seems evident that such a controversial agent capable of demonstrating some clinical efficacy does merit further, serious research.

Before moving on, we might mention the great number of approaches, largely quasi-pharmaceutical, applied in various health spas, predominantly in Europe, which offer clearly experimental and occasionally questionable approaches to slowing the aging process. For a Michelin guide overview of these spas, see the book *The Health Spas* by Robert and Raye Yaller (1974). Among the many approaches are "cell therapy," "embryotherapy," "phylotherapy," "electrosleep," "thallassotherapy," etc. (Popov et al., 1976). It should be evident from even a limited perusal of this area that basic research as well as demonstrable clinical efficacy is clearly lacking. Many of these approaches are blatant charlatanism. They are noted here without judgment. Both caution and further research are called for. Medicine abounds with instances of peasants eating moldy bread for infections, resulting in the discovery of penicillin or the Wassermann reaction for syphilis, which was developed on a totally erroneous assumption while its mode of action still remains ambiguous. Insight and discovery often derive from unlikely sources with the only prerequisite being an analytic curiosity. Suppressing or denying at least the potential of controversial measures most often results in their assuming more importance than they are due.

Brain Chemistry

The third area of consideration in this chapter is that of psychological influences on the biochemistry of aging and longevity. Among the most promising areas of inquiry considered here are the biochemical links between the mind and body, discovery of the body's naturally occurring opiates or endorphins, clinical applications of endorphins in relieving pain associated with aging, and finally the implications of these findings for exploring the placebo response, a phenomenon which can literally swing the balance between illness and health.

Neuroscientists have sought explicit links between brain biochemistry and human behavior since the nineteenth century when the French neurologist Charcot explored the psychosomatic etiology of hysterical seizures (Pelletier, 1979). This research was followed by that of Freud, Jung, Sherrington, Dunbar, Pavlov, Cannon, Selye, and others who began to define the precise neurophysiological mechanisms and biochemical mediators by which psychological states and environmental influences held sway over the body. Due to the observed properties of opiates, ". . . pharmacologists long assumed that specific opiate receptors existed in the brain and possibly in other tissues" (Snyder, 1977). This has now been confirmed. In 1974 an important discovery was made by Choh Hao Li of the University of California School of Medicine in San Francisco. His research focused on the pituitary gland, which produces protein hormones, differentially arranged by enzymes to serve as governing hormones throughout the body. Prior to Li's discovery it was thought that these pituitary hormones affected the body but did not act directly upon the brain or central nervous system. Then Li isolated a potent pituitary protein termed "beta-lipotropin," or "beta-endorphin," for endogenous morphine (Li and Chung, 1976) which played a hormonal role in the body of mobilizing fats. Since that basic discovery, related research has revealed an extraordinary array of such hormones which serve neuroendocrine functions as well as "mediating pain, modulating pleasure and integrating emotions . . . analgesia, addiction, depression and schizophrenia" (Blackwell, 1979). This impressive array is only a hint of the range of possibilities which have arisen through the research of Li and many others since 1974. Not only do these pituitary hormones provide a vital communication within the brain and central nervous system itself, but they also appear to mediate between the brain and the body and between the intangible properties of human consciousness and the biochemical processes they govern.

Following closely upon Li's 1974 work was a virtually simultaneous discovery in 1975 by the two separate research teams of John Hughes and Hans W. Kosterlitz, University of Aberdeen, and Solomon H. Snyder with his colleagues at the Johns Hopkins University School of Medicine. Experiments by Hughes and Kosterlitz provided direct evidence for the existence of naturally occurring opiate-like neurotransmitters. They isolated a morphine-like neurotransmitter, comprising two closely related short peptides, each made up of five amino acid units, from the brains of laboratory pigs. Given the source of this neurotransmitter (Hughes et al., 1975) they formulated the term "enkephalin" from the Greek for "in the head." One of the peptides is "methionine-enkephalin" and the other is "leucine-enkephalin." Where the research of Li and that of Hughes and Kosterlitz converged was that the amino acid sequence of methionine-enkephalin matched a segment of Li's pituitary hormone beta-lipotropin. These substances, which occur naturally in the brain and pituitary gland, produce analgesic effects which are as potent as morphine.

Essential to the understanding of these discoveries is a grasp of the function of receptors in the central nervous system. Information in the nervous system travels to and from the brain in the form of electrical impulses. Between the elongated, finger-like, excitatory neurons which make up the central nervous system are gaps or synapses. Normally, when an electrical impulse arrives at the end of one neuron it triggers the release of chemical carriers of neurotransmitters into the synapse. These neurotransmitters, twenty of which have now been identified, fit into receptors in the next receiving neuron where the impulse again becomes an electrical impulse and so on throughout the central nervous system. When endorphins and enkephalins are released near the synapse, they fit into the opiate receptors and prevent the neurotransmitter from jumping the gap. Such a process may block the ascending pain pathways in the spinal column and brain, resulting in diminished or banished pain. The actual nature of this process remains unknown: ". . . enkephalin inhibition may be indirect. Instead of acting directly on the receiving nerve cell the substance may block the release of excitatory neurotransmitters . . . thereby reducing the receiving cell's excitatory input" (Snyder, 1977). The relations among beta-lipotropin, the endorphins, and enkephalin also remain unresolved. At this point it appears unlikely that they pass directly from the pituitary to the brain, although this is not certain (Bergland and Page, 1979). Endorphins and enkephalins are found in the brains of all vertebrates and are distributed throughout the brain where opiate receptors are most in evidence. Concentrations appear to vary in the ". . . corpus striatum, anterior hypothalamus, amygdala, and periaqueductal gray matter . . . medulla, pons, and spinal cord, this occurrence is exceptionally high in limbic structures and in the hypothalamus, areas involved in emotionality and stress response" (Vereby et al., 1978). This latter observation concerning the role of endorphins and enkephalins as possible mediators of emotional and stress responses has prompted extensive clinical research and application.

Clinical applications of this research have focused on endorphins as the means by which the body inhibits pain perception. Currently it is thought that certain areas of the brain, when appropriately activated, send nerve impulses down the spinal column to block incoming pain signals before they reach the brain. Specifically, researchers believe that ". . . stimulation of the central and periventricular gray areas produces analgesia by causing the release of endorphins" (Marx, 1977). Through the central nervous system process noted earlier, the endorphins subsequently mediate or block the transmission of pain-related nerve impulses. Electrical stimulation of certain areas of the brain has been observed for many years to alleviate pain. Recent research indicates that electrical stimulation of the periaqueductal gray matter in three pain patients resulted in ". . . significant increases (50 to 300 percent) in the concentration of ventricular immunoreactive β-endorphin . . . pain relief . . . may be in part mediated by the activation of the β-endorphin rich diencephalic areas" (Rossier et al., 1979). Furthermore, both laboratory animals and humans ". . . become tolerant to repeated or prolonged electrical stimulation in the same manner that they . . . become tolerant to the analgesic and euphoric effects of morphine" (Marx, 1977). Research by neurosurgeon Yoshio Hosobuchi of the University of California School of Medicine in San Francisco has noted that four patients out of twenty-two receiving electrical implants for pain developed tolerance to beta-endorphin stimulation. His research indicates this may be due to changes in serotonin metabolism and this tolerance may be reversed by "dietary supplements of L-tryptophan" (*Medical World News,* 1979).

Yet another link between endorphin activity, electrical stimulation of the brain, and pain analgesia is acupuncture. Although Chinese medical journals have reported over 400,000 operations between 1966 and 1972 using acupuncture analgesias, the approach remains highly controversial (Bresler, 1979). Most recently acupuncture was given a substantial boost in credibility when Bruce Pomeranz and his colleagues at the University of Toronto reported that acupuncture promoted the release of endorphins which appeared to mediate the resulting analgesia. Pomeranz measured the responses of single neurons in the spinal cords of cats to noxious stimuli. When acupuncture was used for twenty to thirty minutes, the cats did not respond to the stimuli and pain response was suppressed for over an hour after the acupuncture ceased. When "sham" acupuncture points were stimulated, there was no ensuing analgesia. From further research Pomeranz indicated that the pituitary may be the source of the endorphins involved in acupuncture analgesia, since removing the gland prevents decreased pain response in spinal neurons (Pomeranz, 1977). Richard M. Bergland and Robert B. Page of the Harvard Medical School addressed the formidable question of whether pituitary hormones are transported directly to the brain to modify brain function. After a thorough and painstaking review of the research, they concluded ". . . the anatomical bridges between the pituitary and the brain are more complex and numerous . . . and are anatomically well arranged not only to carry neural information to the endocrine system but also to carry endocrine information to the brain. . . . Endorphin and other hormones may be produced in small quantity locally within the brain but transported in larger quantity from the pituitary to the brain on demand" (Bergland and Page, 1979).

Endorphin research appears to be an area with great promise, yielding insight not only into acupuncture but into many other areas: (1) chronic psychosis, drug addiction, rage, paranoia, schizophrenia, and depression have been illuminated by this research (Vereby et al., 1978); (2) activation of the endorphin system stimulates vasopressin, resulting in antidepressant activity, alleviation of some aspects of senile dementia, and restoration of memory (Gold and Goodwin, 1978); (3) function of beta-endorphin appears to regulate "calcium ion flux" in order to inhibit neurotransmitter release (Guerrero-Munoz et al., 1979); (4) enkephalins may enhance learning capacity and induce marked behavioral changes (Arehart-Treichel, 1977); (5) beta-endorphin acts as a mediator of acute stress in a "holistic response of the organism" (Guillemin et al., 1977); (6) beta-endorphin binds to specific, nonopiate receptor sites on human lymphocytes, white blood cells, and may mediate functions such as sleep, epilepsy, headache, as modulators of memory storage processes during stressful events, which helps to deflect or minimize painful psychological experiences, and even orgasm (Hazum et al., 1979). Perhaps more than any single specific area of research, the endorphins illustrate the innate self-regulatory capacity of the human organism.

The Placebo Response

Endorphins are activated not only by the neuroendocrine systems described here, but also through the activity of human consciousness. Placebo response is a ubiquitous aspect of all systems of healing and has received increased and serious attention in recent years. There have been numerous attempts to define placebo. They range from a very restricted dictionary definition: ". . . an active substance or preparation given to satisfy the patient's symbolic need for drug therapy and used in controlled studies to determine the efficacy of medicinal substances. Also, a procedure with no intrinsic therapeutic value, performed for such purposes" (*Dorland's Illustrated Medical Dictionary,* 1974) to elaborate and enthusiastic testimonials. Since a great deal of the relevant research literature has been discussed in *Holistic Medicine* (Pelletier, 1979) as well as in Herbert Benson's *The Mind/Body Effect* (1979), it is not reiterated here. When all of the elaborate literature is considered and distilled, a perfectly adequate definition is given with striking clarity by Jerome D. Frank of the Johns Hopkins University School of Medicine, who terms placebo "the faith that heals" (1975). Beyond that definition is the necessity of reincorporating such a pervasive and powerful influence into clinical practice:

> In its present disregard for the positive placebo effect, medicine has lost a valuable asset, an asset which sustained it for centuries. Such a beneficial element should be reincorporated into medicine. The potential value of nonspecific factors should not be underestimated but must be recognized as a potent and versatile tool. Indeed, neglecting to use the positive placebo effect to its fullest advantage is the poor practice of medicine [Benson, 1979].

In the pharmacological research of the 1950s every attempt was made to eliminate the aspect of suggestion and placebo response. Even

though the "double-blind, random assignment, control group, longitudinal study with periodic follow up" remains the ideal model for
contemporary research, it is increasingly evident that it is only one
of a large spectrum of possible research designs (Campbell and Stanley, 1963) and is itself subject to "experimenter expectancy effects"
(Rosenthal, 1966) or error due to placebo response. When research
efforts were oriented toward the elimination of specific, acute diseases through pharmaceutical interventions, the placebo effect was
minimal and could virtually be eliminated or controlled for by the
double-blind procedure. However, more recent research concerning
the chronic diseases contains an inextricable element of placebo
response since the incidence and alleviation of these conditions are
more dependent upon psychosocial and environmental factors. Positive placebo response and the systematic enhancement of that response is an important area of research in itself, involving such
variables as the "psychological state of the patient," the physician's
"attitudes, expectancies, hopes, and fears" (Benson and Epstein,
1965) as well as situational and environmental influences. Consideration of these variables, although complex, is both possible and neces
sary within the double-blind procedure as well as other designs.

Clinical practice involves the systematic enhancement of placebo.
Jerome D. Frank, in concluding an article examining placebo responses ranging from coronary bypass surgery to the spontaneous
remission of terminal cancer, urged physicians to make more use of
this powerful response:

> In sum, I hope I have succeeded in convincing you that the
> patient's state of mind can affect his body for better or worse.
> Negative emotions such as depression and anxiety can impede
> healing, and positive ones such as expectant faith can enhance
> it. In the patient's eyes we are not only scientifically trained
> physicians, but ministers of healing. By fostering the faith that
> heals, we can enhance our therapeutic power, a goal towards
> which we all continue to strive [Frank, 1975].

While clinicians frequently acknowledge these influences, the absence of quantifiable neurophysiological or biochemical mechanisms
to account for the placebo response has mitigated against systematic

research. To date, the single most important series of research projects involving the placebo response have been those linking positive placebo response to specific biochemical activity involving the endorphins.

Pain and its waxing and waning has remained one of the essential manifestations of the placebo response. Recent research has indicated specific biochemical mediators by which placebo analgesia might function. Even though the research is limited to the analgesic aspects of placebo it does provide a model for the further exploration of the other dimensions of placebo. Perhaps the most eloquent statement of the potency of placebo in inducing analgesic properties as well as swaying the balance between life and death is contained in Boris Pasternak's *Doctor Zhivago*. As Anna Ivanovna lay dying of what appeared to be lobar pneumonia, a powerful transformation takes place as the physician Yura attends to her with the words:

"Will you feel pain? Do the flames find their disintegration? In other words, what will happen to your consciousness? But what is consciousness? Let's see. A conscious attempt to fall asleep is sure to produce insomnia, to try to be conscious of one's own digestion is a sure way to upset the stomach. Consciousness is a light directed outward, it lights up the way ahead of us so that we don't stumble. It's like the headlights on a locomotive—turn them inward and you'd have a crash.

"So what will happen to your consciousness? *Your* consciousness, yours, not anyone else's. Well, what are *you?* There's the point. Let's try to find out. What is it about you that you have always known as yourself? What are you conscious of in yourself? Your kidneys? Your liver? Your blood vessels? No. However far back you go in your memory, it is always in some external, active manifestation of yourself that you come across your identity—in the work of your hands, in your family, in other people. And now listen carefully. You in others—this is your soul. This is what you are. This is what your consciousness has breathed and lived on and enjoyed throughout your life— your soul, your immortality, your life in others. And what now? You have always been in others and you will remain in others. And what does it matter to you if later on that is called your memory? This will be you—the you that enters the future and becomes a part of it.

"And now one last point. There is nothing to fear. There is nothing to fear. There is no such thing as death. Death has nothing to do with us. But you said something about being talented—that it makes one different. Now, that does have something to do with us. And talent in the highest and broadest sense means talent for life.

"There will be no death, says St. John. His reasoning is quite simple. There will be no death because the past is over, that's almost like saying there will be no death because it is already done with, it's old and we are bored with it. What we need is something new, and that new thing is life eternal."

He was pacing up and down the room as he was talking. Now he walked up to Anna Ivanovna's bed and putting his hand on her forehead said, "Go to sleep." After a few moments she began to fall asleep.

Yura quietly left the room and told Egorovna to send in the nurse. "What's come over me?" he thought. "I'm becoming a regular quack—muttering incantations, laying on the hands."

Next day Anna Ivanovna was better.

Though pain was the consideration, life was the result.

At the University of California in San Francisco a team of neurologists and oral surgeons, Jon D. Levine, Newton C. Gordon, and Howard L. Fields, conducted research into the phenomenon of placebo analgesia with fifty patients recuperating from wisdom-teeth extractions. In a double-blind, crossover experimental design, postoperative patients were randomly assigned to three experimental groups where they received morphine, the standard medication for such pain, placebo which they defined as "a class of substances which has been shown to partially relieve postsurgical pain in more than one-third of patients," and naloxone, which "may be somewhat less effective than placebo in terms of pain relief, and theoretically may increase pain" (Levine et al., 1978a). This last observation is due to the fact that naloxone is a known opiate antagonist which is thought to bind receptors influenced by endorphins and therefore block endorphin analgesia. It is interesting to note that there was no control group of patients who would have received neither placebo nor naloxone. Patients were given morphine, placebo, or naloxone in equal volumes by means of an intravenous catheter. In order to evaluate placebo analgesia carefully, the researchers used a "cross-over" element by administering the drugs at three and four hours after surgery in the following manner: One group received placebo (naloxone vehicle) as the first drug and naloxone as the second drug; a second group received naloxone first and placebo second; and the third group received placebo followed by 7.5 mg of morphine sulphate. Pain was evaluated by the patients marking a point on a line ranging from "no pain" to "worst pain ever" at various time intervals and asked to report verbally whether their pain had increased, decreased, or remained the same since the last measurement of their pain level. Results of this study were very significant. First, the patients who received naloxone reported significantly more pain than those who received placebo. Second, the researchers had divided those who received placebo first into two subgroups of "responders" and "nonresponders." Placebo responders were individuals who reported no more pain an hour after they received a placebo injection than they had five minutes before the injection. Nonresponders felt more pain after an hour. Out of these two subgroups the researchers found that naloxone injections increased pain for the responders but not for the nonresponders.

Although inferences from this result are complex, it is likely the placebo responders induced an internal endorphin response which was reversed by the endorphin antagonist naloxone. According to the researchers, "The experiment provides evidence that an endogenous morphine-like factor is released in a clinical situation and is consistent with the observations that in man, analgesia produced by diencephalic stimulation or acupuncture is reversed by naloxone . . . further . . . pain is an important activating factor of the endorphin-mediated analgesia system" (Levine et al., 1978a). In reporting the results in *Lancet,* the researchers also concluded:

> If, as the present study suggests, the analgesic effect of placebo is based on the action of endorphins, future research can proceed with an analysis of variables affecting endorphin activity rather than simply recording behavioural manifestations of

placebo effects. Greater understanding of endogenous mechanisms of analgesia should lead to more effective management of clinical pain with a combination of pharmacological, behavioural, and physical methods [Levine et al., 1978b].

Commenting on previous studies by other researchers, Levine and his colleagues noted that experiments using artificially induced rather than clinical pain have failed to demonstrate pain enhancement with naloxone. They have hypothesized that "... the prolonged duration of the pain or the added stress of the clinical situation accounts for this difference. That stress may be a factor is indicated by the strong positive correlation between plasma levels of adrenocorticotrophin (as stress indicator) and endorphins" (Levine et al., 1978b).

The consideration of stress as a factor begins to link the psychosocial and biochemical levels of analysis. In reporting the results of the preceding experiments to the Second World Congress on Pain in Montreal (*Medical World News,* 1978d), there was some degree of controversy, although the many dolorologists present did eventually agree with both the noncontrol group design and the experimental results. When a conservative presentation draws controversy, then it is understandable why the researchers limited their discussion to a single mention of either the "stress" or "behavioral" factors by which endorphin response might be initially triggered. It is hoped ongoing research will address these issues, since the consideration of the consciousness of the individual is an inextricable aspect of positive placebo response just as the systematic involvement of the patient is an integral part of clinical biofeedback. These factors were briefly considered in a *Psychology Today* article by Howard L. Fields when he concluded, "Perhaps the most intriguing question is whether this system can be activated voluntarily; that is, can people will themselves to feel less pain or learn some mental trick to set the pain-suppressing mechanism in motion?" (Fields, 1978). Many of the same internal, psychological processes which alleviate pain perception under conditions of "alpha EEG feedback" (Pelletier and Peper, 1977) might also mediate the activation of the endorphin response as well as identify those patients most amenable to acupuncture analgesia.

Throughout the history of medicine approximately 30 percent of any given group of patients has been shown to respond positively to placebo. Responders to hypnotic suggestion, acupuncture, inert pharmaceuticals, clinical biofeedback and related clinical approaches which involve a high degree of placebo response may be the same one-third. However, an even more intriguing and equally likely possibility is that there might emerge a means of matching patients with a particular treatment suited to them which would enhance the positive placebo response with the result of pushing the already established 30 percent to even higher levels. It is interesting to note, for instance, that hypnosis analgesia is not reversed by opiate antagonists and thus might operate by altogether different psychological and biochemical processes. A way of matching patients and treatment might result in the effective treatment of a wide variety of disorders for divergent groups of patients, with minimal or no pharmaceutical intervention.

Endorphin research provides objective information regarding one aspect of placebo response. Subjective reports and clinical case studies offer the greatest insight into the psychosocial variables. One of the best subjective accounts of placebo response is that of Norman Cousins of the UCLA School of Medicine, beginning in 1976 with the already classic article, "Anatomy of an Illness (As Perceived by the Patient)" (1976), followed by "The Mysterious Placebo: How the Mind Helps Medicine Work" (1977) and "What I Learned from 3000 Doctors" (1978). It was in the placebo article that Cousins concluded:

> The placebo is only a tangible object made essential in an age that feels uncomfortable with intangibles, an age that prefers to think that every inner effect must have an outer cause. . . . The placebo satisfies the contemporary craving for visible mechanisms and visible answers. But the placebo dissolves on scrutiny, telling us that it cannot relieve us of the need to think deeply about ourselves.
>
> The placebo, then, is an emissary between the will to live and the body. But the emissary is expendable. If we can liberate ourselves from tangibles, we can connect hope and the will to live directly to the ability of the body to meet great threats and challenges. The mind can carry out its ultimate functions and powers over the body without the illusion of material intervention. "The mind," said John Milton, "is its own place, and in

itself can make a heaven of hell, and a hell of heaven" [Cousins, 1977].

Another striking instance of the regenerative capacity inherent in placebo response was documented in the *New England Journal of Medicine* by Neil Fiore of the University of California at Berkeley. Writing from both a personal and a professional perspective, Fiore told of his recovery from an "embryonal carcinoma with pulmonary metastases" (Fiore, 1979). As a psychologist he recognized that ". . . faith placed in an unreliable placebo could backfire," and he describes his search through the literature and within himself for the most efficacious combination of medical and psychological intervention. In this sense it is a balanced approach similar in many respects to that of Cousins. Fiore concludes, "Compliance with cancer therapy, and patient will to life, will increase as therapies include methods of demonstrating to patients that they have the potential for lives that are better than the ones they had before the cancer developed" (Fiore, 1979). That same statement is true for virtually every major, chronic disease, and suggests a clear direction for future research.

At the present time there are a number of experiments demonstrating and clarifying the psychological dimension of the placebo response: (1) men were given a placebo beverage which was supposed to be alcohol and then manifested the behavioral changes associated with moderate intoxication as judged by independent raters (Woolfolk et al., 1979); (2) anxious or depressed patients who are "socially acquiescent" and have a higher than usual concern for social approval and conventional values responded most positively to placebo antidepressant medications (McNair et al., 1979); and (3) research by Martin Corne found that highly hypnotizable subjects tolerated pain from immersing their arms in ice water better than subjects who were rated as unhypnotizable and has hypothesized that hypnosis operates through "quite different mechanisms" than placebo (Holden, 1979).

While the consideration of the neuroendocrinology of endorphins and enkephalins as well as the complex phenomenon of the placebo response may seem tangential to longevity, it is in fact at the heart of the matter. An experiment in a nursing home can serve to illustrate how these factors can swing the balance between life and death as well as health and illness. Judith Rodin and Ellen J. Langer of

Harvard University explored the relationship between patient responsibility and positive placebo enhancement in a nursing-home setting. Ninety-one elderly patients were randomly divided into two groups and each patient was given a small plant. Patients in the "responsibility-induced group" were told that they would be responsible for caring for and watering their plants. Patients in the second control group were told that the staff would take care of their plants. As simple as this involvement was, the results were astounding. From the data collected eighteen months later Rodin and Langer noted, "Patients in the responsibility-induced group showed a significant improvement in alertness and increased behavioral involvement in many different kinds of activities, such as movie attendance, active socializing with staff and friends, and contest participation" (Rodin and Langer, 1977). These findings were based on both nurses' and physicians' independent ratings. Even more striking was the general improvement in the "responsibility group's" physical health, averaging 25 percent over an eighteen-month period in the nursing home. After eighteen months of caring for their plants the "responsibility group" evidenced a 15 percent mortality rate while the control group suffered a 30 percent mortality rate.

In interpreting these data Rodin and Langer noted that the nurses played a vital role in the outcome: "Once the patients began to change, the nurses must have responded favorably to improved behavior, sociability, and self-reliance. . . . Nurses' evaluations of the patients and not the overall health ratings were more closely related to subsequent life and death" (1977). Finally, these two sensitive researchers acknowledged that such findings reflected a holistic approach to patient responsibility and noted, "The long-term beneficial effects observed in the present study probably were obtained because the original treatment was not directed toward a single behavior . . . . [It] instead fostered generalized feelings of increased competence in day-to-day decision making where it was potentially available" (1977). Giving responsibility for a single plant to elderly patients had a profound effect upon them and their entire psychosocial system. A heightened sense of efficacy and participation ensued from this task and appeared to slow and even reverse degenerative disorders and lessen mortality. Research such as this gives a clear indication that psychological factors play as vital a role in the determination of longevity as the biochemical and neurophysiological variables considered up to this point. Without consideration of the role of human consciousness, which is detailed in the next chapter, there are many dimensions of the phenomenon of longevity which would remain enigmatic and insoluble.

Placebo response, like many other techniques in holistic medicine, has definite negative effects and instances where caution or even contraindications are warranted. Given the fairly recent widespread applications of relaxation methods, nutrition therapies, aerobic exercise, and placebo enhancement experimentation, there is not a well-developed body of information concerning the potentially negative effects of these practices. Many of the areas where medical supervision or even contraindications are called for have been outlined in *Holistic Medicine* (Pelletier, 1979). While the areas of caution are relatively clear regarding nutrition and exercise, they are less well-defined in the more psychological interventions of stress management, meditation, clinical biofeedback, and placebo enhancement. Given the longer developmental history of clinical hypnosis and autogenic training as compared to more recent self-regulating approaches, the areas of caution have been better explored. *Clinical Hypnotherapy* (1968), by gynecologists David B. Cheek and L. M. Le Cron, and the series of volumes on *Autogenic Training* by Canadian physician Wolfgang Luthe (1963, 1969a, 1969b, 1976, 1977) are worth mentioning here. Among the many potentially reported and adverse reactions are hypotension, insulin shock, psychomotor seizure, hyperthyroidism, and a range of psychological disturbances, including latent psychosis. Clinicians working with biofeedback have begun to compile a comparable body of information, and it is increasingly evident that interventions previously dismissed as "placebo," "psychosomatic," or even "palpable quackery" (Relman, 1979) do have demonstrable negative as well as positive effects. As the field of inquiry matures there is certain to be more precise evidence of both indications and contraindications.

There are extremely important ethical issues involved in giving placebos, particularly in clinical situations. For an extensive consideration of these complex issues, there is an excellent article in *Scientific American* by Sissela Bok (1974) where she cautions ". . . that the benevolent deception exemplified by placebos is widespread, that it carries risks not usually taken into account, that it represents an inroad on informed consent, that it damages the institution of medicine and contributes to the erosion of confidence in medical personnel." These concerns are hardly recent, since a seventeenth-century engraving in the Philadelphia Museum of Art of medical street vendors has a prominent Latin inscription which translates as "the public wants to be deceived." While many researchers and clinicians are striving to elevate placebo from a term of dismissal to a potent therapeutic agent, there is evidence nevertheless of abuse and improper utilization.

A recent survey of physicians and nurses at three New Mexico hospitals of rheumatologist James S. Goodwin and his colleagues indicated that ". . . most of them are unaware of the proved effect of placebos" and that placebos were frequently given to patients who were considered to be 'overdemanding' and 'complaining' " (Goodwin et al., 1979). While those patients most often received placebo they are least likely to respond, since previous research has indicated that patients who respond positively to placebos tend to be self-sufficient, highly educated, stoic in confronting pain, and cooperative with medical staff. By contrast, the Goodwin Study indicated four patterns of placebo misuse: (1) to prove the patient wrong. As reported by one senior resident, "Placebos are used with people you hate, not to make them suffer but to prove them wrong"; (2) withholding the "gift" of real analgesia and substituting placebos for "undeserving patients"; (3) using placebos when the primary treatment is failing and in order to demonstrate that the patient was "faking it"; and (4) "the use of placebo as a weapon in conflicts between difficult patients and hospital staff" (Goodwin et al., 1979). These results cannot be dismissed nor are they to be taken as a condemnation of medical practices, because many of these behaviors stem from an understandable but not excusable misconception by medical personnel of the potent placebo effect. Medical personnel are often not well informed of either the positive or negative effects of placebo.

While the rendering of an inert chemical constitutes an area of potential ethical issues, the circumstances under which a diagnosis is given are equally problematic. In order not to hold out false hope physicians are often abrupt to the point of negative suggestion that the outcome is likely to be dire or even terminal. It is in these areas where placebo abuse is most overlooked where it is of considerable potency.

> . . . there is also a dark side to the placebo effect. Not only can positive therapeutic effects be achieved by suggestion, but negative side effects and complications can similarly result. . . . Explicit suggestion of possible adverse effects causes subjects to experience these effects. Recent hypotheses that heart attack may follow coronary spasm indicate physiological mechanisms by which explicit suggestions, and the stress that may be produced by them, might prove fatal. Thus, the possible consequences of suggested symptoms range from minor annoyance to, in extreme cases, death [Loftus and Fries, 1979].

These issues cannot be resolved by a readily stated formula or protocol but it is evident that they must be considered in matters concerning a patient's health and longevity. Among the steps which can be taken are the rigorous evaluation of patient response and circumstances under which an inert substance is given, continuing diagnostic efforts of underlying causes even when the patient responds to inert substance or the purely psychological placebo of reassurance, and awareness among clinicians of their own motivations in prescribing placebos. Overall, any contact involving diagnosis and discussion of an illness needs to be considered in this context:

> . . . when a specific risk is disclosed, it should be discussed in the context of placebo effects in general, why they occur, and how to guard against them. A growing literature indicates that just as knowledge of possible symptoms can cause those symptoms, so can knowledge of placebo effects be used to defend against those effects [Loftus and Fries, 1979].

From this discussion of the neuroendocrinology of endorphin and enkephalin response and their recent connection to the analgesic aspect of the placebo effect, it is hoped that the fact that psychological factors play a key role in both health and longevity is clear. Psychological factors per se are extremely important in longevity, as is discussed throughout this book, especially as initiators and mediators of biochemical processes conducive to degeneration or regeneration. While the route to such conclusions through the labyrinth of biochemistry may seem circuitous or even irrelevant, it provides a basis for understanding the most promising frontier of health care, which is the regenerative capacity inherent in the influence of mind over matter.

The Regenerative Capacity of the Body

Up to this point the processes involving regeneration and longevity have been biochemical, neurophysiological, and psychological. When regeneration of limbs is considered, as in the instance of the salamander, another kind of process needs to be considered. Electromagnetic principles underlie regeneration and suggest a subtle, pervasive connection between mind, matter, and environment.

There is no doubt that the human organism is designed with redundant systems providing a wide safety margin. Citing the pioneering work of Harvard University biologist Walter B. Cannon, who first formulated the fight-flight response, the contemporary philosopher Jacob Needleman has noted:

A man may live quite normally . . . with only one kidney—indeed, two-thirds of each kidney may be taken without serious disturbance. One-tenth of adrenal tissue is all that is really necessary for the body, and four-fifths of thyroid substance may be removed without abnormal effects. Only one-fifth of the pancreas is needed to furnish the insulin which the organism requires, and as for the busiest and most versatile organ of the body, the liver, three-fourths of it may be lost without serious harm. Ten feet of the small intestine (normally twenty-three feet long) were taken out of one patient and in many cases almost all of the large intestine was cleared away with results that actually seem to have been beneficial. . . . Blood sugar and calcium level, systolic pressure, lung capacity, are all greater than need be. Even great areas of the brain are expendable [Needleman, 1978].

Recent research concerning biological functions and innovations in microsurgery have demonstrated an even greater safety margin in specific body systems. Human beings, however, appear to be virtually devoid of the capacity for regeneration which is so clearly evidenced in lower organisms.

Healing of injuries is a basic property of all life. Three means of healing are: scarring; tissue replacement where cells are renewed as in the gastrointestinal tract; and, in some species, regeneration, which can perfectly restore a single cell or an entire organ. The first recorded experimentation on regeneration was a paper written in 1768 by Italian physiologist Lazzaro Spallanzani (Garrison, 1914). His data included two observations which still remain accurate: "The younger the animal, the greater its capacity for regeneration; and the lower an animal is on the evolutionary scale, the greater its capacity for regeneration" (Schiefelbein, 1978). Other research in the late 1700s indicated but did not demonstrate or prove that whenever an injury occurs, an electrical charge is generated at the site and is proportional to the severity of the wound. It was not until over two hundred years later that this phenomenon was termed the "current of injury" and began to play a major role in research.

Regeneration of limbs in animals not normally capable of this was first demonstrated in 1945 by S. Meryl Rose, who is currently a professor of anatomy at Tulane University College of Medicine. Rose bathed the stump of a frog's amputated foreleg in a strong salt solution and noted that half of each amputated limb regrew, including bone, muscle tissue, and even a single digit in some instances. Then in 1946 Lev Vladimirovich Polezhaev of the Institute of Developmental Biology in Moscow obtained similar results by repeatedly puncturing the amputated stumps with a needle. Following these experiments, Marcus Singer of Case Western Reserve University refined the data in a series of experiments in the 1950s. He produced renewed growth by transplanting nerves from the hind legs into the stumps and indicated that ". . . regeneration would occur if at least 30 percent of the tissue at the amputation site consisted of nerve" (Becker, 1975). Then in 1958 Russian scientist A. V. Zhirmunskii measured the electrical current on the unbroken skin of various organisms and showed slight differences in electrical potential between any two points. When a wound occurred, the current between the site of injury and the surrounding undamaged tissue changed sharply in a phenomenon termed the "current of injury." Zhirmunskii also demonstrated that the current of injury was related to the amount of nerve tissue in the wound area. Despite this finding, scientists tended to dismiss this phenomenon as merely a by-product of the injured cell membranes. It was not until the late 1950s that orthopedic surgeon Robert O. Becker of the Veterans Administration Hospital in Syracuse, New York, suggested that the current of injury might trigger regeneration and initiated research into electromagnetic induction of limb regeneration.

Beginning in 1957 Becker and his colleagues studied salamanders and frogs since they are closely related but with only the salamander capable of regeneration. They amputated a foreleg of frogs and salamanders and measured the current of injury with a microvoltometer until the limit of regrowth occurred in each of the animals. Although the current of injury was the same for frogs and salamanders on the first day at a positive voltage of 20 millivolts (thousandths of a volt), this declined to zero in the frog by the second day. For the salamander the voltage shifted to a negative polarity between the third and fifth days and gradually declined to zero when the regeneration of the limb was complete.

Such regeneration is extraordinarily complex since it must progress from undifferentiated to differentiated cells for full regeneration to take place:

> It is important to characterize true regenerative growth accurately as the process that begins with the formation of a blastema. This mass of primitive and apparently undifferentiated cells formed by a variety of cellular processes can differentiate into the complete range of cell types necessary to replace the missing part [Becker and Spadaro, 1972].

This same phenomenon and its complexity is reviewed by Peter J. Bryant and his colleagues at the University of California at Irvine, where they have studied regeneration in the limbs of the cockroach and newt (Bryant et al., 1977). To account for organized limb regeneration is an extraordinarily complex issue, which is compounded by the fact that the mechanism must be relatively simple since it is most developed in primitive organisms lacking the complex nervous system of higher-order animals. This apparent paradox has led Becker to hypothesize the existence of a primitive data transmission system comprising perineural cells common to both lower and higher organisms. Early in the 1960s Becker noted: "We found that the potentials are organized into an electrical field, represented by lines of force, which roughly parallels the pattern of the nervous system. . . . Electrical potentials in a conducting medium such as the nerve cell implies there is also a direct current (DC) flow" (Becker, 1975).

Later this basic hypothesis was refined into a sophisticated blend of theory and research data which is the basis for an understanding of the latent regenerative potential for the human species:

> . . . the nerve was not the tissue that transmitted the healing control signal after all. However, we discovered that another thin tissue had bridged the gap in the nerve. In late 1973, we identified this tissue as the Schwann cell sheath, which surrounds each peripheral nerve. We now believe that the Schwann cell sheaths transmit the healing signal, at least in the limbs.
>
> More important, our experiments provided a clue to the source of the entire primitive data transmission system. The Schwann cells are part of a group of cells known as the perineural cells. These are derived from the same tissue that forms the nerve, and they form a complete network that pervades the entire central nervous system, extending from the Schwann cells, which surround even the smallest peripheral nerve, to the glial cells, which form a complex mass in which the brain cells are imbedded. It was known that the glial cells have different electrical properties than the nerve cells, such as slow waves and steady potentials, yet their function was largely unknown. Our work indicates that all the perineural cells link together to form the primitive data transmission system we sought [Becker, 1975].

Operation of this perineural DC potential nervous system was first evidenced in Becker's research with bone, which is one part of the human organism which can regenerate even though it has far less nerve tissue than other body systems. By observing the electrical potential in bones when they were bent, Becker and his colleagues determined that the compressed side became electrically negative while the stretched side became positive. Through systematic experimentation Becker and Columbia University orthopedic surgeon C. Andrew L. Bassett implanted electrodes in the hind legs of adult dogs. After two weeks, considerable new bone growth was found around the negative electrode but none at the positive electrode, which appeared either to prevent new growth or dissolve it as fast as it occurred. Also they discovered that DC currents of 2-5 microamperes produced the most growth. Next Becker and Bassett attempted actually to regenerate the broken leg bones of frogs and noted that the electrical field depended partly on intact nerves to the site, since the potentials dropped nearly to zero when the nerves to the site were severed. Under a microscope, they also noted that there were cell changes in the blood clot surrounding the fractures that led to the formation of a mass which differentiated into new bone. From these results they concluded, ". . . the electrical field found at the fracture site controlled the cellular changes that led to regeneration. Most important, we were able to determine very precise ranges of voltage and current that most effectively produce the desired changes" (Becker, 1975). Further research with rats led them to speculate that if a laboratory rat, whose red blood cells contain no nuclei, could form a blastema, then it was increasingly likely that humans could do so as well. From his results with bone regeneration Becker formulated a theory suggesting a similar control system capable of regulating regeneration in other tissues which do not evidence the renewal typical of the skeletal system.

Higher organisms such as humans lose their regenerative ability as they increase in complexity, because more of their nerve tissue is concentrated in the brain with less available for the rest of the body. Applying these theories to increasingly higher-order organisms, Becker undertook experiments in 1972 to regenerate the amputated legs of laboratory rats through currents applied by implanted electrodes. Not only did regeneration occur but these researchers were able to determine the very precise voltages which produced the most extensive regeneration versus those voltages which actually seemed to destroy the tissue even further. In Becker's words:

> Animals with medium-current devices (5 nanoamperes at 75 millivolts) showed varying degrees of regeneration. The best results occurred in one rat with a device that produced 8 nanoamperes at 100 millivolts with a 10 megohm (million ohms) resistor. This regenerated the missing portion of the upper limb down to the elbow joint, including regrowth of muscle, nerve, bone, and blood vessels [Becker, 1975].

This extraordinary regeneration took place in just three days. At approximately the same time, Stephen Smith, who was then a graduate student of S. Meryl Rose, reported the first complete regeneration of a frog's amputated leg in 1973.

Breakthroughs such as these rapidly accelerated the research, including experimentation with rabbits, to explore the mechanism of arthritis in which injured cartilage heals only by scarring. Research also focused on the relationship between the central nervous system and the regenerative potential. In a series of experiments Becker broke a small bone in a rat's hind leg but left the nerves intact and examined the healing process. Next, he broke the same bone and removed a quarter-inch segment of the main nerve to the hind leg. Despite this, the bones did heal but it took twice as long as in the first experiment. Third, nerve segments were removed two and three days before the break. This resulted in the fracture actually healing faster than when the bone was broken and nerve cut at the same time although not as fast as normal. Finally, the nerve segments were removed five and six days before the break. Most surprisingly, the bones healed in the normal amount of time. Since the nerve could not have regrown in such a short time, Becker examined the severed nerves under the microscope and noted that the Schwann cell sheath was the tissue which had bridged the gap in the severed nerves. Although the healing process was partially dependent on intact nerves to the fracture or wound site, an even more important discovery was the "perineural DC potential nervous system" noted earlier. It became clear that the current of injury might only trigger regeneration and that the necessary current for full regeneration was furnished only when a certain proportion of nerve tissue was present. Since the voltages regulating this phenomenon are of a minute order of magnitude, they are subject to fluctuations in electrostatic fields (EFS). This implication has been more thoroughly researched in recent years and a unique interaction between EFS and biological systems has been discovered:

> . . . in this group the electromagnetic field does not supply the energy for a given process but merely furnishes the energy to control or trigger it. The more sensitive the particular system that is affected by the electromagnetic fields, the smaller is the energy required to produce the effect. Since low-level, trigger effects induced by electromagnetic fields do occur in mammalian systems, the question arises whether such effects could be induced by ESFs [Marino et al., 1974].

Perhaps even more important than the regeneration research per se, this finding has uncovered a profound link between all organisms and the electromagnetic environment which surrounds and permeates them.

For the human being the clinical applications and implications of this research are indeed profound. A great deal of current research is being focused on nerve regeneration since, when this process is incomplete, permanent disability results:

> Usually when a nerve tract is severed or severely injured, the damage is not repaired. The nerves may grow for a while in some haphazard and uncoordinated way but they rarely establish normal connections with their target organs. . . . an understanding of the signals in the first place and what caused them to develop into one type of nerve cell or another may provide clues to the regeneration puzzle [Marx, 1979a].

Observation of patients paralyzed by a spinal cord injury showed that the healing of bone below the injury site occurred at twice the normal rate. Other reports tell of two newborn infants in London who lost their fingers, which spontaneously regenerated. Phenomena such as these became more comprehensible given the regeneration research. These findings have resulted in a range of clinical applications where bone growth has been induced in thirteen patients through "low intensity direct current stimulation" (Becker et al., 1977). All the patients were selected because they were not responding to the standard procedures used to enable fractures to heal normally. Success was reported in "77 percent" of the cases, which is quite promising considering that prior interventions had been demonstrated to be inadequate. In another research project "electrically generated silver ions" from a silver-nylon fabric were applied to the bone surface in order to treat "chronic osteomyelitis," an orthopedic infection usually treated with antibiotics but with varying degrees of success. Over a three-year period, Becker and his colleagues treated fourteen patients, which resulted in ". . . control of the infection in twelve of the fifteen treatment attempts and in healing of the non-union after follow-up ranging from three to thirty-six months. The other three attempts led to two partial and one complete failure" (Becker and Spadaro, 1978). An additional, unexpected benefit was the deposition of substantial amounts of new bone produced during the treatment with a surface silver-nylon fabric rather than an implanted electrode.

Clinical applications of the electromagnetic processes involved in regeneration have also been extended to a sophisticated understanding of acupuncture. According to the Chinese theory of acupuncture, there is a flow of a basic, or Chi, energy throughout the body along twelve pathways, or meridians. Imbalances in these meridians cause pain and disease which can be prevented or treated by inserting various types of needles at specific points in the meridians in order to alter and balance the Chi energy. Acupuncture charts commonly specify approximately 350 points on the 12 meridians where needles can be inserted. More recently it appeared that applying DC or AC electrical potentials at these designated sites had an effect comparable to the insertion of needles. As Becker and his colleagues considered the descriptions of the properties of the acupuncture meridians and the stimulus points they were struck by the fact that the existence of this system was consistent with their theory concerning a perineural DC system. Acupuncture meridians had the properties of a subtle DC electrical system and given that quality, principles of electrical engineering would dictate that amplifiers or boosters should exist at points in the transmission lines in order to compensate for "cable constants" such as resistance and capacitance which cause drops in current strength.

Many of these hypothesized properties are also consistent with the observations of Nobel Laureate Albert Szent-Györgyi in *Introduction to a Submolecular Biology* (1960) that "solid state mechanisms" account for specific electronic properties of biological systems. That was precisely what Becker hypothesized to be the case:

> Since our data indicate that the operational signal levels of the biological DC system are in the millivolt and nanoampere ranges, one can predict the need for structures functioning as operational amplifiers along the channels of DC transmission. This analysis leads one to consider the acupuncture meridians as DC communication channels and the points as sites of operational amplifier location. . . . If we are correct, the points should show lower resistance and higher conductance than nonpoint areas of skin and both resistance and conductance factors should show an organized field pattern around the point. . . . This concept offers an opportunity to objectively assay the system of acupuncture meridians and points in a scientific fashion within the framework of a viable theory [Becker et al., 1976].

In order to test this hypothesis the researchers made skin resistance measures on two readily accessible acupuncture meridians, the large intestine (Li) and pericardium (P). Using a Wheatstone bridge as a resistance indicator, they assessed these two meridians on each of seven subjects. Seventeen acupunture points were evaluated ten times each on the seven male and female subjects. They found that "greater electrical conductance maxima," an indication of reduced electrical resistance, was evidenced at the acupuncture points as compared to control points. Their results indicated that

> . . . three out of eleven acupuncture points on the large intestine meridian and two out of six points on the pericardium meridian were found to exist on all seven subjects. A total of thirteen points out of seventeen were found on at least five subjects. Thus the results establish that most of the acupuncture points studied

objectively exist on most of the subjects measured. It is presently not possible to determine why all acupuncture points are not found on all subjects [Reichmanis et al., 1975].

A more detailed discussion of these procedures and results was written up one year later, and the conclusion was quite unequivocal:

> Electrical correlates have been established for a portion of the acupuncture system and indicate that it does have an objective basis in reality. Thus far, the data are supportive to our general theory of the action of the acupuncture technique as influencing a primitive data transmission and control system [Becker et al., 1976].

These studies were followed by research indicating that the points of low resistance actually functioned as sources of DC emission and that a moving DC potential could be detected from point to point. From these observations it appears that the perineural DC system could function as an information processing system which antedates and underlies the more complex central nervous system. Although some researchers and clinicians insist that acupuncture has no basis in biological systems, the data from electromagnetic regeneration and endorphin research suggest otherwise.

Evidence is accumulating from basic research that the restoration of the regenerative capacity of humankind may prove to be possible. Among the research findings to date are: (1) pioneering research by Clarence Cone of NASA, which recently received a United States patent for Cone's research, indicating that nerve cell regeneration could be stimulated by altering the ". . . concentrations of sodium, potassium and chloride or by direct electromagnetic charge across the cell surface" (Cone, 1976). Prior to Cone's successful mitosis of neurons in the laboratory, it was thought that central nervous system neurons, unlike peripheral nerves, could not regenerate; (2) research by Gideon A. Rodan and his colleagues at the University of Connecticut School of Medicine into the mechanism which would account for the findings that, "Electrical stimuli, applied in various ways, promote appositional and longitudinal bone growth in birds, limb regeneration in amphibia, and fracture repair in dogs, rabbits, and humans" (Rodan et al., 1978). In searching for a genetic mechanism, the researchers found that a specific, external, oscillating electrical field generated sodium and calcium fluxes which triggered DNA synthesis in cartilage cells. This may provide a means of understanding the "mechanical modulation of bone growth"; (3) exploration of axon regeneration in lower organisms since "spinal transection in humans is considered to result in an irreversible loss of functions mediated by the damaged fibers" (Wood and Cohen, 1979). By studying the healing of severed neurons in the spinal cord of the lamprey eel, Malcolm R. Wood and Melvin J. Cohen of Yale University have detailed the regenerative process which leads to "Normal swimming activity . . . in the spinally transected animals, although the regenerated synapses are in atypical regions of the spine" and may ". . . serve as model for . . . functional recovery of the injured vertebrate CNS" (Wood and Cohen, 1979); (4) research using an electromyogram (EMG) to detect the electrical activity of muscles, by Gerard C. Gorniak and his colleagues at the University of Michigan. They have formulated a nonevasive method of monitoring and predicting more precisely the well-documented phenomenon of "muscle fiber regeneration after transplantation" (Gorniak et al., 1979) in autografts with cats. Nondestructive monitoring methods are necessary for the further definition of the mechanisms involved in related instances of regeneration, particularly in humans; (5) an extremely important study by Katherine Kalil and Thomas Reh of the University of Wisconsin at Madison, indicating not only that severed CNS (central nervous system) nerves in baby hamsters could regenerate but could regenerate in a functionally useful way. When pyramidal tract axons were cut in the adult hamster, the fibers degenerated both above and below the cut, resulting in abnormal paw function. However, the researchers severed the same tract in twenty-seven baby hamsters and three months later injected them with a radioactive chemical in order to travel the route of the severed pyramidal tract nerves. From their findings they determined ". . . on infant hamsters . . . there is massive regrowth of the severed axons via a new brainstem pathway to their appropriate terminal sites in the medulla and spinal cord. In contrast to previous studies, these results suggest that axons in the mammalian central nervous system damaged early in life may regenerate in a functionally useful way" (Kalil and Reh,

1979); and finally, (6) a major finding by Stephen J. Buell and Paul D. Coleman of the University of Rochester School of Medicine that lends great insight into the phenomenon of senile dementia discussed in the previous chapter. Senile dementia has usually been considered to be due to deterioration of the central nervous system with neuron death and regression of dendrites in the remaining cells. However, the research by Buell and Coleman has indicated that while some cells do deteriorate, others continue to grow. Based on autopsy samples of the "parahippocampal gyrus" from fifteen human brains, they noted major differences between the brains of "nondemented" adults and adults diagnosed as "senile dementia." According to their analysis:

> In nondemented aged cases (average age, 79.6 years), dendritic trees were more extensive than in adult cases (average age, 51.2), with most of the difference resulting from increases in the number and average length of terminal segments of the dendritic tree. These results provide morphological evidence for plasticity in the mature and aged human brain. In senile dementia (average age, 76.0), dendritic trees were less extensive than in adult brains, largely because their terminal segments were fewer and shorter. . . . These data suggest a model of aging in the central nervous system in which one population of neurons dies and regresses and the other survives and grows. The latter appears to be the dominant population in aging without dementia . . . the conclusion is inescapable that growth of dendrites prevails over regressive dendritic changes in at least one region of the aging brain. . . . The rate at which this shift takes place is probably a function of genetic and nongenetic or extrinsic (taxicological, behavioral, infectious) factors [Buell and Coleman, 1979].

Acknowledging external influences on an internal neurological process underlying senile dementia is a movement toward a holistic yet empirically based model of regeneration.

It is very important to bear in mind that this overview of the relatively new complex field of electromagnetic regeneration represents only a limited number of research projects and researchers and is far from comprehensive. Also, the juxtaposition of these data lends a sense of coherence to the field which is not accurate since a great deal of the research is hyperspecialized and fragmented, with researchers in closely related areas not even citing the data of colleagues. In that sense the field mirrors the field of longevity as a whole.

The significance of research in the area of electromagnetic regeneration goes beyond its immediate applications. While the chasm between the psychological activity of mind and the biochemistry of the brain and body may seem insurmountable, electromagnetic fields may provide an observable bridge. Consideration of these properties may also be related to the holographic description of the human brain discussed in Karl H. Pribram's pioneering *Languages of the Brain* (1971) as well as in *Toward a Science of Consciousness* (Pelletier, 1978). It is becoming increasingly clear that psychological processes produce detectable variations in the electrical and biochemical activity of the entire central nervous system. Minute electromagnetic potentials appear to govern basic biological functions manifested in recovery from injury as well as regeneration. Biological processes can be influenced directly by manipulation of these electrical potentials through electrical stimulation and classic acupuncture. Perhaps the perineural DC system is the link between human consciousness and its influence on the endorphin and enkephalin response as manifested in the placebo response as well as certain aspects of spontaneous remission.

Understanding of this link may make it possible systematically to direct consciousness to regulate these internal electrical and biochemical processes, in a manner analogous to the now common practices of clinical biofeedback. While the speculations are as yet unproven, there is substantial evidence that these are fruitful lines of inquiry. When one considers the alternatives—pharmaceutical panaceas rained down upon passive patients, replacement of skeletal joints by prosthetics and even "bionic limbs" (Teresi, 1979), and the limited yield from increasingly exorbitant technology—these possibilities appear more and more attractive:

We have already helped to repair broken bones that refused to mend by themselves. Soon we may be restoring the damaged joint cartilage that leads to arthritis. And I believe that, in time, we can induce total regeneration in man, not only in his limbs, but also in his heart and other vital organs [Becker, 1975].

The salamander, once again, holds out such a promise; it is capable of regenerating up to 50 percent of its heart. At the frontier of research into longevity is the potential for the human organism to activate its regenerative capacity. If that could be achieved, many of the age-related and life-shortening infirmities of advanced age could be minimized or eliminated.

Although the presentation of the research in this area has focused primarily on the research of Robert O. Becker and his colleagues, there are many other researchers who have made major contributions. Becker's work makes a good illustration of this exciting field because his research looks beyond basic research and its clinical applications to long-range implications, as well as related contemporary issues.

There is now some evidence for central nervous system regeneration and also data that the target cells, organs, and limbs can respond to the regenerated nerves, provided the appropriate linkages exist. A fundamental research problem is to promote the conditions under which the central nervous system neurons will regenerate axons over longer distances to find out how they establish connections with the target cells. However, there are many equally important unanswered questions regarding regeneration:

> We do not yet know either the age at which this process starts (if not during early development [19]) or the age at which the surviving, growing neurons no longer predominate. Nor is it known whether there is in normal aging a limit to the potential for the growth of healthy neurons [Buell and Coleman, 1979].

Actually it remains to be resolved whether selective neuron death in certain areas of the brain is actually as uniformly negative as has been assumed. Richard Dawkins, a zoologist at the University of Oxford, reported in *Nature* that neuronal extinction is not only not random but might actually be an underlying mechanism of information storage and memory in the brain and neuron death interpreted as a sorting out of least-utilized pathways. According to Dawkins, "All that is at issue is whether neurones die at random, or selectively, in such a way as to store information. Students of evolutionary theory will be sceptical to say the least of the idea that 100,000 deaths per day could be functionally completely random" (Dawkins, 1971).

From the level of DNA replication to human limb regeneration, the potential is evident but not the means of systematically eliciting and sustaining the process. It appears that ". . . higher organisms have maintained a reserve repair capacity" and its activation ". . . should lead to reduction in mutagenesis and degenerative diseases in higher organisms" (Smith-Sonneborn, 1979). Researchers have noted that animals or parts of animals that regenerate are not susceptible to cancer. When a tumor is implanted in a lizard's nonregenerative body it soon becomes terminal. However, if it is implanted in the regenerative tail, the tumor disappears (Schiefelbein, 1978). Perhaps the same processes which regulate regeneration could be utilized to check or reverse the unbridled proliferation of malignancies. There are clear indications of an interaction between specific hormonal functions and the perineural DC system since, when the adrenals are removed from a lizard, it loses its capacity to regenerate its tail. When the hormone prolactin is injected, the regenerative capacity is regained.

Electromagnetic Pollution

Moving outward from the realm of internal electromagnetic and neuroendocrine activity in the central nervous system, there appears to be a vital link between the electrical potentials of the human organism and those of the physical environment. Electromagnetic fields which pervade the environment have pronounced effects on the human body. Prior to the last decade the predominant scientific paradigm held that the "nonionizing radiation" of radio, television, high-tension wires, radar, and microwaves had no effect on biological systems except for a few scattered reports concerning effects on snails, fruit flies, moths, and worms. The effects of electromagnetic radiation were thought of simply in terms of ionizing radiation, which can result in destructive heating of the organism. However, that model and its limited view of the effects of the nonionizing radiation of electrostatic fields is no longer accurate from either a theoretical or an experimental position. In an extremely complex article Francis X. Hart and Andrew A. Marino (1976) employed a mathematical model which predicts that there are definite biological effects associated with exposure to nonionizing radiation:

> . . . biologic effects [are] induced by electromagnetic fields at frequencies and intensities that do not induce heating. . . . In this group the electromagnetic field does not supply the energy for a given process but merely furnishes the energy to control or trigger it. The more sensitive the particular system that is affected by the electromagnetic fields, the smaller is the energy required to produce the effect [Marino et al., 1974].

The importance of this last statement cannot be overemphasized because it allows for the possibility that an infinitesimal amount of energy can affect a biological system. We have seen such a possibility earlier with regard to the "cascade amplifier" effect of psychological influences on the neuroendocrine system. Furthermore, there is considerable evidence that humans may have the highest sensitivity and susceptibility among biological organisms.

This property of humankind is consistent with the solid state properties and their semiconductive qualities postulated by Albert Szent-Györgyi (1960). "This high mobility of the charge carriers makes them particularly susceptible to external electrical and magnetic fields and changes in these fields will produce corresponding perturbations in the potentials in a semiconductive lattice" (Becker et al., 1976). This means that the entire human organism is highly sensitive to both internal and external electromagnetic currents and voltages. Electromagnetic fluctuations can affect local cell responses directly or by influencing the system as a whole. This theory evokes an image of the human species aswim in an ocean of electromagnetic fields.

Unfortunately, some of the sources of electromagnetic activity which are rapidly proliferating have demonstrably negative effects upon higher-order organisms. These deleterious effects are the shadow side of the electromagnetic regeneration techniques discussed earlier. Since 1967 a growing body of evidence has demonstrated the negative effects of both electrical and magnetic activity occurring in fields of "extremely low frequency" (ELF), which are those below 100 Hz, or cycles per second, and referred to as "electronic smog," according to ophthalmologist Milton M. Zaret (1979). Electrical activity of 60 Hz is used by virtually all electrical power systems and is common to the modern environment. Studies have distinguished between acute exposure and chronic exposure, more than three days, with the greatest effects observed under chronic conditions. An excellent overview of the earlier studies primarily with lower organisms is contained in "Biological Effects of Extremely Low Frequency Electric and Magnetic Fields: A Review" by Robert O. Becker and Andrew A. Marino (1977), where they cite and review 122 studies. Among the observations were fatal effects on *Drosophila,* bees, and mice; decreased reaction time in rabbits; the detection of, and reaction to, ostensibly innocuous electromagnetic fields by amoebas, eels, and salmon; ELF fields which appear to cause bone tumors in laboratory rats; specific frequencies which cause cataracts in laboratory animals; and many other negative consequences, such as depressed body weights in chicks and decreased egg production in adult hens, increased lipid levels, increased triglycerides, lowered hemoglobin count, and reduced body weight. Research by Robert O. Becker and his colleagues has clarified the nature of some of these electromagnetic threats to living organisms:

> In our laboratory, we found that rats exposed to a sixty hertz electric field for one month exhibited hormonal and biochemical changes similar to those caused by stress. The study employed an electric field comparable in strength to that produced at ground level by a typical high-voltage transmission line. In another experiment, we continuously exposed three generations of rats to the electric field and found increased infant mortality and severely stunted growth. Our results appear to indicate that the applied electric field primarily affects the central nervous system and activates the stress-response mechanism. Chronic stress can produce a wide variety of diseases and pathological conditions [Becker and Marino, 1978].

While these studies are sufficient for concern, the data from human exposure and experimentation are of greatest concern. As early as 1973, research by Dietrich E. Beischer of the Naval Aerospace Medical Research Laboratory reported that chronic exposure to 45 Hz electrical fields resulted in "elevated serum triglycerides" (Beischer et al., 1973), which is a documented indication of stress as well as being related to arteriosclerotic disease. Physician W. Ross Adey, of the Brain Research Institute at UCLA, and his colleagues have observed the ". . . effects of weak electric and electromagnetic fields on the behavior of man and animals" (Adey, 1973) and noted significant effects on specific areas of the brain but even more importantly on the brain as an integrated system. Based on his research Adey has concluded that nonionizing, electromagnetic radiation exerts a detectable and significant influence on behavior and that ". . . the brain is an organ uniquely constructed of vast numbers of excitable elements and that it may be subtly influenced in ways that have no counterpart in liver, muscle, or kidney. . . . We may therefore anticipate that responsiveness to weak electromagnetic fields in cerebral tissue is a manifestation of collective properties of its numerous cellular elements, which may not be discernible in the separate behavior of isolated elements" (Adey, 1975). This observation that the effects of electromagnetic fields on the human organism must be approached in a holistic manner has been made by other researchers as well. Other studies with human subjects reviewed in the Marino and Becker publication show a preponderance of negative effects. Future experimentation will therefore need to proceed most cautiously since ethical issues are involved.

Research in the Soviet Union has been based primarily upon epidemiological studies of personnel exposed to the strong electrical fields emanating from the Russian electrical power system. Physical examinations of 45 switchyard workers in high-voltage areas indicated that 41 evidence some neurological or cardiovascular disorders, ". . . instability of pulse and blood pressure, tremors of the extremities, and hyperhidrosis" (Asanova and Rakov, 1966). These preliminary findings were confirmed in subsequent studies of 386 workers in high-voltage substations and 319 workers in stations near overhead transmission lines. These studies as well as over 100 others in the Soviet Union resulted in the formulation of "Hygienic Rules"

(Korobkova et al., 1972) which carefully govern the permissible exposure of Russian workers to electromagnetic fields of various intensities. Similar studies in the United States did not confirm this hazard. One study of 142 employees exposed to similar fields indicated no increase in physician visits (Strumza, 1970); another study of 11 linemen servicing 345 KV transmission lines revealed no detectable effects (Singewald et al., 1967). However, this is far less than the field intensity of 500 to 750 KV in the Russian research. While the results of experimentation with lower organisms is fairly consistent, research with higher organisms appears to be equivocal. A further complicating factor is that the implications of such research involve formidable political, economic, and environmental issues (Schiefelbein, 1979, and Davis, 1978). With all due respect to the complexity and conflicting data of the research regarding electromagnetic fields, however, the preponderance of the evidence supports the conclusion of Robert O. Becker:

> We therefore now believe that low-level electrical currents and potentials, produced either by direct injection or by rectification and induction from a field, have the capability of bringing about very major biological effects of a very basic nature. . . . the present rapid proliferation of techniques and devices utilizing electrical currents and potentials in the treatment of various clinical conditions seems to be unjustified and indeed alarming . . . . [We] also feel concern for a much broader problem, which is the continuous exposure of the entire North American population to an electromagnetic environment in which is present the possibility of inducing currents or voltages comparable with those now known to exist in biological control systems [Becker, 1972].

Larger historical and ecological evidence also confirms a need for caution. Reversals of the earth's magnetic field are related to extinction of various animal species (Becker and Marino, 1978). The earth's magnetic field during magnetic storms is statistically related to abnormalities in human behavior, including an increase in myocardial infarction (Malin and Srivastava, 1979). Finally, well-known links exist between the earth's magnetic field and the migratory and homing activity of animals and birds (Southern, 1975). Electromagnetic fields are clearly an invisible two-edged sword. On the one hand there is the promise of activating the potential of the human species to regenerate the central nervous system, organs, and perhaps complete limbs. An understanding of electromagnetic processes may help us discover how human consciousness may affect the neuroendocrine system, and perhaps induce the placebo response or spontaneous remission. At the other extreme are the destructive influences of specific electromagnetic activity. "Electromagnetic pollution" poses an invisible but potentially deleterious effect upon the entire ecosystem and all its inhabitants. Electromagnetic fields have been demonstrated to function as a "biological stressor" (Marino and Becker, 1978) and need to be evaluated along with other behavioral and environmental stressors. All biological organisms emerge as being able to perceive and react to infinitesimally weak electromagnetic fields and exposure to very strong fields can cause death.

Conclusion

To review the various influences on rejuvenation, regeneration, and longevity discussed in this chapter, the following appear to be worthy of further research: (1) selective dietary restriction of specific nutrients at specific developmental stages throughout the life of the organism as well as during adult years; (2) deliberate reduction of core body temperature of warm-blooded mammals resulting in periodic episodes of hypothermia; (3) addition of naturally occurring and synthetic antioxidants which scavenge free radicals; (4) gerontological pharmacology oriented toward the enhancement and restoration of memory and intelligence; (5) enhancement of the placebo response by naturally occurring endorphins and enkephalins of the neuroendocrine system; (6) psychophysiological aspects of the placebo response and spontaneous remission; (7) electromagnetic field effects which govern regeneration and may provide the link between the activity of consciousness and the neuroendocrine system. These approaches, it should be pointed out, share a common emphasis upon the noninvasive measures and utilization of the human biological and psychological potential.

Cloning is an obvious omission from this list. It has been brought to public awareness through David Rovik's *In His Image* (1978) and numerous television sensations, while the reality is still much tamer. A good overview is provided by Robert Gilmore McKinnell's textbook *Cloning* (1978) with its subtitle *Nuclear Transplantation in Amphibia: A Critique of Results Obtained with the Technique, to Which Is Added a Discourse on the Methods of the Craft.* At the moment, cloning is a process with considerable potential in the generation of replacement organs within an individual rather than the replication of the total person, which is still a distant although theoretically possible application. During cloning, an unfertilized egg is removed from an animal, such as a frog, and the nucleus is destroyed by ultraviolet radiation. At the same time, a tadpole provides the donor cell for transplantation into the unfertilized frog's egg. Surgically, the tadpole's intestine is removed and some of the epithelial cells that line its intestine are separated out. Then an epithelial cell's nucleus is inserted into the frog's egg which begins to multiply and divide. Cellular division results in hollow blastula comprised of a single layer of cells. Finally, the blastula progresses and differentiates into a normal tadpole, identical to the original donor, and ultimately into a complete frog. Implications of this procedure for the human species are as profound as they are controversial. Cloning may ultimately have great potential but the emphasis in this book is upon extending the human life expectancy to its biological potential through the systematic application of existing knowledge and its immediate refinements.

Estimates of the longevity potential of humans range from a minimum of 120 years upward to 200 or 300 years and beyond. Attaining that potential is dependent upon the systematic introduction of the variables discussed in this and later chapters, throughout the life of the individual. From this perspective the present fixation upon artificial organs is shortsighted. Artificial organs represent an interim stage necessary until the process of actually regenerating these organs is more fully developed. Biotechnological and pharmaceutical developments may proliferate and some will be of great benefit, but they are ultimately of limited application, are extremely costly to develop and apply, and involve undesirable side effects. Such an approach is of course consistent with the prevailing biomedical paradigm, and focuses only on problems of aging. Its roots in the status quo lend it undue influence on the future direction of health care. By contrast, approaches to enhancing the regenerative potential and optimum health capacity of the human species constitute a "positive strategy" (Breslow, 1979) emphasizing prevention, and the potential of increased longevity. Perhaps the greatest potential of these approaches is to magnify and clarify the nature of internal processes and then to restore them to the control of healthy individuals, as in biofeedback.

The research into longevity discussed in this chapter cannot be considered apart from our immediate psychosocial, physical, economic, and political environment. Critiques of holistic medicine have often noted that such approaches overemphasize individual measures. "The question is how much control the individual can exert over certain learned behaviors and coincidentally over the social conditions under which one lives" (Berliner and Salmon, 1980). Unquestionably there is merit to this criticism, but it is equally evident that individuals can assert a great deal more influence in their individual health than previously believed. *Holistic Medicine* (Pelletier, 1979) addressed these issues, which cannot be dismissed in any comprehensive system of health care. When these concepts of preventive and holistic medicine are applied to longevity, the implications are quite clear:

> We have regarded the modern health problems as inevitable consequences of "aging" and put many of the victims away, mainly in costly institutions of dubious quality. . . . Looking ahead, we can visualize a positive health strategy, focused on defined risk factors for unnecessary premature mortality, extending by several years the healthy lives of millions of Americans in the decades that lie before us [Breslow, 1979].

From the standpoint of clinical practice, assessments of cost effectiveness, as well as its impact upon the physical, economic, and psychosocial environment, "prevention does work" (Breslow, 1979) and holistic medicine is a reality with even greater potential yet to be realized. Data cited throughout this chapter have ranged from experimentation confirmed for nearly half a century to highly speculative innovations and theories. Boundaries of inquiry have been and need to be extended even further if the quest is to go beyond a narrow focus on the aging process to a search for the biological potential for longevity inherent in the human species.

FIVE

Lifestyle and Longevity: Mind Over Matter

Mark Twain once quipped, "Age is a case of mind over matter; if you don't mind it, it doesn't matter!" Psychological factors have been demonstrated to be the single most significant predictor of both optimum health and longevity. Genetic and biological influences on longevity are highly dependent on the presence or absence of specific lifestyle influences. Over forty years ago, John Dewey reflected on the phenomenon of aging:

> Biological processes are at the root of the problem and of the methods of solving them, but the biological processes take place in economic, political, and cultural contexts. They are inextricably interwoven with these contexts so that one reacts upon the other in all sorts of intricate ways. We need to know the ways in which social contexts react back into biological processes as well as to know the ways in which the biological processes condition social life [Dewey, 1939].

That statement was contained in Dewey's introduction to the classic book *Problems of Aging* and remains as accurate today as it was then.

Despite the acknowledgment of this relationship, researchers in disparate areas of specialization persist with reductionist models, looking for the absolute dictates of one variable rather than the relative influence of multiple factors. Research into the psychological influences on the biological processes involved in longevity requires this latter approach.

It is clearly evident that psychosocial variables and lifestyle practices established as early as adolescence are the single most significant predictors of adult health and longevity, and even the timing and nature of the experience of death. Psychosocial factors are of such formidable influence that they actually hold sway over the genetic and biological determinants. As surprising as these observations might seem, the research evidence from a wide range of sources to be considered in this chapter indicates: (1) Stress is a major influence governing whether or not even the average life expectancy is attained. (2) Several major prospective studies indicate the capacity of prior lifestyle variables to predict adult health status as well as longevity. (3) A most significant and consistent research finding is that women live longer than men due to lifestyle rather than biological variables. Not only has this trend been apparent since the turn of the century but it is increasing and accelerating. (4) Studies of isolated and identifiable small communities both in the United States and in cross-cultural research have clarified the nature of the interaction between lifestyle and social support systems in enhancing health and life expectancy. (5) There are clear indications that psychosocial factors influence both the time and nature of the death experience. Taken as a whole, these highly diverse studies point to a common conclusion: The health and longevity observed in later years is largely determined by factors at work both internally and externally throughout the life of the individual. The longevity potential is dependent upon the entire developmental process and is not an epiphenomenon which randomly or inexplicably occurs at the end of life.

Stress and Longevity

At this point in time it is virtually axiomatic that stress is a major factor governing all states of optimum health as well as illness. The means which individuals and institutions develop to manage both the positive and negative aspects of stress are of greater importance than the stressors themselves. Professional meetings and journals are as glutted as the popular media with the most recent experimental evidence. During May 1979, ABC World News Tonight aired an excellent five-part series with Jules Bergman entitled, "Stress: Are We Killing Ourselves?" which is available in videotape from ABC in New York. The huge response to that series was one indication of the widespread concern with stress and its effects. There are innumerable books and articles concerned with stress; they will undoubtedly proliferate even further.

The immediate result of this renewed attention is that stress has emerged as a more complex process than had previously been proposed. Pioneering research since the early 1940s by Hans Selye still remains the primary source of the stress concept:

> Stress is the stereotyped part of the body's response to any demand. It is associated with the rate of wear and tear on the human machinery that accompanies any vital activity and, in a sense, parallels the intensity of life. It is increased during nervous tension, physical injury, infections, muscular work, or any other strenuous activity, and it is connected with a nonspecific defense mechanism which increases resistance to stressful or "stressor" agents [Selye, 1974].

Elaboration of this basic concept in experimentation and clinical practice has evolved into a model described by C. David Jenkins, Director of the Department of Behavioral Epidemiology at Boston University School of Medicine:

Realizing that only a multidisciplinary approach can begin to capture the wholeness of human experience, this research paradigm anticipates that stressors, adaptive capacities, defenses, alarm reactions, and pathological end-states will take place at the biological, psychological, interpersonal and sociocultural levels simultaneously and successively [Jenkins, 1979].

Undoubtedly the previous reductionistic approach to stress and related phenomena will persist by virtue of habit and the number of researchers and grants invested in that approach.

Following periods of insightful discovery there is an abundance of research oriented toward replicating or refuting the original work. While refinement of the concepts does occur during this time, major insights are at a minimum while resolution of increasingly minute and isolated phenomena are at a maximum. This appears to be the present status of stress research. While caution and careful evaluation are obviously necessary, the adoption of certain practices is at least as dependent upon swaying vested economic and political interests as on whether or not the data are accurate or definitive. Addressing this issue is John W. Farquhar, Stanford University cardiologist and author of *The American Way of Life Need Not Be Hazardous to Your Health* (1978):

Scientific conservatism is another influence that can contribute to our passive adaptation to preventable cardiovascular death and disability. This conservatism is two-pronged. First, there is an inevitable time lag between a discovery and the synthesis of that discovery into coherent action. . . . Second, an underlying conviction held by a large proportion of medical researchers is that all the pieces of the puzzle should be at hand before making the first move to devise coherent action. . . . Thus, we should continue to support basic research while *simultaneously* implementing our best efforts for appropriate preventive measures, rather than sit passively and wait for the basic research to yield conclusive findings on *all* facets of the complex puzzle [Farquhar, 1978].

This need for action is particularly true in the field of stress. Through the systematic, clinical application of present knowledge it is possible to prevent the premature morbidity and mortality due to stress-related disorders. The means to do this are discussed in *Mind as Healer, Mind as Slayer* (Pelletier, 1977) and *Holistic Medicine* (Pelletier, 1979) and are not reiterated here. A few more recent studies confirm that stress is a major contributing factor in determining whether or not an individual attains the present average life expectancy.

Prospective research is particularly significant since it is less subject to biased interpretation and preventive measures can be built right into the study. One of the most significant prospective studies demonstrating an interaction between psychological states, physical health, and longevity was recently published by Harvard University psychiatrist George E. Vaillant and his colleagues. From an original sample of 204 men in the Harvard sophomore classes between 1942 and 1944, a research team followed 185 for over 40 years. During this period of time the men received periodic psychological and physical assessments and responded to interviews and annual questionnaires. Factors considered indicative of the relative degree of illness in the population were psychiatric treatment, little occupational progress, job dissatisfaction, unhappy marriages, little recreation time, and general psychological instability. From the prospective assessments it was evident that psychological health not only predicted physical health but that physically healthy men who reacted poorly to stress or evidenced psychological instability ran a significantly higher risk of developing serious health problems or dying before reaching their fifties. According to George E. Vaillant: "Of 59 men with the best mental health, assessed from the age of 21 to 46 years, only two became chronically ill or died by the age of 53. . . . Of the 48 men with the worst mental health from the age of 24 to 46, 18 became chronically ill or died" (Vaillant et al., 1979). All of the men in the study moved through the ages of 42 to 53 between 1964 and 1975. Overall it was clear that "poor adult adjustment between 21 and 47 years of age seemed strongly associated with the deterioration of physical health" during the years of middle age. The analysis controlled for such interaction variables as alcohol consumption, tobacco use, obesity, and the life-span of the subject's ancestors. Although the study is not oriented toward analyzing for longevity at the present time, it did clearly indicate that the deterioration and decline of aging is preventable. In discussing the data Vaillant indicates that "tentative conclusions" are that:

> . . . in this sample chronic anxiety, depression and emotional maladjustment, measured in a variety of ways, predicted early aging, defined by irreversible deterioration of health. The data suggest that positive mental health significantly retards irreversible midlife decline in physical health. . . . Stress does not kill us so much as ingenious adaptation to stress (call it good mental health or mature coping mechanisms) facilitates our survival [Vaillant et al., 1979].

These conclusions are consistent with a great deal of recent research indicating that responses to life stressors are accurate predictors of psychological stability, physical health, and longevity in the sense of achieving at least the average life expectancy.

Recent studies have been increasingly sophisticated and tended to confirm that the individual's innate or learned response to stress is more important than the stressors per se. Research by Richard S. Lazarus (1976) of the Department of Psychology at the University of California at Berkeley has emphasized the role of "psychological mediators" governing the actual psychophysiology of the stress response. Findings such as these are sources of optimism because they elevate the individual from the status of passive victim to an active participant in determining how to manage the inevitable and often stimulating stress of life. Among the more recent findings in stress research are studies dealing with: (1) life change events as predictors of depression, schizophrenia, and neurosis (Rahe, 1979; Rahe and Arthur, 1978); (2) use of four cardiorespiratory symptoms to predict premature mortality from heart disease and to develop preventive measures (Todd et al., 1978); (3) applications of "catatoxic" chemicals which activate the body's defenses to stressors as well as preventing if not regressing the aging effects of stress:

> *Continual exposure to stressors can make a person look older than his years and accelerate the aging process. Aging produces*

physical scars and wrinkles that we can see, and it also produces chemical scars that we can manipulate in a laboratory. I can accelerate aging in a young rat by feeding it a special diet that promotes the development of the chemical by-products of aging. After four weeks on the diet the rat's skin wrinkles, its eyes cloud with cataracts, its back curves and weakens. *If I feed the rat's littermate the same diet but add catatoxic chemicals, the aging diet produces no changes* [Selye, 1979];

(4) links between stress and arteriosclerosis. An extremely important study by Eugene Sprague of the University of Texas demonstrated that "Arterial inner-wall disease was approximately two times greater in monkeys who received daily doses of cortisol with a high cholesterol diet than in monkeys on a high cholesterol diet alone" (Silberner, 1979). Since adrenal steroid cortisol is a multifunction hormone released under stress, it is the first direct instance of a biochemical link between stress and the development of athero-sclerosis. Cortisol also makes the arterial wall more prone to choles-terol deposits. Finally, this study begins to clarify the role of stress mediators in determining whether or not consumed cholesterol will manifest itself in the form of elevated serum cholesterol; (5) stress and acute cardiac conditions. A simple assessment termed the "dive reflex," where a person submerges his face in water while he is monitored on an ECG, has shown that ". . . difficult life situations may precipitate near fatal or even fatal arrhythmias" possibly even in the absence of an "underlying cardiac lesion" (Wolf, 1979).

Another major prospective study deserving of mention has been developed from the well-known research of Caroline Bedell Thomas and Karen R. Duszynski (1974) of the Johns Hopkins School of Medicine. Their earlier study of 1,337 medical students for over 30 years has yielded great insight into the links between stress, lifestyle, and subsequent illness. During 1978 the research team analyzed some prospective data which had been collected by psychiatrist Barbara Betz from 45 students randomly selected from the Johns Hopkins Medical School class of 1948. At that time Betz classified the students into three groups based upon psychological assessments. Subjects were classified as "alphas" who were "cautious, steady, self-reliant, slow to adapt and nonadventurous"; "betas" who were "lively, spontaneous, clever, and flexible"; and, "gammas" who were "the most complicated: although often brilliant, gammas were also mercurial and confused. They tended toward extremes—sometimes they were overly cautious and self-deprecating, other times heedless and tyrannical" (Seligman, 1979). By 1978 most of the 45 students were practicing physicians in their middle fifties. Then the researchers screened their records for hypertension, heart attacks, cancer, and severe emotional illness. From the results it was evident that the gammas had the worst medical history with 77.3 percent evidencing severe illness as compared to 25 percent of the alphas and betas. As a further test Caroline Bedell Thomas selected 127 additional students from the classes of 1949 to 1964 and Betz classified them according to her original scheme based upon the prospective assessments of these 127 students. Again the gammas had both the highest rates of illness and death, with thirteen deaths in the gammas while the betas had none. According to Barbara Betz, who is now a staff psychiatrist with the Kaiser-Permanente Medical Center in Los Angeles, the psychological styles reflect individual neuroendocrine profiles and these chronic lifestyles represent a "thread of vulnerability" for the gammas. Most importantly, Betz and Thomas do not advocate attempts at radical personality change but note that gammas ". . . should try to accept the unevenness in their characters. Such self-acceptance may help the tense gammas to relax, and conceivably prolong their lives" (Seligman, 1979). This last observation is the key point in the interaction between stress and longevity. Individuals can learn to adapt more positively to stress in order at least to achieve their average life expectancy. Volumes have been and will be written regarding the psychophysiology of stress, its effects, and the clinical treatment of stress disorders, which are rapidly increasing. For the most part these are concerned with health maintenance and are not oriented toward longevity. However, there are related research and observations of centenarian communities which indicate that stress and psychological factors are major determinants of longevity as well.

The Lifestyle Factor

Despite the sophistication of genetic, biochemical, and neuroendocrine research, the single most accurate predictor of longevity is lifestyle. Researchers have isolated and assessed the relative contribution of genetic, medical, and psychosocial variables in longevity and have found that these latter are paramount. One particularly important predictor of longevity is work satisfaction (Brill, 1978). Early research by Erdman Palmore, Professor of Medical Sociology at Duke University Medical Center, attempted to clarify the interaction between "physical, mental, and social factors" by developing a Longevity Quotient (LQ) which would give both the relative weight or influence of each of these and how they would correlate with longevity. Taking 39 variables, including previous medical history, parents' ages at death, various IQ scores, and socioeconomic data, Palmore conducted a 13-year longitudinal study of 268 community volunteers between the ages of 60 and 94 at the beginning of the study. From these initial examinations Palmore was able to ". . . improve the accuracy of longevity predictions by about one-third over predictions based on actuarial life expectancy alone" (Palmore, 1969a). Employing various statistical analyses, Palmore concluded: ". . . work satisfaction was the best single predictor among men aged 60 to 69, and physical functioning was the best single predictor among women aged 60 to 69 and among negroes. . . . The evidence suggests that maintaining health, mental abilities, and satisfying social roles are the most important factors related to longevity" (Palmore, 1969a). Following up on his initial research, Palmore studied the same group at a 15-year interval and confirmed his initial observations. In addition to verifying the earlier data, he also refined the results into more specific predictors:

(a) work satisfaction, (b) happiness rating, (c) physical functioning, and (d) tobacco use are the four strongest predictors of longevity when age is controlled by the use of a Longevity

Quotient. . . . The most important ways to increase longevity are: 1. maintain a useful and satisfying role in society, 2. maintain good physical functioning, and 3. avoid smoking [Palmore, 1969b].

These findings are consistent with the lifestyle practices noted among centenarian communities and discussed in Chapter VII.

In later writings Erdman Palmore weighed nutrition, exercise, lifestyle, etc., with genetic factors. "There is considerable evidence that environment factors such as nutrition, disease, stress, psychologic attitudes, social roles, and lifestyle probably outweigh the hereditary factors influencing the actual life-span of given persons" (Palmore, 1971). Although the genetic and biological factors discussed in Chapter III exert considerable influence, they are not deterministic. Issues of genetic versus lifestyle variables are similar to the nature/nurture controversy which persists as an anachronistic vestige of the single-variable experimental paradigm. Both genetic and lifestyle variables interact in a manner which remains inexplicable at the present time. Research in Holland by Sven Danner and Arend Dunning of the University of Amsterdam focused on 100 Dutch people who were at least 90 years of age. These Dutch cardiologists observed that the lives of these people were marked by two world wars, a bitter and prolonged economic depression, and an overall life of poverty and toil. Despite this adversity these aged people had exceeded their average life expectancy and evidenced fewer coronary risk factors. Extensive physical examinations were given to the nonagenarians as well as complete familial and personal histories. These profiles revealed ". . . the people . . . belonged to the lower social class. . . . The men had been unskilled laborers; the women had raised several children . . . 2% had smoked . . . only 10% were seriously overweight . . . only 28 had any clinical manifestation of heart disease . . . cholesterol was remarkably low . . . a rather high ratio of HDL-cholesterol to total cholesterol" (*Medical World News,* 1978e). Of particular interest to the cardiologists were dietary influences. ". . . they tended to eat less than the Dutch population as a whole but had approximately the same relative contribution of protein, fat, and carbohydrate as their countrymen. Although their cholesterol consumption was low, their relative cholesterol intake—

compared with findings of recent Dutch population studies—was high" (*Medical World News,* 1978e). When the researchers addressed the role of genetic endowment, they did not find it to be significant, and they concluded that "a major familial influence could not be shown." Overall, the Dutch cardiologists concluded, ". . . a life of hard work without the hazards of affluence is typical of people who live to healthy old age." Family history and long-lived parents are important, but the modifiable lifestyle variables are at least equally important, per se as well as determining whether the genetic potential is realized or not. Although severe social conditions were imposed upon the Dutch nonagenarians, their adaptation resulted in extended rather than decreased life expectancy. Adversity is not uniformly destructive and can be an asset depending on the responses of the individuals.

Among other research findings relating lifestyle to longevity are: (1) married couples who are residing together live longer than the single, widowed, or divorced (Brody, 1979); (2) positive religious attitudes were correlated with happiness, feelings of usefulness, adjustment, and longevity (Blazer and Palmore, 1976); (3) there is evidence of a "longevity syndrome." The personality profiles of 79 people between 87 and 103 years of age indicated that they possessed good health, feelings of well-being, were physically and mentally active, were creative, and generally enjoyed living (Jewett, 1973). It is increasingly evident that modifiable lifestyle factors are major influences on longevity. Socioeconomic forces cannot be discounted here: ". . . studies of noninstitutionalized aged persons with a high occupational status, higher income, more education, greater social activity, and greater life satisfaction all have been found to be significant predictors of greater longevity" (Palmore, 1971). It should be abundantly clear that productivity, psychological adjustment, and overall life satisfaction are essential factors in increasing life expectancy. Shortsighted public health measures exclude these variables as extraneous and minimize the preventive potential while maximizing efforts at managing pathology and disease.

Gender and Longevity

Closely related to the interaction between lifestyle and longevity is the fact that in all modern societies women tend to live longer than men. Recent releases from the United States Census Bureau indicate that women over 65 outnumber men over 65 by 3 million and this gap is expected to become greater. Prior to the early 1900s the ratio of 104 to 106 male births to 100 female births offset the toll of wars and occupational hazards through the second and third decades of life, but this is no longer the case. The most immediate and obvious reaction to higher female life expectancies is to attribute it to genetic or neuroendocrinological differences between males and females. This appears not to be the case even under conditions of laboratory experimentation.

In a series of excellent articles entitled "Why Do Women Live Longer than Men?" Ingrid Waldron, of the University of Pennsylvania, conducted an extensive inquiry into the possible biological basis for such a widespread difference. These articles contain an in-depth analysis of the role of influences such as greater male susceptibility to disease due to X-chromosome-linked recessive mutations, the role of female hormones such as estrogen, which does tend to prevent atherosclerosis in premenopausal women, effects of oral contraceptives, as well as cross-cultural studies of this mortality differential. From this extensive review only the cross-cultural differentiation proved to be of significance, based on existing research. Higher female mortality was observed most frequently in nonindustrial countries. For the ten postindustrial nations evidencing the highest average life expectancy, women consistently outlive men (Favazza, 1977). Although genetic and hormonal factors are partially responsible for this differential, the conclusion of Waldron's studies unequivocally implicates lifestyle as the major influence:

> Therefore, we have considered both cultural and genetic factors in our analysis of the specific causes of the sex differential in

mortality in the contemporary United States. . . . Behavioral factors emerge as important determinants for each of the causes of death listed (24 causes listed). . . . These causes of death with clear behavioral components are responsible for one-third of the excess male mortality, and arteriosclerotic heart disease is responsible for an additional 40 percent of the excess deaths among males . . . men have higher death rates for arteriosclerotic heart disease in large part because they often develop the aggressive, competitive coronary-prone behavior [Waldron, 1976].

In accounting for other identifiable factors contributing to the overall incidence of a 60 percent higher mortality for men than women in the United States, Waldron also noted:

One third of the sex differential in mortality is due to men's higher rates of suicide, fatal motor vehicle and other accidents, cirrhosis of the liver, respiratory cancers and emphysema. Each of these causes of death is linked to behaviors which are encouraged or accepted more in males than in females; using guns, drinking alcohol, smoking, working at hazardous jobs, and seeming to be fearless. . . . Thus, the behaviors expected of males in our society make a major contribution to their elevated mortality [Waldron, 1976].

In view of the higher incidence of arteriosclerotic disease, suicide, accidents, cirrhosis, and respiratory diseases, virtually all of the sexual differential in mortality is accountable for by lifestyle factors which are modifiable. New epidemiological studies throw light on the relationship between cardiovascular disease and sex difference. The incidence of cardiovascular disease has decreased dramatically for all ages, both sexes, and all races between 1968 and 1976 by 20.7 percent. This decline came as a surprise to epidemiologists and was unnoticed for a period of time. Then, physician Michael P. Stern of the University of Texas Health Science Center at San Antonio published an extensive overview on the scientific studies which might explain that decrease. According to his article this decrease is due to several contributing factors evident in that time period, which are

". . . a decrease in high cholesterol–high animal fat diet. . . . Concomitantly, consumption of polyunsaturated, cholesterol-free vegetable fat has tripled . . . a decline in cigarette smoking . . . improved physical fitness . . . and steady improvement during the 1960's and 1970's in high blood pressure control in the United States" (Stern, 1979). These findings are noted here since even with the decline, the male to female mortality differential has remained virtually unchanged while a slight increase in female mortality has been noted in those women who have increased smoking. Although cardiovascular disease appears to be decreasing due to these multiple influences, it still affects many more individuals than is necessary and exacts its greatest toll among men. Neither men nor women attain even their average life expectancy, because of hazardous lifestyle factors. On the positive side this indicates that it may be possible to attain the average life expectancy and beyond by changes in the psychosocial and economic pressures which give rise to lifestyles which presently elevate male mortality.

Marked differences between the patterns of male and female morbidity as well as mortality are complex but do indicate a major source of insight concerning the interaction between psychosocial factors and longevity. This is increasingly imperative since the trends indicate that this difference is increasing and more in evidence now than at the turn of the century. Not only has there been an overall increase in the afflictions of civilization but a crossover effect has occurred during that same time period for males and females. At the beginning of this century females still had a higher mortality than males but this is now completely reversed. In analyzing these trends, Abdel R. Omran of the Department of Epidemiology at the University of North Carolina has formulated a theory of Epidemiologic Transition to account for this phenomenon. According to the Epidemiologic Transition theory:

(1) Mortality is a fundamental factor in population dynamics; (2) there are three major successive stages of the epidemiologic transition; (3) the most profound changes in health and disease patterns occur among children and young women; (4) the shifts in health and disease patterns of the transition stem from socioeconomic changes related to modernization; and (5) there are

three basic models of the epidemiologic transition [Omran, 1977].

Omran applies his theory to account for the "extremely high (almost explosive)" increase in the degenerative and "man-made" diseases since the turn of the century. Perhaps his greatest contribution has been to clarify the crossover effect in male and female morbidity and mortality. Applying his theory to epidemiological graphs of mortality incidence and trends, Omran has concluded:

> The changing pattern of causes of death reflects and characterizes in a major way this sex differential. In the 19th century and earlier, when the leading causes of death were infectious diseases, females were more affected than males for several reasons. Adult women at that time usually filled the roles of wife, mother, nurse, cook, and maid simultaneously. With high fertility and the repeated stresses of pregnancies, lactation, and childbearing, they were susceptible to maternal and communicable diseases. When the era of infectious diseases subsided, coupled with the increasing status of women and lower fertility rates, a shift in excess mortality occurred in their favor [Omran, 1977].

Not only is this trend clearly evident but it is increasing. According to even more recent data compiled by George C. Myers, Director of the Center for Demographic Studies at Duke University, this trend is continuing and diverging even more for eleven of the major postindustrial nations, including the United States. From World Health Organization data it is clear that there is a continued strong decline in mortality rates for females with a somewhat mixed profile for males but remaining higher overall:

> The reductions in USA mortality for elderly males and especially for females during the first half of the 1970s can be viewed as a continuation, but at an accelerated pace, of the long-term secular trend toward lower death rates in the older ages. . . . However, it must be emphasized that the death rates themselves are nearly twice as high for males as for females at the same ages and this differential is increasing as a result of sharper declines in the rates for females [Myers, 1978].

Furthermore, there has been a sharp overall reduction in female mortality of over 2 percent per year in the 1970s, but the factors contributing to this decline are not known. Of particular interest is that the decline is greatest in the later years after age 80 and indicates that at least a small portion of the United States is evidencing greater longevity.

Trends such as these are even greater in Finland, Denmark, and Japan, although the influences remain unknown in these countries. While the quantity of life extension is evidenced in these trends, they do not give any indication of the quality of life experienced by these long-lived individuals. An immediate and obvious result of this divergence between male and female mortality is an increasing number of long-lived widows. Given the increase in this trend, it is imperative that further research be undertaken to identify the factors contributing to this trend and, most importantly, to diversify research away from purely quantitative data, focused primarily on mortality, toward studies of the quality of health in these individuals. To date, only one study has indicated that psychosocial variables were not adequate predictors of longevity, and that was undertaken with males over the age of 80. During 1973 Arthur H. Richardson of the School of Hygiene and Public Health at Johns Hopkins University randomly surveyed 1,366 retired United Auto Workers' men and 1,913 veterans of the Spanish-American War. Both groups were considered to be "advantaged" because of their relatively high retirement income and access to health services. For the younger members of the two populations Richardson's data confirmed the accuracy of psychosocial predictors of longevity as ". . . higher social class position, superior role satisfactions, being married, more social activity, and better behavioral adjustment" (Richardson, 1973). However, for the octogenarian males this was not the case. For men over 80 these psychosocial variables were found to have minimal accuracy and importance in predicting survival over a one-year follow-up period. By contrast, "medical care utilization" was found to be the most significant predictor. In interpreting these results, Richardson has hypothesized that, "Possibly social attributes lose their potency as predictors among the *very* aged because biological and constitutional variables are so powerful and because economic barriers to medical care are less for the two octogenarian groups studied" (Richardson, 1973). Clearly these preliminary findings indicate a pressing need for further research.

Perhaps enhancing the known psychosocial influences in earlier years can increase functional longevity as well as decrease medical care utilization in later years. Also, if longevity is dependent to a large degree upon access to medical care in the advanced-age groups, more effective and reduced fee access is imperative although contrary to the present trends. Projections of an increased number of widows living to an advanced age but denied access to necessary health care is a grim prospect. This tendency of women to outlive men has unfortunately resulted in denigrating stereotypes applied to older women. According to Barbara Payne and Frank Whittington, there is an "old woman" stereotype which depicts that woman as "sick, sexless, uninvolved except for church work, and alone" (Payne and Whittington, 1976). Such observations are emphatically not accurate overall, although they are too often true in the tragic particular. For that reason alone some shifts in values away from male "macho" models toward respect for other ideals, including age and experience, would benefit society as a whole.

Following the work of Waldron as well as that of others, Allan Johnson of the Department of Sociology at Wesleyan University undertook a more recent examination of the sex mortality differentials in the United States. Recently there have been references in the research literature and speculations in the popular press that there might be an increase in female morbidity and mortality due to their greater participation in traditionally male roles. This issue was addressed by Johnson, who examined "age-adjusted" or age specific mortality rates rather than the "crude" death rates utilized most frequently. By using age-adjusted death rates, it is possible to control for the fact that as the percentage of elderly people increases the number of deaths will inevitably increase, even though the age specific rates remain stable. When this procedure was applied to the most recent population data of 1960 to 1974 regarding twelve causes of death, Johnson concluded: "With few exceptions, we shall find that women are enjoying increasingly low mortality risks and an increasing advantage relative to men" (Johnson, 1977). Among the exceptions were a slight increase in cirrhosis of the liver among women and a few equivocal instances.

As definitive as this analysis appears to be, it may not reflect current trends but rather current status. This is due to the fact that psychosocial, stress, and lifestyle influences exert their effects progressively over time and results of any shift are unlikely to be observed in less than five- or ten-year increments. Unfortunately, by that time the contributing factors are not only obscured but are in inextricable interaction. Chronic disorders take a long time to develop, and any increases in female morbidity and mortality would not be evident yet, although there are potential indicators. Addressing this issue in *New England Journal of Medicine,* Charles E. Lewis and Mary Ann Lewis of the UCLA School of Medicine have speculated on the potential impact of sexual equality on both male and female health. Changes in psychosocial roles and pressures not only affect the women involved in them directly but also have a marked impact upon both sexes through family dynamics, career interactions, and avocational interests and behavior. These researchers acknowledge that the major differences "related more to their behaviors and roles in society than to their biologic inheritance." If a shift in roles and lifestyle has occurred, and if this has an impact on women's health, they have pinpointed certain indicators:

> As sex roles change, will those health-related behaviors that seem highly linked to sex also change—i.e., will women demonstrate a pattern of decreased use of services? Will they experience, as younger women physicians do, a relative increase in mortality as compared to men? Will they gain equity in death rates for most diseases as they already have for cancer of the lung? Certainly, they will accumulate greater risks as they drive or fly greater distances and acquire different stresses related to occupational responsibilities [Lewis and Lewis, 1977].

Changes in these patterns will have an effect upon the entire social order which may be evidenced as an increase, decrease, or an equality in the male to female ratio in morbidity and mortality. Since any one of these alternatives is possible, it will be important to detect a disproportionate increase in disorders due to changes in female lifestyles and health trends indicated by the measures noted above.

Within contemporary society the emergence of women as an even greater social influence than before is heralded by many and decried by a few. A relatively neutral assessment of this evolution has been described by Alice S. Rossi noting:

> Over the past half century, increased longevity and fertility control have had a marked effect on family structure. Women now devote a smaller proportion of their adult life to the rearing of children. They have also achieved higher levels of education, facilitating more egalitarian relations between husbands and wives and increasing the proportion of married women who are capable of holding jobs [Rossi, 1972]

This emergence is undoubtedly a positive trend but not without its hazards. It is hoped the hazards evidenced in male lifestyle can be minimized or eliminated by learning from the tragic experiences of the past. Optimism is infused by Lewis and Lewis, who concluded their excellent study by posing several literally vital questions:

> . . . the concept of equality need not imply that females change to match a male "standard." In contrast, men could benefit enormously if their sex-role changes carried with them some of the protective effects associated with a diminished "macho" stance. . . .
>
> If we are striving for a nonsexist society, with equal opportunity for all, it would be better to seek increased opportunities for women in occupation, business and commercial affairs, and a reduction in the morbidity and mortality of men. Perhaps this proposal evades the fundamental question: What is the better measure of equality—for women to die like men, or for men to live (a little bit) like women? Can we not have the benefits of sexual parity in terms of equal opportunities for personal achievement, as well as individual survival? [Lewis and Lewis, 1977].

For a suggestion of what healthier male behavior might look like, a research project by Charles L. Rose and his colleagues is of particular interest. By interviewing the next-of-kin of 500 deceased males, the researchers analyzed the biographical data on 77 selected independent variables. From their extensive analyses the optimal male profile, the one correlated with longevity, included these observations: "less worried, older than spouse, conserving energy, longer lived mother, looked younger than age while under 40, and not easily aggravated" (Rose et al., 1967). At this point in time it is virtually impossible to make a statement regarding evolving roles and influences of women without eliciting controversy. Unequivocally it is a laudable trend and long overdue. However, the need for changed lifestyles in both sexes must be emphasized. Only in this way can a society evolve based on optimum health and longevity for women and men alike.

Cross-cultural Perspectives

Placing the numerous psychosocial influences in an appropriate context reflecting their relative values is a formidable task. There are many variables outside of the immediate social role and lifestyle which exert considerable influence. An innovative study by Richard F. Tomasson of the Department of Sociology at the University of New Mexico attempts to integrate a number of variables. Statistics of the World Health Organization indicate that Sweden has been the country with the lowest overall male mortality and the highest male life expectancy in the world since the early 1960s. For Sweden the average life expectancy for men is 72.0 and 77.4 for women (Favazza, 1977). In his study, Tomasson researched the factors which appeared to account for the extended life expectancy for Swedish males as compared to men in the United States. By contrast to Sweden, men in the United States have a 68.7 life expectancy and women a 76.5 life expectancy (Favazza, 1977). Using age-adjusted mortality rates, Tomasson recorded three life periods when relative differences were the greatest: ages under 1, ages 20 to 24, and ages 50 to 54. From these observations and related research he suggested seven factors which would account for the male mortality differential:

(1) Sweden's system of compulsory, national health insurance dates only from 1955. . . . The point is that medical care, like education, has been regarded as both a communal responsibility

and an individual right in Sweden long before the advent of the modern welfare state; (2) Sweden has progressed further than the United States in absorbing its lower classes (as distinct from the working class) into the conventional living standards of the greater society; (3) Sweden has a highly structured and "tight" social structure in which internal constraints are strong. Constraint has been suggested . . . as a factor in explaining mortality differentials; (4) . . . extremely low infant mortality that prevails in Sweden is due to the smaller percentage of births to women under age 20 and at ages 35 and over; (5) There is an activist approach toward lessening the dangers of existence in Sweden, part of the enormous emphasis in this society on rectifying social problems. . . . The early attack on the problem of industrial pollution is another example of Swedish activism toward social problems. (6) Consumption of cigarettes and alcohol are both much lower in Sweden than in the United States. (7) Diet, exercise, and weight are factors known to be associated with mortality. Dietary differences between these two populations are greater than might be expected in the two most affluent societies in the world. Meat and sugar consumption, for example, is lower in Sweden than in the United States, and the consumption of fish much higher. Average daily caloric consumption in Sweden was 2,850 for 1970–71, low for a modern society [Tomasson, 1976].

Taken as a whole, these wide-ranging factors place the various influences in a perspective, although even this survey is not definitive.

One further point noted in the study was that "At the upper ages there is a reversal of the differential with United States white males having lower mortality than their Swedish counterparts." This is consistent with the findings noted earlier of Arthur H. Richardson as well as those of George C. Myers. One possible interpretation is that access to superior medical services in advanced age may be responsible for this reversal. If so, it is still an instance of "too little, too late," indicating that medical care is disproportionately focused on the later years. There is no need to probe very far before the economic and political issues become apparent. Leslie S. Libow, Chief of Geriatric Medicine at Mount Sinai City Hospital Center in

Elmhurst, New York, has suggested the implications of similar data for the future development of a health care system. His research addressed itself to the interaction of medical, biological, and behavioral factors in an 11-year longitudinal study by the National Institute of Health of 47 healthy men with a mean age of 70 years. These men underwent extensive assessments at the outset and again at 5 and 11 years with the aid of 22 researchers. Emphasis was on the process of aging in healthy, elderly males who were free of obesity and hypertension at the outset. By studying healthy men Libow was able to distinguish between the effects of aging and the effects of disease. Libow concluded:

> A number of findings in this study have implications for clinical and preventive medicine. These include the relationship of lighter weight and higher systolic blood pressure to mortality, the demonstrated benefit of discontinuing cigarette smoking even late in life, and, possibly, the finding of diminished serum albumin preceding the development of gastrointestinal cancer. The relationship of mortality to environmental losses and to diminished scores on mental function tests also suggests clinical and preventive health actions. These findings concerning late life surely suggest insights into early and midlife problems. It is only for society and health professionals to decide if findings such as these should lead to further efforts to enhance the quality of life of our older citizens [Libow, 1974].

When the results of laboratory research, cross-cultural data, epidemiological analyses of the male and female mortality differential, and results of psychosocial research are considered overall, it is pressingly clear how much more can and should be undertaken to enable individuals to attain even their average life expectancy while remaining in sound health.

Cross-cultural studies are full of evidence that certain lifestyles and attitudes developed early in life do optimize and predict adult health and longevity. There are several studies of groups of individuals, such as the "Old Order Amish" (Cross, 1976), a group of Mormons in Utah (Enstrom, 1978), and several major longitudinal studies of other identifiable groups, which indicate the interconnection between psychological and physical health. In a survey of the attitudes and lifestyles of 1,006 people in California, the California Department of Mental Health found that "positive self-esteem" most accurately predicted higher levels of health even over "relations with others, physical environment, heredity, and availability of medical and psychological services" (California Department of Mental Health, 1979). Another prospective research project by Marjorie Honzik of the University of California at Berkeley found that "teenage personality traits" of "calm, dependability, self-satisfaction, even temper" and others were accurately predictive of psychological and physical health in the forties and fifties (Honzik, 1979).

In the Mormon study mentioned above, James E. Enstrom of the UCLA Department of Public Health studied the church records for 15,500 California Mormons during 1968 to 1975 and for 55,000 Utah Mormons during 1970 to 1975 to examine cancer incidence. Using age-adjusted statistics, Enstrom noted that for "religiously active Mormons" the death rate of active Mormons compared to comparable United States white males was "38% for ages 35–64 . . . and 50% for ages 35 years and above" (Enstrom, 1978). For purposes of his study Enstrom defined "active" Mormons as those men who were chosen to be "High Priests and Seventies" usually before age 50. These individuals are observed to adhere to certain church doctrines and lifestyle patterns, and are more involved in church activities than those he classified as "inactive" Mormons. Overall, both the active and inactive Mormons were matched according to most variables, including demographics and socioeconomic status, with the most notable exception that "inactive Mormons tend to smoke and drink about as much as the general population."

Comparisons between the lifestyle-related longevity of the active Mormons, comparable United States males, and inactive Mormons were highly significant. For active Mormon men the average life expectancy is over seven years longer than for comparable United States males. When the specific causes of morbidity and mortality are analyzed, they indicate a "mortality ratio of 50% for all cancer" or half of the incidence observed in comparable males. Furthermore, when he analyzed the comparisons between active and inactive Mormons, he noted a higher incidence of cancer in inactive Mormons. "These comparisons indicate that most of the mortality difference between active and inactive Mormons occurs in the smoking-related cancer sites." Enstrom concluded, "Active Mormons are healthier than Mormons as a whole and rank among the lowest in mortality when compared with other groups of healthy males." These are very significant findings since they involve comparable groups of relatively healthy individuals. Taking the study one important step further, Enstrom postulated that this fact is due to the adherence of the active Mormons to their "Word of Wisdom" which proscribes a certain lifestyle. Although the variable of smoking accounted for the most significant portion of higher mortality in the three groups, Enstrom concluded:

> It appears that the mortality differences are only partially explained by lack of smoking. Several additional factors are possibly important: low consumption of alcohol, coffee, tea, soft drinks, and drugs; certain dietary habits; general health practices, including exercise and proper sleep and weight; various social and psychological aspects connected with the nature of their religion; selection factors related to obtaining leadership roles in the Church; and heredity [Enstrom, 1978].

Although this study concentrated on cancer incidence, it can and needs to be extended to consider other causes of mortality.

Comparable research with both Mormons and Seventh-Day Adventists indicate lower mortality than comparable populations in cancer, coronary artery disease, and myocardial infarction. Longitudinal research conducted by the Loma Linda University School of Medicine has focused on the Adventists since their church proscriptions advocate abstention from alcohol and tobacco. Half are lactovegetarians who eat dairy foods and eggs but no meat, poultry, or fish, and about 2 percent are strict vegetarians. Of greatest interest is their rate of cancer of the colon, associated with low-fiber diets and animal product consumption, which is 72 percent of that for the general population. However, detailed analysis indicates dietary factors alone cannot account for this observed difference, since there was no difference between the vegetarian Adventists and the nonvegetarians (Wynder et al., 1959). Complex subtleties in the research with population subgroups in the United States and abroad indicate the necessity of caution in reaching conclusions. However, these are promising indications which require further inquiry.

From numerous research studies it is clear that religious beliefs and the lifestyles they advocate have a significant influence on health, usually in a positive direction. After an extensive analysis of these studies Kenneth Vaux has written, "Beliefs prompt moral behaviors; these in turn affect health." Drawing on the research data comparing specific religious groups to control groups from the general population, the results indicate such findings as:

Mormons in Utah have 30% lower incidence of most cancers. . . .

Seventh-Day Adventists have from 10–40% fewer hospital admissions for epidermoid and nonepidermoid malignancies. . . .

Regular church-attenders in Washington County, Maryland, have 40% less risk from arteriosclerotic heart disease. . . .

Jews living in Brooklyn have twice the expected incidence of leukemia. . . .

Jewish men in New York City have decidedly lower rates of lung cancer than Protestant or Catholic men [Vaux, 1976].

It is important to note that the fourth item indicates that the effects are not uniformly positive. There is no intention here to advocate religious beliefs as a prerequisite to health and longevity. However, a strong belief, and a sense of purpose in life, whether they are identifiably religious or not, have a profound impact on health. Later in the article Vaux cites other instances: low incidence of cervical and penile cancer among Jews in New York City as due partially to religiously dictated circumcision; the high incidence of coronary disease in the Bible Belt due to its repressive orientation, and the classic Washington County study indicating a 50% less incidence of arteriosclerotic heart disease in men 45 to 64 who attended church regularly. There are other such correlations indicating both the positive and negative influences of strong beliefs as reflected in religious doctrines and practices.

Consideration of specialized religious organizations, secular groups of inordinately healthy and long-lived individuals, or of centenarian communities is not a naive attribution to them of a lost wisdom or advocacy of rural, pastoral virtues and countercultural values. While these are frequent attributes of these groups, they are not uniformly the case nor are the attributes uniformly positive. The relative purity and isolation of ethnic and religious groups is rapidly disappearing as they become increasingly assimilated by, and susceptible to, the stressful adaptations demanded in a complex social order. However, the positive influences on health of their traditions is worth noting. Moreover, it is now possible to exercise choices involving "voluntary simplicity" and related measures, exemplified by these populations. In that sense they are valuable prototypes. Among the communities receiving research attention have been the Amish people who are commonly referred to as the "Pennsylvania Dutch," although they live throughout Pennsylvania, Ohio, Indiana, and the Middle West. Amish people originated in the Canton of Berne, Switzerland, and during the 1700s migrated to the Pennsylvania area. They were the subject of a major sociological study in the early 1960s (Hostetler, 1963). Among the early researchers was Harold E. Cross of the Department of Ophthalmology of the University of Arizona College of Medicine, who became interested in the "Old Order Amish" of Pennsylvania. Even though the intent of his work was to consider the relative genetic purity of the Amish people, it actually demonstrated the importance of lifestyle and psychosocial variables.

It is apparent that the Old Order Amish have several attributes that make them useful to human geneticists. Members are easily identified by their distinctive dress and customs. Their communities were founded by a limited number of ancestors, with identifiable origins. They maintain a closed population with virtually no dilution of the original gene pool. Families are large, illegitimacy rates are low, and the membership constitutes a relatively immobile society concentrated in specific geographical areas. Several additional features are of particular value to the medical geneticist: relatively stable socioeconomic values, uniform environment, high standards of living and medical

care, a great interest in medicine, and strong resistance to insti-
tutionalisation of the chronically ill [Cross, 1976].

Many of these characteristics are common to isolated social groups
as well as to the centenarian communities to be discussed in Chapter
VIII. In 1976 Cross observed that, "In spite of their effective isolation
from the external world, and evident internal stability, the Amish
exhibit signs of stress that may indicate their eventual acculturation,
at least to some degree, with the larger rural community." It is
unlikely that the relatively good health of the Amish is determined
primarily by genetic endowment, since genetic selection is a relatively slow process and would not be responsible for the negative
changes evidenced in recent morbidity and mortality trends.

More recent research by Richard F. Hamman and his colleagues
of the Department of Epidemiology at Johns Hopkins University
School of Hygiene and Public Health has noted a slight decline in
Amish health, although they remain healthier than comparable
populations as a whole. Over a period of several years the research
team studied the morbidity and mortality of 680,000 male and female
Amish and non-Amish people in three of the largest settlements of
the Amish in Pennsylvania, Ohio, and Indiana. "These data suggest
that Amish males, at least, through their combined alterations in
lifestyle and genetics may have avoided the excess male mortality
experience that is characteristic of 45 to 65-year-old non-Amish
males, and have achieved age specific all cause mortality rates like
those of women over age 45" (Hamman et al., 1978). This is particularly significant since the actual leading causes of mortality for the
Amish are identical to those for the general population. "Cancer,
cardiovascular and respiratory disease and accidents represent over
75 percent of all deaths in the Amish." Overall the male mortality
is significantly lower than the United States mortality in all four
areas except for a higher incidence of lymphoma-leukemia. This may
be due to factors such as animal viruses and the chronic exposure to
chemical fertilizers and pesticides which the Amish use in farming.
Although the trends were similar for females, they were less clear-
cut, and the data was more equivocal.

In accounting for the lower morbidity and extended life expectancy noted in these studies and others, it is important to note the

characteristics of Amish lifestyle: (1) "All Amish are rural living and nearly all are farmers" (Cross, 1976); (2) they are strictly endogamous, do not proselytize, and outside marriages with non-Amish are strictly forbidden; (3) there is strict monogamy and since children are highly desirable, contraception is the exception rather than the rule and families are large. It is interesting to note that female reproductive span is longer and birth intervals shorter than among comparable populations. This is consistent with research by Pierre Phillippe and Louise Yelle of the Department of Social and Preventive Medicine at the University of Montreal. In a prospective study of the effect of family size on a mother's longevity, they found, "We show that 1 to 5 pregnancies is associated with the greatest longevity in weakly inbred women and 11 pregnancies is associated with the greatest longevity in more inbred women" (Phillippe and Yelle, 1976). One of their interpretations was that the positive stress engendered during childbirth under supportive circumstances may actually strengthen the mothers and endow them with a "greater physiological capacity," especially inbred women; (4) Amish exercise heavily, especially the men, and use horses to farm as well as for transportation; (5) their community is a primarily spiritual one without distinct geographical boundaries and the population is relatively stable; (6) there are "no electricity, no autos, and no telephones" (Hamman et al., 1978); (7) although the Amish consume a diet "rich in animal fats, carbohydrates, and calories" (Hamman et al., 1978), they evidence low cardiovascular disease; blood pressure and cholesterol are lower due to heavy exercise for males and minimal smoking for both males and females. Highly significant and positive interactions have been noted between diet and physical activity as discussed in Chapters VI and VII of *Holistic Medicine* (Pelletier, 1979); (8) alcohol consumption is moderate and cigarette use is rare; (9) there is an overall good standard of living and adequate but not excessive medical care; and finally (10) "in spite of their usual pacifism and strong belief in nonviolence, there is considerable internal strife" (Cross, 1976).

Communities such as the Mormon, Amish, and Seventh-Day Adventists are not utopian, but there are valuable lessons to be learned from them if a social consciousness is to emerge that will create a true health care system. Amish in particular have chosen a lifestyle where they live and work in an isolated and supportive culture. That lifestyle and culture is virtually identical to rural America a hundred years ago and not unlike a lifestyle that many have suggested is healthier than our present one. It is not a coincidence that the lifestyle, high environmental quality, relative isolation, and strong psychosocial system evidenced in these groups are remarkably similar to those of the centenarian communities to be discussed in Chapter VIII. The possibility of such biological longevity seems less improbable, since these populations are present in the United States. At the very least these communities show that choices can and must be made to stem the excessive morbidity and premature mortality evident in our society.

Midlife Transitions and Longevity

Potentially middle-aged people are the most influential generation at any given time since they are the wealthiest, most powerful, and socially and politically skilled. Despite this great potential and the fact that most individuals have achieved a state where their material goals have been attained, middle age is considered to be a period of "midlife crisis. Free-floating anxiety or symptom formation of various types may develop in middle age due to the stresses that threaten personal, physical, and social integrity. Depression, in a variety of forms, is perhaps the most common illness, as it follows losses with increasing frequency in the middle years" (Greenleigh, 1974). During a recent annual meeting of the American Academy of Science someone quipped, "The middle aged male seems to have replaced the white rat and the college student as the psychological research world's foremost subject." The consensus among researchers is that there is an abundance of myth and a dearth of data regarding the complexities of adult development (Greenberg, 1978). There is a high degree of individual variation which determines whether these years are a period of agonizing turmoil or extraordinary opportunity.

To date, the most definitive research on adult psychological development is that of Daniel Levinson of Yale University Medical School, who published his findings in the excellent book, *Seasons of a Man's Life* (1978). It was Levinson's theories and research which provided the basis for the popularized accounts in Gail Sheehy's *Passages*. It is important to note that the much criticized concept of invariate and predictable adult developmental stages or "crises" is not derived from Levinson's research but rather from popularized and reductionistic models which may be appealing but do not accurately or adequately reflect the original research. Early research by George L. Maddox and Elizabeth B. Douglass appears to be as accurate now as in 1974 when they reported the results of a 13-year, longitudinal study of 106 men and women ranging in age from 60 to 94. Their conclusion based on six periods of assessment of psychological and physical indicators over the 13 years was: "The data presented here provide evidence that development, change, and growth continue through the later years of the life-span in spite of the decrement of social, psychological, and physiological functioning which typically accompanies the aging process" (Maddox and Douglass, 1974). Later research by this team and others, including Levinson's pioneering research, has confirmed this conclusion. For over ten years Levinson and his colleagues studied forty men between the ages of 35 and 40 through a series of interviews lasting from ten to twenty hours. Other data were drawn from plays, novels, and autobiographies of that life period and assembled by the interdisciplinary research team. The main point here is that their findings demonstrated the existence of a "life structure" which is a complex and dynamic process with distinct periods of transition characteristic of various stages. Approximately 80 percent of the men in the study found the "Midlife Transition" to be a period of "tumultuous struggles" both internally and vis-à-vis the external world. However, the finding of greatest importance here is that a few of the men underwent a manageable transition without crisis. These men seemed to recognize that such periods of transition challenged the assumptions, illusions, and vested interests of their previous lifestyle and that it offered the opportunity for further development.

Psychiatrist Lawrence Greenleigh has suggested that during this period a "midlife inventory" occurs in which a person "examines his life to see where he is, where he has been, and where he is going" (1974). Among the many issues are the relationship to adolescent children where "unconscious incestuous feelings . . . will bring about harsh, critical attitudes and distancing," where a reevaluation of marriage occurs since "the excuse of staying together for the children is no longer valid," a period when "gray hair, wrinkles, sagging breasts, and the climacterium, as well as having children leaving home and other family changes, make women clearly aware of their age," and also this is a time when widowed men evidence a "death rate during the six months following bereavement that is 40 percent above the statistical rate for married men of the same age" (Greenleigh, 1974).

These are representative concerns but they are hardly exhaustive or new. The same stages and predictable crises were formulated by Carl G. Jung in a 1933 essay entitled, "The Stages of Life." However, the concept of highly divergent means of managing these transitions is quite recent. Rather than viewing these periods as stages of inexorable conflict, it is possible to understand all of adult development as an ongoing process of increased awareness on the part of each individual regarding his or her lifestyle. To the degree that these external questions are denied, and life stagnates, the greater will be the ensuing disruption and crises. Even then, as in the dramatic instances of "regenerative psychosis" (Perry, 1962) and "spontaneous remission" (Simonton et al., 1978), these periods of great disruption are potentially positive occurrences. The outcome is dependent upon the individuals' prior lifestyle as well as the psychological and physical resources brought to bear on the rite of transition. Although most of the research has focused on populations of males, there is a pressing need for greater sensitivity to the transitions of both males and females since it is highly likely that men have a great deal to learn from women. In considering the research by Daniel Levinson and his colleagues, a journalist has formulated the transitions as a period when Truman Capote's other voices in other rooms are heard:

> He hears the voice of an identity prematurely rejected, of a love lost or not pursued or a valued interest or relationship given up in acquiescence to parental or other authority; of an internal figure who wants to be an athlete or nomad or artist, to marry for love or remain a bachelor, to get rich or enter the clergy or live a sensual carefree life—possibilities set aside earlier to become what he now is. During the Midlife Transition, he must

learn to listen more attentively to these voices and in the end, to decide what part he will give them in his life [Robbins, 1978].

For both men and women there are reevaluations, choices, and priorities to be determined. These decisions will profoundly influence their future health and longevity.

These issues of course do not suddenly arise in the middle years. Lifestyles developed and maintained throughout life swing the balance from turmoil to transition. Aging is a phenomenon which is most evident during middle age and is a fundamental aspect of the turmoil. The potential for longevity begins at birth and transforms middle age into a period when the positive adaptations of earlier lifestyles become manifest. If individuals have realized from youth onward to engage in life with flexibility and ongoing reassessment of goals and lifestyle, then their adaptation to the critical middle years will enhance optimum health and longevity.

The research of George Vaillant, as described in *Adaptation to Life: How the Best and Brightest Came of Age* (1977), is a most vivid portrayal of these issues. In the study the men were followed for over thirty-five years in order to "make a systematic inquiry into the kinds of people who are well and do well." The study made it evident that adult development is complex, and involves continual change and adaptation not characterized by a predictable succession of easily identifiable stages. Furthermore, childhood disruption does not necessarily predict adult functioning, although patterns of early adolescent adaptation appear to be a significant predictor of adult health. The book sounds a clear note of optimism that even the most pronounced turmoil often results in optimum adaptation and that the most healthy men had developed ingenious methods for managing stress and crisis. In his book Vaillant details the developmental profiles of thirty-six of the men and the self-descriptions are as informative as the research analyses. One man succinctly stated the reason for his midlife tranquillity as, "You discover that your experiences and whatever sense you have gathered in the course of your life are needed." Out of this study came an important insight:

Perhaps the most important conclusion of the Grant Study has been the agonizing self-appraisal and instinctual reawakening at age forty—the so-called "middle crisis"—does not appear to portend decay. However marred by depression and turmoil middle life may be, it often heralds a new stage of man [Vaillant, 1977].

Results of the Grant Study indicate middle and late life adaptation is dependent upon the progressive development of skills throughout an entire lifetime. Further study of this group of men as well as other groups, especially of women, can yield data indicating whether a positive midlife transition is reflected in maximum life expectancy.

Psychosocial Influence and the Nature of Death

It is increasingly evident that psychosocial factors determine both how and when an individual dies. Just as positive psychosocial factors induce optimum health and longevity, negative influences can elicit premature and excessive mortality. As with the other major points of transition in adult development, death is not an isolated event. In the context of a meaningful life, it need not be a source of inordinate fear, as it is in our present culture. Stating this position most eloquently is Robert N. Butler in *Why Survive? Being Old in America:*

After one has lived a life of meaning, death may lose much of its terror. For what we fear most is not really death but a meaningless and absurd life. I believe most human beings can accept the basic fairness of each generation's taking its turn on the face of the planet if they are not cheated out of the full measure of their own turn. The tragedy of old age in America is that we have made absurdity all but inevitable. We have cheated ourselves. But we still have the possibility of making life a work of art [Butler, 1975].

Such a point of view acknowledges that attitudes and lifestyles in effect for many years prior to the actual event of death have a profound influence on the timing as well as the very nature of that occurrence. Since the clarification of thanatos, or death wish, by Sigmund Freud, there has been increasing acceptance of the fact that psychosocial variables determine an individual's death to a great degree:

> The subintentioned death is one in which the person plays some partial, covert, subliminal, or unconscious role in hastening his own demise. The evidence for such a role might be found in a variety of behavior patterns: poor judgment, imprudence, excessive risk-taking, neglect of self, disregard of a life-extending medical regimen, abuse of alcohol, misuse of drugs—all ways in which an individual can advance the date of his death [Shneidman, 1973].

The role of psychosocial factors in cardiovascular disease and subsequent coronary-caused death is the subject of a large body of literature. Since the classic studies of "voodoo death" by Walter B. Cannon in the 1930s to the "sudden death syndrome" research by Bernard Engel in more recent years, both the neurophysiological mechanisms and psychosocial influences have been explored and classified. It has become evident that psychosocial stress factors not only contribute to cardiovascular disease but also trigger the actual moment of death by eliciting fatal ventricular arrhythmias. Research by Patrick T. Donlon and his colleagues of the University of California School of Medicine in Davis had indicated that ". . . in some cases psychologic stress may be a more potent factor than exercised in precipitating pathologic cardiac effects" (Donlon et al., 1979). Increasingly sophisticated research has defined the neurological pathways from the "retina, to the telencephalon, to the amygdala, back through the telencephalon to the brain stem and the motor neurons" (McCann, 1979), through which stressors to the higher nervous system are transferred in milliseconds throughout the heart and body. A sympathetic storm of activity through these pathways can lower the threshold for potentially lethal ventricular fibrillation, induce tachycardia, and elevate blood pressure. When there is underlying coronary artery disease this excessive sympathetic activity acts as "a major contributor to destabilization of normal cardiac rhythm and, in turn, to sudden death" (DeSilva and Lown, 1978). There is other evidence that even in instances where there is no underlying coronary artery disease, this excessive sympathetic activity can cause sudden death by inducing a "coronary spasm" in which one or more coronary arteries suddenly and transiently occlude. The result may be angina pain or, under conditions of prolonged duration, a heart attack not unlike that induced by a clot in the coronary arteries (Bishop, 1979).

Elaboration of the psychosocial influences and neurophysiological mechanisms underlying these events are considered in *Mind as Healer, Mind as Slayer* (Pelletier, 1977) as well as in chapter five of *Holistic Medicine* (Pelletier, 1979). While the earlier data were highly preliminary and suggestive, these more recent research findings have confirmed the role of psychosocial influences in both premature morbidity and mortality. One physician who has extended his observations beyond the realm of cardiovascular disease is S. J. Breiner of Michigan State University. In his research Breiner examined the mortality statistics for the leading causes of death for both men and women in the United States for the year 1971. For his study Breiner analyzed both the pathophysiology and psychosocial influences pertaining to "accidents, suicide, congenital malformations, diseases of infancy, cancer, diabetes, pneumonia and influenza, arteriosclerosis, cirrhosis, emphysema, heart disease, and stroke." His conclusion is quite remarkable:

> By weighing the physical and the psychological elements in each category of mortality statistics, new percentages emerge for the cause of death. As a result the "psychological" category (conscious and unconscious) becomes the number one epidemiologic "toxic agent," accounting for approximately 40% of all deaths [Breiner, 1978].

Such findings are clearly controversial and subject to interpretation but it is likely that Breiner's findings will be extended beyond cardiovascular disease into a wide range of premature mortality. A number of influences remain highly speculative. For instance, the often discussed impact of retirement upon morbidity and mortality has led to inconclusive and inconsistent results. One study found "elevated mortality after early retirement" but also determined that "normal retirement, per se, is not obviously detrimental to survival" (Haynes et al., 1978). Psychosocial influences, occurrences such as retirement and death of a spouse, and the alarming rate of increasing suicides among the elderly constitute an important area for research as well as public policy.

Some of these psychosocial factors can be dealt with only on a political and public policy level. Studies in Massachusetts of "zones of excess mortality" have concluded that ". . . the extreme mortality rates in these areas described are unlikely to be the result of chance, but are part of a biosocial gradient, with lesser degrees of social deprivation tending to be accompanied by lesser rates of mortality." Individuals with excessive mortality in Massachusetts tend to live in "severe economic deprivation, poor housing, a mixture of overcrowding and loneliness, family breakdown, personal disability and social instability" (Fielding and Russo, 1977). Many of the population are elderly and issues of cause and effect are clouded. There is a well-known "drift hypothesis" which shows that people with fewer economic resources move into economically deprived zones after their health has begun to decline. Social conditions of deprivation are clearly among the most potent influences on health and longevity, particularly among the elderly. These conditions can provide justification for increased medical care expenditures or else prompt the more formidable endeavor of modifying the destructive psychosocial conditions.

Prospects for the Future

Improved health and longevity in the future will come from changes in lifestyle and environmental and socioeconomic factors rather than from the medical care system. The psychosocial structure of particular groups in the United States, the cultural systems evident in centenarian communities, and the lifestyles of women can serve as prototypes for efforts to curb the incidence of premature morbidity and mortality in our society. It is important to note that the most cogent critiques of the present unrealistic and excessive dependency upon medicine to deliver health and longevity come from within medicine itself. Robert S. Mendelsohn of the University of Illinois has written a radical critique of medicine in *Confessions of a Medical Heretic* (1979):

> I believe that more than 90 percent of modern medicine could disappear from the face of the earth—doctors, hospitals, drugs, and equipment—and the effect on our health would be immediate and beneficial. . . . Modern medicine is now better geared for killing people than for healing them. . . . We're using drugs and surgery in cases where they were never meant to be used . . . . The dangers of bottle-feeding are well documented. . . . 90 percent of the major categories of tranquilizers are not just useless, they are absolutely hazardous. . . . Immunizations are very controversial inside of medicine. Even the polio immunization. Sabin and Salk point out that three fourths of all the cases of polio in the last ten years have been vaccine-induced. . . . The great advantage that chiropractors have is that by law they are not permitted to use drugs or surgery, and therefore, they cannot do as much harm as the physician can. . . . Linus Pauling now has some statistics that show that life expectancy is dropping for adults, and I think he's right [Mendelsohn, 1980].

These statements may seem extreme, especially when taken collectively, but they are based on hard data and empirical research. While Mendelsohn's statements have been viewed as needlessly castigating by many in the medical profession, many others acknowledge that his writing has verbalized their latent fears and concerns.

The major significance of such criticism is to pose serious questions which have been ignored or pushed aside. Since the predominant state of research and public policy ignores such issues and their implications, it is inevitable that they be stated in stark and controversial terms. The medical profession needs to be roused from a lethargic and inattentive state to greater clarity and awareness. All of the above observations, or accusations, depending on your point of view, are symptomatic of a profound period of transition in medicine and society at large.

The task of the next century will be to alter the conditions which have given rise to the afflictions of civilization and prevented the human species from attaining its full biological potential. The exceptions to these conditions need to be researched more thoroughly for indications of their reversibility. Increased longevity and decreased infant mortality, however, present a different threat to the world. Global population is more than 4 billion, compared with 2 billion only 50 years ago. By the year 2000 the population is projected to be close to 6 billion with an increase of more than 90 million people. Declines in mortality and increased longevity will enhance this phenomenon. Certain cynical analysts feel we should be content with the present average life expectancy. However, the population dangers of increased longevity and decreased infant mortality could be offset by lower birth rates and redistribution of planetary material resources and food supplies. In China, with more than one fifth of the world's population, the population growth rate has dropped from 2.3 to 1.2 percent in the years 1971 to 1978 (Population Reference Bureau, 1980). Trends such as this have not defused the population bomb but suggest that the dire projections are not inevitable.

At the conclusion of his classic *Youth in Old Age,* Harvard University gerontologist Alexander Leaf made population regulation a prerequisite of increased longevity. Any attempt to extend the present life expectancy and to cut down the excessive mortality of the afflictions of civilization needs to be carefully weighed in the context of global population control and equitable distribution of resources.

> If the life span can be extended with vigorous, enjoyable, active years, then the population control should be on the birth rate. The obligation must be to the living, not to the unborn who potentially are almost limitless in numbers. If we improve the quality of life for the present living, those born later will share the benefit. . . . I believe that the same conditions are necessary for all to have a full life regardless of length. It seems never too soon to create the conditions [Leaf, 1975].

There is no denying that the potential hazards of overpopulation could far outweigh the benefits of extended longevity: increased demand upon limited food and energy resources, increased psychosocial stress, and overall familial and cultural disruption. However, dire consequences such as these are preventable since they would result only if the social, political, ecological, and economic conditions which now exist were to remain inflexible. If longevity is achieved through well-thought-out social change and combined with control of population, then the negative consequences can be avoided. By contrast, a blind pursuit of pharmaceutical or biotechnological panaceas with no thought to their social, ecological, and economic implications might produce an extension of life expectancy that was worthless in terms of quality of life.

The definition of an epidemic is a disease affecting 6 percent of a given population, and a pandemic is one affecting more than that. Psychosocial influences limiting health and longevity are of epidemic and pandemic proportions. Just as major modifications were undertaken in the external environment to stem the infectious plagues, equally significant measures need to be undertaken with both the physical and psychosocial environment to eliminate the modern plagues. We are in a major period of transformation, evidenced in myriad ways: global ecology movements, antinuclear demonstrations, human potential movements, gay liberation, new-age politics, proliferating spiritual communes, maturation of holistic medicine, and most significantly in the women's rights movement. Collectively these represent an emerging consciousness and suggest an evolutionary trend. Profound changes in human lifestyle could result in a balance of male and female longevity and a fulfillment of the biological potential for both sexes. It will be of critical importance for men to learn from the healthier, newly awakened lifestyles of women, rather than for dysfunctional male lifestyles to be preserved to the detriment of all.

Twentieth-century consciousness was characterized by overemphasis on the rational, self-assertive, linear, and scientific mode of awareness. There was an emphasis on dominion over nature and scientific progress outstripping archaic religions. Longevity is a matter of regaining a balance between the masculine, Yang, and feminine, Yin, modes of the human species in the twenty-first century. Through a life-preserving balance of activity and contemplation, competition and cooperation, rational knowledge with intuitive wisdom, the human species can attain its longevity potential.

SIX

Nutrition and Longevity: A Question of Balance

For nearly half a century nutritional and dietary influences have been demonstrated to extend the life expectancy of laboratory animals. Morris H. Ross of the Institute for Cancer Research in Philadelphia accomplished the longest recorded life extension of rats, to more than 1,800 days, corresponding to approximately 180 years in human life, through dietary restriction (Ross, 1976). Although there has been an abundance of research with laboratory animals confirming results such as these, their profound implications for human longevity has been inadequately addressed. It is evident that these dietary manipulations are too extreme to apply to humans, since there are undesirable effects such as stunted growth, delayed maturation, musculoskeletal compromise, "increased risk of bacterial infection and impairment of specific functional systems" (Kent, 1978). Nevertheless, there are major, unanswered questions regarding the optimum diet in youth, young adulthood, middle age, and advanced age. Nutritional needs are subject to variations due to psychological and physiological changes that accompany aging. Documented instances of changes in human physiology which both affect and are affected by nutrition are: ". . . a decline in efficiency of renal function; a redistribution of body content, with a decrease in protein and an increase in fat; and changes in the nervous system, particularly the gradual loss of neurons in the brain (Busse, 1978). Findings such as these raise the question whether moderate dietary adaptation throughout the life of the individual could influence the occurrence of the degenerative diseases, as well as exert an influence on longevity.

Human nutrition is an exceedingly complex and increasingly controversial area of research and clinical applications. Controversy arises not necessarily out of objective disagreement but due to the fact that nutrition is an emotionally charged subject and is inextricably linked to social, political, and economic considerations. This chapter is neither an exhaustive nor comprehensive consideration of dietary influences on health but rather a suggestion of how the basic principles and procedures discussed in *Holistic Medicine* (Pelletier, 1979) can be modified and adapted to enhance an individual's likelihood of attaining the maximum life expectancy and beyond in a state of optimum health. The following issues will be addressed: (1) the psychosocial, political, and economic context of nutrition; (2) the relationship between physiological changes in the human alimentary tract, food consumption and absorption, and subsequent health and longevity; (3) specific disorders which increase with aging and which are preventable, in part, through adequate nutrition. Among the disorders considered are obesity, organic brain syndromes, and cardiovascular disease; (4) the Pritikin diet and exercise program as an example of an optimum diet; (5) the documented capacity of specific dietary restrictions and antioxidant supplementation significantly to enhance true longevity. Finally, the chapter concludes with (6) a look at the Tarahumara Indians as living prototypes of a culture with an optimum diet and consequent longevity. This last section is a preview of Chapter VIII which will deal with other long-lived societies.

The Context of Nutrition

Most of the research concerning dietary influences during development has focused on physiological changes in the alimentary system
from the mouth through the gastrointestinal tract, and thus fails to
consider the interaction between lifestyle, economic restrictions, and
subsequent dietary practices. These issues are clearly acknowledged
in the government publication *Dietary Goals for the United States*
(McGovern, 1977) as well as in *Healthy People: The United States
Surgeon General's Report on Health Promotion and Disease*
(Califano, 1979), and they will assume even greater importance as the
emphasis on prevention grows over the next decade.

Another concept frequently neglected in discussions of nutrition
is that of "biochemical individuality" as propounded by Roger J.
Williams. ". . . although the kinds of nutrients needed by all human
beings are the same, the amounts needed differ from person to person" (Williams, 1978). When the wide range of individual variability
in metabolic requirements is acknowledged, a degree of objectivity
is restored in the midst of rapidly proliferating, unfounded opinion.
Although individual nutritional requirements were elaborated by
Williams in *Biochemical Individuality* (1956) they have not been
widely adopted since they stand in direct opposition to the plethora
of "faddist" diets which ". . . suggest that certain foods are good for
all people at all times without allowing for individual requirements
or for the variation in individuals' normal eating habits" (Williams,
1978).

In navigating through the conflicting opinions, several books
which are extremely useful are *The Heinze Handbook of Nutrition:
A Comprehensive Treatise on Nutrition in Health and Disease* (Burton, 1976), *Handbook of Nutritional Science* (Williams, 1977), and
Diet and Nutrition: A Holistic Approach (1978) by physician Rudolph
Ballentine. From these books it is clear that just as there is an
enormous range considered normal in the aortic branching of the
human heart, size and position of the stomach, as well as virtually

all human biological systems, there is also a wide range of normal individual dietary requirements. Computer assessments of an individual's dietary consumption, food preparation, vitamin supplementation, lifestyle, and level of physical activity is a promising step toward adapting global dietary prescriptions to an individual's actual dietary requirements. Administration of these assessments must be undertaken in a context where the results are discussed and adapted further to individual dietary practices, whether those are of the "omnivore," "lactovegetarian," "lacto-ovo-vegetarian," or "total vegetarian" (Crosby, 1975) variants.

Compounding the delicate interactions between metabolic individuality, lifestyle preferences, and psychosocial factors is the fact that these requirements and practices vary in the course of normal human development. By acknowledging this complexity, and gaining some understanding of the biochemistry of the aging and regenerative processes discussed in Chapters III and IV, it is possible to examine the research literature and explore the interaction between nutrition and longevity. Despite the complexity of nutrition a limited number of dietary practices appear to share the common effect of reducing the incidence of a wide range of chronic diseases as well as enhancing longevity. Emphasis here is not on diet as a therapeutic approach to obesity, alcoholism, psychopathology, or eternal youth but rather on the role of dietary principles throughout the life of the individual in leading to optimum health and longevity. Qualitative and quantitative differences in the longevity of laboratory animals have demonstrated that the degree to which dietary influences are effective is dependent on:

1) the specificity in dietary requirements of the individual and the manner with which it is used for growth, 2) the stage of life when the dietary manipulation is begun, 3) the genetically determined growth potential and 4) the magnitude of the long-lasting effects of a prior regimen [Ross, 1977].

Not only have such dietary restrictions doubled the life expectancy of laboratory animals but they decreased the rate, frequency, severity, or time of onset for numerous age-related disorders, including some malignant tumors, autoimmune diseases, diabetes, cardiovascular disease, including myocardial fibrosis and periarteritis of mesenteric arteries, aging of collagen, hyperlipidemia, glomerulonephritis, and a range of other disorders. By contrast, the incidence of these diseases in overfed and obese laboratory animals is greatly increased, to as high as 40 percent above normal. From these studies it is evident that "There may well be periods of life when an organism is especially sensitive to one set of conditions and another period for another set" (Ross, 1977). This concept of developmental specificity is of great significance since it indicates that the influence of nutrition on longevity is a lifelong process and that specific steps can be initiated throughout the life cycle. Much of the conflicting data regarding dietary factors may be due to global prescriptives being inflexibly applied when specificity and timing are the real concerns. Just as the discovery of receptor sights, which are sensitive to particular molecular structures, has emphasized the importance of exact thresholds of response in the neuroendocrine system, the concept of developmental specificity explains why dietary excesses or restrictions at specific periods in life can have particular negative and positive effects.

Roger J. Williams has suggested the term "genetotrophic diseases" from the Greek *genesis* (birth) and *trophikos* (feeding), which suggests that ". . . every individual has, because of genetic make-up, distinctive nutritional needs that must be met to achieve optimum well-being" (Williams, 1978). When these changing needs are not met, then the genetotrophic diseases, ranging from neuroendocrine disorders to alcoholism, become manifest, particularly in advanced age. On a more positive note, "If the genetotrophic theory is correct, it should be possible to meet the nutritional needs of any individual at any stage of life, provided these needs are known" (Williams, 1978). While this is a theoretical possibility, clinical application is limited at the present time.

One exception is the Nutrition Program for Older Americans (NPOA) developed by physician Donald M. Watkin of the Administration on Aging under the Department of Health, Education, and Welfare. Five basic principles underly the NPOA, and these are excellent guidelines for any comprehensive program:

First, nutrition, health, and aging form an integral triad affecting all. . . . Second, in North America, malnutrition is a sequitur of disease, whether physical, metabolic, emotional, or attitudinal. . . . Third, since aging is a lifelong process, good nutrition and health practices must be applied throughout life. This basis will become effective only when the present image of the aged improves to the point that younger persons will strive for effective longevity. . . . Fourth, changes in lifestyle to avoid risks have positive value. This basis requires professional and political leadership if it is to become widely adopted. . . . Fifth, acute illnesses and accidents require immediate attention to nutritional and other factors if needless morbidity and mortality are to be avoided. . . . All these bases are the infrastructure for other actions directed at improving the image of today's aged and thereby diminishing the fatalism of younger persons and augmenting their determination to adopt lifestyles compatible with long, active, happy and productive lives [Watkin, 1978].

These postulates and their implementation through the requisite political and economic institutions such as Medicare and Medicaid are the basis for any national program concerned with the nutritional aspects of aging and longevity as a whole. Health-inducing lifestyles and nutritional practices, even when adopted late in life, will improve the effective longevity of aging individuals. Information concerning these practices is not widespread or well understood and "much sad experience to date has indicated that the elderly and their families and friends have excessive implicit faith in pills and injections but very little understanding of the critical need for appropriate nutrition" (Watkin, 1978). While the greatest efficacy results when nutrition and dietary practices are adopted early, there is evidence that:

Changes in lifestyles have been postulated to increase significantly the average age at death, even when initiated at age 45. No acceptable data have indicated success associated with such changes in persons aged 60 or older. Nonetheless, it is hard to believe that elimination of alcohol and drug abuse, of use of tobacco, of gluttony, of diets high in fat, of food faddism and medical quackery, of insufficient physical activity, of too little rest or sleep, of the lack of regularly scheduled relaxation and recreation, of careless driving and failure to wear seat belts, and of failure to seek and follow qualified and indicated medical diagnosis and treatment could not improve morbidity and mortality statistics among the elderly [Watkin, 1978].

These observations and programs are the logical base for a program of optimum nutrition conducive to effective longevity.

Access to adequate food sources does not appear to be enough, since an optimum diet does require work and fairly diligent adherence. One unfortunate finding in animal experimentation reveals that: "Rats, permitted to choose freely among three different diets, selected precisely those combinations which maximized their incidence of degenerative disease and minimized their life span. Some even shifted dietary preferences during the course of life to select precisely those diets which were the most noxious at that particular time" (Stunkard, 1976). An overabundance of food choices apparently constitutes a potentially lethal hazard for animals as well as the human species.

Diet and Aging

What are the disorders related to nutrition which lead to premature morbidity and mortality in the general population and what can be done to prevent their occurrence? Among the more prominent incidences of these disorders are atherosclerosis and coronary heart disease, gastrointestinal tract disorders, certain forms of cancer, osteoporosis, obesity, chronic fatigue, and a host of subclinical deficiency disorders. While assertions such as these were formerly relegated to obscure journals, recent government publications such as the McGovern Committee report, *Dietary Goals for the United States* (1977), as well as statements by the American Medical Association (*American Medical News,* 1979) and the National Cancer Institute (Broad, 1979) are clear indications that that era has passed. Precedent-breaking guidelines suggested by the National Cancer Institute are in keeping with the *Dietary Goals for the United States* (1977) and specify that ". . . fat intake be limited to a third of total calories, that more whole grains and fresh fruits and vegetables be eaten to provide necessary vitamins and minerals, and that alcohol consumption be limited to 2 oz. a day" (*Medical World News,* 1979c). Overall, these reports have tended to focus on the prevention of diseases known to be associated with certain dietary practices. Rather than discuss specific diseases and their relationship to diet, this chapter focuses on dietary practices which appear not only to prevent certain diseases but to enhance longevity.

The American Health Foundation in New York City has undertaken a study of 15,000 children in sixteen countries on the assumption that health risk factors in children are directly related to chronic disease in adults. According to AHF president, Ernst L. Wynder, the preliminary results are alarming. Data on the children's height, weight, blood pressure, skin-fold thickness, serum cholesterol, and physical fitness indicate "Cancer, heart disease and stroke are going to be even more prevalent when today's children reach maturity." Hope lies in the fact that "Children can be trained to live an appropriate lifestyle just as they can be trained to read and write" (*Medical World News,* 1979c). Deciding what is to be taught to both children and adults is likely to constitute an area of great scientific and social controversy. One means of moving toward a consensus is to adapt broad dietary guidelines and check these through periodic computer assessments sensitized to the physiological changes attendant to normal aging. Although this is not possible at present, there is a basis for such an undertaking in specific areas. Physiological changes in the central nervous system, cardiovascular functions, renal function, gastrointestinal system, and musculoskeletal functions appear to dictate corresponding changes in dietary requirements.

Considerable research has focused on changes in the central nervous system due to aging:

> Brain weight decreases linearly with age. . . . The brain atrophies during aging . . . caused by a loss of cells in the central nervous system. . . . Other substances and brain cells also change during aging. . . . There is no longer any doubt that significant ultrastructural alterations in nerve and glial cells occur in the aging brain. Among these are increased instances of dendritic degen-

eration, distortion, or swelling. . . . Neurotransmitter uptake capacity declines with aging. . . . Studies have only recently been initiated to study possible changes in brain neurotransmission during aging, but many aspects of this process seem to be altered during senescence. . . . The most striking changes described thus far appear to involve the catecholamine neurotransmitters dopamine and norepinephrine. [Lytle and Altar, 1979].

Extensive research over the last ten years at the Massachusetts Institute of Technology has clearly indicated that brain chemistry and function can be influenced by a single meal. Diet has a marked effect upon the formation of the primary neurotransmitters in the brain since it determines how much of the chemical precursors for these neurotransmitters is actually available. Specifically, the neurotransmitter serotonin is immediately affected by the amount of its dietary precursor, the amino acid tryptophan; norepinephrine is influenced by the dietary amino acid tyrosine; and acetylcholine is determined by its precursor, choline. Among the disorders associated with acetylcholine deficiency are tardive dyskinesia, a chronic twitching of the limbs induced by long-term use of antipsychotic medications, and some aspects of senility and memory deficit. John D. Fernstrom of MIT has observed, "Choline is normally present in the diet as a constituent of lecithin (a fatty acid found in eggs and fish). Eating lecithin raises blood and brain choline levels and stimulates acetylcholine formation" (Fernstrom, 1979). Relationships such as these exist between all ten to fifteen neurotransmitter compounds and their dietary precursors, although the direct relationships are usually more complex than the connection between choline and acetylcholine. As a note, commercial lecithin supplements provide very minimal amounts of choline, while research-quality lecithin is both highly purified and quite expensive.

Among the possible future applications of such dietary measures on central nervous system functions are supplements of tryptophan to "stimulate growth hormone secretion, to produce analgesia, and to lower blood pressure" and ingestion of tyrosine, which "elicits a dramatic reduction in blood pressure. This effect appears to be caused by the stimulation of norepinephrine synthesis within the brain" (Fernstrom, 1979). Dietary supplementation of natural amino acids and other substances may become an effective, relatively inexpensive, safe, nonpharmaceutical means of treating and preventing a range of age-related disorders. "The idea that normal diets can affect brain metabolism is becoming established. . . . Many researchers . . . are investigating the possibility that the synthesis of brain products other than serotonin, acetylcholine, and the catecholamines may also be affected by diet" (Kolata, 1976). Since dietary factors influence the abundance or deficiency of the precursors of these neurotransmitters, then it is more important rather than less important that elderly individuals consume an optimum diet. That is not the case at present. ". . . socioeconomic factors, such as poverty isolation, or ignorance about good dietary practices, may cause the individual to select foods that are nutritionally inadequate for normal health . . . nutrition-induced changes in the central nervous systems of the elderly may be more insidious and commonplace than once was thought" (Lytle and Altar, 1979). Through adequate diet perhaps the incidence of central nervous system deterioration evidenced in premature senility, memory impairment, and other decreased abilities in higher-order mental functions can be effectively reduced.

Increases in the proportion of fat in the human body, as well as elevations in blood pressure and serum cholesterol, are so pervasive that they are often considered to be inevitable consequences of aging. Since these are among the major contributing factors to coronary artery and coronary heart disease, the inescapable conclusion would be that cardiovascular disease would remain the leading cause of morbidity and mortality in the postindustrial nations. However, there are "populations in the world that age to the life-span appropriate to the human species without developing clinical evidence of atherosclerosis" and "there is considerable difference in the prevalence rate in various parts of the world, probably related to factors other than age per se" (Bierman, 1978). Recent decreases in the incidence of cardiovascular disease in the United States are at least partially attributable to a decline in fat consumption during the years 1965 to 1977. There is adequate evidence of deviation from the ostensibly inevitable development of the risk factors associated with cardiovascular disease to indicate that while the incidence is an "average" it is not necessarily "normal."

Even if body weight remains constant throughout life, there are changes in body composition. As an individual ages the caloric requirements decrease because of decreased physical activity and decreased cell mass. Under these conditions there is a decline in the lean body mass of muscle and bone with a reciprocal increase in the proportion of fat tissue, sometimes resulting in obesity. Active protein tissue is slowly replaced by fat even in a person who is not overweight. Compounding this trend is the fact that "the basic metabolic rate declines 16% between 30 and 70 years of age . . . caloric requirement decreases approximately one third . . . therefore, gradual loss of weight is desirable after 60 years of age" (Busse, 1978). However, weight increase is the tendency. According to physician Myron Winick of the Institute of Human Nutrition at Columbia University School of Medicine, "The latest RDA (set forth in 1974) calls for a 10% reduction in caloric intake once a person is over fifty years old, though the basis for this reduction has not yet been precisely determined" (Winick, 1978). Consistent findings from laboratory animal and human research confirm that "The heavier the animal, the shorter was its life span" (Kent, 1978). Data from life insurance actuarial tables confirm that "leanness in humans may also decrease morbidity and enhance longevity" (Schlenker et al., 1973). As early as 1959 the American Society of Actuaries published a massive report entitled *The Build and Blood Pressure Study* which analyzed the life-spans of over 170,000 people. From the report, the persons who were five to ten pounds under the average weight for their height and build exhibited the longest life expectancy and the occurrence of many common diseases were delayed until much later in life. There is a clear necessity of decreasing total caloric consumption during the course of adult development but at the same time, the nutritional requirements not only remain constant but actually increase in some instances. Protein requirements remain relatively constant: ". . . minimum protein needs of healthy adults do not change significantly during a normal lifetime. The recommended daily protein intake for healthy adult men and women of almost any age is 56 g and 46 g respectively" (Winick, 1978). In laboratory experimentation and observations of human dietary practices there is some suggestion that a diet relatively restricted in protein at certain early stages and with later moderate protein intake will result in increased longevity.

Consumption of Fats

Closely related to the excessive consumption of saturated fats and refined carbohydrates among the elderly is hyperlipidemia, or elevated serum cholesterol levels. Normal concentrations of serum cholesterol are considered to be 230 mg/100 ml from age 1 to 19, 240 for 20 to 29, 270 for 30 to 39, 310 for 40 to 49, and 330 for 50 and over. To a degree, these levels are genetically determined through cholesterol production in the human body. Values in excess of these levels are considered to indicate hyperlipidemia. While there is great concern over the relationship between hyperlipidemia and cardiovascular disease, it is evident that there is not a one-to-one relationship. Hyperlipidemia remains a risk factor but not as powerful a predictor as cardiac arrhythmias, heart enlargement, or electrocardiographic abnormalities. Furthermore, both the concentrations and effects of elevated serum cholesterol levels are modifiable to a degree through diet and physical exercise. Deep relaxation reduces hypercholesterolemia or elevated serum cholesterol levels (Cooper and Aygen, 1979), as does ingestion of yogurt (Hepner et al., 1979). Cholesterol and serum levels are also modified through the presence of high-density lipoproteins (HDL) which are increased in turn by "moderate alcohol consumption" (Darby, 1978) as well as exercise (Mann, 1977). Even though all the facts are not in yet, it does appear beneficial to reduce overall saturated fat consumption, particularly in middle age and beyond. According to Jean Mayer:

> . . . I wish it were true that the production of cholesterol by the body is automatically decreased by the same amount that is consumed. But, again, although there is some adjustment of cholesterol production in relation to cholesterol intake, the fact is this correction is far less than complete. The consumption of large amounts of dietary cholesterol still increases blood cholesterol (1976).

Overall experiments clearly show a significant effect of dietary cholesterol upon subsequent serum cholesterol levels. "The relation between dietary cholesterol and serum cholesterol levels is curvilinear, with the magnitude of effect decreasing at higher intakes" (Hausman, 1978). Apparently, within the normal ranges of consumption of dietary cholesterol, the potential negative effects are most pronounced (Mattson et al., 1972; Keys et al., 1965; Porter et al., 1971).

Planning a diet low in cholesterol and saturated fatty acids can be complex, however. While the term "polyunsaturated fatty acids" has virtually become synonymous with prevention of cardiovascular disease in both popular and medical journals, recent research indicates a potential hazard in polyunsaturated oils when they have been refined out of their naturally occurring state in grains, vegetables, and fruits. In *Diet and Nutrition,* Rudolph Ballentine cites such studies: "A closer look at the people who have changed to vegetable oils has shown that while deaths from heart attacks decreased, overall mortality rates did not fall. As deaths from heart disease fell, deaths from cancer began to increase . . . an unusual frequency of malignant melanoma" (Ballentine, 1978). Findings such as these are consistent with the observation by biochemists that free radical interactions occur frequently in the oxidation of polyunsaturated fatty acids (Harman, 1978). Data derived from these studies are not definitive nor should they be taken as a source of alarm. However, the potential hazards of refined polyunsaturated oils clearly need further study.

Finally, there are other factors associated with dietary modification by the elderly which can be briefly considered: (1) noted Harvard University nutritionist Jean Mayer has observed that "Deficiencies in the fat-soluble vitamins A, D, and E in the aged are frequently due to consumption of a diet very low in fat, to the interference in absorption caused by habitual ingestion of mineral oil as a laxative (the mineral oil drains away the fat-soluble vitamins), or to disease" (Mayer, 1974); (2) "What elderly people eat is greatly influenced by real or imaginary connections between the food ingested and the response of the body, and overconcern with bodily functions may become a problem. Loss of teeth, unsteady hands, and other disabilities must be considered in the preparation and serving of food" (Busse, 1978); and most importantly, (3) "The decreased need for quantity of food means that the *quality* of the diet must be higher than for younger, more active people" (Mayer, 1974). Reduced consumption of saturated fats, reduced body weight, moderation in balancing ratios of saturated to polyunsaturated fats, while maintaining a high quality of nutrients in the diet, are among the concerns which must be incorporated into a diet planned for older people.

Another factor in coronary heart disease, known for over twenty-five years, has received increasing attention. Men with coronary heart disease exhibit low blood levels of high-density lipoprotein (HDL). Proteins are required to transport fats such as cholesterol through the relatively watery medium of the circulatory system. There are two basic forms of the proteins involved in this transport function, which are HDL and low-density lipoprotein (LDL). Both are produced by the intestine and liver and secreted into the bloodstream where they bond with serum cholesterol. However, there is a critical difference in HDL and LDL function: "LDL seems to serve as a delivery truck, picking up cholesterol and depositing it in cells, including those of our blood vessels. HDL, on the other hand, apparently resembles a garbage truck that collects the excess cholesterol —perhaps even removing it from cells—and (probably) carries the material back to the liver, where it can be excreted" (Bennett, 1978). From these findings physician William Castelli, who is Director of the Framingham Study, has formulated a more accurate cardiovascular risk index based on the ratios of total cholesterol to HDL cholesterol. (The lower the ratio the better, since that indicates a higher percentage of HDL.) Using these ratios, Castelli has observed that for individuals in the United States:

> . . . an average man has a ratio of 5.0; in women, who suffer less from heart disease, the average is about 4.5. Babies are born with a ratio of about 2.3, a value that adults can only approach, it appears, if they adhere to strict vegetarian diets. . . . [The] goal for anyone with a value above 4.5 should be to bring the ratio back down to that level. A ratio in the range of 7 to 9 doubles the standard risk of a heart attack [Bennett, 1978].

Overall, women tend to have higher HDL levels than men at all ages after puberty and this difference may help to explain partially the greater resistance of women to cardiovascular disease.

Details of HDL and LDL function have been discussed in chapters six and seven of *Holistic Medicine* (Pelletier, 1979). There are specific measures which lower the serum cholesterol to HDL cholesterol ratio such as cessation of smoking, caloric reduction, reducing animal fat and cholesterol consumption, ingesting fish, garlic, brewer's yeast, lecithin, and exercise. Charles Glueck and his colleagues at the University of Cincinnati College of Medicine have identified two groups of people who appear to be genetically endowed with either high HDL or low LDL concentrations. In either case their life-spans are as much as five to ten years longer than average. "It does not seem to matter whether the HDL are up or the LDL are down. Either way they are protected" (Marx, 1979e). The results of Glueck's studies are based on data derived from 18 kindred of families with extensive histories of "familial hypobeta and familial hyperalpha lipoproteinemia" (Glueck et al., 1976) or families with an LDL to HDL ratio of approximately 1:1. In a related study Glueck and his colleagues tested "16 octogenarian kindred" (Glueck et al., 1978) and found that the offspring of families where "either two siblings or a parent and child lived to age 80" did evidence elevated HDL levels. From these studies Glueck has hypothesized a "longevity syndrome" since he has observed that the "people's lifestyles— their diet or whether they smoke, for example—do not seem to matter either" (Marx, 1979e). As with all research which attempts definitively to sort nature from nurture, this hypothesis remains to be proven. It is likely that the genetic predisposition can be greatly modified or even negated by subsequent psychosocial and environmental influences.

Alcohol

"Moderate alcohol consumption" (Darby, 1978) is one dietary factor found to increase HDL levels. "Moderate" is defined as the equivalent of 1.5 ounces of pure alcohol, which translates into "4 ounces of 80 proof whiskey, roughly equivalent to 40 ounces of ordinary American beer (4.5 percent), . . . or half a bottle (four 3.5 ounce glasses) of table wine" (Darby, 1978). Although there is considerable research evidence that these levels are safe and moderate, half that amount may be a wiser quota. While biochemistry may allow a certain level, the difficulty many people have in regulating alcohol consumption makes it exceedingly unwise to encourage the levels suggested by Darby's findings. Even half that amount requires caution. Certainly there are safer and equally effective means to alter HDL concentrations. Excessive levels of alcohol have a reverse effect on health. "Six or seven drinks a day for a period as short as two weeks can throw the digestive system into reverse . . . the intestine will go into a secretory state where it will pour out liquids, resulting in a loss of minerals and vitamins. . . . The public thinks cirrhosis of the liver is the main danger of drinking. But approximately 16 percent of the people who drink get it. A much, much larger proportion develop the nutritional or intestinal effects of alcohol" (Mekhjian, 1979). Nevertheless, there are major studies indicating benefits to be derived from moderate alcohol consumption: (1) a study of ischemic heart disease in eighteen developed countries indicates a "strong negative correlation" between wine consumption and subsequent heart disease in the populations (Leger et al., 1979); (2) "a strong negative association between moderate alcohol consumption (up to 60 ml per day), mainly from beer, and the risk of nonfatal myocardial infarction and death from coronary heart disease" (Yano et al., 1977); (3) positive benefits of moderate alcohol consumption with postcoronary patients (Klatsky et al., 1979); and (4) positive effects with eighty long-term psychogeriatric patients who consumed three ounces of wine per day for ten weeks with a six-month follow-up indicating "reduction in chloral hydrate to induce sleep" (Mishara and Kastenbaum, 1974) as well as other positive behavioral effects. Alcohol is so frequently abused in our society that any indication of its positive effects in moderation draws controversy. However, it is far more constructive to acknowledge and apply its benefits rather than attempt to undertake a moralistic prohibition. Caution needs to be exercised especially in the offspring of alcoholic parents, since they are more sensitive to alcohol. "Blood acetalhyde concentrations were significantly elevated after a moderate ethanol dose" in twenty men with family histories of alcoholism (Schuckit and Rayses, 1979). It must also be pointed out that Mormons, Amish,

Seventh-Day Adventists, and other groups show considerable health and longevity in the virtual or total abstinence of alcohol consumption.

Alimentary Tract Deterioration

Alterations in the stomach, gastrointestinal tract, and renal or kidney functions in advanced age also have a pronounced effect upon nutrition and subsequent health. General atrophy of the gastric system and the diminished secretion of hydrochloric acid by the stomach's parietal cells results in reduced absorption of iron and vitamin B12. An immediate result is iron-deficiency anemia, which is very common in the aged of both sexes and compounds the problem of poor nutrition in the elderly. For vitamin B12 the potential detriments are even greater since partial deficiencies in B12 have been linked to the chronic fatigue and mental confusion noted in older people. "In a double blind study of 35 elderly subjects ranging in age from 65 to 90 years, all of whom had previously complained of fatigue . . . researchers observed that on administration of vitamin B12, the symptoms of fatigue disappeared in 89% of the participants" (Schlenker et al., 1973). In actual clinical practice, the issue of partial B vitamin deficiencies is of great significance: "If the confusion of vitamin deficiency is misdiagnosed as an irreversible effect of old age, the elderly person may be wrongly confined to a nursing home. If the diet there is inadequate and the desire to eat is further reduced by lack of companionship, the patient's mental condition may go from bad to worse" (Mayer, 1974).

Another factor affecting nutrition in the elderly is impaired renal or kidney function. According to Myron Winick, renal function is gradually impaired in three primary ways: "(1) the renal blood flow and glomerular filtration rate (GFR) decline; (2) the maximal tubular excretory capacity (Tm) for glucose and para-aminohippuric acid (PAH) declines; (3) the ability to form either concentrated or diluted urine decreases" (Winick, 1978). Each decline in renal function has an effect on dietary and nutritional requirements for the elderly, primarily in regard to protein and amino acid requirements. While there is some information concerning protein requirements throughout the life cycle, there is very little information known about essential amino acid requirements. Some data is available on the requirements for threonine and tryptophan, two essential amino acids, but there is literally no information about requirements for the remaining six essential amino acids. Another result of declining renal function is decreased ability to eliminate excessive glucose. There is an unfortunate tendency for elderly people actually to increase their refined carbohydrate and sugar consumption during a period of life when decreases are in order. Normal blood sugar concentrations or glucose levels are absolutely essential to the body's cells as a primary energy source. Virtually all of the sugars and more complex carbohydrates consumed in a person's diet are processed into glucose in the body. Metabolism is slow and maintains glucose levels within relatively narrow normal ranges with excess amounts stored in the liver as glycogen or converted into fats for longer-term and often unnecessary storage.

Sugar consumption

While specific glucose levels are essential to biological functions, the excessive consumption of sucrose has markedly negative effects. Sugar or sucrose, a 12-carbon molecule, resulting from the linkage of glucose to fructose, is the product obtained from the refinement of sugar cane or beets. According to recent estimates "the average American consumes an astounding 128 pounds of sugar per year, accounting for almost one quarter of our total calorie intake" (*Harvard Medical School Health Letter,* 1978). Furthermore, the actual consumption of refined sugar has remained relatively stable at just under 100 pounds but the amount of "hidden sugars" as additives to common processed foods has jumped from 13 pounds per person in 1960 to 30 pounds in 1977. These hidden sugars, derived from corn syrup, sugar, and sweetener, are in great abundance in common processed foods: 29% of Heinz tomato ketchup is sugar; 30% of Wish-Bone Russian dressing and 65.4% of Coffee-Mate is sugar, to cite but a few instances. A listing of the "Added Sugar in Processed

Foods" is contained in the August 1979 issue of *Nutrition Action* and is a necessity for anyone wishing to avoid hidden sources of excessive sucrose.

Excessive sugar consumption is not linked in a causal manner to diabetes, although it is thought to be indirectly linked, as a major factor, to obesity. Excessive sucrose or refined carbohydrate intake has many other hazards: (1) "increases the serum cholesterol level and thus makes the individual prone to cardiovascular attack; [2] affects the pancreas resulting in adult diabetes in a certain fraction of older people" (Schlenker, 1973); (3) "blood glucose levels increase progressively with age in most population studies, and hyperglycemia in turn appears to play a significant role in the development of atherosclerosis . . . superimposed environmental factors, such as caloric excess, amplify the age-related effect . . . triglyceride and cholesterol levels in whole populations are also important, since they appear to increase with age" (Bierman, 1978); (4) possible contribution to hypoglycemia. This requires careful interpretation of a five-hour oral glucose tolerance test in order to provide an accurate rather than an impressionistic and fashionable diagnosis.

These findings are of particular importance to the elderly since they often live alone and make extensive use of processed convenience foods which contain hidden sucrose. When an individual is faced with the prospect of cooking for one, the usual solution is to resort to processed foods. Edward W. Busse, Dean of Allied Health Education at the Duke University Medical Center, has investigated the multiple factors influencing elderly diets. One important observation of his is that there is a decline in the number of taste buds per papilla on the tongue beginning at middle age. Taste buds located on the anterior of the tongue which detect sweet and salty tastes are the first to decline. As a result those that detect bitter and sour tastes remain. From these changes Busse has noted, "This progressive loss has been offered as an explanation for the complaint by some older people that all foods taste bitter or sour" (Busse, 1978). The progressive impairment of the ability to gauge sweet or salt tastes may also result in elderly people consuming both excessive sucrose and excessive salt, which is unequivocally related to hypertension. Excessive sucrose consumption can be curbed through labeling of processed foods. Contrary to what is popularly believed, excessive sucrose consumption early in life does not result in a subsequent preference for glucose after the onset of puberty. Judith J. Wurtman and Richard J. Wurtman of the Massachusetts Institute of Technology have found that ". . . the amount of sucrose consumed during the early postnatal period bears no clear relationship to the amount consumed electively during subsequent development and maturation" (Wurtman and Wurtman, 1979). Excessive sucrose consumption is a modifiable aspect of nutrition, dependent upon public education and lifestyle. Altered functions in the stomach, gastrointestinal tract, and renal system in interaction with socioeconomic and nutritional factors make such steps of even greater importance in advanced age.

Fiber

As many as 50% of Americans have lost their teeth by 65 years of age and this percentage increases to 66% by age 75. As dentures replace the lost teeth the elderly increasingly avoid or minimize high fiber foods. This is further exacerbated by a slowing down of the passage of food through the digestive tract. When there is little fiber in the diet ". . . the stomach contents take longer to move through the intestines, and the result is hardening of the stools, constipation, and for some diverticulitis" (Winick, 1978). Constipation is common and often leads to excessive use of mineral oil, contributing to fat soluble vitamin deficiencies, and extensive laxative abuse. As discomforting as these conditions are, they might be a tolerable aspect of a low fiber diet if it were not for further complications. At the present time there is "a growing body of evidence that low fiber intake may contribute to certain gastrointestinal diseases common to the elderly, including diverticulitis, gallbladder disease, and cancer of the colon" (Winick, 1978).

The concern over "dietary fiber" was initiated by noted cancer researcher and surgeon Denis P. Burkitt, who found that certain diseases common in Western countries are virtually unknown in the developing countries of Africa (Burkitt, 1979). Since Burkitt's initial paper in 1973 there has been a great controversy over the benefits of dietary fiber. Although dietary fiber may seem relatively simple, it is an extraordinarily complex matter. Even the terminology has evolved, from "crude fiber" to "dietary fiber." Gene A. Spiller and his colleagues of Syntex Research in Palo Alto have suggested the term "plantix," which refers to "dietary fiber and will include cellulose, lignin, water-insoluble hemicellulose, pectins, gums, and mucilages" (Spiller et al., 1978). Increased dietary fiber has the following effects:

* decreases the intestinal transit-time of the feces (the reproducibility and importance of this finding is still debated),
* increases peristalsis and fecal bulk, thus diluting potential carcinogens and decreasing their contact time with the bowel mucosa,
* possibly affects the composition of the intestinal flora,
* and inhibits the bacterial degradation of bile acids, and possibly other, potentially carcinogenic, fecal constituents [Kochen, 1979].

As might be predicted, there are critics such as the late Franz J. Ingelfinger of Harvard Medical School who has noted, "Nothing catches on as fast in medicine as a dietary fad. . . . The popularity of stuffing oneself with bran, lignin, or even grass will wane" (Ingelfinger, 1979). Undoubtedly there are extreme versions and advocates of dietary fiber, and fad diets are obviously rampant both within and outside of the medical profession. However, in instances where dietary fiber is greatly reduced, moderately increasing its presence appears to be beneficial. Actually, this is in keeping with another statement by Dr. Ingelfinger: "In the long run, the optimum human diets tend to be those that are well balanced" (1979). Moderation is the key, as we have said before. At the present time the average intake of dietary fiber in the United States ranges from 5 to 8 grams per day with vegetarians consuming as much as 12 to 24 grams per day. Precise recommendations for any given individual are dependent upon multiple factors which can be weighed by means of computer-based dietary assessments. A simple increase in dietary fiber so as to prevent or alleviate a specific disorder is as questionable as any other single panacea. In the etiology of the gastrointestinal disorders cited above, there are clearly factors other than dietary fiber in interaction: ". . . besides the reduction in consumption of fiber there are such things as excessive consumption of refined carbohydrates, animal fats, cigarettes, and alcohol, and insufficient physical exercises, just to list a few. Further, if one eats fiber, it may displace other items that would be eaten in its place" (*Medical World News,* 1974).

With these reservations, the preponderance of evidence does clearly indicate that increased dietary fiber is both necessary and beneficial, especially for the elderly. Such evidence includes: (1) research showing that "reduction of caloric intake alone cannot account for the significant protection against colonic carcinoma given by bran" (Fleiszer et al., 1978); (2) data on the danger of laxatives. "All laxatives can produce harmful effects, especially when taken chronically. Prescribing laxatives seems to be as addictive as taking them. . . . It therefore would seem advisable to recommend the use of foods that would provide a moderate amount of fiber in the diets of the elderly to alleviate constipation and improve intestinal function" (Zimring, 1978); (3) After a lengthy consideration of dietary fiber as well as the psychosocial variables which mediate the effects, Robert A. Levine, who is Professor of Medicine and Head of Gastroenterology at New York's Upstate Medical Center in Syracuse, concluded: "Certainly, a high fiber diet is more natural, cheaper, and safer than the laxatives currently available. . . . A high fiber diet can also be recommended as prophylaxis when the problem of constipation is likely to increase, during pregnancy, in the elderly, in chronically hospitalized patients, and immediately following myocardial infarction when straining at stool may be dangerous" (Levine, 1978); (4) Gene A. Spiller and his colleagues of Syntex Research concluded that "It appears that a sensible increase in plantix intake should be recommended to a population consuming a Western-type diet. It also appears that the wisest choice is a balanced mixture of cereal, legume, fruit, and vegetable plantix" (Spiller et al., 1978). A recent article by Denis P. Burkitt recommends the per diem ingestion of "22 grams (about 3/4 oz.) of dietary fiber. This is equivalent to 6 grams of crude fiber from miller's bran . . . recommended as a daily supplement" (Burkitt, 1978). As a further point, Burkitt indicates that "cereal fiber is more effective in lowering cholesterol or blood sugar than fiber from fruits, vegetables, or nuts" (Burkitt, 1978). All the degenerative diseases and the increased mortality they entail do have multiple causes but lack of dietary fiber appears to be an important factor, and one that is easily corrected. While an attempt to prevent or eliminate the range of gastrointestinal disorders among the elderly through dietary fiber supplementation alone is simplistic, such a change seems both simple and beneficial. Furthermore, the negative effects of increased dietary fiber are nil, apart from increased flatulence in the initial stages. It is a readily modifiable factor in nutrition, likely to enhance both health and longevity.

An Optimum Diet

This chapter is neither an exhaustive nor comprehensive consideration of dietary influences on health but rather a suggestion of how the basic principles and procedures discussed in *Holistic Medicine* (Pelletier, 1979) can be modified and adapted to enhance an individual's likelihood of attaining the maximum life expectancy and beyond in a state of optimum health. If dietary and nutritional influences on longevity are to be more fully explored and developed, methods for assessing the complex interactions between lifestyle, economic, alimentary tract, and nutritional variables need to be developed. Computer assessments, in conjunction with face-to-face evaluations and educational programs, though in their infancy, do provide evidence of efficacy as well as the possibility of low cost dissemination. At the present time there is a plethora of nutritional panaceas of highly dubious benefit. In contrast to most of these are the guidelines and practices designed by Nathan Pritikin and in use at his Longevity Center in Santa Monica, California. His approach consists of a twenty-six-day program of a low fat and cholesterol diet and several miles of walking per day. While the dietary aspects of the program are both hotly promoted and condemned, the associated exercise protocol is frequently overlooked or not even mentioned. The effects of the exercise program, psychosocial support system, and patient education interaction with the diet may prove to be more significant than the nutrition program per se. These issues will only be resolved by future research. Although the overall efficacy of the Pritikin Program is yet to be evaluated, it is at least consistent with many of the dietary factors outlined earlier, which have been shown to enhance health and longevity. Details of the Pritikin diet and program are readily available in Pritikin's book *The Pritikin Program for Diet and Exercise* (Pritikin and McGrady, 1979) as well as in numerous abbreviated magazine articles (Isaacs, 1977).

Extensive case histories have been presented to document the Pritikin Program, including a powerful study of three patients in two segments of the CBS program *60 Minutes* (Wallace et al., 1978). These of course do not constitute definitive proof. Nevertheless, the Pritikin Program, as opposed to the Pritikin diet per se, appears to constitute a potentially effective approach to the stabilization and prevention of cardiovascular disease, thus permitting individuals to attain their average life expectancy. Whether or not the program actually reverses cardiovascular disease, specifically the atherosclerotic process, or induces longevity beyond the average life expectancy, remains to be demonstrated. All too often, approaches such as the Pritikin program are either prematurely dismissed by health professionals or uncritically embraced by others.

An interesting sideline to this discussion is the prevalence of a wide variety of dietary practices among health professionals. The public is rarely aware of this. Recently, the highly respected professional newspaper *Medical Tribune* carried an article on its front page entitled, "What the Experts Do—Unofficially—to Dodge Cancer" (McCann, 1978). The gulf between professional opinion and recommendations on the one hand and idiosyncratic personal practices on the other is often denied by the practitioners themselves. During a conference of the American Cancer Society, *Medical Tribune* correspondent Jean McCann asked the authorities who were present to discuss their personal strategies to prevent cancer. "Those polled often are quick to point out that their strategies are based only on scanty scientific evidence and are not to be taken as gospel by the public, but are apt to mutter such sober-scientist pieties on one side of the mouth while ingesting megadose vitamins with the other" (McCann 1978). Under the cover of the obligatory "I-won't-swear-this-is-good science" disclaimer, the statements and actual practices make the Pritikin Program seem positively conservative. (1) Arthur C. Upton, Director of the National Cancer Institute: "I take vitamin C and a multiple preparation; I do not drink heavily. . . . I minimize my intake of animal fat. I also take a substantial amount of fiber, including a large amount of green leafy vegetables, and I eat bran for breakfast, and I try to control my weight. I guess you might say I try to hedge my bets!"; (2) Ernst L. Wynder, President of the American Health Foundation: "I think a high fiber intake is important in preventing colon cancer. The evidence for carbohydrates is somewhat complicated, but we think fat—both saturated and unsaturated —is what's important"; (3) Philip R. Lee, Director of the Health Policy Program at the University of California School of Medicine in San Francisco: "I eat what I consider a prudent diet. . . . I eat considerably less meat than I used to eat . . . also with alcohol consumption, I am not a heavy drinker, but I don't abstain"; (4) Linus Pauling, winner of two Nobel prizes, had a more predictable response: "I myself take 10 grams of vitamin C, 25,000 units of vitamin A, and good amounts, several times the MDR's, of other vitamins. . . . I abstain from smoking and take regular exercise . . . practices of this sort can decrease the incidence of cancer by as much as 75%"; (5) Roger J. Williams, biochemist at the University of Texas in Austin: "I try to eat wholesome foods and avoid sugary things and too much alcohol. . . . I take vitamin supplementation . . . . In addition to this I take extra vitamins C, E, B₆, folic acid, calcium, and magnesium. I also exercise by walking about three miles daily"; (6) the late John H. Knowles, President of the Rockefeller Foundation: "I take three grams of vitamin C a day plus a Super B complex . . . my diet is low in fat, high in roughage. I get seven-and-a-half to eight hours sleep. At five-foot ten, I keep my weight at 148, which is what I weighed in college, by playing squash four times a week" (McCann, 1978).

Many of the personal practices of these eminent scientists are contradicted by or at least not supported by data or experimental evidence. Of particular note is the use of vitamin supplements, which is almost uniformly rejected by the pathology management industry and yet clearly widespread among individual physicians. Lay people and professionals alike do not wait for scientific validity to be established to plan their personal health programs.

Dietary Restriction and Longevity

The next two sections address two fundamental areas of research: (1) the effects of specific dietary restrictions upon life expectancy; and (2) the effects of antioxidants on health and life expectancy. During the late 1920s Clive M. McCay of Cornell University performed a series of classic experiments with laboratory mice. In one experiment McCay compared the life expectancy of a group of normally fed mice to another group which was fed the necessary vitamins and minerals but one-third the amount of calories. From this experiment McCay noted that the oldest animal in the "ad libitum," free-feeding, group was 969 days as compared to an age of 1,465 days for the calorie-restricted group (McCay et al., 1939). The extended longevity was due to a prolonged period of adolescence with the mice remaining normally active and intelligent but with some impairment of normal growth. "Rats were retarded in growth for periods of 300, 500, 700 and 1000 days before being allowed to grow to maturity. . . . Retardation of growth by diets, complete except for calories, affords a means of producing very old animals for studying aging. Animals that are retarded for even 300 days can never become as large as those that mature normally. After 1000 days of retardation only part of the rats were able to resume growth when adequate energy was allowed in the diet" (McCay et al., 1939).

Since that experiment, that basic observation has been confirmed and refined in experiments which show two main approaches. One involved global or single-factor dietary restrictions early in the laboratory animal's development while the other researched the effects of dietary restriction on adult animals. Results clearly indicate that the earlier the dietary restriction occurs, the more dramatic are the instances of extended longevity (Weindruch et al., 1979). Although there are also definite benefits to later dietary restrictions, the results are more limited. This point underscores a fundamental distinction between simply retarding the aging process and longevity. Extended longevity is the result of multiple biological and psychosocial factors, many of which are effective only when they are introduced at critical developmental stages early in the life of the organism. Longevity is dependent upon measures occurring throughout the lifetime of an individual and not restricted to heroic measures undertaken in the later developmental years.

Refinements in McCay's pioneering experimentation continue to yield further information considering both the specific measures of dietary restriction and the mechanisms by which longevity is achieved. There were some adverse effects of prolonged dietary restriction noted in earlier experiments, but more specific data have indicated that these consequences appear to be preventable. Recent research by Paul E. Segall and Paola S. Timiras of the University of California at Berkeley has focused on diets restricted in total calories or deficient in specific constituents such as the amino acid tryptophan. For one series of experiments five groups of three-week-old female rats were placed three in a cage at weaning and fed five different diets. Segall and his colleagues found "Long term feeding of rats low in calories or deficient in tryptophan appears to increase the average and extreme lifespan and to delay the age of tumor onset, the age-related cessation of reproductive function, and the decline of homeostatic competence" (Segall et al., 1975). To account for those findings and those of their other experiments they have noted "alterations in body and organ growth, in anterior pituitary morphology and in neurotransmitter development in selected brain areas" (Segall et al., 1977).

These observations are consistent with the neuroendocrinology of aging described in the previous chapter. Results such as these indicate that early dietary restrictions, particularly of tryptophan, are key regulators of aging. Tryptophan is the necessary precursor for the neurotransmitter serotonin which places a central role in the growth and development of the central nervous system. It is hypothesized that diets deficient in tryptophan or restricted in calories affect maturation and aging by ". . . interfering with CNS protein synthesis, or neurotransmitter metabolism, or both" (Segall and Timiras, 1975). A deficiency in either of these functions, especially in early developmental stages, appears to arrest or retard some aspects of brain and neuronal maturation with attendant effects on the organism as a whole. Partial confirmation of this mechanism derives from other experiments where the chronic administration of d1-parachloro-phenyllalanine (PCPA) which inhibits the brain synthesis of seroto-nin resulted in a similar state of delayed maturation as in the caloric and tryptophan restrictions. Furthermore, the caloric restriction appears also to affect the pituitary gland. This finding offers the possibility of uncovering the underlying neuroendocrine interaction as well as suggesting a means of preventing some of the negative side effects of the restrictive diet (Ooka et al., 1978). According to Segall and his colleagues, the dietary restrictions result in ". . . pituitary hyposecretion and such reduction could contribute to the extension of lifespan seen in these animals. The supplementation of these hypopituitary animals with endocrine hormones such as those of the thyroid, adrenals and gonads might alleviate some adverse consequences of the pituitary-insufficient state and a further delay of aging may be achievable" (Segall et al., 1978).

Numerous other research projects have confirmed that dietary restriction does influence the pituitary, resulting in diminished activity of the anterior pituitary and target gland hormones except for ACTH (adrenocorticotrophic hormone) and the corticosteroids, which are usually increased (Everitt, 1973). Among the many positive effects of caloric and tryptophan restriction have been: (1) delays in the onset of tumors and cataracts; (2) better coat condition and hair regrowth; (3) prolonged ability to reproduce. Restricted-diet mice reproduced between 17 and 28 months while none of the ad libitum mice reproduced after 17 months; and (4) extended longevity as noted, "The average lifespan (in months = the standard error of the mean) of the rats recovering from the long-term tryptophan-deficient diets was 36.31 $\pm$ 2.26 while the control rats survived an average of 30.25 $\pm$ 1.90 months" (Segall, 1976). Again, these results were most pronounced in those animals placed on the restricted diet early in life. One further observation by Segall and Timiras is that by restricting dietary tryptophan, they have also been able to influence the animal's "thermoregulatory competence" or ability to maintain a constant body temperature which diminishes with advanced age. Their experiments involved the capacity of mice to recover to a temperature of 37°C following a three-minute immersion in ice water. As predicted, this capacity diminishes with age, but the mice on tryptophan-restricted diets recovered more rapidly and Segall and

Timiras concluded, ". . . tryptophan-deficient diet retards physiological aging, at least with respect to temperature homeostatic capacity . . . . It is interesting to speculate that tryptophan deficiency may stop the action of a 'biological clock' governing both growth and aging" (Segall and Timiras, 1975).

Also considering the mechanisms of dietary restriction is Johan Bjorksten, who has suggested a process consistent with cross-linkage theories: ". . . low caloric intake may favor longevity because the oxidation then proceeds more completely, with less possibility for accumulation of polyfunctional intermediates . . . and other known cross-linking agents" (Bjorksten, 1963). There are many unknown factors and potential risks in human applications of these principles. As an example, there is an indication that nerve myelination is interfered with by restricted nutrition (Cheek et al., 1970). If comparable effects occurred in humans, the result could be permanent damage to susceptible areas of the central nervous system. Resolution of these complications will depend upon research to determine both the specific dietary elements which can be safely and productively restricted as well as the precise timing and duration of such measures in the early stages of development and throughout life. Speculations such as these may be related to Denckla's aging theory. At this point such measures are restricted to laboratory experimentation.

Despite over fifty years of research, Richard H. Weindruch and his colleagues from the UCLA School of Medicine have concluded, "The mechanisms behind these various effects of controlled dietary restriction (i.e., undernutrition without malnutrition) are poorly understood at present" (Weindruch et al., 1979). In their search to define these mechanisms, Weindruch and his peers have explored the effects of postmaturational dietary restriction. Laboratory rats have been placed on restricted diets after 70 days, 300 days, and upward of 365 days of life in various experiments with positive results (Ross, 1972; Ross et al., 1976). After a brief overview of the research they note that the results suggest that ". . . life expectancy and possibly maximum life span may be increased in the mature and even middle-aged rat by appropriate underfeeding" (Weindruch et al., 1979). Most recently, Charles L. Goodrich of the Gerontology Research Center in Baltimore reported that even periodic fasting appears to promote longevity and more vigorous activity late in the life of laboratory rats. His research consisted of observing both the efforts of fasting and access to an exercise wheel of five groups of paired male rats. One group served as a control group; one was fed every other day and had access to the wheel; another group was fed on the same schedule but had no access, and the remaining two groups ate ad libitum with only one group having access to the exercise wheel. Outcome measures indicated that the fasting rats lived longer than the ad libitum feeding ones. Also, of the ad libitum rats, those that exercised lived longest. Mortality of the rats ranged from 100 days for the ad libitum, nonexercising rats to over 180 days for the rats fed every other day. Exercise did not appear to add to increased longevity between the two groups of fasting rats. From these results, Goodrich noted, "The amount of voluntary wheel exercise was significantly increased for the rats fed every other day when compared with the voluntary wheel exercise of controls, and these differences were especially impressive and consistent late in the life span" (Goodrich, 1979). Research such as this demonstrates that periodic fasting, as opposed to the restrictive measures noted earlier, appears to promote a vigorous and extended life.

Effects of life enhancement and extension measures may not be detectable until late in the life-span. It is this absence of immediately detectable negative consequences of self-destructive lifestyles that permits individuals to destroy health and curtail even their average life expectancy. For the same reason, it is necessary to understand the future outcome of positive practices or it is unlikely they will be sustained. Dietary restriction appears consistently to delay the onset of the common "spontaneously occurring diseases" (Cheek et al., 1970) of advanced age such as myocardial degeneration, cardiovascular disease, tumor onset, nephrosis, and a wide range of disorders. These laboratory findings may also throw light on the extended longevity recorded in centenarian communities located in various regions of the planet. This controversial and complex subject is considered in Chapter VIII, but at this point it is important to note that the research results of both dietary restriction and periodic fasting are consistent with the indigenous practices evidenced in the centenarian communities.

Antioxidants and Longevity

Among the dietary influences on longevity is the activity of antioxidants. Antioxidants are chemical substances, both naturally occurring and pharmaceutical, which appear to inhibit cross-linkage and reverse collagen damage. These substances act by removing intermediate free radicals in the lipid and aqueous phases of the cell and prevent such reactions from becoming self-perpetuating. Biochemical properties of antioxidants would perhaps receive scant attention outside of research laboratories if it were not for the fact that one of the most effective antioxidant agents is the controversial vitamin E. According to Aloys L. Tappel of the University of California at Davis, "It is a paradox that oxygen, which is absolutely essential for all animal life, is toxic under conditions that allow its reaction with sensitive biological compounds of the animal body. . . . Peroxidation involves the direct reaction of oxygen and lipid to form free radical intermediates and to produce semistable peroxides" (Tappel, 1968). Antioxidants, including vitamin E, inhibit peroxidation. For many years vitamin E deficiency has been linked to aging in animals. By contrast, supplementation with vitamin E appears to prolong life expectancy in both cells and organisms under laboratory conditions. In addition to vitamin E, antioxidants include the equally controversial vitamin C, which might also potentiate the effects of E, methionine, selenium, and the synthetic butylated hydroxytoluene (BHT) used as a standard food preservative.

Of all of these substances, vitamin E has clearly attracted the most research attention. One researcher who has conducted extensive research on these antioxidants is Lester Packer, who has summarized this work as follows:

> If free radical injury constitutes a major environmental cause of aging, then increased dietary concentrations of suitable forms of antioxidants and free radical scavengers should afford some protection and could contribute to an organism's ability to real-

ize its maximum life span. Several studies have shown that dietary supplementation with vitamin E or other antioxidants can, indeed, significantly increase life span and retard aging changes [Packer and Walton, 1977].

When this hypothesis is evaluated under experimental conditions, the results are quite extraordinary considering the range of applications and the uniformity of the positive results. Among Packer's many experiments is one which attempted to determine the influence of dl-α-tocopherol, one form of vitamin E, on the number of population doublings of the normal human cells (WI-38 cells) used in Leonard Hayflick's cultures. Although the results have been difficult to replicate with a high degree of reliability, Packer reported, "... free radical mediated oxidative damage of membrane lipids may be averted by the naturally occurring free-radical scavenger, vitamin E, and may increase the potential of WI-38 cells growing in culture to proliferate" (Packer, 1976). In related experiments, the addition of hydrocortisone to the culture medium extended cell life by 40 percent and cells cultured at reduced oxygen increased their population doublings as did cells supplemented with vitamin E or albumin.

Among other experiments with vitamin E are the following: (1) Addition of dl-α-tocopherol quinone to the culture medium of roundworms prolongs life-span by 30 percent and delays the appearance of lipofuscin (Epstein and Gershon, 1972). (2) Inclusion of vitamin E in the medium of the nematode *Turbatrix aceti* prolonged life-span by 17 percent (Bolla and Brot, 1975). (3) Administering vitamin E and other antioxidants to mice resulted in decreased lipofuscin accumulation in the heart and testes, although no significant increase in life-span was noted (Tappel et al., 1973). (4) Dietary vitamin E decreased the incidence of malignant growths in laboratory mice, and vitamins E and C, as well as BHT protected mice from skin cancer and cultured human cells from the damage of ultraviolet and visible light (Pereira et al., 1976). There are other experiments with vitamin E and other antioxidants which have indicated no effects (Kohn, 1971), although the weight of current evidence is in favor of some benefits from vitamin E. "On evaluating the overall results obtained by antioxidant and free radical scavenger feeding of animals, it appears that some benefit is being achieved in terms of prevention of disease and general extension of lifespan" (Cutler, 1976). Recently Lester Packer has reevaluated his earlier experiments with vitamin E, since in nineteen subsequent culture series the addition of that antioxidant did not reproduce his original findings. From this later analysis he has concluded, "A synergism between vitamin E and some component (S) in the first of two lots of serum used in the original experiments seems the most likely explanation for our earlier findings" (Packer and Smith, 1977). Results such as these emphasize the tenuous nature of even the most stringent laboratory data as well as the fact that longevity is dependent upon multiple, systemic influences rather than upon any single causative agent. While the claims of vitamin E cults will continue to vie with the caution of "hard science," neither extreme is probably accurate. However, the predominance of evidence does indicate that vitamin E and other antioxidants have positive effects at the cellular and the organismic level.

At the human level these results have been interpreted to indicate that antioxidants retard the aging process by inhibiting harmful environmental influences, by reducing the oxidation of essential dietary nutrients, and through both of these processes preventing the degenerative processes initiated by free radicals. There is some evidence that inhabitants of geographical areas rich in the antioxidant selenium, which is a water-soluble free radical scavenger, have a significantly lower death rate from cancer. After reviewing such findings, Lester Packer noted, "This type of finding may provide a basis for developing preventive measures. . . . Antioxidants may prevent various carcinogens from being activated to the more carcinogenic epoxides" (Packer and Walton, 1977). This is a very important conclusion since it indicates that cancer incidence is not necessarily related to environmental exposure to carcinogens. While exposure is unquestionably a factor and environmental protection and reclamation measures are of the highest national priority, resistance and susceptibility must also be considered in any holistic model.

Related to the issue of antioxidants is an apparent dilemma involving the balance between saturated and unsaturated fat in the human diet. While saturated lipid reduction is a positive strategy, substantial increases of polyunsaturated lipids have potentially negative consequences. In the metabolic process, polyunsaturated fats are particularly susceptible to the lipid peroxidation reactions which give rise to free radicals. According to Bernard L. Strehler, "It may well turn out that the benefits one gets from using unsaturated fats in the diet are offset by the increased production of age pigments!" (Strehler, 1979). One mediating factor in the saturated to unsaturated ratio is vitamin E. Concerning this phenomenon, Aloys L. Tappel has written an excellent overview entitled "Will antioxidant nutrients slow aging processes?" and has concluded, ". . . vitamin E can inhibit lipid peroxidation and the production of damaging free radicals. To suppress atherosclerosis, a diet rich in polyunsaturated lipids appears appropriate. . . . The proper balance between the intake of polyunsaturated lipids and biological antioxidants is essential and may be important in slowing aging processes" (Tappel, 1968).

Among the many researchers exploring this question is Denton Harman, who has conducted research with mice and rats, feeding them unsaturated lipids. After reviewing his own experiment and those of other researchers, he concluded, "The result of this study as well as other dietary fat investigations (seven studies cited) are compatible with the possibility that *in vivo* lipid peroxidation contributes to the breakdown of biological systems, but is not the major factor determining the mortality rate when the diet contains lipid antioxidants in the amounts normally employed to prevent signs of vitamin E deficiency" (Harman, 1973). It is also known that vitamin E deficiency is enhanced when the diet is high in polyunsaturated fatty acids. While final conclusions are not possible now, it is still possible to pursue a moderate course of action as recommended by Denton Harman:

> . . . it is reasonable to expect that one or more inhibitors [antioxidants] added to a properly selected, acceptable, natural diet may increase the useful life span of humans by 5 to 10 years. . . . Following the dictum "do no harm," some alterations could be made now in human diets. . . . Thus, increasing the weekly intake of vitamin E by 300-500 mg would not be detrimental even though it is not yet certain that this increase would have a beneficial effect on the healthy human life span [Harman, 1973].

Stating a similar and perhaps more forceful opinion is Lester Packer:

> It seems that if we can optimize the cellular environment, we should be able to delay some of the degenerative changes that accompany the aging process and give rise to a modest extension of life span by enabling an organism to approach its full genetic potential. Our results point to a role of antioxidants in the protection against cancer and aging. We must now seek information on the combination of antioxidants that will afford maximum protection in a particular environment. *Antioxidants* eventually may be considered as *essential dietary ingredients, much like vitamins* [Packer and Walton, 1977; emphasis in original].

This is a conservative hypothesis by most standards and it does suggest a reasonable, positive strategy which could be pursued until the evidence is in.

Other Dietary Approaches to Longevity

Antioxidants and dietary restrictions are fairly well-documented and researched. Before leaving the subject of diet and longevity, there are a number of other approaches which are more tenuous but need to be mentioned. There is the large and growing area of "gerontological pharmacology" (Kormendy and Bender, 1971) with an emphasis on pharmaceutical agents known to retard aging or mitigate its toll. While these areas are of considerable interest, they are not considered at length here since they are one more instance of the search for panaceas rather than a holistic, preventive approach which would minimize overdependency on pharmaceuticals or render them unnecessary.

Among the more controversial dietary approaches is the work of New York physician Benjamin S. Frank, outlined in his book *Nucleic Acid, Nutrition and Therapy* (1977). According to Frank's theory, the body cannot always synthesize enough ribonucleic and deoxyribonucleic acids, resulting in a progressive breakdown of the DNA genetic encoding which eventually leads to deterioration and death. As an antidote to this degenerative process, Frank contends that the body requires supplemental nucleic acids and nutrients: ". . . Exogenous RNA especially when combined with metabolically associated B vitamins, minerals, amino acids and sugars, will enter the cell and aid in normal regeneration of the decayed metabolic organization of the cell and in so doing will bring about normal enzyme synthesis and activation" (Frank, 1977). A key factor in Frank's theory is that this nucleic acid supplementation increases the rate of adenosine triphosphate, ATP, which induces cell repair and restoration of normal function. Among the many claims for the efficacy of this approach are ". . . improved cardiac function . . . therapeutic effects . . . in patients suffering from atherosclerosis, emphysema, diabetes, peripheral nerve degeneration, glaucoma, hypercholesterolemia and other age related disorders" (Kent, 1977). While there is some minimal research to support some of these claims, the efficacy has clearly not been proven. Furthermore, many of these conditions can be significantly improved by measures totally unrelated to diet and nutrition (Pritikin and McGrady, 1979). Effective intervention and prevention of such conditions will perhaps involve nucleic acid supplementation in conjunction with other approaches. Controversy over nucleic acid supplementation generates the strong emotional reactions characteristic of this field.

While laboratory research into dietary factors in longevity proceeds slowly but surely, there is already significant evidence from projects such as those of the Stanford Heart Disease Prevention Program (Farquhar, 1978) and others that the dietary practices of large populations can be changed toward more beneficial ends. One such study was undertaken in Belgium over the last ten years. During that period of time, Belgians have shifted overall from a low ratio of polyunsaturated to saturated fat in their diet to a higher one with lower total fat and cholesterol. The change was more significant in the northern part of Belgium with approximately 5,554,000 inhabitants, than in the south with approximately 3,212,000. Population statistics in the north show a direct relationship between decreased serum cholesterol and decreased coronary morbidity and mortality. Although saturated fat and the risk factors also decreased in the south, there was still a significant difference between north and south which makes these data of particular significance. To account for these differences a research team from the University of Leuven in Brussels undertook an extensive medical, psychosocial, and dietary study of the population differences which might account for this effect. Coronary risk factors and mortality were examined in the two regions based on data from "Belgian army males (42,755), male postmen (4,782), families from the parent-children study (6,234), and males aged 40–59 (7,212)" (Joosens et al., 1977). Differences in fat intake and serum cholesterol were associated with "striking differences" in morbidity and mortality between the two regions. Also, although not a purpose of the study, the male life expectancy proved to be higher in the north at 68.8 as opposed to 66.4 in the south. Medical parameters and certain lifestyle variables appeared to be of minimum impact, "Possible confounding factors such as blood-pressure, body-weight, and cigarette smoking have been evaluated and only small differences in both directions were found between the regions. Similar results were obtained for sugar consumption and serum-triglycerides" (Joosens et al., 1977). When the researchers examined their data more closely, they found that the most significant variable was public education. Advertising against excessive dairy-product consumption as well as medical and public education was greater in the north than in the south:

> Many of the factors interact—notably, (1) the lower economic status of the north in the past and its gradual improvement so as to overtake the south in recent years; (2) publicity on behalf of butter and other dairy products by the Ministry of Agriculture and related pressure groups; (3) manufacturers' advertisements for margarine on posters and in newspapers; and (4) differences of opinion between northern and southern medical schools about the importance of dietary fats in the genesis of atherosclerosis [Joosens et al., 1977].

The publicity promoting butter in the south led the researchers to the observation that "Our findings cast doubt on the ethics of campaigns for the promotion of butter, as pressed by many European governments and by the Common Market." Results such as these show the importance of the total context as well as suggesting political and economic resistance to any shift in dietary practices.

The Tarahumara Diet

Issues involving strongly vested economic interests cannot be resolved without positive, alternative models. While such models are rare, they do exist and should receive increased attention. Many of the more prominent examples of populations exhibiting optimum health and longevity are discussed in detail in Chapter VIII. An example pertinent here is the Tarahumara Indians of the Sierra Occidental mountains in the north-central state of Chihuahua, Mexico. Several research teams have observed that members of this tribe:

> . . . reportedly run distances up to 200 miles in the competitive sport of "kickball" races which often last several days. Previous observations indicate deaths from cardiac and circulatory complications are unknown. Relatively low blood pressures and pulse rates have been observed. Scattered anthropological reports suggest that the diet of the Tarahumaras consists primarily of beans, corn and squash. . . . These initial observations in the Tarahumaras that they may consume a diet high in vegetables and cereals and low in animal foods and that they are exceptionally physically fit stimulated us to pursue further studies about coronary heart disease risk factors in these people. Exercise effects are obviously of great significance in these findings and are considered in the next chapter since the focus here is upon diet. Eighty percent carbohydrate would ordinarily induce obesity. Markedly reduced animal protein would be expected to have some deleterious effects unless undertaken carefully. A host of other potential risk factors did not produce disease in these people. Quite the contrary, the Tarahumara Indians are an extremely healthy population. Extensive medical and psychosocial histories were taken of 523 men and women of the tribe. . . . Of particular pertinence in this study was the demonstration of a direct correlation between the intake of dietary cholesterol and the plasma cholesterol concentration.

This was the first demonstration with a given population group of such a correlation [Connor et al., 1978].

Specifically, the dietary consumption of cholesterol in the Tarahumaras is very low, 71 mg per day, compared with American intakes of 500 to 750 mg per day and higher. With low serum cholesterol levels in the Indian population ranging from 17 to 144 mg per day, "dietary cholesterol had a close association, probably causative, with plasma cholesterol concentrations" (Connor et al., 1978). Overall, the health profile of the Tarahumaras indicates that death from cardiac and circulatory complications are virtually unknown; they exhibit low blood pressure and pulse rates with none of the sex differences found in virtually all other populations, plasma triglyceride levels comparable to individuals on a fast, and virtually no obesity.

There are many psychosocial variables such as high social cohesiveness, and also the factor of extensive exercise, which account for part of these findings. Nevertheless, there are specific characteristics of the Tarahumara Indian diet which are highly significant: (1) the major caloric sources were corn and beans, which contributed about "90% of the total calories. The remainder of the diet was almost completely derived from other vegetable sources. Meat was seldom eaten"; (2) "the mixture of corn and beans provided a protein intake of 79 to 96 grams per day . . . amounts . . . met the essential amino acid requirements by many times (from 236 to 1,221%)"; (3) "exceptionally low in total fat, between 9 and 12% of the total daily calories, compared to 40% in the American diet"; (4) "the ingestion of fiber and starch was much higher in the Tarahumara than in the American population"; (5) "sugar consumption . . . was exceptionally low at / less than 3% of total calories"; (6) "Despite the fact that this was a physically active population, HDL levels were not increased as has been suggested for subset groups of Americans who run 10 or more miles per day. Indeed the direct opposite seemed to be the case"; (7) "lower intake of sodium chloride"; and (8) "no hypertensive Tarahumara person was encountered and there appeared to be no rise of blood pressure with age" (Connor et al., 1978). These are remarkable findings. Also, there was no evidence of osteoporosis, a progressive loss of bone calcium resulting in a brittle skeletal system and common among the elderly in the United States, which has been related to an excessive level of protein intake. Research by noted nutritionist Sheldon Margen of the University of California at Berkeley with two thousand students since 1965 has indicated a direct relationship between protein intake and increased calcium excretion (Margen, 1974). Perhaps further research will indicate that high protein diets derived from meat sources induce osteoporosis while comparable protein intake from vegetable sources does not. At the present time there is evidence that "... calcium treatment alone does little for ... osteoporosis ... however ... calcium supplementation *before* osteoporosis develops may partially prevent the disease, delay its onset, or at least slow its progress ... adults should consume a minimum of 1 g or more each day" (Winick, 1978). Exceptionally low fat intake such as the 9 to 12 percent in the Tarahamura diet could result in fat deficiencies in the body especially in linoleic acid, which the body cannot manufacture. This is not the case, indicating the adequacy of the Tarahamura diet, which is quite similar to the Pritikin recommendations.

Studies of subpopulations in the United States and of groups such as the Tarahumara Indians cannot necessarily be generalized to the overall population of the United States. However, they are living evidence of the fact that radically different values, lifestyles, and diets from those of the general United States population can produce optimum health and enhance longevity. While such extreme practices may not be desirable or even achievable in our population as a whole, they are worth investigation as an example of the human biological potential. Populations such as the Tarahumara have unwittingly matched many of the practices now under scrutiny in laboratories as factors in longevity. Their example may contain many lessons as we search for the fundamental properties of a true health care system. Chapter VIII will take a more detailed look at these lessons.

Recently Senator Jacob K. Javits of New York summarized the implications of the emphasis upon pathology management for the elderly:

> Americans expect the miracles of modern medicine—technology, service, facilities and personnel—without regard to expense. But the nation's health-care costs have more than tripled

in the last decade: from $38.9 billion in 1965 to $138 billion in 1976. They continue to increase at the rate of approximately $20 billion a year. Despite the staggering expense, this tremendous rise in the price of health care has not been matched by an equivalent rise in the health status of our people. That is not to say that we are spending too much for health care. Rather, the question is whether we are spending too much compared with other costs in the nation, and whether health-care costs are rising so fast as to effectively deny disadvantaged and elderly citizens access to needed services [Javits, 1979].

Increasing numbers of elderly people requiring expensive medical care is a trend which is not inevitable if preventive measures such as positive dietary practices are introduced early and maintained throughout life. Biomedical research must be combined with studies of healthy subpopulations in order to determine what the most beneficial dietary practices might be and what effects are probable.

SEVEN

Exercise and Longevity

When the Olympic Games began in 776 B.C., as a tribute to the Olympian god Zeus, Hippocrates had already observed that intense athletic competition had a harmful effect on the heart and other body organs, and lowered resistance to disease. Evidence of the relationship between physical health and longevity has intrigued paleontologists and medical historians, whether examining the fossils of our most likely ancestor, *Australopithecus africanus,* approximately five million years ago or the records of the first Olympic competition. A passage from Plato's dialogues provides a useful context for this consideration of physical exercise and longevity. A young man named Charmides seeks a headache remedy from Socrates, who explains to him at length that such a remedy is not adequate since, "To treat the head by itself, apart from the body as a whole is utter folly." Ideally, Socrates advises an approach taught to him by a Thracian physician:

> You ought not to attempt to cure eyes
> Without head,
> Or head without body,

> So you should not treat body
> Without soul.

Plato's observation reminds us that physical exercise cannot be studied without attention to the whole person.

The Benefits of Physical Exercise

Other than nutrition, no single area of research is more clouded with unsubstantiated opinion than the realm of physical exercise and its relationship to health. Of even greater uncertainty and controversy is the role of such activity in extending life expectancy. This chapter builds upon the research, programs, and cautions discussed in the chapter entitled "A Sound Mind in a Sound Body" in *Holistic Medicine* (Pelletier, 1979). The basic considerations are not discussed at length here since they are readily available in that chapter as well as in *Fit or Fat* (1978) by Covert Bailey as well as in the excellent quarterly reports, *Physical Fitness Research Digest,* of the President's Council on Physical Fitness and Sports. There is now widespread documentation that regular aerobic activity does enhance both physical and psychological functioning. Recently Arthur S. Leon and Henry Blackburn of the Department of Medicine at the University of Minnesota School of Medicine wrote an extensive, critical review of both the animal and human research in this area and summarized the benefits of endurance exercise:

> (1) A reduction in heart rate and blood pressure and morphological changes in skeletal and cardiac muscle, resulting in improved physical work capacity, enhancement of cardiovascular efficiency in delivering oxygen and nutrients to the tissues, and a reduction in myocardial oxygen requirements for any given amount of work. (2) Increased muscular endurance; (3) Possible increased myocardial vascularity, including capillary density, coronary collaterals, and size of the coronary artery tree as demonstrated by animal studies; (4) Reduced blood coagulability and a transient increase in fibrinolysis; (5) Reduction in

weight and adiposity and increased lean body mass; (6) Increased cellular sensitivity in insulin, reducing requirements at any given glucose load; (7) Blood lipid changes including a reduction in serum triglycerides and an increase in the amount of cholesterol carried by high-density (alpha) lipoprotein, low levels of which are reported in population studies to be related to development of CAD. . . . Psychological benefits of regular exercise are difficult to measure; however, there is no doubt that exercise helps relieve muscular tension, makes one feel better and sleep better, and may aid motivation for improving health habits including cessation of cigarette smoking [Leon and Blackburn, 1977].

When exercise is undertaken without an exercise-oriented physical examination or with premature overexertion, there are risks, including sports-related injuries and cardiovascular problems. Physical examinations have many unsolved weaknesses. Evidence of coronary pathology based upon treadmill assessments is not always accurate. While this problem will continue, cardiologist and Editor-in-Chief of *Modern Medicine* the late Michael J. Halberstam noted that current tests are quite reliable: "With the application of rigid criteria for positives and the application of a tincture of common sense and clinical data, false positives should be down in the 5 to 10% range. Anyone who's getting 20 to 30% false positives needs either a new treadmill or a new set of calipers" (Halberstam, 1979). Monitored treadmill assessments are more reliable indicators when undertaken in conjunction with a complete exercise-oriented assessment and history.

Over one million men and women in the United States have engaged in a 20-year study by the American Cancer Society to assess the impact of specific lifestyle variables upon morbidity and mortality. Over 90 percent of the original subjects of the study were followed by 68,000 volunteer interviewers over the entire 20 years and the result was "450 million items of information on the effects of lifestyle on health." This study is the "largest human biological study undertaken of life and death" and as such its results are of great significance. According to the preliminary results, one major finding is: "Physical exercise lengthens life and wards off heart disease and stroke" (Sharfstein, 1979). This was particularly true of men. The death rates among men who did not exercise at all were significantly greater than among those who did and decreased in direct proportion as the amount of exercise increased. Numerous results will continue to be gleaned from this study, but a key point in the results so far is that physical exercise did enable more men and women to attain maximum life expectancy.

Athletic Participation and Longevity

Prior to the early 1970s there were only a few inconclusive and experimentally faulty studies which correlated exercise with health and even fewer which correlated exercise with longevity. Then Anthony P. Polednak and Albert Damon of the Department of Anthropology at Harvard University undertook a study of 2,090 men who attended Harvard College between 1880 and 1916. After an overview of the research literature prior to 1970, Polednak and Damon concluded:

> In summary, no strong association has been established between college athletics and subsequent death from cardiovascular disease. Any tendency is toward a protective effect. As with longevity, follow-up studies on cause of death among former college athletes should take into account the type of sport, degree of participation and achievement, the time period covered, the subjects' physique, and their later habits of exercise (Polednak and Damon, 1970).

In order to rectify some of the variance in previous studies, the researchers selected a fairly homogeneous group of Harvard graduates and divided them into three groups of "major athletes—men who received one or more letter awards" (177), "minor athletes—participants in major sports who did not win letters, plus all regular participants in intercollegiate sports" (275), and "non-athletes—men who had no record of having participated in formal intercollegiate sports" (1,638). At the time of the study a total of 1,900 of the 2,090 men had died, or 90.9 percent, and the age and cause of death were obtained from death certificates. There was an increased longevity noted over time within each athletic category which the researchers attributed to "general environmental and possibly medical advances." After an extensive analysis of the data, Polednak and Damon reported a result which they found "surprising": ". . . minor athletes were generally and for the most part significantly longer lived than major athletes and non-athletic classmates . . . major athletes had shorter lives than their less athletic or less athletically prominent classmates. . . . In percentages of men still alive and in percentages of men reaching ages 70 and 75, minor athletes were consistently and for the most part significantly higher" (Polednak and Damon, 1977). Even with the extended longevity of minor athletes, the three groups did not differ in death rates from infections, neoplasms, suicide, or cardiovascular disease, which was the leading cause of death in all groups. Since a greater proportion of minor athletes were still alive at the time of the study, it is reasonable to expect that their average age at death will be relatively greater than the other two groups, indicating their equal susceptibility to the same causes of death but at a more advanced age.

During 1971, Peter Schnohr of the Department of Medicine in the Copenhagen County Hospital conducted a study of 297 of 307 male "athletic champions" born in Denmark between 1880 and 1910. His results contradicted the Polednak and Damon study: "The male athletic champions had a significantly lower mortality than the general population" (Schnohr, 1971). These findings resulted in a considerable debate. Other researchers noted that the "mean lifespans of the athletes were related to the sport in which they had participated" (Largey, 1972) and that these significant differences were obscured by Schnohr's data. Specifically, the mean ages of football athletes was 57.4 at the low end of the continuum as contrasted to track and field athletes at 71.3, which is clearly a major difference. Some researchers concluded that " 'Brute' sports such as football shorten lifespans while 'endurance' sports such as track lengthen them . . . long distance skiers survived seven years longer than controls. The reduction in mortality is primarily due to the lowered incidence of coronary atherosclerosis in 'endurance' athletes" (Bassler, 1977).

During this period, Anthony P. Polednak refined his research approach to consider "the type of sport, degree of participation and achievement, the time period covered, the subject's physique, and later habits of exercise" (Polednak, 1972). Applying methods similar to his previous research, Polednak studied 8,538 men from Harvard University between 1880 and 1912 and considered all the cited variables except for the later exercise habits. Exclusion of this variable was quite unfortunate, since this has proven to be a major factor and had been demonstrated to be of significance prior to Polednak's study. Difficulty in obtaining such data was the reason for its exclusion from Polednak's study as well as virtually all studies prior to that time and many studies since then. Various factors reduced the original population to 6,303 subjects who were analyzed in relation to longevity and causes of death. Polednak's data confirmed his earlier study, although the differences were not as great:

> Major athletes had the shortest lives, but differences were small. . . . Major athletes died significantly earlier than nonathletes from coronary heart disease; they also died more often and earlier from neoplasms, although differences were not statistically significant for this series. Physique might account for the slightly reduced longevity of major athletes. Using several methods of analysis, longevity of minor athletes was as great as, or slightly (but insignificantly) greater than, that of nonathletes despite the larger body size of the former [Polednak, 1972].

During the same period, physician Curtis Prout of Harvard University studied 172 graduates of Harvard and Yale who rowed at least once in a 4-mile varsity race. From his data Prout found that the average life expectancy for both groups of rowing team members was higher than that for control groups. Prout's conclusion was cautious: "It is tempting to think that rowing itself made these men more long-lived, but other selection factors may be operating" (Prout, 1972). Among the factors considered by Prout were height, the fact that "varsity oarsmen tend to continue to exercise and avoid obesity," also that "people who are successful in various fields tend to outlive their less successful contemporaries," and the variables of "college education and social class." An early, classic study, *Length of Life,* of 28,269 male graduates of eight Eastern colleges (Dublin et al., 1949) indicated the positive effects of social and economic status, and academic honors, upon longevity.

Based on these and other early studies, a more comprehensive approach to the interaction between physical exercise and longevity began to evolve which considered the role of related factors:

> These facts suggest that the athletes are likely to benefit from three factors so far as longevity is concerned: (i) the direct effect of exercise, (ii) the indirect effect of exercise on the control of their obesity; and (iii) the tendency to refrain from acquiring the smoking habit at an early age. The active period of sport participation is short, and those who totally gave up sporting activities after they are 30 years old would gradually lose the beneficial effects of exercise acquired under (i) and (ii). . . . The groups who remain to some degree physically active in their later life would tend to have the additional benefits arising from (i) and (ii) [Khosla, 1972].

This acknowledgment of the mutual interaction among the three variables of obesity, smoking, physical exercise, and the factor of continuity of exercise habits in later life was an important step in understanding the correlation between physical activity and longevity.

During recent years Polednak has undertaken more specific analyses of his data derived from a cohort of 8,393 college men, in particular with regard to his earlier observation that, "Major athletes died significantly more often from neoplasms (cancer) than nonathletes. Mean age at death from neoplasms was significantly lower in major athletes than in both minor athletes and nonathletes" (Polednak, 1976). Further detailed analysis indicated increased risk at the specific sites of the prostate and gastrointestinal tract excluding the colon. In accounting for these findings, Polednak excludes increased traumatic injury as a cause and suggests an as yet undetermined number of influences such as "lifestyle, occupation, personality, and personal habits that are relevant to cancer risk" (1976). However, Polednak does indicate a relationship between excessive athletic activity and destructive effects of stress: ". . . chronic exercise may be viewed as a type of 'stress'; its profound effects on adrenocortical function are of particular interest in view of the effects of adrenocortical steroids on antibody levels" (Polednak, 1976). Such research suggests that excessive physical activity can be as destructive as its absence. This is not noted here to create alarm but to acknowledge that there are potential hazards, particularly after age 35, and that there is controversy regarding the limits of exercise benefits.

Such controversy was fueled when Maryland Congressman Goodloe E. Byron, a 49-year-old veteran marathoner, collapsed and died after jogging 12 miles. Prior to that time California pathologist Thomas J. Bassler had maintained that such a death was a biological impossibility for a nonsmoking marathoner (Bassler, 1977). This point of view was challenged by certain researchers including two who stated the other extreme that ". . . at present there is no conclusive evidence that physical activity is beneficial to health, although there is suggestive evidence that this may be so" (Brown and Milvy, 1977). Byron's autopsy revealed that the cause of death appeared to be progressive atherosclerotic heart disease. Prior to Byron's fatal marathon, he had been warned not to run in view of negative results from an exercise tolerance test which were ignored. According to Samuel M. Fox, head of the cardiology exercise program at Georgetown University, "This clearly demonstrates that one cannot rely on marathon running or conditioning, or running some 20 miles a week to give immunity to coronary-disease progression or coronary events" (*Medical World News,* 1978).

Evidence for the negative effects of competitive levels of athletic activity remains unproven, but such rare events introduce a valid note of caution. In any case, an individual does not need to achieve a professional or even competitive level of fitness to attain an optimum state of health. Over-intensive training, characteristic of competitive sports, may often be counterproductive or even detrimental to sound health. As eminent Swedish physiologist Per-Olof Astrand has emphasized, "As far as health is concerned, it is not the absolute amount and volume of training that is important but the *work in relation to the individual's capacity.* The severe, prolonged training of the top athlete adds no health benefits to those of a submaximal training program twice a week!" (Astrand, 1979). When the goal is physical fitness, it would be unfortunate to subject ourselves to the same overbearing sense of achievement, competitiveness, and mastery so characteristic of Western culture as a whole. The goal is rather to attain an active lifestyle which has five basic exercise characteristics, according to physician Harold H. Bloomfield:

> Enough stretching, twisting, reaching, and bending to maintain flexibility and elasticity, at least two hours of standing every day; a few minutes of moderate exercise that pushes your pulse rate up to 120 and thereby forces your circulatory system to maintain a reserve efficiency, exertion of moderate physical effort once or twice daily, thus maintaining your strength and energy; and enough daily physical activity to burn at least 300 calories [Bloomfield, 1978].

As minimal as these requirements are, the cardiovascular as well as psychological benefits are extensive.

Another variable in the relationship of exercise to health and longevity is the necessity for physical activity to be sustained throughout the lifetime of the individual. Exercise requires an ongoing involvement and has cumulative benefits. When Keiji Yamaji and Roy J. Shephard performed a critical analysis of the seven major studies linking physical activity to subsequent longevity, they emphasized this important aspect: "We may thus conclude there is no relationship between the cause of death and physical activity at university. However, subsequent weight gain, lack of exercise, and smoking habits increase the risk of coronary heart disease and malignant tumors. Former athletes, like nonathletes, should continue to exercise in later life" (Yamaji and Shepard, 1977). Despite the pervasive acceptance of the benefits of exercise, controversy remains, particularly in the area of competitive sports. Perhaps it is the very nature of harsh, highly competitive team athletics which is not conducive to exercise being continued in later life. Moderate aerobic exercise, however, begun early in life and continued throughout adult development, clearly does exert a positive influence on health and longevity.

A Lifetime Exercise Program

Potential benefits of vigorous physical activity outweigh the potential risks associated with inactivity:

> Current scientific evidence does suggest that regular, vigorous exercise has many positive benefits. Among these is the possibility that regular exercise may attenuate several of the risk factors involved in heart disease, such as emotional stress, serum lipids, blood pressure, and obesity—as well as improve cardiovascular-pulmonary capacity and efficiency, retard age-related deterioration in work capacity, promote general health, and improve the quality of life [Bell et al., 1978].

With this assumption in mind, the remaining questions hinge on the nature of an optimum exercise program throughout adult development. There is a high degree of consensus about several components of such a program: (1) Pre-exercise evaluations including exercise-oriented physical, personal medical history, and risk factor assessment for all men and women, especially over the age of 35; (2) warm-up and cool-down periods; (3) intensity of physical activity based upon "target zone pulse rate"; (4) duration of exertion; (5) frequency of exercise; (6) types of exercise; and, (7) psychological variables. Each of these factors has been extensively considered in *Holistic Medicine* (Pelletier, 1979) and will be reviewed only briefly here.

PHYSICAL EXAM

The pre-exercise physical and the cardiovascular physiology underlying such assessments are discussed in the chapter just mentioned. One development which was not included is a relatively simple and yet accurate means developed by the New York State Department of Education for assessing an individual's "Cardiovascular Disease

Risk Factor" prior to the exercise program and six months later. This assessment has been introduced as a key aspect of the comprehensive Xerox Health Management Program (Pfeiffer, 1980).

Another relatively simple means of assessing cardiovascular efficiency is to measure how rapidly the heart rate returns toward normal after moderate exertion. This assessment is the "Step Test" and has different administration and scoring parameters for men and women. Men should select a bench or stool 12 inches high and hold a stopwatch or watch with a second hand. Then step up and down at 24 steps per minute on a metronome. For the correct stepping procedure, proceed in four counts: (1) step up on the bench with the right foot first; (2) then bring up the left; (3) put the right foot down; (4) then put the left foot down and repeat the sequence totaling 96 counts per minute. After stepping for exactly three minutes, sit down immediately on the bench. Within five seconds, count your pulse for a full minute. This is your pulse recovery score. For men, the pulse recovery norms are:

Men's Pulse Recovery Norms

Rating	Heart Rate per Minute
Excellent	75–80
Good	85–90
Average	95–115
Fair	120–125
Poor	130–135

In order to take into account the variability in cardiovascular responses as well as flexibility of men and women, women use a different procedure. Women use an 18-inch stool or bench and step up and down at 30 steps per minute for one full minute. In this case, the counting procedure is 120 counts for only one minute. Immediately after stepping for one minute, sit down and start timing your pulse recovery. Women follow a different procedure; they wait 15 seconds, then take their pulse for 15 seconds; wait 15 seconds more and take a second pulse for 15 seconds; wait 15 seconds again and take a third pulse for 15 seconds. Add the three pulse counts and compare the sum for the women's recovery norms:

Women's Pulse Recovery Norms

Rating	Heart Rate Recovery
Excellent	66–77
Good	80–91
Average	95–109
Fair	112–123
Poor	127–137

This test is one aspect of an exercise-oriented physical examination, and can also serve as a means of periodic assessment of a "conditioning effect" (Ryan, 1978) over time. Trends in cardiovascular fitness programs are toward self-administered assessments such as these to insure a safe and moderate approach.

WARM-UP EXERCISES

Any exercise program should include a warm up period prior to exercise and a cool-down period at the end. This procedure prevents many sports-related injuries to joints and soft tissue. Warm-up and cool-down exercises can also increase the range of motion for joints and minimize postexercise soreness particularly in the initial stages. Sports medicine physician Allan J. Ryan has emphasized the multiple goals of warm-up and training exercises: "The physical qualities that normally must be improved beyond resting or basal activity levels to permit effective performance in a sport include strength, speed, endurance, cardiorespiratory function, agility, flexibility, coordination, balance, and reaction time" (Ryan, 1978). Although there is a high degree of variability in the flexibility exercises which can be utilized, there is general agreement upon basic stretch exercises which extend and flex muscle groups of the Achilles tendon, calf, back, thighs, and major leg muscles. Without the use of illustrations it is not possible to render an accurate description of such flexibility exercises. The intent of this chapter is simply to note that these exercises are vital, particularly in advanced years.

For individuals of any age but especially for anyone over 35, there is a series of excellent illustrated books by physical education and yoga instructor Ruth Bender (1975, 1976, 1978) which provide a wealth of practical instruction. Another graphic source of exercises for both the warm-up and cool-down period is the booklet "One Step at a Time" (1981), which is available at no cost from the President's Council on Physical Fitness.

FREQUENCY, DURATION, AND INTENSITY

The frequency of exercise usually agreed upon is a minimum of three times per week on nonconsecutive days. Frequency is extremely important since: "Improvements achieved by training can be maintained only be repetition, which must be at an average frequency of approximately three times weekly, preferably not consecutive days. Failure to maintain this frequency results in a decay of the improvement to the original baseline for that quality" (Ryan, 1978). The actual duration of the exercise period is often recommended to be in the range of 20 to 30 minutes, at the "exercise heart rate" discussed below, which allows the body time to move from the "anaerobic" to the "aerobic" phase of exertion: ". . . in the anaerobic phase are primarily adenosine triphosphate (ATP) and creatine phosphate with small amounts of glycogen. In the aerobic phase both glycogen and fatty acids are used as fuel. Which is used more depends on the length and intensity of exercise" (Ryan, 1978). Emphasis on the positive aspects of the aerobic phase has been the foundation of the comprehensive system developed by Kenneth H. Cooper in the most recent *The Aerobics Way* (1977) as well as his earlier works (Cooper, 1975, 1976; Cooper and Cooper, 1976).

Whether or not an exercise is aerobic depends on its intensity. It is in this stage that there is the greatest variability due to age and where the greatest caution needs to be maintained even in the presence of a completely clear physical examination. Intensity can be measured by the "exercise heart rate" or "target pulse" (Morehouse and Gross, 1975, 1977). This is the pulse or heart rate which can be safely achieved during physical exercise and which can sufficiently tax the cardiovascular system, without overexertion. Since it is beneficial to maintain a sustained target pulse, these measures can be taken immediately after the period of physical activity. An individual can take his pulse at the radial artery of the wrist or carotid artery of the neck, counting for 10 seconds and then multiplying by 6. An individual should continue to move while taking the pulse. Ideally, the heart rate should be between 70 percent and 80 percent of maximum for an individual's age. The chart below is adapted from one used in the Xerox Health Management Program mentioned above:

TYPE OF EXERCISE

The exercises which most adequately fulfill the criteria of an optimum exercise program are walking, running, cross-country skiing, jazz dancing, swimming, bicycle riding, and similar exercises. They must be personally enjoyable and integrated into a person's ongoing lifestyle. All of these activities constitute moderate aerobic activity involving large muscle groups, primarily of the hips and legs, in a rhythmic and continuous motion which can be maintained over the required time of at least thirty minutes. It is important to note that jogging is only one of many such exercises. Many individuals are actually discouraged by the current fashion for jogging. As one essayist observed, "Long distance runners are lonely because they are insufferable!" Walking may be an excellent alternative: "For the general public, without having to go through stress testing, brisk walking five days a week for at least an hour would give you the same metabolic benefits as the average jogging program without as much risk" (Bloom, 1978).

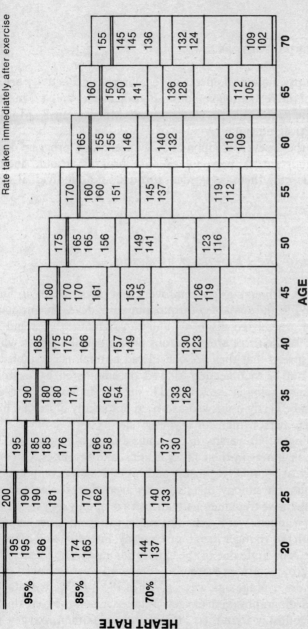

PSYCHOLOGICAL FACTORS

Among the psychological effects of regular physical activity are: (1) elicitation of the relaxation response (Benson et al., 1978); (2) marked reduction in acute anxiety (Bahrke and Morgan, 1978; Morgan, 1979); and (3) significant alleviation of depression (Kostrubala, 1976).

Each of these seven components of an exercise program is extremely important. A personal exercise program should include them all, adapting them, as needed, throughout an individual's lifetime.

Exercise and the Physiology of Aging

It is probable, although as yet unproven, that physical activity initiated early in life and sustained throughout adult development delays the onset of age-related disorders and can significantly extend life expectancy. While there are numerous physiological changes which are so widespread that they are considered normal, it is established that these can be significantly slowed or eliminated by exercise. Exercise is an ongoing process. Initial limitations in flexibility or lung capacity can be vastly improved and need not be any more of a limit for an elderly person than for a young one.

At Washington University in St. Louis a team of researchers has studied male runners in their fifties, sixties, and seventies. Over the period of a year John O. Hollostzy and his colleagues compared the cardiovascular physiology of 14 runners averaging 58 years of age with 10 competitive trackmen with an average of only 23 years. Each of the older runners were men who ran 5 to 10 miles per day and matched with the younger men for frequency, intensity, and duration of training. (As a note, one of the elderly runners was 77 years old.) These two groups of men were also compared to 11 sedentary nonsmokers whose average age was 54. All of the men were evaluated by electrocardiography and oxygen uptake capacity. From the assessments Hollostzy found: (1) "the average maximum oxygen uptake of the older athletes to be almost twice that of the sedentary group and only 14% lower than the young runners' capacity"; (2) "both old and young runners weighed less"; (3) also both groups of runners "had slower heart rates, and showed lower heart and blood pressure responses to varying work loads than did those who normally shunned exercise"; and (4) "studies at several centers point to an average 10% decline in cardiovascular efficiency per decade but the runners tested . . . show only about a 4% falloff" (*Medical World News,* 1979d). Overall, Hollostzy concluded, "It's not that their strenuous regimen stops cardiovascular deterioration; it just slows it down considerably." These findings are consistent with preliminary studies in other laboratories. They indicate that "normal deterioration" is not normal at all but merely average.

In 1958, Nathan W. Shock and his colleagues in the Gerontology Branch of the Baltimore City Hospitals in Maryland started a study of the "physiology of aging" by testing 400 men between ages 30 and 90 and following them for 20 years. Among the types of decline in major functions for men and women from 30 until 90 they found: (1) decrease in blood flow through the kidneys and changes in the kidneys themselves which reduce "the efficiency with which the kidneys process metabolic waste products"; (2) decline in ability to exercise and to work which was measured by "the maximum amount of work a subject can do and have his heart return to normal within two minutes after he stops working"; (3) a drop in the average "grip pressure" in the hands from 28 kilograms at age 20 to 20 kilograms at age 75, indicating a decline in muscle function; (4) decline in cardiac output, amount of blood pumped per minute, and changes in blood pressure. "Although the resting blood pressure in healthy individuals increases only slightly with age, a given amount of exercise will raise the heart rate and blood pressure in old people more than it will in young people"; (5) a decline in the amount of oxygen that the blood takes up from the lungs and transports to the tissues during exercise; (6) decline in respiratory function, reflecting a loss in "simple mechanical efficiency"; (7) changes in the neuroendocrine system adversely affecting a "wide variety of physiological processes, ranging from cellular metabolism to regulating the diameter of small blood vessels and consequently the amount of blood reaching various tissues"; (8) less stability in internal chemistry. "Such factors as total blood volume, acidity, osmotic pressure, protein content and sugar content remain constant in both young and old subjects at rest. But when these variables are deliberately altered, the older person needs a much longer time to recover internal chemical equilibrium"; (9) blood sugar changes. "Although the average blood-sugar level remains quite constant even into advanced age, the rate at which the system removes extra glucose drops significantly in older people"; (10) decline in coordination among organ systems and in those functions which require the simultaneous output of several organ systems, such as physical exercise or sex; (11) loss of weight in individual organs after middle age. "The average weight of the brain at autopsy falls from 1,375 grams (3.03 pounds) to 1,232 grams (2.72 pounds) between ages 30 and 90" and other instances such as muscle mass; (12) a similar decline in the nervous system. "The number of nerve cells in a trunk decreases by 27 percent at advanced ages" (Shock, 1962).

These early observations have been confirmed and refined in many subsequent studies of aging by Shock as well as others. For the most part these deteriorations of aging are assumed to be the end product of aberrant cellular activity, as discussed in Chapter III. However, these common deteriorative changes are unequivocally not inevitable. As we have seen in previous chapters, lifestyle changes, including nutrition, can prevent deterioration. Although specific biochemical explanations for the effects of exercise upon aging are rare, Johan Bjorksten has suggested one hypothesis: "The favorable results reported from physical exercise to the point of exhaustion in treatments to combat degenerative disease may be due to the metal-chelating potency of the lactic acid thus generated, in addition to the resulting physical relaxation and vasodilation" (Bjorksten, 1978). Even within the ostensibly inevitable degenerative processes there is a wide range of individual variability.

One key to understanding aging and particularly to taking action that might extend the human life span can be found in the differences in the rate of aging observed in different individuals. These differences indicate that many factors play a role in aging. When we know why some people age less rapidly than others, we may be able to create conditions that will minimize the loss of functioning cells and tissues thereby enabling many more people to live as long as those who live longest today (Shock, 1962).

Discovering the lifestyles, diets, and physical activities which enable some individuals and large subpopulations to maintain health and prevent the deterioration associated with aging remains a central challenge.

These deteriorative aspects of aging must be carefully monitored in the early stages of an exercise program for previously sedentary individuals. At the very innovative Gerontology Center of the University of Southern California, Herbert A. De Vries has developed such a program by working with two hundred older men and women over a period of five years at the Laguna Hills Retirement Community. His program includes each of the seven components cited earlier with the further observation that, "We believe the trainability of healthy, asymptomatic men and women in their 60s and 70s is not greatly different in a relative sense from that of young men and women. However, the hazards of endurance training may be considerably greater" (deVries, 1979). For these reasons the program emphasized medical screening, individual assessment of exercise response, and careful progression in training challenge. De Vries was particularly concerned about cardiovascular impairment. "Loss in maximal oxygen consumption capability translates into a loss of energy. Men have lost about 50% of this capacity by age 75. Women follow a similar course" (De Vries, 1979). Improvement in this and other capacities was documented:

Over a 42-week training period, oxygen transport in the experimental subjects improved by 29% while the controls showed no significant change. Highly significant improvements were also observed in vital capacity (19%), minute ventilation (Ve) at 90% maximum (35%), and in arm strength (12%). Other significant health benefits included a decrease in skinfold measurements concomitant with weight loss, and a decrease in both systolic and diastolic blood pressure. Exercise also had a highly significant "tranquilizer" effect on resting muscle action potentials, which appeared to be considerably better than that of meproba-mate [De Vries, 1979].

Such programs obviously involve moderate, sustained activity, not strenuous or competitive levels. "A man who jogs a few days a week will reap many of the same benefits as a marathon runner" (*Medical World News,* 1979b). As surprising as that might seem, it is one of the findings of G. Harley Hartung, Assistant Professor of Physical Medicine at Baylor College in Houston. In a study of marathon runners, joggers, and inactive men, Hartung found that the runners and joggers both had higher HDL levels. Runners ate similar diets, and were low to moderate drinkers, which also appeared to influence their HDL levels. Similar results were obtained by Rudolph H. Dressendorfer and Harry Gahagen of the Pennsylvania State University. They checked the triglyceride and total cholesterol levels of 80 runners between 22 and 59 years old. "Though serum-lipid levels of runners increased with age, the researchers found no significant difference in cholesterol levels of men who averaged nine, 18, or 36 miles a week . . . the total cholesterol levels of the runners were 5% to 10% lower than those of sedentary firemen who served as controls" (*Medical World News,* 1979b). The researchers were surprised that the high-mileage runners had approximately the same lipid levels as the low-mileage men. Dressendorfer and Gahagen concluded that "running three miles three times a week can reduce serum cholesterol" (*Medical World News,* 1979b).

In results such as these, there is always the possibility that those people who take part in exercise programs are already endowed with better cardiovascular systems than their inactive contemporaries. That may be the case in a few instances but not overall, according to Stanford University epidemiologist Ralph S. Paffenberger, Jr., who has studied over 17,000 alumni of Harvard University. From his research he has clearly determined that genetic or physical endowment alone is not a sufficient condition for prevention of cardiovascular disease. Paffenberger has confirmed earlier studies that varsity athletes did not retain their low risk status if they did not continue a regular exercise program after graduation. According to Paffenberger, "If anything, they tended to be worse off than nonathletes if they gave up sports after leaving college. On the other hand, some men who weren't particularly athletic in their student days improved their cardiovascular status by keeping up a high level of physical activity after graduation" (*Medical World News,* 1979d). People of any age can benefit from a moderate exercise program when it is judiciously planned and sustained. Images of extraordinary athletic prowess so worshiped in our culture very often intimidate people, especially elders, from beginning a program of physical activity. Findings from studies such as these and an acknowledgment that age-related deterioration is not inevitable can dismiss these misconceptions.

During 1977, Charles L. Rose and Michel L. Cohen investigated 200 variables that might be related to longevity, including their particular interest, physical activity, in order to try to answer the pressing question of "What predicts longevity?" They gathered data on these 200 variables from a study of 2,000 healthy males across all adult ages who were to be followed until their deaths. For many reasons of experimental design as well as expedience the researchers finally limited their study to 69 specific variables for 500 selected white males whose death certificates were recorded in the Boston City Hall during 1965. "In addition to looking at a whole series of longevity predictors including physical exercise and thus determining its relative importance, I [Rose] also looked at the predictors of exercise themselves. . . . In order to get at the relative position of physical exercise in the hierarchy of longevity predictors, one must identify those that are more important and less important than physical exercise . . . eight items were more important than the reference variable (exercise). . . . These were, in order of decreasing correlation: (1) fewer illnesses; (2) younger age appearance; (3) less smoking; (4) less worry; (5) rural residence; (6) sense of humor; (7) higher occupational level; and, (8) off job activity" (Rose and Cohen, 1977). Actually younger appearance at age 40 and over and fewer illnesses were the two best predictors of longevity. Such findings give a sense of the relative importance of exercise in the context of other lifestyle variables. Ralph S. Paffenberger, Jr., has also extrapolated from his data to give exercise its relative place in reducing cardiovascular disease: "A man can reasonably expect to reduce his heart disease risk by 37% through exercise, 61.5% by lowering his blood pressure, another 30% if he stops smoking, and 21.3% if he loses excess weight" (Hales, 1979).

The multiple influences which must be considered in weighing the benefits of physical exercise are also evident in the area of sexual activity in advanced age. There is an abundance of destructive mythology concerning sexuality at all ages but particularly with regard to the elderly. The most pervasive myth is that menopause for women and middle age for men was considered to signal the end of sexual life. While that may be another instance of an average cultural norm, it is neither normal nor inevitable. There are many such myths:

> One of these is that sexual thoughts, needs, and activities cease when we become older. Another myth concerns women in particular—that sexual desire stops at a certain age (menopause). There are so many of these misconceptions. Men always need to ejaculate to enjoy sex; old people are physically unattractive and therefore sexually unappealing; sex and sex appeal are for the young; sexually active old people are dirty, perverse, nasty [Davis and Davis, 1978].

While none of these myths are accurate they do exert a considerable negative effect on the sexual activity of elderly people. Fortunately, these concepts are changing and evolving, as can be seen in many recent books which consider sexuality throughout the entire lifetime. William J. Masters and Virginia E. Johnson were first, with *Human Sexual Response* (1966) and *Human Sexual Inadequacy* (1970), followed by others such as Alex Comfort's *The Joy of Sex* (1972) and Bernie Zilbergeld and J. Ullman's *Male Sexuality* (1978).

It is not the intent here to consider the human sexuality of the elderly in any comprehensive manner except to indicate the vital role of sustained sexual activity in advanced years. Adult sexuality is a complex area but there are certain predictable physiological changes which require adaptation as with diet and exercise. During the menopausal period for women, hormonal imbalances do occur, primarily with a drop in estrogen and progesterone levels while testosterone remains stable. Often this results in an increased female sex drive since testosterone is a key influence for both females and males. At the same time that sexual interest is heightened, the psychological stress of middle years and other physical changes may thwart and confuse these desires: "Women experience relatively minimal sexual change during their forties, but their skin may not be what it was and breast and buttock tone decreases" (Davis and Davis, 1978). Later in the middle years, physical illness or even surgery may further inhibit sexual relations for both men and women. This is due more to fear and self-consciousness than to biological necessity:

> Women who have had a hysterectomy are still capable of full and satisfying sexual lives. Colostomies, mastectomies and other operations that involve physical changes need not put an end to sexual activities. . . . Depression, also, can affect one's sexuality; it can slow down physical responses or even stop them altogether. . . . Again it must be stated, many older people give up sexual activity earlier than is physically necessary [Berlin, 1978].

For men as well as women these complications may prematurely terminate a satisfying sexual relationship. For the male, the change in physiological response which creates the greatest concern is the attaining and sustaining of an erection. Often during middle age, males first notice a lack of response and this generates considerable anxiety as noted by Davis and Davis:

> This failure to erect can be profoundly alarming to the forty- to fifty-year-old male, unless he understands some basic physiology of which you may want to inform him. In almost every case, a male of that age must have direct physical genital stimulation to reach a full erection, and the process may take a little time (Davis and Davis, 1978).

If this relatively minor change in physiological functioning is not recognized it can lead to anxiety focused on "performance" where each "failure" increases the likelihood of future anxiety, possibly resulting in impotence.

Impotence for males after age 40 is seldom based on decreased levels of testosterone. Research indicates that levels either remain stable or drop slowly until age 60 and remain stable from that point on. According to recent research 80 percent of males are still sexually active at age 68 and 75 percent remain active at 78, although there are changes in activity levels: "The male of seventy-eight can expect a 'refractory period' of five to ten days. During that time, no amount of effective psychological or physical stimulation will allow him to repeat the sexual response cycle" (Davis and Davis, 1978). Paradoxically, the males who are most susceptible to psychological anxiety over performance of sexual activity are ones who place a high value upon physical fitness and exercise. Psychiatrist J. C. Little has termed the phenomenon "athlete's neurosis," based on case studies of 44 male patients who exhibited the following characteristics: "(1) an excessive and often exclusive preoccupation with physical fitness, (2) a sudden breakdown occurring at about the age of 40 years, when their physical powers were beginning to wane, and (3) the fact that their breakdown had followed almost immediately some threat to their physical well-being" (Little, 1979). Very often this neurotic reaction has been triggered or aggravated by an anxiety-provoking situation during sexual activity.

These few brief observations are included here only to illustrate the fact that sexuality can be problematic for both sexes during middle age and beyond. Variables such as lifestyle, psychological status, nutrition, and physical exercise will be influenced by and exert a profound influence upon sexuality in advanced years. Rather than dwell upon the vast range of potential psychopathology, it is of greater importance to consider sexuality as an integral aspect of the entire lifetime for women and men alike. Any aspect of physical activity, sexuality included, occurs in a total life context. Larry M. Davis and Vivian E. Davis keep this larger dimension in mind when they work with the sexual concerns of elderly people:

> When we speak of "spirit" we are referring to our special essence, a deeper level than our maleness and femaleness, the level of our basic human life force or energy. . . . We work with our patients and ourselves to move towards integration of mind, body, and spirit believing that this leads to a more total human experience and better balance and happiness [Davis and Davis, 1978].

When such an orientation evolves to become the rule rather than the exception, then the intimacy of advanced years can insure that

". . . even the most difficult lives can be judged worthwhile and satisfying" (Butler, 1975). It is not simply a matter of passively condoning sexuality into advanced years, since passivity can do little to rectify the formidable and dominant sanctions which mitigate against such fulfillment. From the research with the populations of centenarian communities in Russia, Ecuador, Pakistan, and elsewhere it is evident that sexuality in advanced years is advocated, not simply condoned. Nor can sexuality be seen apart from other physical activity and general health. Physical inactivity results in reduced work capacity and diminished cardiorespiratory function which adversely affects all physical functions including sexuality.

Exercise and Life Expectancy

Returning to the effects of exercise in extending life expectancy, it has been empirically proven that the cumulative "training effects" of endurance exercise result in more efficient peripheral vessel activity requiring less oxygen and consequently less heart activity. In addition, coronary arteries may be increased in size, and serum lipid levels are lowered. "Whether these physiological changes promote longevity or confer immunity to coronary atherosclerosis remain unresolved questions" (*MD,* 1979). To evaluate these benefits, however, one must recognize that physical activity does not occur in a vacuum. A recent cover story on running in *MD* magazine noted: "Jogging and especially endurance running require health-promoting habits. Many runners report they have quit smoking, moderated drinking habits, and adopted a sensible diet. Some say that running has cured insomnia, impotence, and bettered their sexual performance" (*MD,* 1979). It is more probable that exercise enhances longevity not only through its own effects but through these multiple influences.

Interactions between lifestyle variables and exercise have also been related to the various body types of individuals in various athletic activities. Cardiologist, marathoner, and author of *Running and Being: The Total Experience* (1978) George Sheehan has postulated that certain "somatotypes" are represented in and developed by certain physical activities, and that this in turn affects the longevity statistics. After reviewing several major studies of the relationship between athletic activity and life expectancy, Sheehan observed that "endomesomorphic football players and weight lifters . . . have a shorter lifespan in our culture . . . the ectomorphic marathoner . . . who leans to withdrawal and asceticism tends to live longer . . . . Given this information, one can understand why Prout found that oarsmen live more than six years longer than randomly selected classmates; why Karvonen's cross-country skiers outlived the national average by seven or more years . . . trackmen lived longer by 14 years than football players" (Sheehan, 1973). These findings can be attributed to the interaction between lifestyle, exercise, and body type. A further variable is found in the fact that the more ectomorphic-type exercises such as walking, running, bicycling, do not depend on team efforts or special equipment and are more likely to be maintained throughout adult development. A comparison between Finnish cross-country skiers and professional major league baseball players in the United States found that

> The national ballgame . . . baseball, appears to be as healthy as cross-country skiing . . . in a study of 10,079 professional major league players . . . the total mortality of the players was 72% of the mortality of U.S. white males of similar age. Even in old age, the physiology of a former champion athlete differs in several ways from that of a non-athlete. The blood pressure . . . was lower. . . . The ex-athletes corresponded to younger "physiological age" than those of the controls. . . . Many of the former athletes continue active exercise habits" [Karvonen, 1976].

To evaluate such results future researchers will need to use more precise measures of body composition than general physical somatype classifications. It may be an error to group athletes according to type of athletic involvement or somatype, since the variables of lifestyle, continued physical exercise, and body composition may be more significant and these cut across all categories. Since obesity is a primary risk factor in advanced age, the determination of actual fat composition in the body may enable researchers to determine more precisely the effects of long-term exercise upon longevity. In *The Aerobics Way* (1977), Kenneth H. Cooper describes a method of determining an individual's percent of body fat by the use of caliper measurements of the four body sites of the chest, axilla, triceps, and suprailiac. From the measurements, it is possible to determine an individual's ideal "lean body weight," which is the total body weight less the result of the calculations. It is different for men and women. A somewhat simplified, self-administered assessment of this sort is contained in the Xerox Health Management Program (Pfeiffer, 1980). Since the overall percentage of body fat tends to increase with age, such assessments can provide a more accurate means of assessing the dimension of body composition over time. From these calculations it has been found that the actual body composition of athletes ranging from football to marathon running might be comparable if an adequate exercise program were maintained throughout the adult years. The ideal form of exercise conducive to longevity again could be defined as one which is sustained throughout life, which maintains a lean body composition, and which is accompanied by an overall reduction of lifestyle risk factors.

The resolution of these issues will ultimately depend upon systematic studies of populations in the United States and abroad who incorporate such forms of exercise in their daily lives. There are now an estimated twenty-five million joggers and runners in the United States alone. Major corporations such as Xerox, Brunswick, AT&T, and others are developing comprehensive health promotion programs with physical exercise as a key component. Over thirty-one major cities have installed outdoor exercise courses. With such a growing interest and large populations of high diversity, it will be possible to assess many hypotheses concerning the effects of exercise on longevity. One interesting study is being conducted at the Harvard Medical School where L. Howard Hartley and his colleagues have developed a program consisting of a medical evaluation, risk factor scores, dietary history, blood samples, blood pressure readings, and an exercise electrocardiogram on a bicycle ergometer performed by two technicians under physician supervision. Over 1,800 people were assessed in a variety of settings such as YMCAs, industries, a ski lodge, hotels, resorts, a police station, and public schools. After a three-year trial Hartley and his colleagues found that their accuracy was comparable to other evaluations and that "The cost of each test was between $60 and $70, which is considerably less than equivalent services at most hospitals (more than $100 for the exercise test alone at six major Boston hospitals). . . . The program appears to be effective, economical, and convenient for the participant" (Hartley et al., 1979). Assessments and exercise education program costs can be reduced even further and can be made more readily available through all of the various settings noted in the Hartley study. Benefits to overall health are likely to be immediately evident.

It is ironic that the simple biological necessity of physical activity has become an elaborate ritual entailing considerable risks and millions of dollars. That need not be the case. It is the absence of "hard physical work" that makes elaborate exercise programs necessary (Kritchevsky, 1979). The study of populations where physical activity remains more integrated into daily life is vital, as a positive model and also as a living indication of the human biological potential. During the Middle Ages, Persian couriers ran over 200 miles in 2 days to carry messages for Turkish sultans. In more recent years the Tibetan monks of the Mahetang order were trained for "swiftness of foot" to carry messages "over rough, mountainous terrain at high altitudes in severe cold conditions, run 300 miles in 30 hours while repeating their sacred mantras in synchrony with their striding and breathing" (*MD*, 1979b). Today there are the Tarahumara Indians who run distances of up to 200 miles in their competitive sport of kickball. This involves races of several days' duration, with one recorded instance of a 500-mile run over 5 days. In addition to the extensive running there was also ". . . a high degree of physical activity, both in carrying out the usual activities of their lives in subsistence farming and in the procurement of water and the other necessities of life" (Connor et al., 1978). This considerable physical activity and restricted diet is certainly a factor in the absence of cardiovascular disease among the Tarahumara people. However, the exact reasons remain unresolved. "Despite the fact that this was a physically active population, HDL levels were not increased as has been suggested for subset groups of Americans who run 10 or more miles per day. . . . HDL cholesterol levels were lower than most normals in the United States. Since total cholesterol and LDL cholesterol are likewise lower . . . this overall tendency . . . may reflect the lifelong low intakes of dietary cholesterol and saturated fat" (Connor et al., 1978). Unfortunately, the Connor study does not consider the possibility of genetic factors playing a role, as suggested by the HDL research of Charles J. Glueck cited in the previous chapter. Such genetic factors may be of considerably greater importance in isolated populations with a limited genetic base. However, even with a strong genetic predisposition operating, lifestyle, diet, and physical exercise remain important. Since the Connor study also did not report on the life expectancy of the Tarahumara Indians, that dimension remains to be explored.

Numerous research studies have noted the tendency of endurance sports to decrease heart rate. Olympic marathon runners have a rate of 58 beats per minute, middle distance runners 63, short distance runners 65, all well below the average male value of 72 beats per minute, this accompanied by significant reductions in blood pressure. Dale Groom of the University of Oklahoma School of Medicine studied eight Tarahumara Indians with no evidence of enlarged or "athlete's" heart. According to Groom's study, the Indians showed an extraordinary drop in diastolic pressure while running. "Tested at the three-quarter mark of a 28-mile race, two recorded diastolic readings of zero and the others ranged from 8 to 40 mm. Hg. After the race diastolic pressure rose to a range from 69 to 80 mm. Hg within a few minutes. All had normal blood pressures before the race and none had an abnormal electrocardiogram" (*MD,* 1979b).

Studies of populations such as the Tarahumara are extremely useful in evaluating the relative role of physical activity and other variables in lengthening life expectancy. There are many variables which have not been considered in existing studies, such as the 7,000- to 8,000-foot-altitude home of the Tarahumara, the absence of electromagnetic smog, the presence of abundant negative ionization, and psychosocial influences. Perhaps their example is a necessary one for our society where the ancient survival value of physical strength and agility is no longer respected. Above all else, the very existence of populations such as the Tarahumara Indians and centenarian communities is a fundamental challenge and alternative to the most basic values of contemporary society. Their environment, lifestyle, diet, and physical activity is in direct contrast to the dominant characteristics of the majority of the earth's population. While it is not possible or perhaps even desirable to emulate their example, they are living evidence of the "road not taken" as well as an unfulfilled biological potential.

As to the role of exercise in extending human longevity, it is obviously important, although tightly interwoven with other factors. Alexander Leaf noted this striking blend of influences in *Youth in Old Age:* "More striking and significant to me than the absolute ages of these elders was their remarkable physical and mental fitness and their obvious joy in life compared to the senility and debility so common among the elders of our society" (Leaf, 1975). Chapter VIII will explore the way of life in certain centenarian communities where physical activity is an integral part of every day.

EIGHT

A Century
of Life

Isocrates, the Athenian orator of 436–338 B.C., lived to be 98; Heraclitus of Ephesus, the Greek philosopher of about 556 to 460 B.C., lived to age 96; and the philosopher and mathematician Pythagoras lived to 91 during about 580 to 489 B.C. These are among the earliest documented instances of extended longevity. From such records and others noted in the first chapter, Alexander Leaf has concluded that "The exceptional survival time of yesterday is still the exceptional survival time of today" (Leaf, 1973). To investigate exceptional longevity Leaf undertook extensive observations of three geographic areas in the world where individuals were reported to live to ages considerably beyond 100 years old. Details of these findings and other related studies are discussed in this chapter. All the variables considered up to this become focused when such societies are studied. Since emotional outpouring in this area of inquiry virtually inundates the relative paucity of evidence, it is essential to establish the working hypotheses upon which this information is presented.

Despite the interest in these biological niches of extreme longevity in isolated geographic areas, it is important to remember that they are not unique and that instances of healthy longevity of 90 to 120 years have been documented in many other societies since at least the sixth century B.C. Such instances are an indication of a biological potential inherent to the human species as a whole.

The Study of Centenarian Communities

To date there have been studies of several major centenarian communities and individuals throughout the world, including the Vilcabamba in the Ecuadorian Andes, the Hunza who live deep in the Karakoram Range of the western Himalayas in northern Pakistan, the Abkhazians in the Caucasus Mountains of Georgia in the Soviet Union, the Mabaans of Sudan, and the Tarahumara Indians of the Sierra Madre Occidental mountains in the north central state of Chihuahua in Mexico. There has also been limited research with centenarian individuals in the United States, and extensive case studies of individuals evidencing extended longevity. Most of this research has been conducted by Alexander Leaf and is clearly of an "observational" nature according to Leaf's own qualifications (Leaf, 1978). Despite the cautions clearly stated by many researchers, there has been a tendency for public and professional journals to overstate the conclusions of such findings. "A public eager to believe that there is really a fountain of youth pouring forth somewhere on this globe is not easily put off by a scientist's natural pessimism. A good segment of mankind has always wanted to believe in paradise" (*Nutrition Today*, 1978). Nor is it only the "public" who are gullible; "scientists" are not all rational skeptics. Now the pendulum has swung from uncritical acceptance of centenarian observations to equally unfounded refutation.

To date there is only one empirical study of one of the reported centenarian communities which has challenged the phenomenon on the grounds of "age exaggeration," though without entirely refuting the earlier findings (Mazess and Forman, 1979). While that study is important and will be considered here, it is equally important to note that evidence for the existence of centenarian populations has been ostensibly refuted many times. Irrational and premature statements abound on both sides of the issue as testimony to the considerable effect elicited in any discussion of longevity. This chapter cannot resolve these issues but it is an attempt to identify and clarify some of the important questions which remain unanswered amidst the emotional din.

The biological potential suggested in the studies of these communities is the focus of the chapter. While biochemical data and observations of centenarian communities cannot prove or disprove the biological potential of humankind, this living evidence merits serious consideration.

World attention focused on centenarian communities in 1973 when *National Geographic* (Leaf, 1973a), *Scientific American* (Leaf, 1973b), and *Hospital Practice* (Leaf, 1973c) all published reports by Alexander Leaf that he had observed three communities of individuals who apparently were living well beyond 100 years of age in extremely good health. His interest had been prompted by reports of earlier research by Ecuadorian physician Miguel Salvador (Salvador, 1972) and a research team of scientists and physicians who had been studying the Vilcabamba. The publication of Leaf's reports stirred up great interest in these communities. Simultaneously, researchers pointed out a small but significant body of data indicating the common phenomenon of "age exaggeration" by the extremely elderly people of populations throughout the world. Exaggeration of age had been studied in the United States (Myers, 1966; Rosenwaike, 1968) as well as in the Soviet Union (McKain, 1967; Medvedev, 1974; Myers, 1965). Overall these studies indicated consistent excesses in the self-reporting of age by elderly people and cast doubt upon subsequent reports of extreme longevity. Commenting on the phenomenon of age exaggeration in the United States, Robert J. Myers, formerly Chief Actuary of the Social Security Administration, has noted: "Overstatement of age seems to be particularly the case among those who claim to be aged 110 or over. Demographers are familiar with the story of the persons at the oldest ages who become some 15 years older between each decennial census" (Myers, 1966).

This acknowledged tendency is often cited to refute longevity. While it may mean that there are fewer centenarians than reported, it does not mean that there are none. Leonard Hayflick is among those who criticize centenarian studies: "Wholly authentic data on the life span of man do not reveal life spans beyond 110 to 120 years and studies of the Abkhazians, using rigid rules of evidence, have largely exploded the myth of their reputed longevity" (Hayflick, 1973b). While extreme ages of 150 are unlikely, instances of ages 110 and thereabouts are thoroughly documented. Leaf did not rely on subjective reports alone, but used baptismal and marriage records, church documents, notations in family Bibles, letters, passports, "the person's memory of outstanding events," and "even carvings on walls and doors that record the birth of a new member of the family" (Leaf, 1973c). Due to the obscure and unwritten Hunza language, Leaf did generally accept the verbal reports of age in that community, which may mean that age exaggeration influences those reports. Other researchers such as Miguel Salvador in Ecuador, Professor G. Z. Pitskhelaurt in the Soviet Union, and S. Magsood Ali of Pakistan have independently verified the ages of the three centenarian communities observed by Leaf. Professor Pitskhelaurt assessed the self-report ages versus documentation with 704 Georgian centenarians and reported, "almost 95% had given correct ages; the rest were within 5% of the correct age. In no case was the stated age more than 10 years above or below the documented age" (Leaf, 1973c). Age exaggeration is a potentially confounding variable, but since subjective reports were not the only indicator of longevity in any of the previous studies, it is not adequate grounds to dismiss their results.

The research generally cited to disprove claims of longevity in centenarian communities was conducted by Richard B. Mazess of the Department of Radiology at the University of Wisconsin and Sylvia II. Forman of the Department of Anthropology at the University of Massachusetts. An earlier research project had been undertaken by Mazess to assess the "bone mineral content" of the Vilcabamba since they were a "population noted for longevity and rarity of fractures and spinal curvature in the elderly" (Mazess, 1978). Such conditions usually accompany loss of minerals in aging skeletal systems. Using a method of direct photon absorptiometry, Mazess assessed the bone mineral content of 188 males ages 5 to 99 and 164 females ages 5 to 95 years. When the data analysis was performed, Mazess adjusted for age, weight, and height since the Vilcabamba have a smaller build relative to whites in the United States but entirely normal for their size. From these data Mazess found the Vilcabambas had a "15% . . . lower amount of bone . . . evident in all age-sex groups" and ". . . the rate of aging bone was almost identical to the rate observant in U.S. whites (4% per decade in males and 10% per decade in females)" (Mazess, 1978). Despite this reduced bone mass, Mazess did confirm the relative absence of "bone deformities in children and the absence of osteoporosis (spinal curvature, fractures) in the elderly" (Mazess, 1978). "Apparently factors other than reduced bone mass may be etiologic in the clinical manifestations of skeletal aging, or there may be compensatory mechanisms which offset the usual pathologic sequelae of aging bone loss. The extent to which this obtains in Vilcabamba, as distinct from other populations, remains to be explored" (Mazess, 1978). It is interesting to note the acknowledgment of multiple influences in an area as specific as bone mineral content and subsequent disease.

In his conclusion Mazess noted: "While this casts doubt on the claims of extreme longevity, it in no way runs counter to the observations that there is a large population of relatively healthy elderly people in Vilcabamba" (Mazess, 1978). After reviewing this research Alexander Leaf himself has concluded, "Thus, though I think the health message that I was trying to promote is still correct, the evidence of unusual longevity in the populations that I visited, is certainly not correct" (Leaf, 1980). Leaf's emphasis on health is important. Interest in extended life expectancy can take attention away from the quality and subsequent quantity of life. The older people in these communities teach us that individuals can remain optimally healthy and actively involved in the entire psychosocial matrix of their culture far beyond the point considered possible at the present time.

Drawing upon some of the age documentation for this earlier study, Richard B. Mazess and Sylvia H. Forman subsequently published an empirical study of actual longevity among the Vilcabambas. Using 1974 census data of approximately 80% of the population of 1,100 people, constructing genealogies for some of the elders, and obtaining actual birth records focused the research on "95 living adults over age 30, and 24 recently deceased persons over the age of 50 years" (Mazess and Forman, 1979). There were several common errors noted by the researchers in previous records, including the use of the same names repeatedly over many generations resulting in mistaking the records of parents for those of their children or later children receiving the same name of a sibling who had died years earlier. With these previous errors accounted for, the researchers performed a "linear regression analysis" which compared the actual ages of the 95 subjects to their reported ages found, "There was little age exaggeration up to 60 or 70 years, but after this systematic age exaggeration was evident. . . . None of the 23 'centenarians' investigated had in fact survived to 100 years. Similarly none of the 15 'nonagenarians' investigated had in fact reached 90 years" (Mazess and Forman, 1979). Many of the famous centenarians noted by Leaf and other researchers were considered in this population and their extreme ages were discounted. The researchers noted another important factor: the age exaggeration ". . . has been worsened by recent scientific and tourist incursions."

These are very significant findings but according to the researchers themselves they do not refute the previous observations, although many subsequent researchers have erroneously attributed that conclusion to the Mazess and Forman study. The original study concludes: "It has not been possible to completely resolve the controversy concerning longevity in Vilcabamba, but we were able, using the above approach, to show the elderly had overstated their ages . . . . While extreme longevity is questionable, our results do provide some support for previous census findings of a high percentage of persons over 60 years in Vilcabamba. . . . There may have been, and may still be, some centenarians in the Vilcabamban region; our results do not exclude this possibility" (Mazess and Forman, 1979). Furthermore, they state, ". . . it appeared many older individuals had died in the past decade. The proportion of elderly may have been higher prior to 1970 when extensive contact with surrounding areas became common" (Mazess and Forman, 1979). Finally, the researchers rightfully call for careful documentation of all aspects of the Vilcabamban society:

On the other hand Vilcabamba, and perhaps the other centers of supposed longevity, seem exceptional in having a relatively large group of elderly inhabitants who remain physically active and who seem to maintain cardiovascular and musculoskeletal health. Hopefully, both longevity and health will be studied in all these communities with greater exactitude in the future [Mazess and Forman, 1979].

This excellent study is insightful, respectful of its limitations, and aware of possible misinterpretations and premature conclusions.

While a person of 96 may not seem so impressive as one of 140 or 150, it is an impressive age by any standards, at any time, in any geographic location. Another 30 or 40 years of healthy life is like another full lifetime. The health of the Vilcabamba elders remains highly significant and thoroughly documented.

More accurate physiological measures of age are clearly needed. Jeffrey L. Bada and Patricia M. Masters of the Scripps Institution of Oceanography in San Diego have adapted methods used in dating the antiquity of fossils. "By examining proteins in the teeth or lenses of the eyes . . . it is possible to calculate the year of birth with only a 10 percent margin of error" (Sobel, 1979). When Russian gerontologists gave the researchers a tooth from a Soviet Georgian, the researchers estimated her age at 91 when her documented age was known to be 96 years old. Such biologically based approaches are promising though they clearly require further development. Even if the results of such inquiries demonstrate 120-year life-spans as opposed to the reported 150-year life-spans, that discovery would be highly significant. Actually there is a great deal more evidence to suggest the possibility of such an extended life expectancy than there is to support a built-in limit at the present average life expectancy. There is sufficient basic and observational data at least to leave open the question of whether or not there are living populations which demonstrate the future biological potential of the human species.

Centenarian individuals and communities may very well be such prototypes since numerous aspects of their biological endowment, lifestyle, and psychosocial order are the very factors conducive to longevity discussed in earlier chapters. Extrapolating from research to the human condition is a formidable task, but it is evident that many influences on longevity suggested in such research are clearly manifested in the lives and social orders of centenarian communities. Such inferences must still be tentative, for the data indicate an enormous range of variation on certain basic themes. Recently the newsletter of the consumer-oriented Committee for an Extended Lifespan published a list of the various alleged panaceas for attaining longevity, drawn from the self-reports of long-lived individuals. Items on the list range from "sleep with your hat on" to "drink a pint of whiskey per day" (Otto, 1979). Clearly there are no universal factors. As this chapter will indicate, this is as true of cultures as it is of individuals and is a testimony to the diversity and complexity of humankind. Focusing too exclusively on what is common among centenarians can exclude the most significant factors.

With that reservation in mind it is possible to outline and clarify certain common denominators and their variants which are characteristic of centenarian populations. These influences are of equal importance, although any one or any subgroup may assume greater emphasis in the ratio for a given person or culture for a given time and circumstances. Among the common denominators of longevity in individuals and cultures throughout the world and in the United States are: (1) hereditary or genetic influences; (2) dietary and nutritional factors; (3) consumption of moderate amounts of alcohol; (4) physical activity throughout life; (5) sexual activity prolonged into advanced years; (6) environmental influences; and (7) psychological factors including continued productive involvement in family and community affairs. Many of these factors were discussed in relation to optimum health in the final chapter of *Holistic Medicine* (Pelletier, 1979). The specific implications of these factors for longevity will be elaborated here.

This list is of course not exhaustive, no one variable is mutually exclusive of others, and future research may yet indicate that all of these are the superficial aspects of a yet undiscovered factor of paramount importance. Even before such final answers are in, research in centenarian communities may have many benefits. By studying people who attain extended longevity in optimum health it may be possible to learn how to enhance these conditions in our own population. Alexander Leaf considered this possibility:

> Much of what we do for our elderly patients represents an attempt to rectify debilitating diseases that have already reached an irreversible stage. Arteriosclerosis, arthritis, and other degenerative diseases are common among elderly Americans. But are such diseases an essential part of the aging process? Are

there not places in the world where a significant proportion of the people live to a ripe old age and yet somehow remain in vigorous health, retaining their mental capacities even to age 100 or more? [Leaf, 1973c].

It seems more likely now than in 1973 that these questions can be systematically explored and resolved. Virtually every aspect of the centenarian communities represents a living alternative to the traditional values of Western culture. These communities are viable instances of the "road not taken": rugged mountain paths instead of freeways, minimal material wealth contrasted to excessive opulence, simplicity of diet and necessary exercise versus overindulgence and sedentary obesity, social cohesiveness, and a sense of purpose rather than fragmentation and ennui. While these conditions have been imposed by necessity upon members of these communities, they present critical value decisions for Western culture. Romantic illusions aside, these lifestyles carry severe limitations and stresses of their own but they remain unique prototypes of another way to live a life.

Genetic Factors

In all discussions of longevity, genetic or hereditary influences are probably cited more often than any other explanation. There is a tendency to attribute any unknown influence to genetic endowment. However, the influences which determine whether or not a genetic predisposition is expressed can occur at any time in an organism's development, and are probably as important as the infinitesimal event of the sperm fertilizing an egg. Addressing the issue of heredity, Alexander Leaf has concluded:

> Heredity is generally thought to be a significant factor in long life, as indeed it is. Several studies of life expectancy of offspring of long-lived parents indicated a significant advantage over that for offspring of short-lived parents. The advantage, however, is a modest one. One study of the inheritance of longevity based upon life insurance records indicated that offspring of long-lived

parents had a life expectancy at age 20 that probably does not exceed by three years the life expectancy of a similar aged group whose parents were short-lived. This was the maximal statistical advantage that could be attributed to heredity according to this study [Leaf, 1973c].

Genetic variables were of particular importance in Leaf's observations since the Vilcabambans are primarily of European-Spanish rather than Indian descent and appear to be highly inbred and isolated. In the Hunza these conditions of inbreeding were also evident and could indicate a genetic expression of longevity. The centenarians of the Caucasus region, however, do not exhibit a limited gene pool. A 1970 census listed ten different ethnic groups. Among the 4,500 to 5,000 centenarians noted in that census, there were Russians, Georgians, Armenians, Turks, and others "suggesting that no single isolated genetic factor is involved in longevity" (Leaf, 1973c).

A possible indication of genetic influences interacting with lifestyle variables is the consistent observation that people of the centenarian communities have a marked absence of cardiovascular and coronary heart disease. Several recent studies have a bearing on this issue. Research by E. Cuyler Hammond and his colleagues from the Department of Epidemiology of the American Cancer Society examined the longevity of parents and grandparents in relation to coronary heart disease and associated variables in their offspring. After examining the records of over 15,000 men and 50,000 women over a period of six years, the researchers concluded, "Death rates from coronary heart disease, hypertensive heart disease, and stroke were found to be considerably higher among subjects with short-lived parents than among subjects with long-lived parents" (Hammond et al., 1971). Since this conclusion is often cited, it is important to acknowledge several contributing influences which make the genetic factor per se more equivocal. One is that the actual mortality age differences were rather small, though statistically significant. Second, the researchers acknowledged that while some risk factors such as "hypertension" and "lack of exercise" were considered, others such as "glucose tolerance" and "serum lipid" were not. The researchers themselves acknowledged: "However, we cannot rule out the possibility that nongenetic transmittal of some factor or set of factors might have accounted for the findings" (Hammond et al., 1971). Though the inextricable interaction between genetic, environmental, and lifestyle variables is consistently acknowledged throughout such research, the myth of genetic causation persists, particularly with regard to centenarian cultures.

Related to the Hammond research is a project by Margaret H. Abbott and her colleagues at the Johns Hopkins Hospital in Baltimore, Maryland, where the team examined the survival of 9,205 progeny, 4,537 females and 4,668 males, of 1,766 nonagenarian parents originally studied in a classic book by Pearl and Pearl (1934). From their data the researchers also noted ". . . a fairly uniform, but weak, positive relationship between the ages at death of the nonlongevus parent and of the progeny, the relationships between mother and child being closer than that between father and child" (Abbott et al., 1974). Following this research, Fu-Sun Yen and a research team from the UCLA Department of Psychiatry attempted a study of the actual chromosome composition of venous blood samples drawn from a small sample of 19 female octogenarians. These were part of an original subject pool of 1,603 twins in a longitudinal study initiated in 1948. The team confirmed ". . . the higher frequency of hypodiploid cells (cells with less than 46 chromosomes) in older compared to younger women . . . an increased frequency of hypodiploidy could not be confirmed for older men" (Yen et al., 1976). Chromosome samples drawn from 19 octogenarian women in 1970 who survived until 1976 were compared to those of 19 of the original sample who had died in that six-year interval. Although there was the hypodiploid difference noted, the researchers concluded that, ". . . none of the differences were statistically significant . . . . So far, no relationship has been detected—either in men or women—with the six-year survival during the ninth decade of life" (Yen et al., 1976). Even at the chromosomal level of analysis, the influence of isolated genetic variables on longevity is not apparent.

In Chapter VI the research of Charles J. Glueck and his colleagues was cited since it implies a strong genetic influence in promoting optimum ratios of HDL to LDL in the 80-year-old kindred of long-lived parents. Although his research does indicate a reduced risk for these kindred, one major study concludes with this overriding qualifier:

The generalizability of the conclusions is sharply redistricted by
our lack of data on additional "risk factors" in the hyperalpha-
and hypobeta-lipoproteinemic octogenarian kindreds; did they
smoke less, did they have a lower blood pressure on average,
were they less obese, etc.? Just as there is a mosaic of interacting
risk factors which potentiate atherosclerosis, there are probably
many "anti-risk factors" (including high C-HDL and low
C-LDL) which are protective [Glueck et al., 1977].

One of the foremost researchers in the area of genetics and longevity
is Irving S. Wright, Chairman of the New York Academy of Medicine's Section on Geriatric Medicine. From his wide-ranging research comes a means of assessing a person's "heredity longevity
potential" based on familial history. Wright believes that this should
be included in any assessment of risk factors, such as in the Health
Hazard Appraisal, since "unless the hereditary longevity potential is
included the most important item will be missing" (Wright, 1978). At
the same time, he clearly recognizes the significance of lifestyle factors which we have discussed: "Tobacco, obesity, untreated hypertension, hyperlipidemia, and excessive stress should be controlled if
we wish to achieve our personal heredity longevity potential"
(Wright, 1978).

This overview of studies citing interaction effects between genetic
and lifestyle variables could be greatly extended. It appears certain
from research with long-lived individuals both within and outside of
centenarian communities that genetic influences on longevity are a
contributing but highly limited factor. Data from a twelve-year study
of the Abkhazians by Georgian cardiologist David Kakiashvili show
how lifestyle influences can affect possible genetic factors. From a
series of electrocardiogram studies Kakiashvili found that these elderly people "do have the usual range of cardiovascular disease."
However, "continuous physical activity develops and maintains an
extensive collateral blood supply to the heart, and . . . if one artery
gets pinched off because of localized arteriosclerosis, the collateral
circulation is sufficient to prevent atrophy of the affected heart muscles" (Leaf, 1973c). Such influences which enhance or suppress genetic predispositions are most often referred to, in a derogatory
manner, as "confounding variables" since they inconveniently con-

taminate or obscure reductionistic models of cause and effect. Every attempt is made to eliminate or "control" such variables. In a similar manner, most researchers dismiss the contaminating influences of "placebo," "consciousness and belief systems," "spontaneous remission," "regenerative psychosis," and a host of phenomena which may be more significant than the effects being researched. Rather than viewing such influences as contaminating and extraneous and attempting to eliminate them, a more holistic approach emphasizes the necessity of multiple variables and their interactions. It is possible to recognize and acknowledge genetic, medical, psychosocial, environmental, and other influences and to determine the ratio of each given factor upon a given individual or culture. While such approaches are considerably more difficult to design and implement, they are not only possible but mandatory in the study of longevity.

From the point of view of people already born, concern with genetic endowment is of course academic. The other six factors in longevity mentioned above are within the control of individuals. As Alexander Leaf has noted, "Since few of us have the opportunity to choose our parents, it is fortunate that improving environmental factors have had such a favorable effect on health . . . if environmental matters are paramount, then many new directions are open to us" (Leaf, 1973c). To provide a context for these new directions, the excellent research and writings of Thomas McKeown, Professor Emeritus of Social Medicine at the University of Birmingham in England, are most helpful. In his classic work, *The Role of Medicine* (1979), McKeown outlines the steps which can be taken to insure health and longevity, and the relatively minor role medicine has and will play in this task:

> The improvement of health during the past three centuries was due essentially to provision of food, protection from hazards, and limitation of numbers. Assessment of the determinants of human health suggests that the same influences are likely to be effective in future; but there is this difference, that in developed countries personal behaviour (in relation to diet, exercise, tobacco, alcohol, drugs, etc.) is now even more important than provision of food and control of hazards. . . . The limitations of the traditional concept of the medical role would have been

recognized much earlier, if health had not been transformed in the past three centuries by other influences.

What is needed is an adjustment in the balance of interest and resources between the three main areas of service referred to above. It is essential to give sufficient attention to the personal and non-personal influences which are the major determinants of health: to food and the environment, which will be mainly in the hands of specialists, and to personal behaviour [McKeown, 1979].

These same principles provide the context for a consideration of the common factors found to be conducive to longevity. Environmental and psychosocial influences conducive to optimum health are also conducive to longevity. While the relative importance of any given factor for an individual or culture is highly variable, they are uniformly present among centenarian communities.

Nutrition

After genetic endowment, the second common denominator conducive to longevity found in observations of centenarians is nutritional and dietary practice. The Vilcabambas are a totally agricultural community where people raise their own vegetables and grain. Their diet is almost exclusively vegetarian with small amounts of protein and fat derived from vegetable sources. According to physician Guillermo Vela of Quito, the daily caloric intake is very low at 1,200 calories. The Hunza are also an agricultural community with diets similar to that of the Vilcabambas. In a survey of 55 adult male Hunzakuts, Pakistani nutritionist Magsood Ali determined their average daily caloric intake at 1,923 calories comprising 50 grams of protein, 32 grams of fat, and 354 grams of unrefined carbohydrate (Leaf, 1973d). Animal protein and fat constituted less than 1 percent of the daily caloric intake. Oil extracted from apricot seeds is used in cooking. Grains, leafy green vegetables, root vegetables, dried legumes, fresh milk and buttermilk, clarified butter and cheese, fresh and sun-dried apricots, mulberries, and grape wine constitute the usual diet. Portions consumed are quite frugal. In summer a typical meal consists of a "... soup made from grain, corn, yuka (a kind of root), beans and potatoes. This mainstay is augmented with oranges, bananas, and a little unrefined sugar. A considerable quantity of vegetables is eaten. ... In winter less fruit is available" (Davies, 1973). Many of the dietary practices and actual recipes of the Hunza have been adapted to ingredients readily available in the United States by Renée Taylor in *Hunza Health Secrets for Long Life and Happiness* (1964).

Among the Hunza, crops of vegetables, grains, fruits, and nuts are often inadequate to last through the severe winters. As a result, "Before the new greens come through in the spring, the people have gone through a period of semistarvation" (Leaf, 1973c). This is a very important observation, consistent with all of the research concerning the longevity enhancement effects of prolonged caloric restriction discussed in Chapters III and IV. These conditions are of course imposed by circumstance rather than voluntarily undertaken. It would be important to examine the constituents of centenarian diets in infancy, since these imposed restrictions may have inadvertently created the particular caloric, protein, and tryptophan moderate deficiencies noted to double the life expectancy of laboratory animals (Segall et al., 1978; Segall, 1979). Examination of early dietary patterns is of great importance since diet during the critical stages of early development appears to be at least as important as, if not more so than, dietary habits during the rest of life.

If all of these data seem to fit the dietary prescriptives discussed in Chapter VI almost too well, then the Georgians of the Soviet Union provide somewhat contrary evidence. When their diet is examined, it is quite a contrast to that of the Vilcabambas and Hunzakuts: "Theirs is a mixed agriculture-dairy economy and they consume animal products almost daily. The people live not only by their vegetables and fruits but also by their herds of cows, goats, and sheep. They drink milk, eat cheese and yogurt three times a day and often have meat" (Leaf, 1973c). Despite these animal products in the diet, the caloric consumption for people over 50 remains low, 1,800 calories, as opposed to an average of 3,300 calories in the United States. Their diet is high in roughage, high in unrefined carbohydrates, low in salt, refined carbohydrate, and refined sugar consumption. All of this is in contrast to the average diet in the United States with its high fat, low roughage, high salt and sugar content. Some aspects of this diet fall short of the nutritional recommendations of the National Academy of Sciences, yet virtually none of the inhabitants have been found to be either malnourished or obese. Although the dairy product intake is higher than might be expected, it is still considerably lower than in the average American diet.

The Abkhazian consumption of dairy and animal products raises the question of serum cholesterol levels. In two journal articles Alexander Leaf reported the results of research by Miguel Salvador, who noted a low level of 219 $\pm$ 10 mgs per 100 ml of serum for 49 Vilcabambans who were ages 60 and over. Reported levels for the Abkhazians were at an astounding 91.8 $\pm$ 4.2 mgs per 100 ml of plasma for males and females (Leaf, 1973c, 1973d). For males in the United States there is a "normal" increase in serum cholesterol from ages 18 to 32 where it tends to level at 250 mgs per 100 ml. For women this same trend begins approximately 13 years later and peaks at age 50. Leaf challenges the normality of such trends by citing data from primitive inhabitants of the Solomon Islands where "there is no tendency for plasma cholesterol to rise with age. Thus even our notions of the 'normal' or average values for the cholesterol may be biased by the prevalence of atherogenic diets in our own culture" (Leaf, 1973d). The figures for the Abkhazians demonstrate that dietary influences alone cannot be divorced from lifelong physical activity and other factors known to modify nutrition and diet.

While the protein intake of the vegetarian Vilcabambas and Hunzakut is low at 35 to 38 grams and 50 grams, respectively, this is not necessarily dictated by their vegetarian diet. When the vegetarian diet of corn and beans of the Tarahumara Indians was discussed in the last chapter, the protein level was quite high at 79 to 96 grams per day. These communities are not undernourished in any dimension of diet but are living examples of the advice of the American Heart Association: ". . . for long life, maintain a moderate caloric intake that generally avoids obesity, and a diet low in animal and saturated fats" (Leaf, 1973c).

Although there is a considerable amount of data concerning diet and nutrition among these three centenarian communities, there are many questions which have not been addressed. Trace substances are an example. "No one has yet studied the intake of magnesium or cobalt or other essential substances in the three areas" (Leaf, 1973c); Another variable may be the quality of the water. The Hunza water supply winds through mountains for many miles before reaching the valley. "By the time it reaches the valley, it has picked up so much silt that it is opaque in a drinking glass. . . . It refuses to precipitate, even if the water is allowed to stand overnight" (Leaf, 1973c). Analysis of the mineral content of such water would be important since it may be a primary source of trace elements or it may be involved in free radical activity both externally and internally. Recent research by Theodore Mill and his colleagues at Stanford Research Institute in Menlo Park, California, has provided a methodology for experimenting with this possibility. Obtaining "natural water" samples from a river, a creek, and a lake, the researchers noted an abundance of "free radical oxidants in natural waters" (Mill et al., 1980). Since an increase in free radical activity in the interior of cells has been found to be a major factor in aging, the presence of free radical oxidants would appear to accelerate rather than retard the aging in centenarian communities. This question cannot be resolved now since the biochemistry involved would be extremely complex, but the analytic methodology of the SRI research team provides a means of addressing this issue. Many of the locals attribute their long life to "various herb teas they drink," according to David Davies (1973) in the Unit of Gerontology of University College London. Mo Siegel, of Celestial Seasonings tea in Boulder, Colorado, noted, "They never heat their teas above 140 degrees Fahrenheit" (Woodfin, 1978). Actual methods of food preparation are a further variable worth studying, since preparation can enhance or nullify nutritional constituents.

With all these questions still unresolved, the influence of nutrition on health, life expectancy, and longevity must still be recognized as of major importance. Thomas McKeown equated the status of nutrition with that of Darwinian evolution: "The case for the significance of nutrition is circumstantial. In this it is like the case for the origin of species by natural selection, which so far lacks confirmation by experimental production of a new species. It is nevertheless a convincing hypothesis because it has stood the test of critical examination in a variety of circumstances over an extended period" (McKeown, 1979).

A third common factor, related to nutrition, in each of these communities is alcohol. Each had its own alcoholic drink with no evidence of alcoholism. The Vilcabambas imbibe a potent liquor made from sugar cane, and the Abkhazian people drink two or three glasses of wine at each meal plus a moderate amount of vodka and brandy (Favazza, 1977). David Davies made this observation of the Vilcabambas: "One particularly remarkable feature is that the inhabitants drink two to four cups of rum a day, and smoke anything from 40 to 60 cigarettes each day. But the rum is unrefined and the cigarettes are home-made, usually from tobacco grown in their gardens, and wrapped in maize leaves (though toilet paper is preferred if available)" (Davies, 1973). Similar observations have been noted for the Hunza, who liberally enjoy a red wine called "Hunzapana," and the Abkhazians, who make a wine as well as a strong vodka from their own grapes. To date there are no actual measures of the alcohol content of these drinks nor of the actual amount consumed or consumption patterns, although drinking alcohol before or with breakfast is not uncommon. Although there are no empirical data concerning alcoholic consumption, reports seem to indicate a level far in excess of the "moderate alcohol consumption" discussed in Chapter VI. Since there is no evidence of alcoholism, such observations need to be explored to consider the role of other dietary effects upon alcohol consumption. Alcohol is consumed in the context of an adequate diet, physical activity interacts with the alcohol to result in optimal HDL to LDL ratios; and there is lack of social stigma as well as active support for the appropriate use of alcohol. All three of these influences are markedly absent in the profile of alcoholics in the United States. When local residents of the centenarian communities are asked to what factor they would attribute their long lives, credit was most frequently given to the local alcoholic beverage, to their vigorous sexual activity, or both!

Physical Activity

Physical activity is the fourth and perhaps the most important factor in the longevity and optimum health exhibited in these centenarian communities. Associated with it is the consistently very important fifth factor, active sexuality. From Alexander Leaf's observations, "The level of physical activity and fitness among the aged was very striking in all three areas . . . the expenditure of physical energy probably is a better explanation of exceptional longevity than any other apparent influence" (Leaf, 1973c). "In all three cultures the people are physically active throughout life since they are primarily farmers who labor by hand and walk a great deal in mountainous terrain or ride horses" (Witte et al., 1967). If hard physical labor seems a dour prescription for longevity, it is also important to note that there are numerous "festivals" among these people and a great deal of toasting with alcohol plus "native dances which are performed for us with such vigor in the mid-day heat" (Leaf, 1973d). There is little evidence of the enforced austerity and rigor which accompanies exercise programs in the United States. Popular writer John Langone has created a witty parody of what passes for the "healthy" life in our society:

> And if I need a creed, I suppose it would be this sketch that some physician drew up of the man least likely to have coronary disease, someone I don't want to be: An effeminate municipal worker or embalmer completely lacking in physical and mental alertness and without drive, ambition or competitive spirit, who has never attempted to meet a deadline of any kind. A man with poor appetite, subsisting on fruit and vegetables laced with corn and whale oils, detesting tobacco, spurning ownership of radio, TV or car, with full head of hair and scrawny and unathletic in appearance, yet constantly straining his puny muscles by exercise, low in income, blood pressure, blood sugar, uric acid and cholesterol, who has been taking nicotinic acid, pyridoxine and

long-term anticoagulant therapy ever since his prophylactic castration [Langone, 1978].

The benefits of physical activity that is well-integrated into a person's entire life rather than confined to mandatory exercise periods is clear from two classic studies undertaken in Great Britain and the United States. J. N. Norris compared the incidence of heart attacks among postal workers in London who delivered mail versus those who had desk positions. Only 51 of 171 postmen suffered myocardial infarctions, while nearly half, or 70, of 143 office workers had heart attacks. Norris also conducted extensive postmortem studies indicating that "men in physically active jobs have less coronary heart disease during middle age, what disease they have is less severe, and they develop it later than men in physically inactive jobs. The hearts of sedentary workers showed the pathology of the hearts of heavy workers ten to fifteen years older" (Leaf, 1977). The other study was initiated by Curtis Harnes, an astute general physician in Evans County, Georgia. Harnes had observed a high incidence of coronary heart disease among his white male patients, but few cases of heart attacks among black male patients. A detailed survey of this observation was conducted by J. C. Cassel, who studied all adults over age 40 and half of the males between the ages of 15 and 39 in Evans County between 1960 and 1962. From 1967 to 1968, 91 percent of this population was reexamined. Three groups of white sharecroppers were identified, and it was clear that two of these groups and the black men had less than half the incidence of coronary heart disease of the third group, who were white nonfarmers. "Analysis of the data revealed that it was the level of physical activity required by the blacks and white sharecroppers which largely protected these two groups from coronary artery disease. Most known risk factors were measured—namely blood pressure, serum cholesterol level, cigarette smoking, body weight, and diet—and could not account for the differences" (Leaf, 1977).

These studies make it clear that physical activity helps to burn excess calories and dispose of undigested fats and thus appears to be a significant factor in preventing cardiovascular disease. Exercise may well prove to be the most significant factor mediating nutrition and help to account for the great individual differences in tolerance for high-risk diets.

After extensive physical examinations of the people of the Caucasian village of Duripshi, Alexander Leaf concluded that physical activity was a potent preventive measure not only against cardiovascular disease such as myocardial infarction and atherosclerosis but other disorders such as osteoporosis. This latter condition, an increased porosity of the bones, is common among the elderly of the United States. When this condition is present, the calcium and salts which harden bones as well as the collagen and cartilage matrix for these components all begin to deteriorate and bones become thin, less dense, and fragile. Studies by the National Academy of Sciences entitled *Human Factors in Long-Duration Spaceflight* (1972) have found that astronauts experienced this condition under physical inactivity under conditions of weightlessness, since reduced stress on the skeletal system caused calcium and phosphate to pour out of the bones. Among the people of the centenarian communities Leaf saw no evidence of osteoporosis and found the people to be consistently strong and active. Donald Whedon, who is Director of the National Institute of Arthritis, Metabolism, and Digestive Disease, has concluded, "We need a major effort to educate middle-aged people to manage their lives to prevent this thinning of bone tissue" (Marx, 1980). Among the measures recommended by Whedon, including increased consumption of calcium, is:

> . . . maintenance of physical activity. Whedon is one of the investigators who showed that deprivation of physical activity, as in patients immobilized in bed, is associated with a dramatic loss of bone mineral. Astronauts living in the zero gravity of space show a similar loss, leading Whedon to conclude that the activity of the muscles working against gravity is needed to maintain strong bones. As yet there is little evidence on whether normally active persons on earth can prevent the bone mineral loss of osteoporosis by increasing their activity—jogging or performing other exercises—but it is clear that inactivity can hasten calcium loss [Marx, 1980].

In an excellent overview of the relationships between physical activity, life expectancy, and enhanced longevity, Arthur S. Leon and Henry Blackburn of the University of Minnesota Medical School have concluded:

> It is now clear that physical inactivity contributes to the reduced work and cardiorespiratory capacity previously attributed to aging . . . small increases in habitual physical activity levels are adequate to reduce the incidence and severity of coronary heart disease . . . a minimum of 30 minutes of vigorous physical activity per week requiring peak energy output of 7.5 kilocalories per minute or more was associated with "protection" against coronary heart disease . . . such changes may be expected to favorably modify the course of CHD and increase functional and actual longevity [Leon and Blackburn, 1977].

This last statement is of particular importance since the two researchers had compiled every major study of physical activity prior to 1977 in this paper. Protective effects appear to be due to the capacity of exercise to increase the lumen or diameter of coronary arteries as noted earlier by Leaf. Beyond the protective effect which allows individuals to attain their average life expectancy there appears to be an absolute and positive effect upon longevity. The researchers also state that regular aerobic activity promotes "increased longevity, independent of its effect on CHD" (Leon and Blackburn, 1977).

Leaf has drawn several generalized conclusions regarding the role of exercise in health and longevity. He has also warned that a competitive level or certain types of sport exercises may have "negative survival effects." Very strenuous exertion may place a sudden large stress on the heart. This may account for the fatal bursts of "ventricular tachycardiafibrillation," hypothesized to be the cause of sudden death in case studies of 18 joggers (Thompson et al., 1980) as well as in 275 cases involving stressful life situations (Engel, 1977). For the people of the long-lived regions of the world, regular exercise derives largely from activities essential to survival: extensive walking, climbing in rugged terrain, farming, and folk dancing. From his research with these individuals, Leaf has identified specific beneficial effects of physical activity: (1) the physically trained person has a slower heart rate at rest and experiences a lesser increase in rate for a given level of exertion than an untrained individual. The heart receives its nutrient blood supply during diastole, which is the period of relaxation between contractions. Thus, a slower heart rate allows a longer time for blood flow in the coronary arteries to supply the heart muscle with oxygen and nutrients; (2) physical training lowers blood pressure since exercise induces vasodilation of muscle arteries. This means that circulating blood encounters less resistance and less effort is required on the part of the heart. Among the elderly people studied, continuous physical exertion contributed to a marked absence of hypertension and cardiovascular disease; (3) exercise apparently increases the ability of the blood to dissolve clots. According to the present thrombogenic theory of atherosclerosis, deposits of the protein fibrin adhere to the inner lining of diseased or injured arteries. Although the role of fibrin deposits in the development of atherosclerosis remains unclear, it is a regular constituent of atherosclerotic plaques. In light of his research Leaf asserts that "Exercise of a vigorous nature stimulates fibrinolytic activity—fibrin dissolving activity—and may in this manner also protect against the development of atherosclerosis" (Leaf, 1977); (4) exercise has a positive effect on the concentration of lipids in the blood. Leaf cites both laboratory research and the results of longitudinal studies in San Francisco, Albany, Hawaii, and Georgia and notes that "physical exercise increases the concentration of the protective high-density lipoproteins (HDL)" (1977). (5) Finally, demands on the heart muscle for any given level of exercise decrease with physical fitness. This allows an increased level of exercise and exertion before the supply of oxygen to the heart muscle limits further activity.

Summarizing his research concerning the relationship between exercise, optimum health, and longevity, Leaf states:

> In these, and possibly other ways, exercise seems to protect against the development of atherosclerosis, that is, circumvent its deleterious effects by increasing collateral circulation to an ischemic area of heart muscle, or actually promote the regression of the atheromatous process. . . . The beneficial effects of exercise on the development of coronary artery disease may even outweigh what are regarded as deleterious effects of diet [Leaf, 1977].

These observations are borne out among centenarian communities, where the people sustained a high level of vital organ function due to the conditioning effects of prolonged continuous exercise made necessary by farming rugged terrain and hillsides. For anyone, it is clear that exercise needs to be regular, frequent, and continued throughout life.

Sexual Activity

Sexual activity prolonged into later life is the fifth major common denominator noted by researchers in the centenarian communities. Aging is generally associated with a gradual decrease in the number of cells in certain organs, including the male testes. Cells that produce sperm are the first to be affected, but later the cells producing testosterone may also diminish. For females the ovaries gradually cease functioning during the late forties or early fifties. Despite these tendencies, sexual potency in the male and sexual interest in the female do persist into advanced age. Sexual interest is more evident in females of advanced age than in males. This is not a recently discovered fact, although there is a tendency in our culture to believe that sexuality was invented in the 1960s. Actually the classic Kinsey report of 1953 stated, "There is little evidence of any aging in the sexual capacities of the female until late in life." Later research has indicated that "a longitudinal study of aged married couples in their sixties and seventies [showed] that some women actually show an increase in sexual interest and activity" (Fisher, 1973). Another demonstration of continued sexual interest by both sexes is a report by Herman Brotman of the Department of Health, Education, and Welfare. Each year "there are some 3,500 marriages among the twenty million Americans over the age of sixty-five, and . . . sexual activity is cited along with companionship as one reason for these late unions" (Leaf, 1973).

Although there is no systematic research concerning sexual activity in the centenarian communities, there is anecdotal evidence. Healthy sperm specimens have been obtained from a supposedly 119-year-old Abkhazian man; Vilcabamban women bear children in their late fifties and are usually observed to assume the initiating role, especially in advanced age. By contrast our present attitudes reflect a "sexual inhibition in intimacy as a heritage of Victorian attitudes and repressive religious thinking" (Butler, 1975). Vestiges of Victorian censures persist for the elderly despite a relative sexual revolution among younger people. Colloquialisms such as "out to pasture, fogy, geezer, over the hill, dirty old man" (Butler, 1975) reveal a great deal about attitudes toward the elderly with regard to sexuality. Sexist thinking includes the elderly. An older man with a younger woman is clearly more acceptable than an older woman with a younger man, even though there is no rational reason for such a judgment. Freedom from these censures and anachronistic attitudes will portend freedom for both sexes. In Vilcabamba there are no comparable stigmatizing terms for the elderly, who are respected. "Los viejos" is the name for those approaching or beyond the century mark.

Sexuality is not limited to sexual intercourse but has infinite expressions. A variety of physical sexual contact can be clearly noted among the centenarians. Although researchers have referred to such polymorphous sexuality, that aspect of these communities has been neglected except in the work of some writers who have visited these people. One person who has documented this fact in both print and film is Gene Ayres, a Junior Fellow with the Metropolitan Applied Research Center of New York. Ayres studied the Vilcabamba people primarily and reported that one Miguel Carpio Mendieta was sexually active at 123 years of age. Ayres also pointed out that the cardiologist Miguel Salvador observed that "in Vilcabamba there exist no stresses, including sexual hangups. Extramarital children were the rule rather than the exception" (Ayres, 1973). Other writers such as Grace Halsell, author of *Los Viejos—Secrets of Long Life from the Sacred Valley* (1976), noted a clear sexual interest in her by one Vilcabamban male named Gabriel Brazo, aged 132. Extramarital relationships and children are not taken as an indication of promiscuity in these cultures. However, Leaf has noted that: "Strong taboos against sex outside of marriage and equally strong traditions about the sanctity of the family probably limit extramarital sex in all three areas, . . . everywhere I saw couples who had been married for 80 years or more" (Leaf, 1973c). Among the Caucasians, Professor

Pitskhelaurt believes that a happy marriage and a prolonged, active sex life clearly contribute to their unusual longevity. The Abkhazians themselves concur most heartily. Unmarried individuals are the exception, with 44 percent of the families with 4 to 6 children and 5 percent with 10 to 15 children. Some have over 20. Even in our culture it has been observed that married individuals tend to live longer and often remarry soon after the death of a spouse.

As with any single factor in the dynamic process of longevity, it is important not to overemphasize the factor of sexual activity among centenarian people. Certainly no direct causation has been proved nor advocated by any of the centenarians. All too often the small amount of information concerning long-lived individuals is presented in a sensationalist manner or relegated to the status of a curiosity, and certainly their sexual attitudes and habits are subject to such exploitation. Rather than seeing these magnificent people as curiosities, it is more rewarding to look for the wisdom in their lifestyles. Whatever the relationship between longevity and continued sexual activity, both indicate a life of activity and fulfillment.

Social Environment

The single most important and most frequently overlooked factor in longevity is the psychological dimensions. This includes prolonged and productive involvement in family and community affairs, an acquired status of dignity and wisdom, and an enduring sense of the meaning and purpose of life itself. The role of human consciousness in the process of longevity is the reason that any search for a simple formula, recipe, secret, etc. is doomed to failure. This dimension is generally relegated to minor status in research with centenarians since it is impossible to quantify consciousness or dissect it under a microscope. In her insightful and sensitive book, *Los Viejos,* Grace Halsell suggests the importance of this dimension:

> The viejos could not imagine why those who came to study them put so much emphasis on their years. They had not aspired to old age, nor pursued regimens to arbitrarily add years to their

lives. They were beneficiaries of a mysterious process, and were not concerned about the biology of it. They would look at me disbelievingly when I kept inquiring into possible causes and reasons. I finally realized that they far preferred to talk about the challenge of *today,* rather than the fact that they had defied actuarial tables [Halsell, 1976].

Cross-cultural research has shown that people of comparable biological age perceive themselves as "middle-aged" versus "old" at very different times of life stages (Shanas, 1970). It is not known how much their expectations actually contribute to their extended life-span, but several researchers have agreed upon their positive influence. Leaf noted that when people in centenarian communities were asked how long they expected to live, they would answer, "To a hundred." In proposing a toast to guests in Vilcabamba, they employ an obvious exaggeration and say, "May you live to be 300!" But as Leaf has noted, "100 years as the normal lifespan is firmly established in their minds" (Leaf, 1973c). From studies of involuntary retirement and in the limited number of instances where people leave the centenarian cultures and rapidly decline in health, it is evident that this intangible element of belief and social support systems plays a vital role. Numerous studies have found clear links between "loneliness, disease, and death" (Lynch and Convey, 1979), but few researchers have considered the protective effect of supportive communities. From studies of populations in Borneo and elsewhere, physician and anthropologist Stewart Wolf of the University of Texas in Galveston has concluded, ". . . human relationships may function to prevent disease and death. . . . It seems appropriate to supplement our consideration of emotional stress with attention to forces that counteract stress and sustain the person. . . . These are forces that appear to be at work among the Abkhazians in Russia's Caucasus that are among the longest lived and healthiest people on earth" (Wolf, 1977).

An intact and ongoing social system may play a part in longevity more important than any nutritional, exercise, environmental, or other factors. Alexander Leaf has noted, "It is characteristic of each of the areas I visited that the old people continue to be contributing, productive members of their society . . . people who no longer have a necessary role to play in the social and economic life of their society generally deteriorate rapidly" (Leaf, 1973a). Increased age is accompanied by increased social status, such as presiding over community councils. Meanwhile, the elders remain active in the chores of farming and other natural labor. Retirement is unknown, and daily hikes, swims, and horseback rides are common. None of the Vilcabamba live alone and unproductive idleness is unknown. Sula Benet has pointed out that the Abkhazian elderly are

> a life loving optimistic people. . . . Unlike so many very old dependent people in the United States who feel they are a burden to themselves and to their families [the Abkhazians] enjoy the prospect of continued life . . . in a culture which so highly values continuity in its traditions. The old are indispensable in their transmission. The elders preside at important ceremonial occasions, they mediate disputes and their knowledge of farming is sought. They feel needed because they are [Benet, 1965].

When these factors of involvement are considered, the parallels independently observed between the Ecuadorians, the Abkhazians, and the populations of Roseto, Pennsylvania, and of Brunei, Borneo, by Stewart Wolf (1977) are very striking. Active participation and community involvement have been demonstrated to be of major significance in determining an elderly person's level of functioning in later years.

The attribution of dignity and wisdom to the aged of the centenarian communities is perhaps the pivotal point between health and illness, life and death. In carefully considering the effect of such intangibles as the "prestige of the elderly," Alexander Leaf has concluded:

> I am now convinced that when the social environment encourages one to feel socially useful and needed in the economy, and to be looked up to and revered as a wise figure, the extremely elderly keep their mental faculties and physical abilities so that they can respond appropriately. This is quite contrary to prevailing trends in modern industrialized societies, which tend to emphasize youth and to regard old people as useless and standing in the way of progress [Leaf, 1973c].

Evidence of the potency of such an influence on both health and longevity has been made clear by two kinds of research from outside these communities: (1) studies of the effects of ongoing, purposive activity on health into advanced age; and (2) studies showing a direct relationship between prominence and recognition late in life and extended longevity. Physician Leslie S. Libow, of the Mount Sinai Hospital Center in New York, conducted an eleven-year longitudinal study of twenty-seven "optimally healthy" men compared to twenty men of "average" health, with the mean age being 70 years old. His research sought to determine the interaction between medical, biologic, and behavioral factors in the aging, adaptation, and survival of these forty-seven individuals. In addition to finding the normal aging changes such as decreases in serum albumin, peak occipital EEG frequency, and cerebral metabolic utilization of glucose, this study confirmed the Framingham Study indicating increased mortality with increased systolic blood pressure. However, most significant in the findings was "the role of psychosocial factors in contributing to mortality, for example, the increased mortality related to environmental losses. . . . Behavioral variables with the greatest accuracy in predicting mortality were the mental status test and organization and complexity of daily behavior" (Libow, 1974). Among the "optimally healthy elderly people" it was evident that "upward mobility and striving in midlife were related to better adaptation in late life . . . highly organized, purposeful, complex and variable daily behavior together with the absence of cigarette smoking were highly correlated with survival for these healthy elderly men" (Libow, 1974).

Other studies have confirmed a high level of "life satisfaction" as a precondition of extended longevity (Palmore and Cleveland, 1976; Bell, 1974). Research data also indicate that an active lifestyle allows "development, change and growth to continue through the later years of the lifespan in spite of the decrement of social, psychological and physiological functioning which typically accompanies the aging process" (Maddox and Douglass, 1974). Such observations throw into question the appalling practice of relegating elderly people to geriatric centers or the enforcement of arbitrary retirement age. Only in a youth- and performance-fixated culture would the normal decrease in peak performance be viewed as pathological or as a way of rationalizing neglect of the elderly. Advanced age is not inherently a period of physical or psychological impairment in any sense. However, the expectation of decline can result in a self-fulfilling prophecy. Among the historical instances of productive longevity are Titian, who painted prolifically until he died of the plague at age 99; Picasso, who was productive until his death at 92; Grandma Moses, who did not become an artist until age 76 and finished her last canvas shortly before her death at 101; philosophers George Santayana, who published at 88, and Bertrand Russell, at 91; statesmen Charles de Gaulle, who held office until age 78, and Winston Churchill, until 80. Certain professions have been identified as particularly long-lived, such as symphony conductors (Ford, 1979). Data from 6,239 men in *Who's Who in America* shows extended longevity for clergymen, educators, military men, and especially among scientists (Quint and Cody, 1970). A list could be extended at great length of "those who defied the conventions of age by remaining vigorous and creative into the late winter of their lives" (Favazza, 1977). While these individuals are the exceptions, they are nonetheless indicative of an untapped biological potential of the human species as a whole.

In the centenarian communities it is evident that the "viejos" remain active at a level of participation suited to their mental and physical abilities. Although they remain highly active, they also have the wisdom to recognize futile, stress-inducing striving and "have learned to accept things as they are, if they cannot change them" (Stanyan, 1976). When Alexander Leaf pressed 117-year-old Gabriel Chapnian of the Caucasus to say whether anything disturbed him, he responded cheerfully, "Oh, yes, there are a number of things that are not the way I would want them to be, but since I can't change them I don't worry about them" (Leaf, 1973). Perhaps that philosophy is at the heart of the prolonged health and longevity sustained by these people. In 1969, Joshua Green, philanthropist and chairman of the Seattle, Washington, People's National Bank, turned 100. Since he had been a friend of everyone from Rudyard Kipling to recent presidents of the United States, his birthday was a subject of national news coverage. From the enormous amount of mail he received, Green was prompted to formulate seven constants constituting a "syndrome of longevity" (Green, 1974). These consisted of constant cheerfulness, good heredity, regular physical activity, maintaining good health especially in the "dangerous years" between fifty and seventy, self-imposed discipline such as no smoking, always working throughout life on something you enjoy, and high emotional stability. While there are individuals who violate all of these constants with impunity and also live beyond 100, these guidelines are in keeping with the observations of others. Throughout the research literature into the habits of centenarian people there are anecdotes and personal profiles that substantiate Green's philosophy. In Alexander Leaf's *National Geographic* article, "Every Day Is a Gift When You Are Over 100," there are folk dancers, musicians who strum mandolins, their hands free of arthritis, eyes that are full of life and light, and mountain utopias farmed by people more than a hundred years old. When all research is in on these people, an unknown magic will still remain. In the words of an old Abkhazian woman, "I can't explain it in scientific terms, but there just seems to be something special in the life here" (Strauss, 1973).

Physical Environment

Environmental factors among the centenarian communities are the seventh and last major influence on longevity. They are also the least researched. In a few instances the quality of the water and the mountainous terrain in these geographic areas have been described but not systematically. Of the three major communities observed by Alexander Leaf, Vilcabamba in the Andes is located at an elevation of 4,500 feet, Hunza communities are spread over a mountainous area ranging from 3,500 to 7,000 feet at the palace of Mir, and in the Caucasus region the elevations were lower, with most centenarians living between 3,000 and 5,000 feet. "In none of these areas is the altitude high enough above sea level for the atmosphere to be rarefied. Rather, the significant factor seems to be the mountainside existence and the incredible amount of physical exertion necessary just to attend to the daily business of living" (Leaf, 1973c). Again this indicates an interaction in this case between lifestyle factors and environment rather than a cause and effect relationship between the physical environment per se and longevity. There is some preliminary evidence from the research of Marian C. Diamond of the University of California at Berkeley that "environmental stimulation," including physical as well as mental stimuli, can result in an increase in nerve cell branching on the cerebral cortex even in advanced age. Although the research has been conducted with laboratory animals, this "increase in mammalian cerebral cortex" (Diamond, 1980) could indicate a regenerative potential in the human nervous system. These are the areas of the brain involved in higher-order thinking. At present Diamond's research is being extended to consider the precise nature of the environmental stimulation which would enhance such nerve growth in advanced age.

Purely environmental determinants in these communities also need study to consider variables such as: further analysis of the water and soil to determine trace-element concentrations, relative concentration of negative ions which are in greater abundance in proximity to water or at high altitudes, presence or absence of carcinogenic agents, presence or absence of naturally occurring antioxidants, the absence of electromagnetic activity generated from power lines and media stations. Numerous other variables will undoubtedly be found which make these environments different from those of postindustrial nations.

Even the actual causes of death among these people are virtually unknown since autopsies are infrequent. Differences in morbidity between the centenarians and other comparable communities have been noted by David Davies:

> In 1965, a study was made in Hungary of all the country's 23 centenarians. Like the majority of the Vilcabamba centenarians, most of them were brought up in small, rural villages, and carried on rural occupations. Six were farm hands (one male and three females), six were housewives; five farmers (four males and one female); two were seamstresses; and there was one tailor, one shepherd, one white cooper and one washer woman. In contrast to the Vilcabambans, who generally carried on some kind of work until within a few days of their death, the Hungarians were being kept alive by modern medical knowledge. The causes of death were also different. In the Hungarian group, death usually resulted from arteriosclerosis or malignant tumours, while in the people of Vilcabamba accidents, or dis-

eases brought from outside the area, were the usual cause of death [Davies, 1973].

Among the Vilcabamba, Davies noted, "Hypertension, heart disease, and cancer are comparatively uncommon. Death is usually the result of an accident, or of catching influenza from the few outsiders who visit the place" (Davies, 1973). There is one recent report of autopsies performed on two individuals whose ages were verified: Russian Ivan Sztchebeitka, 118, Turk Zaro-Aga, 130, both of the Caucasian region in Russia. From these autopsies it was found that the Russian had died of a renal disease of vascular origin and the Turk had died of pneumonia. "The postmortem examination revealed that old and very old men die of an illness, e.g., examples of pneumonia or of heart failure and so on. A natural death of old age *(Maramus senilis)* does not exist" (Scheidegger, 1977). Although the centenarians are not immortal and eventually do succumb to many of the same major disorders evident in other cultures, the incidence is much later in life. They enjoy relatively good health and activity right up to the time of death, which usually ensues after a brief illness and without morbid fear or preoccupation. Both physical environmental and psychosocial conditions clearly contribute to this phenomenon, although the physical variables remain unexplored.

Prior to the 1972 International Congress of Gerontology in the Soviet Union, the Russian Novosti Press Agency prepared a report on the centenarians of their various regions and concluded:

Long life is apparently related to various factors which exist in Daghestan. The geographical and climatic conditions of the mountainous part of that republic; the simple dairy, vegetable, and meat food; life-long physical work (farming) in which the residents are engaged; adequate rest; activity (physical exercise, sports, various amusements and dancing); meaningful cultural traditions and customs transmitted from generation to generation; satisfying family life; humor and a "strong" nervous system; well-developed folk medicine; good heredity; and the constant improvement of the population's material and cultural standards with special emphasis on all inclusive health services, all appear to have varying effect [Novosti, 1970].

But these isolated communities are all threatened by modernization and the pollution it can bring. Dramatic negative effects upon both health and mortality can be seen when outside influences begin to permeate these societies. An instance of invasive and disruptive change has been noted by Ecuadorian physician John Lovewisdom, who first went to Ecuador in 1940 and is considered the first person to have studied the Vilcabamba. Since the influx of researchers and tourists, Lovewisdom has noted, "The worldwide publicity that followed Vilcabamba's discovery produced the very thing I came here to escape. Good roads and tourist traffic brought modernization, farming with chemical sprays and fertilizers, and the centenarians have been destroyed completely by drugs introduced to them by visiting medical doctors, and made available at a local drugstore. I am now forced to move again, to get away from the pollution" (Otto, 1979b). Guillermo del Pozo, physician for the Vilcabambas, has stated that twenty-five of the oldest residents have died during this period of modernization and "I don't think it's a coincidence" (Goodman, 1979). If the delicate balance and harmony of these societies are upset, their health and longevity may be severely affected. For the dignity and integrity of these centenarian people, researchers and reporters should be aware of the pollution they may bring.

The Human Biological Potential

Human longevity is a biological reality. Evidence for potential human longevity exists from basic biochemical research, laboratory experimental studies, single case reports, and in observations of centenarian communities. While this extensive body of research and data clearly predict and support the possibility of extended human longevity, there is virtually no research proving that it is impossible. There is actually far more evidence to support the possibility of longevity than there is to explain the present rates of life expectancy. Although centenarians are relatively rare, the fact of their existence could indicate an inherent but latent biological capacity. In an appendix to *The Coming of Age* (1972) Simone de Beauvoir cites several

French research projects which involved 600 to 700 documented centenarians, and another of 400 people over 100 years old:

> Most of the people in this group make careful plans for the future; they are interested in public affairs and are capable of youthful enthusiasm. They have their little fads and a sharp sense of humor; their appetites are good and they have great powers of resistance. They usually enjoy perfect mental health; they are optimistic and they show no sign of being afraid of death [1972].

Her book, which is essential reading for anyone concerned about longevity, emphasizes that centenarians are not exclusively isolated in remote geographic regions, with questionable birth certification, but are increasingly evident in Europe. There are a sufficient number of documented instances to indicate that this longevity potential can be made manifest. For instance, John Turner of England died on March 22, 1968, at the documented age of 111 years and 281 days, and British woman Ada Roe is documented to have died on January 11, 1970, at age 111 years and 339 days (Davies, 1973). A lengthy and excellent cover-story article entitled "The Days of Our Years" (1977) by Armando R. Favazza, Associate Editor of *MD*, noted numerous documented instances such as French-Canadian Pierre Joubert of 113 years, 124 days, and American John Sailing, who died in 1959 at age 113 years and one day. Further documented instances are an Irish spinster named Katherine Plunkett, who died in 1932 at 111 years and 329 days, or Milwaukee woman Louise K. Thiers, who also lived to be 111 years, 138 days, and died in 1926 (Scheinfeld, 1973). More recently a United Press International release noted an extraordinary centenarian not only because of her age but because of an unusual instance of biological regeneration. Ai Beebal of Karachi, Pakistan, is 146 years old, and "growing a new set of teeth" (*San Francisco Chronicle,* 1978). According to research reported by the Soviet Union's Novosti Press Agency, the oldest Russian, named Shirali Mislimov, died on September 2, 1973, at the age of 168 (Leaf, 1973c). Adam Akhmedov, age 127, and his wife Manna Aliyeva, age 125, were still alive as of 1970 in the village of Sanakari in the Soviet district of Dakhadayevski. Finally, Ashura Omarova in the village of Kadar was reported to be an astounding 195 years old (Novosti, 1970). In these latter instances it is highly likely that "age exaggeration" is a factor, but there is no reason to discount all of the reports.

The reported health of many individuals at extreme ages is of far greater importance than the absolute number of years, even according to the centenarians themselves. Although this interaction of health and longevity is frequently overlooked or dismissed, it emerged as an important theme when United States Representative Claude Pepper sponsored the testimony of eight centenarians to a House committee. Pepper, a Florida Democrat, is 80, making him the oldest member of the House of Representatives. Pepper has noted that when he was born, in 1900, the life expectancy was 49, as compared to the current average of approximately 72 years. Individuals ranged from 100-year-old W. L. Pannell, who still practices medicine in East Orange, New Jersey, to 111-year-old George Washington White, who used to be a fireman on the Southern Railway's famous Number 97 Crescent Limited. After the varied and lively testimony of these eight centenarians, Pepper stated that they represented "living evidence of whole new horizons for life extension." Going one step further, Pepper noted a "centenarian explosion." "Only 3,200 Americans lived past their centennial in 1969, today that number exceeds 13,000" (*San Francisco Chronicle,* 1979). These people, it must be emphasized, are not located in relatively inaccessible regions of the world. Longevity has been observed in a great diversity of places and throughout history. It is not a restricted greenhouse phenomenon but is manifest under a wide range of circumstances. One of the oldest documented centenarians was Charlie Smith, who died at age 138 in 1979 at a veterans' hospital in the United States. Longevity is a reality here and now.

In any new area of research, caution needs to be exercised, but that is not an adequate reason to retard the dissemination and implementation of current knowledge concerning longevity. In his excellent book *The American Way of Life Need Not Be Hazardous to Your Health* (1978) John Farquhar urges: "Thus we should continue to support basic research while simultaneously implementing our best efforts for appropriate preventive measures, rather than sit passively and wait for basic research to yield conclusive findings on *all* facets of the complex puzzle. The combination of a normal lag and 'let's wait' attitude can erect impressive barriers to preventive action" (Farquhar, 1978). Virtually all of the recommendations of the Farquhar program are initial steps which could allow more individuals to attain at least the average life expectancy and perhaps beyond. More recently Thomas McKeown has addressed the same issue:

> It is sometimes suggested that action cannot be taken to modify influences which may promote or damage health until evidence of their effects is complete. . . . It is fortunate that this requirement was not always imposed in the past. When Snow protected a London population from cholera in the mid nineteenth century by removing the handle of the Broad Street pump, the evidence of the relation between the disease and the water supply was anything but complete; indeed neither micro-organisms nor tests of significance had been discovered. If thalidomide had not been withdrawn on the basis of an observed association between the drug and limb deformities and when knowledge of teratogenesis was very deficient (as it still is), many thousands of children would have been born with malformations. If the argument that an association does not prove causation and only experimental evidence is conclusive had been accepted, quite a number of people who found the relation between cigarette smoking and lung cancer sufficiently convincing would have died of the disease before beagles had been taught to smoke [McKeown, 1979].

McKeown suggests a "burden of prudence" where action is indicated by "high, or even moderate probabilities" rather than "a burden of proof," since ". . . it should be recognized that conclusive evidence of harm or benefit to health is often an unrealistic requirement" (McKeown, 1979).

The statements by both Farquhar and McKeown are focused on preventive measures to enhance the quality of life and attaining average life expectancy with no mention of longevity. However, given the inextricable interaction between quality and quantity of life, these same arguments for cautious implementation are clearly applicable. Furthermore, the measures conducive to the enhancement of the quality and quantity of human life are noninvasive, with a low risk factor and extremely high positive potential. The reason such measures continue to be overlooked is a matter of economics and politics, as is the utilization of dangerous drugs such as thalidomide, diazepam-based tranquilizers, or risky practices such as thyroid irradiation or the highly contested coronary bypass procedure. Virtually all of the measures conducive to longevity adhere to the most fundamental tenet of the Hippocratic oath: *Primum nil nocere,* or "do no harm." When the average life expectancy in ancient Greece was 22 years (Greenblatt, 1977), the present life expectancy in the seventies would have seemed extraordinary, and the nonagenarians Isocrates, Heraclitus, and Pythagoras no doubt seemed almost immortal. The rare instances of optimum health and longevity then and now spur us on in our quest to fulfill the biological potential of the human species.

NINE

Intimations of Immortality

From 1802 to 1804, while William Wordsworth composed "Ode: Intimations of Immortality," he found himself entranced by the questions of longevity and immortality. In a letter to accompany the poem Wordsworth reflected on his state of mind during the writing of the ode: "I was often unable to think of external things as having external existence, and I communed with all that I saw as something not apart from, but inherent in, my own immaterial nature" (Perkins, 1967). Throughout the poem Wordsworth attempts to reconcile his own internal sense of immortality with the evidence in nature of the waxing and waning of seasons as well as his own failing physical and mental capacities. Not only did Wordsworth reflect upon such issues but his personal habits and concerns were all conducive to optimum health and longevity. Numerous historical records, letters, and anecdotes recount that he did not smoke or drink, gained little weight in his lifetime (he lived to be 80), unlike many of his closest friends avoided opium and other social drugs of his time, and purposely lived and worked in the open air. "De Quincey estimated that Wordsworth walked between 175,000 and 180,000 miles during his life, and if so he must have averaged nearly ten miles a day for sixty years" (McKeown, 1979).

Actually there was widespread concern with self-care during this period. Historians have noted many parallels with the end of the twentieth century. England in the 1800s was pressured by the Industrial Revolution; environmental pollution from coal was a major concern; there was considerable experimentation with social drugs such as opium and cocaine, and there were major social movements concerned with a return to a more pastoral and rural lifestyle. While Wordsworth attained a predictably long life, it is equally well-documented that both he and his sister, Dorothy, suffered from a great deal of minor morbidity such as headaches, toothaches, gastrointestinal problems, and numerous other stress-related disorders. Wordsworth's letters and lifestyle have regained considerable interest for many of these reasons among several researchers, including Thomas McKeown, who has noted, "What Wordsworth's history illustrates is that there is no necessary close relation between morbidity and mortality. The diseases that shorten our lives are not usually the ones that diminish their quality from day to day" (McKeown, 1979). Certain issues were as great a concern in the nineteenth century as now and still remain unresolved. Of even greater importance than the specific issues of health and longevity exemplified by Wordsworth's lifestyle are his musings on immortality. There is an unfathomable quality to any consideration of longevity which permeates the reflections of Socrates, Plato, Kant, Spinoza, Pascal, Goethe, Emerson, Charles Darwin, Albert Schweitzer, Tagore, René Dubos, and is epitomized in Wordsworth's final lines to "Intimations of Immortality": "To me the meanest flower that blows can give,/ Thoughts that do often lie too deep for tears." Meditations in the realm of longevity and immortality yield a dimension of human consciousness which is irreducible and not easily put into words.

New Horizons

Metamorphosis is the shedding of one form to assume another. Perhaps the greatest contribution of an inquiry into human longevity is that it can illuminate the present metamorphosis in our attitudes toward health. Concerns over the excesses of a pathology management industry are not unique to this period of history by any means. Any random sample drawn from historical records indicates the "divided legacy" documented by Harris Livermore Coulter (1977), the ongoing dialectic between holistic and reductionistic approaches to health. Growing out of the populist health movements of late-nineteenth-century England were remarkably similar concerns. The physician Frank B. Wynn characterized Christian Science and similar movements as

> . . . a natural protest against the materialistic trend of modern medicine. For forty odd years the hue and cry of advancing medicine has been for a sign, a demonstration—in physiology, chemistry, pathology, and bacteriology; find the micro-organism and prove its relationship to the disease; locate the lesion and ablate it by the knife—always a material enemy to be subdued by material means. . . . So intent upon demonstrable scientific achievements, the profession has not seen or properly evaluated the mental and moral factors in the cause and cure of disease. In years gone by the general practitioner was an artist in the practical application of these principles. But with the advent of specialism dividing the human body into a multiplicity of departments, to be treated in a cold, mechanical way, the practitioner lost sight of the coordinated, pulsing, reacting organism as a whole. Medical practice, like the practitioner, lost its soul and spirit to the tyranny of materialism. Cases in which mental treatment or spiritual ministration was indicated were still treated by material means resulting in failure, which condemned the methods employed and fed the growth of a cult. Healing through the mind, or through benignant moral or spiritual influences became a lost art. Out of the ruins of our failure a medico-religious cult has builded its temples and inculcated its teachings [Reed, 1932].

While these observations are stated in the extreme, they do reflect the pervasive and long-standing search for a balance between psychosocial and biomedical approaches to health and longevity. Holistic medicine addresses itself to these concerns. The study of longevity may help broaden the realm of inquiry, as well as being an important area of research per se. When we look at the distant horizons of inquiry, the present tasks do not seem so impossible or even formidable. One instance of this common phenomenon is the 4-minute mile. On May 6, 1954, Roger Bannister, who is now a prominent physician and government sports advisor, became the first man to break the "impossible" barrier of the 4-minute mile with his time of 3 minutes, 59.4 seconds. That infinitesimal amount of .6 of a second marked the end of an ostensibly insurmountable barrier and the beginning of further reductions in time for running the mile. While such barriers are partially a matter of physiology, they are equally important as psychological barriers which limit our reality.

Inquiries into possibilities of longevity may serve to extend the boundaries of what is known of the human condition. Many limitations and barriers are seen to be surmountable, with implications astonishing enough to make the controversy over holistic medicine seem conservative and pale by comparison. Writing in *The Medusa and the Snail* (1979), Lewis Thomas included an essay entitled "On Warts." Although this hardly seems a subject for provocative inquiry, he notes:

> The strangest thing about warts is that they tend to go away. Fully grown, nothing in the body has so much the look of toughness and permanence as a wart, and yet, inexplicably and often very abruptly, they come to the end of their lives and vanish without a trace. . . . If my unconscious can figure out how to manipulate the mechanisms needed for getting around that virus, and for deploying all the various cells in the correct order for tissue rejection, then all I have to say is that my unconscious is a lot further along than I am. . . . Whatever, or whoever, is responsible for this has the accuracy and precision of a surgeon. There almost has to be a Person in charge. . . . Some intelligence or other knows how to get rid of warts, and this is a disquieting thought [Thomas, 1979].

Speculations such as these are more and more common, and are an aspect of a fundamental revision of the realms of inquiry. Quantum physicists have led the way with such concepts as negative mass, black holes which distort time and space, probability waves, time flowing backward, and subatomic events inexplicably linked in a "synchronicity," beyond present concepts of causality.

Attitudes toward so-called medical miracles have also changed. Physicians at Lourdes, France, have examined over 5,000 supposed miracles since 1858. Sixty-five cases have been stringently reviewed under three major criteria: instantaneous alleviation of an acute, unequivocally organic disease for which there is absolutely no known cure. It is important to note that if such strict criteria and screening were applied to any other research, there would be virtually no suitable subjects or any data. Instances of miracle cures include "blindness of cerebral origin," multiple sclerosis for periods of up to six years, and "sarcoma of the pelvis" according to the case publications and records of medical director Theodore Mangiapan (1980). A cover-story article in *Medical World News* in December 25, 1978, explored the implications of the Lourdes data, comparing it with applications of positive beliefs systems by surgical teams as well as innovative, clinical programs (Marwick, 1978).

Still on the frontiers of medical research is a study which shows striking correlations between spontaneous remission, miracle cures, and, on the other end of the spectrum, the phenomenon of voodoo death. According to Richard A. Kalish of the University of California at Los Angeles Department of Public Health there are seven criteria for miracle cures and their converse:

1. The disease must be serious and impossible or at least very difficult to cure. Conversely, a voodoo death, to be authentic, must not involve an organism diseased in any serious fashion.
2. The disease must not have reached a stage at which it is liable to disappear shortly of its own accord. The voodoo death victim must not have a disease that has reached the stage at which it might become serious of its own accord.
3. No medical treatment can have been applied, or if it were, it must be shown to have been ineffectual. A voodoo death would be all the more impressive if medical treatment had been attempted. In this context, one noted psychologist and physician, M. Erik Wright, Professor of Psychology and of Psychiatry at the University of Kansas, has attested to observing a West Australian aborigine, previously healthy, who

showed every medical sign of shock and imminent death and for whom medical treatment proved worthless. When the medical director threatened the person responsible for the bone-pointing with murder, the curse was lifted, the patient informed, and recovery followed shortly.

4. The cure must be sudden. Most voodoo deaths are not sudden.
5. The cure must not be preceded by any crisis. The death must be attributable only to the curse, and not to any crisis.
6. The cure must be completely due to natural causes at the expected time. The death must be completely due to voodoo curses, with timing not particularly relevant.
7. There must be no relapse after the cure. Presumably, the converse would be that there must be no returning from the dead following the death.

The similarities—or, if you prefer, the distinctions—between miracle cures and voodoo deaths suggest to this author the possibility of similar mechanisms of intervention [Kalish, 1970].

The distinction between miracle cure and voodoo death parallels the distinction between the positive and negative aspects of placebo response discussed in Chapter IV. The mechanisms behind these phenomena may be related to the psychophysiological and psychoimmunological mechanisms considered in Chapters III and IV. This is not an attempt to "explain" miracle cures but rather to support the substantial and growing body of literature showing that human consciousness holds profound sway over both health and longevity.

Before the Answers Are In

Holistic medicine and longevity research has tended to focus upon psychobiological processes characteristic of individual organisms. Such an approach is necessary but not sufficient to address the profound transformations taking place on social, political, economic, and ecological dimensions. There are numerous influences on both health and longevity which are not under the immediate influence of an individual or even small groups of individuals. If the transformation of human life is to complete its cycle, then aggregates of individuals must exercise their social, political, and economic influence.

Group action is of course needed on environmental and social problems which undermine health. Among the burgeoning areas of inquiry are the following: (1) Studies showing that airplane accident fatalities increase just after newspaper stories about murder and suicide. Evidence indicates that the reporting of these events actually "triggers subsequent murder-suicides, some of which are disguised as airplane accidents" (Phillips, 1978); (2) Research indicating a clear correlation between significantly higher rate of cancer of the "lung, the nasal cavity and sinuses, and the skin" in a survey conducted from 1950 to 1969 of counties in the United States where the petroleum industry is most heavily concentrated (Bot et al., *Business Week,* 1977); (3) The "clinical ecology" approach developed by physician Theron G. Randolph (1964, 1965, 1978), who has demonstrated that the pervasive introductions of chemicals into clothing, food, environment, and air has resulted in severe allergies: "10,000 people are allergic to the twentieth century." Chemical exposure and the resulting allergic reactions are manifest as headaches, arthritis, cardiovascular disease, and certain forms of cancer; and (4) A very substantial and growing body of evidence indicating a clear connection between "electromagnetic and noise pollution," particularly near airports and urban areas in general, with a wide range of physical disorders ranging from high infant mortality to hypertension (Becker and Marino, 1978). As disparate as these phenomena are, they all offer a similar choice: between the continued management of the pathology induced by such conditions or implementation of health measures to decrease the risk. This is not to suggest that solutions are at hand in the immediate future but to show where the focus must be put if optimum health and extended longevity are serious goals.

Even in areas where research has gone on for years, underlying questions remain. Despite the widespread concern and research focusing on cardiovascular disease, and despite its recent decline in incidence over the last five years due to undetermined, but multiple, influences, the precise processes underlying vascular and heart disease are still not clearly understood. Writing in the *Journal of the American Medical Association,* Earl A. Burch, Jr., of the University of South Carolina School of Medicine, underlines these lingering questions:

> Despite the relative frequency and prognostic importance of congestive heart failure, there is no general agreement on diagnostic criteria that might be used in epidemiologic studies or therapeutic trials to define the development, amelioration, or prevention of this condition. . . . Empirically determined criteria have been described and successfully used in epidemiologic studies and natural history studies . . . but no systematic assessment of the reliability and validity of these criteria has been made [Burch, 1979].

Burch points out that the much more controversial diagnosis of "schizophrenia" could be substituted for "congestive heart failure" with no change in the validity of the statement. Even in the presence of clearly diagnosed organic pathology such as congestive heart failure, the research and clinical practice is not as definitive as it is assumed to be or as it is often presented. In a more speculative area, such as longevity, even more patience is required. Such inquiries may require many decades and cannot be prematurely dismissed if they do not yield immediate results.

Recently the *Harvard Medical School Health Letter* (February 1980) rendered an excellent overview of the progress to date in understanding cardiovascular disease as well as the issues that remain unresolved. It is now evident that the process of atherosclerosis is due to cholesterol deposits on the arterial wall or endothelium, that platelets and LDL cholesterol appear to interact in an unknown manner to increase the likelihood of damage to the arterial walls, and that cells underlying the damaged arterial lining appear to proliferate to repair the damage with the resulting formation of a plaque which further deforms the arterial wall and increases the degenerative process. Defining this process has been and is an arduous and painstaking process which has resulted in many modifications of initial theories as well as early experimentation.

Meanwhile, the falling death rate from atherosclerosis suggests that Americans are doing something right—but nobody is certain what it is. The recent decline suggests that "environmental" causes are ultimately responsible for the high prevalence of atherosclerosis, as does the fact that some other countries have very low rates. But nobody can say with certainty whether changed diet, reduced smoking, increased exercise, better control of high blood pressure, or improved treatment methods for heart attacks account for the recent decline. . . . Enough is now known to justify the simple measures that should be common knowledge to all persons at risk [*Harvard Medical School Health Letter,* 1980].

These observations confirm those of Thomas McKeown in regard to infectious disease: "Control of the infections resulted mainly from modification of the conditions under which they occurred, and there are theoretical as well as historical reasons for believing that the same approach is required for an attack on many of the disease problems that remain" (McKeown, 1979). Such an approach with multiple methods of inquiry undertaken over decades into the area of longevity is likely to yield even greater results than inquiries into a specific disease process.

Any approach to longevity must go beyond an attack on simple diseases. Elimination of cardiovascular disease and cancer would result in an increase of the overall life expectancy of less than seven years. For individuals already over 70, the resulting increase would be one and a half to two years at maximum.

There are only a few major disease processes that are now identified as being the major causes of death in man. As a consequence, much medical research has been focused on obtaining an understanding of these disease processes. However, the importance of these diseases to the overall health and longevity of the general population is frequently over-emphasized and the importance of the general aging process labored. . . . The elimination of one disease process would immediately uncover another disease process, and so forth. It is therefore apparent that the elimination of these specific diseases, even if successful, will not result in a uniform maintenance of health, which is necessary for a more useful and enjoyable lifespan. A more general approach to the maintenance of health is necessary [Cutler, 1976].

Politics and Longevity

A shift in both public policy and clinical practice from a pathology management industry to a health care system has profound political and economic consequences. A *Time* magazine cover story entitled "Medical Costs: Seeking the Cure" pointed to some of these. "Medicine has become an industry employing costly technology as sophisticated as that found in the space program" (*Time*, May 28, 1979). At the present time the political lobby of the American Medical Association is the largest, most active, and most well-funded lobby in Washington. In the balance is the $250 billion-plus budget of the pathology management industry. Less than 1 percent of this is allocated to preventive care or health promotion programs. When slightly over 9 percent of the United States' gross national product is involved, it is easy to see why political, economic, and special interest group pressures have far more to do with the nature and structure of health care in this country than the actual effectiveness of any program. Neither optimum health nor extended longevity for the population as a whole can be achieved through more expenditures and increased technology. However, there are signs of change. ". . . National health costs continue to mount and threaten to climb even more steeply. Given this situation, and the governmental commitment to continued and increased subsidization of the cost of health care, disease prevention has become more attractive" (Hirsch, 1980). According to other analysts, a preventive approach is more than attractive, it is imperative. Further urgency is introduced by the fact that the postwar baby boom generation is getting old and will create a disproportionate demand upon existing health care systems beginning as early as the year 2000. While government agencies and policies are not particularly influenced by evidence, logic, or foresight, they are certainly influenced by the sheer numbers of highly vocal individuals who are now reaching middle age with a heightened awareness of holistic approaches to health care. These concerns are not peripheral as they were in previous generations but are central for this influential group.

One of the most outspoken individuals of this population is Roy R. Anderson, a vice-president with Allstate Insurance Company. Anderson statements sound more like articles in new-age magazines than those in insurance and occupational counseling journals. Anderson writes of "ecological pollution," "threat of the misuse of nuclear energy," "worldwide unemployment and economic inflation," "inability to control and guide the development of technology," "loss of faith by people in institutions of all kinds" (Anderson, 1979). He draws attention to the need for a complete change of attitude.

> . . . these movements that relate to holistic health *do* seem to come as a surprise to the medical establishment and to us in the health insurance business. The nearest we seem to be able to come to the concepts of holistic health is to talk in terms of the need for "preventive medicine." But this is a negative concept. It relates to a state of non-sickness. We need to turn the coin over and think in the positive terms of attaining health: physical health, mental health, and spiritual health [Anderson, 1978].

These are not the statements that would be expected by the "Casualty Actuarial Society and the Society of Actuaries," but that is precisely where they were delivered. An interest in longevity requires a new mode of thinking. It also requires the involvement of people at every level, in the social and environmental ecology of the planet. Historians and philosophers of science have pointed out that Galileo was censured by the church when he drew his sketches of the moon in *Siderius Muncius* in 1610. This was not because of the discovery per se, but because he persisted in publishing the works in contemporary Italian rather than in the scholarly Latin and that made the work accessible to larger numbers of people and threatened the authority of the organized church.

Longevity and Philosophy

Paul K. Feyerabend of the University of California at Berkeley advocates caution in embracing "scientism—the faith in the existence of a unique method whose application leads to exclusive truths about the world" (Broad, 1979). Rather than excessive dependency upon external authority and definitive pronouncements, Feyerabend advocates an "epistemological anarchism" or the necessity of maintaining an open and inquisitive mind which is not unduly constrained by current social conventions. In a recent biographical sketch in *Science,* Feyerabend notes that he actually practices his "epistemological anarchism" and that his health has been improved not only by the work of an acupuncturist but by faith healers and astrologers as well. According to Feyerabend, "Respect for all traditions will gradually erode the narrow and self-serving rationalism of those who are now using tax money to destroy the traditions of the taxpayers, to ruin their minds, to rape the environment, and quite generally to turn living human beings into well-trained slaves" (Broad, 1979).

This attitude of "epistemological anarchism" needs to be adopted toward the question of longevity. The search for longevity is an ongoing process without a fixed end-point. The Ten Oxherding Pictures of Chinese Buddhist tradition depict the life of a man as a series of encounters with an ox. In the first illustration the man initiates a quest for his lost ox, symbolizing the deeper sources of latent wisdom within every individual. In the second picture he finds traces of the ox; in the third he sees the ox; in the fourth he catches hold of the resisting animal; in the fifth he leads the now docile creature; in the sixth the oxherd is seated on the animal's back; the seventh shows the man meditating without the ox being near; in the eighth both man and ox have gone out of sight; in the ninth the man has returned to his beginning point in peace and tranquillity. In the tenth a sublime moment is recorded in which the man, now having his enlightenment, walks down a lane in the most ordinary way, in ordinary clothing, with nothing to mark him from any other peasant.

The search for longevity embodies the potential for wisdom implied in this arcane allegory. For many individuals the quiet introspection characteristic of meditation remains elusive or inaccessible. The Zen Buddhist practice of *zazen* is considered to have three parts: "to sit down, to sit still, and to sit long" (Baker-roshi, 1978/1979). During this process there emerges a profound sense of trust and acceptance: "Eventually this developing faith and trust in yourself will allow you to sit still and be able to look at, see, and accept the particular person you are. In this way our mental and emotional life become as stable and precise as the physical world" (Baker-roshi, 1978/1979). Through this process an individual begins to see the inherent teaching and wisdom of every event, person, and life situation. When this pervasive sense of meaning persists throughout the day as well as during meditation, the state of awareness or enlightenment can be achieved.

Standing by the stream waiting for the moon to rise.
But knowing how impatient I am, the moon takes its time.
Tired of waiting, I return to my study and close the door.
The moon leaps over a thousand peaks [Yang Wan Li].

The search for longevity may eventually lead more individuals to lives of reflection, for which the advanced ages are ideally suited.

Longevity will require a collective heightening of human consciousness. When there is fear of disease, the technology of medicine governs life; when there is fear of poverty, economics holds sway; when there is fear of death, then religious dogma asserts control. When these fears dominate the search for longevity, the result is a fixation upon the life-extension technologies of cryogenics, bionic limbs, cloning of total organisms, and other twenty-first-century variants of the Fountain of Youth. Thoughtful reflection upon these fears and assumptions can banish the hold of these distortions over the clear perception of the human condition. Longevity does not require denial of death but freedom from that fear. There are historical records of the "death of Zen masters." Master Soen Nakagawa faced death in his ninety-fifth year: "My body and mind are now made clear and clean, and I am ready to die any time. But if all people are troubled, I may live a little longer. I will close the curtain of my worldly show at the best season of the year, not so hot, not so cold" (Sato, 1974). Charles Darwin may have had such an enlightened human being in mind when he wrote a friend, "Believing as I do that man in the distant future will be a far more perfect creature than he is now, it is an intolerable thought that he and all other sentient beings are doomed to complete annihilation after such a long, continued, slow progress" (Wolfgang, 1978). The instances of longevity evident in every region of the planet and throughout history show a latent biological potential which may become manifest in the next evolutionary stage of the human species.

BIBLIOGRAPHY

ABBOTT, M. H., MURPHY, E. A., BOLLING, D. R., AND ABBEY, H. The familial component in longevity, a study of offspring of nonagenarians. II. Preliminary analysis of the completed study. *Johns Hopkins Medical Journal,* January 1974, *134* (1): 1–16.

ABELSON, P. H. Cost-effective health care. *Science,* May 14, 1976, *192* (4240). Editorial page.

————. Cancer—opportunism and opportunity. *Science,* October 5, 1979, *206* (4414). Editorial page.

ABRAHAM, J., SHEETY, G., AND JOSE, C. J. Strokes in the young. *Stroke,* May-June 1971, *2* (3): 258–267.

ADAMS, C. W. Human longevity. *Chest,* April 1970, *57* (4), 308–309.

ADELMAN, R. C. Overview of the biology of aging—introductory statement. *Federal Proceedings,* 1979, *38* (6).

————, AND BRITTON, G. W. The impaired capacity for biochemical adaptation during aging. *BioScience,* October 1975: 639–643.

ADER, R., AND COHEN, N. Behaviorally conditioned immunosuppression. *Psychosomatic Medicine,* 1977, *37,* 333–340.

ADEY, W. R. The influence of impressed electrical fields at EEG frequencies on brain and behavior. Symposium paper delivered to

"Behavior and Brain Electrical Activity," Houston, Texas, November 1973.

————. Introduction: Effects of electromagnetic radiation on the nervous system. *Annals of the New York Academy of Sciences,* 1975, *247:* 15–20.

Agricultural Research. Dietary fiber reduces egg cholesterol. 1979, *27*(10): 6.

AHLERT, G. Genetics of senescence. I. *Zeitschrift für Alternsforschung,* 1978, *27*(1): 1–8.

AIROLA, P. *How to Get Well.* Phoenix: Health Plus Publishers, 1974.

————. *Are You Confused?* Phoenix: Health Plus Publishers, 1977.

ALFIN-SLATER, R. B. Nutrition and aging—introduction. *Federation Proceedings,* 1979, *38*(6): 1993.

ALIKISHIEV, R.S.H. Certain data on the longevity in the Dagestan ASSR. *Gig Sanit,* August 1968, *33*(8): 70–74.

ALMY, T. P. The stress interview: Unfinished business. *Journal of Human Stress,* December 1978, 308.

ALVAREZ, W. C. "A normal diet and length of life." *Geriatrics,* April 1971, *26*(4), 81–82.

American Heart Journal. Emotional and sensory stress factors in myocardial pathology. 1966, *72:* 536–564.

American Medical News. No place for junk food promo. January 5, 1979: 5.

————. Physician's role in prevention is emphasized. January 12, 1979: 25. (a)

————. Unneeded surgery contention disputed. January 5, 1979: 1 and 4. (b)

————. AMA publishes new series of guidelines on nutrition, health. December 7, 1979: 27.

ANDAY, G. J., SPARKES, R. S., AND MINDLIN, H. J. 13–14 chromosome translocation and longevity in man. *Oncology,* 1974, *29*(1): 90–97.

ANDERSON, F., AND COWAN, N. R. Survival of healthy older people. *British Journal of Preventive and Social Medicine,* December 1976, *30*(4): 231–232.

ANDERSON, R. R. The Future: A challenge to the actuarial profession. Paper presented to the joint meeting of the Casualty Actuarial Society and the Society of Actuaries, April 10, 1978.

————. The challenge of our future. Paper delivered to LIMRA Agent Management Conference, May 21, 1979.

ANDZEL, W. D. Effects of moderate prior exercise and varied rest intervals upon cardiorespiratory endurance performance. *Journal of Sports Medicine and Physical Fitness*, 1978, *18*(3): 245–252.

APA Monitor. Califano sacked, squeezes in prevention message on departure. September/October 1979: 24.

AREHART-TREICHEL, J. NGF may hold the key—but to what? *Science News*, May 21, 1977, *116:* 330–335.

————. Enkephalins: More than just pain killers. *Science News*, July 23, 1977, *116:* 59–62.

————. Questioning the new genetics. *Science News*, September 1, 1977, *116:* 154–156.

————. Senility: More than growing old. *Science News*, October 1, 1977, *112:* 218–221.

————. Enzymes: Medicine's new gold mine. *Science News*, July 22, 1978, *114* (4): 58–60.

————. The pituitary's powerful protein. *Science News*, November 25, 1978, *114* (22): 374–381.

ASCHOFF, J. Circadian systems in man and their implications. *Hospital Practice*, May 1976, *11*(5): 51–97.

ASTRAND, P. O. *Health and Fitness.* Canada: Ministry of National Health and Welfare, 1979.

————, AND RODAHL, K. *Textbook of Work Physiology.* New York: McGraw-Hill, 1970.

————, AND RODAHL, K. *Manuel de Physiologie de l'Exercise Musculaire.* Paris: Masson et Cie, 1972.

ATTERHOG, J. H., Jonson, B., AND SAMUELSON, R. Exercise testing in Sweden—survey of procedures. *Scandinavian Journal of Clinical and Laboratory Investigation*, 1979, *39* (1): 87–92.

AUDY, J. R. Health as a quantifiable property. *British Medical Journal*, November 24, 1973, *4* (5890): 486–487.

AUSTIN, J. E., AND QUELCH, J. A. United States national dietary goals—good industry threat or opportunity. *Food Policy*, 1979, *4* (2): 115–128.

AZBEL, M. Physicist looks for patterns to decode DNA. *Brain/Mind Bulletin*, October 2, 1978, *3* (22): 1.

BAGNARA, J. T. ET AL. Common origin of pigment cells. *Science,* February 1979, *203* (2): 410–415.

BAHRKE, M. S., AND MORGAN, W. P. Anxiety reduction following exercise and meditation. *Cognitive Therapy and Research,* 1978, *2* (4): 323–333.

BAILEY, C. *Fit or Fat?* Boston: Houghton Mifflin Company, 1978.

BAKER-ROSHI, Z. Foreground and background meditation. *The Wind Bell,* Winter 1978/1979, *16* (1).

BALL, K. P. Cigarette diseases: The most preventable epidemic. *Social Health Journal,* January-February 1970, *90* (1): 40–42.

BALLENTINE, R. *Diet and Nutrition: A Holistic Approach.* Honesdale, Pa.: The Himalayan International Institute, 1978.

BARBER, T. X., ed. *Biofeedback and Self-control.* Chicago: Aldine-Atherton, 1970, 1971.

BARNOTHY, M., ed. *Biological Effects of Magnetic Fields.* Vol. 2. New York: Plenum Publishing Corp., 1971.

BARROWS, C. H. Nutrition and aging: The time has come to move from laboratory research to clinical studies. *Geriatrics,* March 1977, *32* (3): 39, 41.

BARRY, H., III. Longevity of outstanding chess players. *Journal of Genetic Psychology,* September 1969, *115* (1): 143–148.

BARSKY, A. J. Patient heal thyself: Activating the ambulatory medical patient. *Journal of Chronic Diseases,* 1976, *29:* 585–597.

BARTEL, A. G. Exercise stress-testing—current status. *Cardiology,* 1979, *64* (3): 170–189.

BASSETT, C. A. L., AND BECKER, R. O. Generation of electric potentials by bone in response to mechanical stress. *Science,* 1962, *137:* 1063–1064.

BASSLER, T. J. Marathon running and atherosclerosis. *British Medical Journal,* 1977, *1:* 229.

BATCHELDER, L. E. Foods for the upper age group and nutritional implications. *American Journal of Public Health,* 1956, *46* (10): 1329–1335.

BATESON, G. *Steps to an Ecology of Mind.* New York: Ballantine, 1972.

———. "The pattern which connects." *The CoEvolution Quarterly,* Summer 1978: 5–16.

BATKIS, G. A. Problems of longevity. *Zdravookhraneniye Rossiiskoi Federatzii,* 1968, *12* (9): 3–5.

BAUER, G. Cardiac transplantation: Reflections of a cardiologist. *Medical Journal of Australia,* November 16, 1968, *2*(20): 915–917.

BAUMANN, B. Diversities in conceptions of health and physical fitness. *Journal of Health and Human Behavior,* 1961, *3:* 34–46.

BAZELOH, M., FENICHEL, G. M., AND RANDALL, J. Studies on neuromelanin. *Neurology,* May 1967, *17:* 512–519.

BEAL, J. B. Electrostatic fields, electromagnetic field, and ions—mind/body environment interrelationships. *Proceeding of Symposium and Workshop on "The Effects of Low-frequency Magnetic and Electric Fields on Biological Communication Process."* Sixth Annual Meeting of the Neuroelectric Society, Snowmass-at-Aspen, Colorado, 1973, Vol. 6.

BEALE, G. Social effects of research in human genetics. In W. Fuller, ed., *The Social Impact of Modern Biology.* London: Routledge & Kegan Paul, 1971.

BEAUVOIR, SIMONE DE. *The Coming of Age.* New York: G. P. Putnam's Sons, 1972.

BECKER, R. O. The bioelectric factors in amphibian limb regeneration. *Journal of Bone and Joint Surgery,* 1961, *43-A:* 643–656.

———. The biological effects of magnetic fields: A survey. *Medical Electronic and Biological Engineering,* 1963, *1:* 293–303.

———. Geomagnetic environment and its relationship to human biology. *New York State Journal of Medicine,* 1963, *63:* 2215–2219.

———. The electrical control of growth processes. *Medical Times,* 1967, *95:* 657–669.

———. The effect of magnetic fields upon the central nervous system. In *Biological Effects of Magnetic Fields.* Vol. 2., pp. 207–214. New York: Plenum Publishing Corp., 1969.

———. Augmentation of regenerative healing in man, a possible alternative to prosthetic implantation. *Clinical Orthopaedics and Related Research,* 1972, *83:* 255–262.

———. Electromagnetic forces and life processes. *Technology Review* (MIT), December 1972: 32–38.

———. Stimulation of partial limb regeneration in rats. *Nature,* 1972, *235:* 109–111.

———. The basic biological data transmission and control system influenced by electrical forces. *Annals of the New York Academy of Sciences,* 1974, *238:* 236–241.

————. Boosting our healing potential. In *Science Yearbook,* pp. 40–45. Chicago: World Book Encyclopedia, 1975.

————. The current status of electrically stimulated bone growth. *O.N.A. Journal,* 1975, *2,* 35–36.

————. An application of direct current neural systems to psychic phenomena. *Psychoenergetic Systems,* 1977, *2:* 189–198.

————. Microwave radiation. *New York State Journal of Medicine,* 1977, *77:* 2172.

————, BACHMAN, C. H., AND FRIEDMAN, H. The direct current control system: A link between the environment and the organism. *New York State Journal of Medicine,* 1962, *62:* 1169–1176.

————, AND MARINO, A. A. Biological effects of extremely low frequency electric and magnetic fields: A review. *Physiological Chemistry and Physics,* 1977, *9:* 131–147.

————, AND MARINO, A. A. Electromagnetic pollution. *Science,* 1978, *18:* 14.

————, REICHMANIS, M., MARINO, A. A., AND SPADARO, J. A. Electrophysiological correlates of acupuncture points and meridians. *Psychoenergetic Systems,* 1976, *1:* 105–112.

————, AND SPADARO, J. A. Electrical stimulation of partial limb regeneration in mammals. *Bulletin of New York Academy of Medicine,* 1972, *48,* 627–641.

————, AND SPADARO, J. A. Treatment of orthopaedic infections with electrically generated silver ions. *The Journal of Bone and Joint Surgery,* 1978, *60A*(7), 871–881.

————, SPADARO, J. A., AND MARINO, A. A. Clinical experiences with low intensity direct current stimulation of bone growth. *Clinical Orthopaedics and Related Research,* 1977, *124:* 75–83.

———— ET AL. Geomagnetic parameters and psychiatric hospital admissions. *Nature,* 1963, *200:* 626.

BEDNY, I., SILINA, E. D., AND LIUBARSKAIA, B. L. Longevity in cities according to data of the years 1959 and 1970. *Zdravookhraneniye Rossiiskoi Federatzii,* 1972, *16*(4): 22–27.

BEHARI, J., AND ANDRABI, W. H. Generation of Hall voltage in bone. *Connective Tissue Research,* 1978, *6*(3): 181–184.

Behavior Today. December 18, 1978: 7.

————. Pacific mutual: Behavioral research + maintenance = lower health costs. December 25, 1978: 2–4.

————. News roundup. January 1, 1979: 7.

————. Cruikshank: Times story on "selfish" elderly: "A complete distortion." January 8, 1979, *9*(52): 1–2.

————. News roundup. January 8, 1979, *9*(52): 7.

————. News roundup. January 15, 1979: 7.

————. News roundup. January 22, 1979: 8.

————. Papers presented at the AAAS meeting in Houston: A first report. January 22, 1979: 3–4.

————. "Holistic" emphasis at OTA helps spearhead obstetric reassessment. February 5, 1979: 3–5.

————. November 26, 1979a: 7–8.

————. Researcher finds prison life significantly retards the aging process. February 14, 1980: 5–6.

————. News roundup. March 3, 1980: 77.

BEIER, W., BREHME, K. H., AND WIEGEL, D. Vitality, aging and biological efficiency of a multicellular system. *Mechanisms of Ageing and Development,* March 1973, *1*(5): 313–318.

BEIGEL, H. G., ed. The possibility of sexual happiness in old age. In *Advances in Sex Research.* New York: Hoebel-Harper, 1963.

BEISCHER, D. E., GRISSETT, J. D., AND MITCHELL, R. E. *Exposure of Man to Magnetic Fields Alternating at Extremely Low Frequency.* Naval Aerospace Medical Research Laboratory, Pensacola, Florida, NTIS No. AD 770140, July 1973.

BELL, B. D. Cognitive dissonance and the life satisfaction of older adults. *Journal of Gerontology,* 1974, *29*(5): 564–571.

BELL, C. W., FORKER, A. D., AND ELIOT, R. S. How to advise your middle-aged patients on exercise. *Modern Medicine,* September 30–October 15, 1978: 93–99.

BELLER, S., AND PALMORE, E. Longevity in Turkey. *Gerontologist,* October 1974, *5*(14): 373–376.

BELLOC, N. B. Relationship of physical health status and health practices. *Preventive Medicine,* 1972, *1:* 409–421.

————. Relationship of health practices and mortality. *Preventive Medicine,* 1973, *2:* 67–81.

BENDER, R. *Yoga Exercise for Every Body.* Avon, Conn.: Ruben Publishing, 1975.

————. *Be Young and Flexible After 30, 40, 50, 69 . . .* Avon, Conn.: Ruben Publishing, 1976.

————. *Yoga Exercises for More Flexible Bodies.* Avon, Conn.: Ruben Publishing, 1978.

BENDITT, E. P. The origin of atherosclerosis. *Scientific American,* February 1977, *236*(2): 74–85.

BENET, S. *Abkhasians: The Long Living People of the Caucasus.* New York: HREW, 1965.

————. *How to Live to be 100.* New York: Dial, 1976.

BENNETT, W. I. High-density lipoprotein and heart disease. *Harvard Medical School Health Letter,* December 1978, 4(2).

BENSON, H. *The Mind/Body Effect.* New York: Simon & Schuster, 1979.

————, BEARY, J. F., AND CAROL, M. P. The relaxation response. *Psychiatry,* 1974, *37:* 37–46.

————, DRYER, T., AND HARTLEY, L. H. Decreased VO_2 consumption during exercise with elicitation of the relaxation response. *Journal of Human Stress,* June 1978: 38–42.

————, AND EPSTEIN, H. D. The placebo effect: A neglected asset in the care of patients. *Journal of the American Medical Association,* 1965, *232*(12).

————, AND MCCALLIE, D. P. Angina pectoris and the placebo effect. *New England Journal of Medicine,* 1979, *300:* 1424–1429.

BERG, A. Self-destructive habits. *New Physician,* September 1977: 45–46.

BERG, A. O., AND LOGERFO, J. P. Potential effects of self-care algorithms on the number of physician visits. *New England Journal of Medicine,* March 8, 1979, *300:* 535–537.

BERG, R. L. The high cost of self-deception. *Preventive Medicine,* December 1976, *5*(4): 483–495.

BERGLAND, R. M., AND PAGE, R. B. Pituitary-brain vascular relations: A new paradigm. *Science,* April 6, 1979, *204,* 18–24.

BERLIN, H. Your doctor discusses: Sexuality in maturity. *Planning for Health, 1979, 21*(4). Kaiser Permanente Hospital, Oakland, California.

BERLINER, H. S., AND SALMON, J. S. The holistic health movement and scientific medicine: The naked and the dead. *Socialist Review,* 1979, *4*(1), 31–52.

————, AND SALMON, J. S. The new realities of health policy and influences of holistic medicine. *Journal of Alternative Human Services,* Summer 1979, *5*(2): 13–16.

————, AND SALMON, J. S. The holistic alternative to scientific medicine: history and analysis. *International Journal of Health Services,* 1980, *10*(1): 133–147.

BERMAN, J. L., WYNNE, J., AND COHN, P. F. Hemodynamic correlates of increased R wave sum in multiple lead treadmill exercise tests. Abstract. *American Journal of Cardiology,* 1979, *43*(2): 354.

BERNARDI, F., AND NINIO, J. Accuracy of DNA-replication. *Biochimie,* 1978, *60*(10): 1083–1095.

BERRY, W. T. Nutrition and growth. *Community Health* (Bristol, England), March-April, 1972, *3*(5): 237–244.

BERTRAND, C. A. On coffee and your heart. *Executive Health,* 1979: *15*(5).

BEVILACQUA, C. On the conditions of social hygiene of the aged population of the city of Trieste. *Rass Int Clin Ter,* July 31, 1967, *47*(14): 769–783.

BEZOLD, C. *The Rise of Alternatives to Drug Therapies and the Implications for Pharmaceutical Research and Development.* Washington, D.C.: Institute for Alternative Futures, Antioch College, February 1979.

BIERMAN, E. L. Atherosclerosis and aging. *Federation Proceedings,* 1978, *37*(14): 2832–2836.

Biofeedback and Self-control. Chicago: Aldine Publishers, Annual volumes 1970–1978.

BISHOP, J. E. Puzzling incidents of coronary spasms suspected as one cause of heart attacks. *The Wall Street Journal,* November 14, 1979, 20.

BJORKSTEN, J. Aging, primary mechanism. *Gerontologia,* 1963, *8:* 179–192.

————. The crosslinkage theory of aging. *Journal of the American Geriatrics Society,* 1968, *16*(4): 408–427.

————. Approaches and prospects for the control of age-dependent deterioration. *Annals of the New York Academy of Sciences,* June 7, 1971, *184:* 95–102.

————. Some therapeutic implications of the cross-linkage theory of aging. *Advanced Experimental Medical Biology,* 1977, *868:* 579–602.

————. A unifying concept for degenerative disease. *Comprehensive Therapy,* January 1978, *4*(1): 44–52.

BLACK, D. Medicine and the mind. *Playboy,* April 1980: 120–221.

BLACKWELL, B. The endorphins: Current psychiatric research. *Psychiatric Opinion,* October 1979.

BLAKEMAN, M. C. Self-care for health problems: An idea whose time is coming. *San Francisco Examiner,* November 19, 1979.

BLAUSTEIN, A. T. *National Advisory Council on Economic Opportunity: 11th Report.* Washington, D.C.: U.S. Government Printing Office, June 1979. Stock #041-008-00017-2.

BLAZER, D., AND PALMORE, E. Religion and aging in a longitudinal panel. *Gerontologist,* February 1976, *16*(1): 82–85.

BLOOM, M. Fitness in America: Is medicine keeping up? *Medical World News,* November 27, 1978: 66–76.

BLOOMFIELD, H. H. Holistic health: More than the absence of disease. *Medical World News,* December 11, 1978: 87.

———, AND KORY, R. *The Holistic Way to Health and Happiness.* New York: Simon & Schuster, 1978.

BLOT, W. J., BRINTON, L. A., FRAUMENI, J. F., AND STONE, B. J. Cancer mortality in US counties with petroleum industries. *Science,* October 7, 1977, *198:* 51–53.

BLUM, H. L. Personal communication to Arthur T. Blaustein, Chairman, National Advisory Council on Economic Opportunity, 1978. (a)

———. Proposal to National Advisory Council on economic opportunity. Berkeley: University of California, School of Public Health, 1978. (b)

Board of Medical Quality Assurance, Department of Consumer Affairs, State of California. Reviewing the legal definition of medicine in California—A proposal for Foundation support from the Adolph Foundation. 1979.

BOHN, R. C., AND STEILZNER, D. J. Regeneration of optic axons from one eye to the other eye in frogs *(Rana pipiens). Anatomical Record,* 1979, *193*(3): 486–487.

BOIARSKI, A. I. A. Average life expectancy. *Zdravookhraneniye Rossiiskoi Federatzii* 1968, *12*(9): 3–5.

BOK, S. The ethics of giving placebos. *Scientific American,* 1974, *231:* 17–23.

BOLLA, R., AND BROT, H. Age dependent changes in enzymes involved in macromolecular synthesis in *Turbatrix aceti. Archives of Biochemistry and Biophysics,* 1975, *169:* 227–236.

BONNEVIE, P. The concept of health. *Scandinavian Journal of Social Medicine,* 1973, *2:* 41–43.

BORTZ, W. Doctor's prescription for living to 120. *San Francisco Chronicle,* December 11, 1978: 1.

BOTWINICK, J. A crude test of a hypothesis relating rate of growth to length of life. *Gerontologist,* Autumn 1968, *8*(3): 196–197.

BOWEN, D. M. Accelerated aging or selective neuronal loss as an important cause of dementia. *Lancet,* 1979, *2*(8106): 11–14.

BOWERMAN, W. G. Centenarians. *Transactions of the Actuarial Society of America,* 1939, *40:* 361–378.

BOWERS, D. Electrocardiogram of nonagenarians. *Geriatrics,* May 1969, *24*(5): 89–92.

BREINER, S. J. Causes of death—unconscious dimensions. *Current Concepts in Psychiatry,* March/April 1978: 17–22.

BRESLER, D. E., AND TRUBO, R. *Free Yourself from Pain.* New York: Simon & Schuster, 1979.

BRESLOW, L. A quantitative approach to the World Health Organization definition of health: Physical, mental and social well being. *International Journal of Epidemiology,* 1972, *1:* 347–355.

———. A policy assessment of preventive health practice. *Preventive Medicine,* June 1977, *6*(2): 242–251.

———. A positive strategy for the nation's health. *Journal of the American Medical Association,* November 9, 1979, *242*(19): 2093–2095.

———, AND KLEIN, B. Health and race in California. *American Journal of Public Health,* April 1971, *61*(4): 763–775.

BRILL, N. Q. Are psychiatrists physicians, too? *Psychosomatics.* August 1977, 5–6.

BRILL, P. Work satisfaction best predictor of longevity. *American Medical News,* December 1, 1978: 16.

BRISSOT DE WARVILLE, J. P. *New Travels in the United States of America, 1788.* Cambridge, Mass.: The Belknap Press of Harvard University Press, 1964.

BROAD, W. J. Paul Feyerabend: Science and the anarchist. *Science,* November 2, 1979, *206:* 534–537.

———. New strength in the diet-disease link? *Science,* November 9, 1979, *206:* 666–668.

BRODY, J. E. Marriage is good for health and longevity, studies say. *The New York Times (Science Times),* May 8, 1979: C1–2.

BROOKE, M. H., CARROLL, J. E., DAVIS, J. E., AND HAGBERG, J. M. Prolonged exercise test. *Neurology,* 1979, *29*(5): 636–643.

BROSSE, C. A psychophysiological study. *Main Currents in Modern Thought, 1978, 4:* 77–84.

BROTMAN, H. B. The fastest growing minority: The aging. *American Journal of Public Health,* March 1974, *64*(3): 249–252.

————. Life expectancy: Comparison of national levels in 1900 and 1974 and variations in state levels, 1969–1971. *Gerontologist,* February 1977, *17*(1): 12–22.

BROWN, B. *New Mind, New Body.* New York: Harper & Row, 1975.

BROWN, D. D. Gene organization: Another surprise. *Science News,* July 28, 1979, *116:* 72.

BROWN, G. W. ET AL. Life events and psychiatric disorders, Part I —some methodological issues. *Psychological Medicine,* February 1972, *3:* 74–87.

BROWN, J. P. Role of gut bacterial flora in nutrition and health: A review of recent advances in bacteriological techniques, metabolism, and factors affecting flora composition. *CRC Critical Reviews in Food Technology,* January 1977, *8*(3): 229–336.

BROWN, K. S., AND MILVY, P. A critique of several epidemiological studies of physical activity and its relationship to aging, health, and mortality. *Annals of the New York Academy of Sciences,* 1977: 103–119.

BROWN, W. T. Human mutations affecting aging. Review. *Mechanisms of Ageing and Development,* 1979, *9*(3-4): 325–336.

BRUCK, D. Fitness, exercise, age and human sleep. *Australian Psychologist,* 1979, *14*(2): 203.

BRYANT, P. J., BRYANT, S. V., AND FRENCH, V. Biological regeneration and pattern formation. *Scientific American,* July 1977, *237* (1): 66–81.

BUELL, S. J., AND COLEMAN, P. D. Dendritic growth in the aged human brain and failure of growth in senile dementia. *Science,* November 16, 1979, *206:* 854–856.

BURACK, R. There is no epidemic of cancer in the United States. *The New York Times,* "Letters to the Editor," April 15, 1979.

BURCH, E. A. The congestive heart failure model of schizophrenia.

Journal of the American Medical Association, May 4, 1979, *241*(18): 1923–1925.

BURCH, G. E. People live no longer anymore. *American Heart Journal,* February 1972, *83*(2): 285–286.

Bureau Medical de Notre-Dame de Lourdes. Cures of Lourdes recognized as miraculous by the church. Compiled as of January 1, 1979.

BURKE, D. C. The status of interferon. *Scientific American,* April 1970, *236*(4): 42–50.

BURKITT, D. P. The link between low-fiber diets and disease. *Human Nature,* December 1978, 34–41.

————. Is dietary fiber protective against disease? *Executive Health,* December 1979, *16*(3).

BURNET, F. M. *Immunologic surveillance.* New York: Pergamon, 1970.

————. A genetic interpretation of aging. *Lancet,* September 1, 1973, *2*(827): 480–483.

BURNS, P. Noise and death rates. OMNI, March 1979: 40.

BURTON, B. T., ed. *The Heinze Handbook of Nutrition: A Comprehensive Treatise on Nutrition in Health and Disease.* New York: McGraw-Hill, 1976.

Business Week. The skyrocketing costs of health care. May 17, 1976: 144–147.

————. Using cancer's rates to track its cause. November 14, 1977: 69–75.

————. Unhealthy costs of health. September 4, 1978: 58–68.

BUSSE, E. W. How mind, body, and environment influence nutrition in the elderly. *Postgraduate Medicine,* March 1978, *63*(3): 118–122, 125.

BUT DANG-DOAN. Notes on physician mortality. *CAH Sociol. Demogr. Med.,* April-June, 1977, *17*(2): 73–76.

BUTLER, R. N. Aging: A challenge to medicine. *Journal of the Tennessee Medical Association,* August 1977, *70*(8): 585–586, 588.

————. Research programs of the National Institute of Aging. *Public Health Report,* January-February 1977, *92*(1): 3–8.

————. *Why Survive? Being Old in America.* New York: Harper & Row, 1975.

————, AND LEWIS, M. *Aging and Mental Health: Positive Psychosocial Approaches.* St. Louis: C. V. Mosby Company, 1973.

California Department of Mental Health, Office of Prevention. *In Pursuit of Wellness.* San Francisco: 2346 Irving Street, #108, 94122, 1979.

CAMERON, E., AND PAULING, L. Supplemental ascorbate in the supportive treatment of cancer: Prolongation of survival times in terminal human cancer. *Proceedings of the National Academy of Science,* October 1976, *73*(10): 3685–3689.

————, AND PAULING, L. On cancer and vitamin C. *Executive Health,* January 1980, *26*(4).

CAMPBELL, A. Subjective measures of well-being. *American Psychologist,* March 1976: 117–124.

CAMPBELL, D. T., AND STANLEY, J. C. *Experimental and Quasi-Experimental Designs for Research.* Chicago: Rand McNally and Company, 1963.

Canadian Medical Association Journal. Putting humanity back into medicine. April 8, 1972, *106*(7): 744–745.

CANNON, W. B. *The Wisdom of the Body.* New York: W. W. Norton, 1942.

CAPLAN, R. D. *Job Demands and Worker Health: Main Effects and Occupational Differences.* Ann Arbor, Mich.: Institute for Social Research, Box 1248, 48106, 1970.

CAPRA, F. Modern physics and eastern philosophy. *New Dimensions,* Summer 1974, *3*(2).

————. *The Tao of Physics.* Berkeley: Shambala, 1975.

CAQUETTE, M. Gynecological problems in geriatrics. French. *Vie Medicale au Canada Français,* 1979, *8*(1): 174.

CARLSON, R. J. *The End of Medicine.* New York: John Wiley & Sons, 1975.

————. The healthy corporation. Unpublished manuscript, 1980.

CARLSON, S. A. Nutrition in old age. In S. A. Carlson, ed., *Symposia of the Swedish Nutrition Foundation,* Vol. X. Uppsala, Sweden: Almqvist & Wiksell, 1972.

CARMODY, T.-P., FEY, S. G., CONNOR, W. E., AND MATARAZZ, J. D. "Family-based model for the dietary-treatment and prevention of hypertension." *Preventive Medicine,* 1979, *8*(2): 142. Meeting abstract.

CARP, F. M. Impact of improved living environment of health and life expectance. *Gerontologist,* June 1977, *17*(3): 242–249.

CASEY, A. E., CASEY, J. G., DOWNEY, E. L., AND GRAVLEE, J. F. Longevity from non-mechanized farm labor and dairy food in upland Irish bog. *Alabama Journal of Medical Sciences,* April 1972, *9*(2): 164–170.

CASTANEDA, C. *The Teachings of Don Juan.* New York: Ballantine Books, 1968.

————. *A Separate Reality.* New York: Simon & Schuster, 1971.

————. *Journey to Ixtlan.* New York: Simon & Schuster, 1972.

————. *Tales of Power.* New York: Simon & Schuster, 1974.

CERAM, C. W. *Gods, Graves, and Scholars.* New York: Alfred A. Knopf, 1952.

CHANG, C. C., D'AMBROSIO, S., SCHULTZ, R., TROSKO, J. E., AND SETLOW, R. B. Modification of UV-induced mutation frequencies in Chinese hamster cells by dose fractionation, cycloheximide and caffeine treatments. *Mutation Research,* 1978, *52:* 231–245.

————, PHILIPPS, C., TROSKO, J. E., AND HART, R. W. Mutagenic and epigenetic influence of caffeine on the frequencies of UV-induced ouabain-resistant Chinese hamster cells. *Mutation Research,* 1977, *45:* 125–136.

CHARV, A. T. J. Various problems of old age and aging. *Bratislavske Lekarske Listy,* October 1972, *58*(4): 385–388.

CHASE, A. The real story of medicine. *Medical Tribune,* November 21, 1979: 15.

CHEBOTAREV, D. Fight against old age. *Gerontologist,* Winter 1971, *11*(4): 359–361.

CHEEK, D. B., GRAYSTONE, J. E., AND READ, M. S. Cellular growth, nutrition and development. *Pediatrics,* February 1970, *45* (2): 315–334.

————, AND LE CRON, L. M. *Clinical hypnotherapy.* New York: Grune & Stratton, 1968.

CHEN, M. M., AND WAGNER, D. P. Gains in mortality from biomedical research 1930–1975—Initial assessment. *Social Science & Medicine,* 1978, *12*(3-4C): 73–81.

CHERASKIN, E., RINGSDORF, W. M., AND BRECHER, A. *Psychodietetics.* New York: Bantam, 1976.

CHOW, C. K., AND CHEN, C. J. Influence of dietary selenium on the age-related susceptibility of rat erythrocytes to ixidative stress. *Federal Proceedings,* 1977, *38*(3): 391.

CHOW, E. *Applications to Experimental Health Manpower Project, State of California, Department of Health, for Approval of Pilot Project: Training Holistic and Cultural Health Educators/Practitioners.* San Francisco: East West Academy of Healing Arts, 1977.

CHRISTEN, N. J., GALBO, H., HANSEN, J. F., HESSE, B., RICHTER, E. A., AND TRAPJENS, J. Catecholamines and exercise. *Diabetes,* 1979, *28*(S1): 58–62.

CHRISTENSEN, C., AND GAGNON, J. Sexual patterns in a group of older never married women. *Geriatric Psychiatry,* 1972.

CIRENEI, F. Apropos of extreme longevity: Clinical and hemato-chemical study of a 104-year-old subject. *Acta Gerontology* (Milano), October-December 1969, *19*(4): 245–248.

CLARK, B. A. Physical activity and aging—Shepard, R. J. Book review. *Journal of Gerontology,* 1979, *34*(2): 280.

CLEMENS, J. A., AND FULLER, R. W. Chemical manipulation of some aspects of aging. *Adv. Exp. Med. Biol.,* 1978, *97:* 187–206.

Clinical Psychiatry News. Type A behavior further analyzed. May 1978, *6*(5): 43.

————. Geriatrics now popular, but the elderly are not. December 1978, *6*(12): 1.

————. Mood disorders seen in 20% of sample of Irish male alcoholics. January 1979: 10.

————. Biomedical model said to exclude patient. April 1979: 8.

————. Greater longevity raises need to cope with effects of aging. May 1979: 36.

COBB, S., AND ROSE, E. M. Hypertension, peptic ulcer and diabetes in air traffic controllers. *Journal of the American Medical Association,* April 1973, *224:* 489–492.

COBB, W. M. Immortality, aging, and differentiation. *Journal of the National Medical Association,* April 1, 1977, *69*(4): 205–206.

COCHRANE, A. L. Effectiveness and efficacy: Random reflections on health services. *British Medical Journal,* 1974, *4:* 5.

COHEN, B. L. Saccharin: The risks and benefits. *Nature,* February 9, 1978, *271*(5645): 492.

COHEN, D. Magnetic fields of the human body. *Physics Today,* August 1975, *4*(30): 34–43.

COMFORT, A. Test-battery to measure ageing-rate in man. *Lancet,* December 27, 1969: 1411–1415.

————. The biological basis for increasing longevity. *Medical Opinion and Review,* April 1970: 18–25.

————. *The Joy of Sex.* New York: Crown, 1972.

————. *A Good Age.* New York: Crown, 1976.

————. On healing Americans. *Journal of Operational Psychiatry,* 1978, *9*(1): 25–36.

————. Gerontology and geriatrics in aerospace-medicine. Editorial. *Journal of the Royal Society of Medicine,* 1979, *72*(2): 85–87.

COMMONER, B. *The Poverty of Power: Energy and the Economic Crisis.* New York: Knopf, 1976.

————, AND BOKSENBAUM, H., eds. *Energy and Human Welfare: The Social Costs of Power Production,* Vol. 1. New York: Macmillan Information, 1975.

CONE, C., AND CONE, C. M. Induction of mitosis in mature neurons in central nervous system by sustained depolarization. *Science,* 1976, *192:* 155–158.

————. *Connecticut Medicine.* Impact of an aging population on utilization and bed needs of Connecticut hospitals. 1978, *42*(12): 775–781.

CONNOR, W. E. ET AL. The plasma lipids, lipoproteins, and diet of the Tarahumara Indians of Mexico. *American Journal of Clinical Nutrition,* July 31, 1978: 1131–1142.

CONOLEY, G. Living may be hazardous to your health. *American Way,* February 1980: 37–44.

Consumer's Union. Nutrition as therapy. January 1980: 21–24.

COOPER, K. H. *The New Aerobics.* New York: Bantam, 1975.

————. *Aerobics.* New York: Bantam, 1976.

————. *The Aerobics Way.* New York: M. Evans & Co., 1977.

————, AND COOPER, M. *Aerobics for Women.* New York: Bantam, 1976.

COOPER, M. J., AND AYGEN, M. M. A relaxation technique in the management of hypercholesterolemia. *Journal of Human Stress,* December 1979: 24–27.

COOPER, R., STAMLER, J., DYER, A., AND GARSIDE, D. Decline in mortality from heart-disease, U.S.A., 1968–1975. *Journal of Chronic Diseases,* 1978, *31*(12): 709–720.

COOPER, T., AND MITCHELL, S. C. Preventive medicine: The approximation of paradise? *Preventive Medicine,* March 1972, *1*(1): 15–19.

COSTE, C. In search of wellness: New dimensions in health care. *The New Physician,* September 1977, 25–27.

COULTER, H. L. *Divided Legacy: A History of the Schism in Medical Thought.* Volumes 1, 2, 3. Washington, D.C.: Wehawken Book Co., 1977.

COUSINS, N. Anatomy of an illness. *New England Journal of Medicine,* 1976, *295:* 1458–1463. Reprinted in *Saturday Review,* May 28, 1977: 4–51.

————. The mysterious placebo: How the mind helps medicine work. *Saturday Review,* 1977, *5:* 9–16.

————. What I learned from 3000 doctors. *Saturday Review,* February 18, 1978: 12–16.

————. The conquest of pain. *Saturday Review,* March 17, 1979: 12.

————. The holistic health explosion. *Saturday Review,* March 31, 1979: 17–20.

CRANMER, M. F. Estimation of risks due to environmental carcinogenesis. *Medical and Pediatric Oncology,* 1977, *3*(2): 169–198.

CREMER, H. D. Nutrition, aging, and life expectancy. *Zeitschrift für Ernahrungswissenschaft Suppl.,* 1973, *15:* 130–138.

CRICK, F. H. C. Nucleic acids. *Scientific American,* September 1957, *197*(3): 188–200.

————. The genetic code. *Scientific American,* October 1962: 66–74.

————. The genetic code: III. *Scientific American,* October 1966: 55–62.

————, WANG, J. C., AND BAUER, W. R. Is DNA really a double helix? *Journal of Molecular Biology,* 1979, *129*(3): 449–461.

CROSBY, W. H. Can a vegetarian be well nourished? *Journal of the American Medical Association,* 1975, *233:* 898.

CROSS, H. E. Population studies and the old order Amish. *Nature,* July 1, 1976, *262:* 17–20.

CRUSE, J. P., LEWIN, M. R., FERULANO, G. P., AND CLARK, C. G.

Co-carcinogenic effects of dietary cholesterol in experimental colon cancer. Letter. *Nature,* 1978, *276*(4690): 822–825.

CRUSE, J. P., LEWIN, M. R., AND CLARK, C. G. Dietary fiber and experimental colon cancer. *Lancet,* 1979, *1*(8112): 376.

CUMMING, E., AND HENRY, W. E. *Growing Old.* New York: Basic Books, 1961.

CUMMINGS, J. H. Dietary factors in etiology of gastrointestinal cancer. *Journal of Human Nutrition,* 1978, *32*(6): 445–465.

CUSACK, R., AND DOUGLASS, J. Pre-exercise stress tests. *New England Journal of Medicine,* February 7, 1980, *302*(6): 349–350.

CUTLER, R. G. Cross-linkage hypothesis of aging. DNA adducts in chromatin as a primary aging process. In K. C. Smith, ed., *Aging, Carcinogenesis and Radiation Biology.* New York: Plenum Publishing Corp., 1976.

———. Alterations with age in the informational storage and flow systems of the mammalian cell. *Birth Defects: Original Article Series,* 1978, *14*(1): 463–498.

DANIELLI, J. F., AND MUGGLETON, A. Some alternative states of amoeba, with special reference to life-span. *Gerontologia,* 1959, *3:* 76–90.

DARBY, W. J. The benefits of drink. *Human Nature,* November 1978: 31–37.

DAVIDSON, D. M., TAYLOR, G. B., DEBUSK, R. F., HOUSTON, N., AND AGRAS, W. S. Comparison of treadmill exercise testing with and without psychological stress. Meeting abstract. *Clinical Research,* 1979, *27*(1): 3.

DAVIDSON, W. Drugs for eternal youth—scientific attempts to combat aging. *Journal of Drug Issues,* 1979, *9*(1): 91–104.

DAVIES, D. A Shangri-la in Ecuador. *New Scientist,* February 1, 1973: 104–106.

———. *The Centenarians of the Andes.* Garden City, N.Y.: Anchor Press, 1975.

———. Progress toward the assessment of health states. *Preventive Medicine,* September 1975, *4:* 282–295.

DAVIS, C., AND FESHBACH, M. Life expectancy in the Soviet Union. *The Wall Street Journal,* June 20, 1978: 7.

DAVIS, K. Health and high voltage. *Sierra,* July/August, 1978: 23–25.

DAVIS, L. M., AND DAVIS, V. E. Golden sexuality. *Behavioral Medicine,* December 1978: 16–19.

DAVIS, P. J. What's new and important about aging and endocrine function? *Medical Tribune,* June 6, 1979: 7–8.

DAVIS, R. G. Increased bitter taste detection thresholds in Yucatan inhabitants related to coffee as a dietary source of niacin. *Chemical Senses and Flavor,* 1978, *3* (4): 423–429.

DAVISON, W. Drugs for eternal youth—scientific attempts to combat aging. *Journal of Drug Issues,* 1979, *9* (1): 91–104.

DAVITZ, J., AND DAVITZ, L. *Making It: 40 and Beyond.* New York: Winston Press, 1979.

DAVY, J. Death's tourists. *San Francisco Sunday Examiner & Chronicle,* July 17, 1979: 2–6.

DAWKINS, R. Selective neurone death as a possible memory mechanism. *Nature,* January 8, 1971, *229:* 118–119.

DAWSON, A. M., AND BALLER, W. R. Relationship between creative activity and the health of elderly persons. *Journal of Psychology,* September 1972, *82* (1): 49–58.

DeDUVE, C., PRESSMAN, B. C., GIANETTO, R., WATTIAUX, R., AND APPELMANS, F. Tissue fractionation studies: 6. intracellular distribution patterns of enzymes in rat liver tissue. *Biochemical Journal,* 1955, *60:* 604–617.

DELAYE, J., DELAHAYE, J. P., CANICAVE, J. C., JANIN, A., PINEL, A., AND GONIN, A. 1st attack of myocardial-infarction during sporting exercise in young subjects—report of 12 cases. *Lyon Medical,* 1979, *241* (2): 81–87.

DENCKLA, W. D. A time to die. *Life Sciences, 16:* 31–44, 1974.

———. Interactions between age and the neuroendocrine and immune systems. *Federal Proceedings,* April 1978, *37* (5): 1263–1267.

DENHOLM, J. G. Longevity of women G.P.S. *British Medical Journal,* April 14, 1973, *2* (858): 119.

DeSILVA, R. A., AND LOWN, B. Ventricular premature beats, stress, and sudden death. *Psychosomatics,* November 1978, *19* (11): 649–661.

DETRE, K., MURPHY, M. L., AND HOLTFREN, H. Effect of coronary bypass surgery on longevity in high and low risk patients. Report from the V.A. Cooperative Coronary Surgery Study. *Lancet,* December 17, 1977, 2(8051): 1243–1245.

DEVOR, M., AND GOVRINLI, R. Selective regeneration of sensory fibers following nerve crush injury. *Experimental Neurology,* 1979, 65(2): 243–254.

DE VRIES, H. A. Tips on prescribing exercise regimens for your older patient. *Geriatrics,* April 1979, 34(4): 75–81.

DEWEY, J. Introduction. In E. V. Cowdry, ed., *Problems of aging.* Baltimore: Williams & Wilkins, 1939.

DIAMOND, M. C. Using your brains. *The Independent & Gazette,* Berkeley, California, February 13, 1980: 3.

DICKEY, L. *Clinical Ecology.* Springfield, Ill.: Charles C Thomas, 1976.

DILLARD, C. J., LITOV, R. E., SAVIN, W. M., DUMMELIN, E. E., AND TAPPEL, A. L. Effects of exercise, vitamin-E and ozone on pulmonary-function and lipid peroxidation. *Journal of Applied Physiology,* 1978, 45(6): 927–932.

DILMAN, V. M. The elevational mechanism of aging and cancer, paths to prevention through limitation of disorders in bodily energy and reproductive homeostasis caused by increased resistance of the hypothalamus to change with age. *Voprosy Onkologii,* 1970, 16(6): 45–53.

————. Age-associated elevation of hypothalamic threshold to feedback control, and its role in development, ageing, and disease. *Lancet,* June 12, 1971: 1211–1219.

DISHMAN, R. K. Biological and behavioral—influences on exercise adherence. Meeting abstract. *Medicine and Science in Sports,* 1979, 11(1): 80.

DLIN, B. M. Risk factors, life style and the emotions in coronary disease. *Psychosomatics,* 1977, 18: 28–31.

DONLON, P. T., MEADOW, A., AND AMSTERDAM, E. Emotional stress as a factor in ventricular arrhythmias. *Psychosomatics,* April 1979, 20(4): 233–240.

DORMANDY, T. L. Free radical oxidation and antioxidants. *Lancet,* March 25, 1978: 647–650.

DOWNEY, G. The next patient right: Sex in the nursing home. *Modern Health Care,* June 1974: 56–60.

DOYLE, A. E. The dilemma of mild hypertension. In *Hypertension and Stroke Control in the Community*. Geneva: World Health Organization, 1976.

DOYON-GODINIAUX, F., LOMBARDO, E., PARMENTIER, N. C., AND JAMMET, H. Comparative study of life span of radiologists and physicians of other specialties. *Annales de Radiologie* Paris, 1969, *12*(11): 1009–1014.

DUBLIN, L. I., LOTKA, A. J., AND SPIEGELMAN, M. *Length of Life*. New York: Ronald Press, 1949.

DUBOS, R. *Man Adapting*. New Haven, Conn.: Yale University Press, 1965.

———. Man adapting. In W. Ewald, Jr., ed., *Environment for Men*. Bloomington: Indiana University Press, 1967.

———. *So Human an Animal*. New York: Scribner's, 1968.

———. Humanizing the earth. *Science*, 1973, *179:* 769.

———. Bolstering the body against disease. *Human Nature*, August 1978: 68–73.

DUHL, L. J. The psychiatrist's role in dealing with social turmoil. *American Journal of Psychiatry*, August 1970, *127*(2): 143.

———. The health planner: Planning and dreaming for health and wellness. *American Journal of Health Planning*, October 1976, *1*(2): 7–14.

———. Health services for the poor. Unpublished report, University of California, Berkeley, 1980.

———, AND DEN BOER, J. *Making whole: Health for a New Epoch*. Elmsford, N.Y.: Pergamon Press, 1980.

DYCHTWALD, K. Aging: The elder within. *New Age*, 29–33.

———. *Bodymind*. New York: Pantheon, 1977.

EASTON, J. *Human Longevity*. London: Salisbury, 1979.

EASTWOOD, M. A., AND KAY, R. M. Hypothesis for the action of dietary fiber along the gastro-intestinal tract. *American Journal of Clinical Nutrition*, 1979, *32*(2): 364–367.

Editorial. How to grow old without aging. *Journal of the American Medical Association*, May 28, 1973, *224*(9): 1289.

———. Population and the new biology. *Lancet*, October 13, 1973, *2*(833): 834–835.

————. Causes of death: Ancient and modern. *South African Medical Journal,* February 1974, *48*(6): 198.

————. Dietary goals for the United States. 2. Reaction statement by the American Dietetic Association. *Journal of the American Dietetic Association,* 1979, *74*(5): 529–533.

ELLERBROEK, W. Language, emotions, and disease. OMNI, March 1978: 93–95.

ELLIOT, O. The constitutional aspect of host factors in disease. *Singapore Medical Journal,* February 1972, *13*(1): 57–64.

ENGEL, G. L. Studies of ulcerative colitis: The nature of the psychologic process. *American Journal of Medicine,* 1955, *19:* 231.

————. Perspectives in biology and medicine: A unified concept of health. 1960, *3:* 459–485.

————. A life setting conducive to illness—a psychological setting of somatic disease: The giving-up—given-up complex. *Bulletin of the Menninger Clinic,* 1968, *32:* 355–366.

————. The psychosomatic approach to individual susceptibility to disease. *Gastroenterology,* 1974, *67:* 1085, 1093.

————. Psychologic factors in instantaneous cardiac death. *New England Journal of Medicine,* March 18, 1976, *294*(12): 664–665.

————. The need for a new medical model: A challenge for biomedicine. *Science,* April 8, 1977, *196*(4286): 129–136.

————. Sudden death. *Psychology Today,* November 1977: 18–22.

————, AND SCHMALE, A. Conservation—withdrawal: A primary regulatory process for organismic homeostasis. *Physiology, Emotion and Psychosomatic Illness.* CIBA Foundation Symposium 8, Elsevier, N.Y., 1972.

ENGLE, B. T., NIKOOMANESH, P., AND SCHUSTER, M. M. Operant conditioning of rectosphincteric responses in the treatment of fecal incontinence. *New England Journal of Medicine,* 1974, *290:* 646–649.

ENSTROM, J. E. Cancer and total mortality among active Mormons. *Cancer,* October 1978, *42*(4): 1943–1951.

EPSTEIN, J., AND GERSHON, P. Studies of ageing in nematodes IV. The effect of antioxidants on cellular damage and life span. *Mechanisms of Ageing and Development,* 1972, *1:* 257–264.

EPSTEIN, L. H. Relationshhip between exercise intensity, caloric intake and weight. *Addictive Behaviors,* 1978, *3*(3-4): 185–190.

ERDMAN, P. Predicting longevity. *Gerontologist,* 9(4): 247–250.

ESTES, J. W. As healthy a place as any in America: Revolutionary Portsmouth, New Hampshire. *Bulletin of Historical Medicine,* Winter 1976, 50(4): 536–552.

EVERETT, M. D. Strategies for increasing employees' level of exercise and physical-fitness. *Journal of Occupational Medicine,* 1979, 21(7): 463–467.

EWIN, D. M. ET AL. Behavioral approaches to patient care. *Patient Care,* April 30, 1979: 26–106.

EWIN, D. M. ET AL. Putting behavior therapies to office use. *Patient Care,* May 15, 1979: 60–105.

EXTON-SMITH, A. N. Maintenance of health in old age. *Transcripts of the Medical Society of London,* 1971, 87: 175–184.

EYRE, D. R. Collagen: Molecular diversity in the body's protein scaffold. *Science,* March 21, 1980, 207: 1315–1322.

EZHOVA, N. N. Socioeconomic shifts and the health of the population of the Udmurt Assr. *Sov-Zdravookhr,* 1978, 51–54.

FARQUHAR, J. W. Stress and how to cope with it. *The Stanford Alumni Magazine,* Fall/Winter, 1977.

———. *The American Way of Life Need Not Be Hazardous to Your Health.* Stanford, Calif.: Stanford Alumni Association, 1978.

FAVAZZA, A. R. The day of our years. *M.D.,* October 1977: 19–101.

FELDMAN, D. J. Chronic disabling illness—holistic view. *Journal of Chronic Disease,* 1974, 27: 287–296.

FELDMAN, R. E. Collaborative consultation: A process for joint professional-consumer development of primary prevention programs. *Journal of Community Psychology,* 1979, 7: 118–128.

FERENCZI, S. An attempted explanation of some hysterical stigmata. In *Further Contributions to the Theory and Technique of Psychoanalysis.* London: Hogarth Press, 1926.

FERGUSON, T. *Medical Self-care.* Box 717, Inverness, Calif.: 1981.

FERNSTROM, J. D. How food affects your brain. *Nutrition Action,* December 1979: 5–7.

———, AND WURTMAN, R. J. Nutrition and the brain. *Scientific American,* February 1974: 84–91.

FIELDS, H. L. Secrets of the placebo. *Psychology Today,* November 1978: 172.

————, AND BASBAUM, A. I. Brainstem control of spinal pain—transmission neurons. *Annual Review of Physiology,* 1978, *40:* 217–248.

FINCH, C. E. Neuroendocrinology of aging: A view of an emerging area. *BioScience,* October 1975, *25*(10): 645–650.

————. Extra-ovarian mechanisms in reproductive aging: Evaluation of possible pituitary and hypothalamic roles. Conference of NIA, Endocrine Society, and Veterans Administration. Bethesda, Maryland, October 18–20, 1979.

————. Neuro-endocrine mechanisms and aging. *Federal Proceedings,* 1979, *38*(2): 178–183.

————, AND HAYFLICK, L. *Handbook of the Biology of Aging.* New York: Van Nostrand Reinhold Company, 1977.

FINKLE, A. A sexual function during advancing age. In I. Rossman, ed., *Clinical Geriatrics,* p. 477. Philadelphia: J. B. Lippincott, 1971.

————, TOBENKIN, M. I., AND KARG, S. J. Sexual potency in aging males. I. Frequency of coitus among clinic patients. *Journal of the American Medical Association,* 1959, *170:* 113–115.

FINNERTY, F. A., JR., SHAW, L. W., AND HIMMELSBOCH, C. K. Hypertension in the inner city—detection and follow-up. *Circulation,* January 1973, *47:* 76–78.

FIORE, N. Fighting cancer—one patient's perspective. *New England Journal of Medicine,* February 8, 1979, *300*(6): 284–289.

————. Fighting cancer—patient's perspective—reply. Letter. *New England Journal of Medicine,* 1979, *300*(21): 1220–1221.

————. Letter to the Editor. *New England Journal of Medicine,* May 24, 1979: 1220.

FISHER, G. How to deal with stress. *U.S. News & World Report,* November 6, 1978: 65–66.

FLEISZER, D. ET AL. Protective effect of dietary fibre against chemically induced bowel tumors in rats. *Lancet,* September 9, 1978: 552–553.

FLOERSHEIM, G. L. Influencing of the aging: From the future ghost to a biological research object. *Praxis,* October 10, 1972, *61*(41): 1279–1282.

FLYNN, M. A., NOLPH, G. B., FLYNN, T. C., KAHRS, R., AND

KRAUSE, G. Effect of dietary egg on human-serum cholesterol and triglycerides. *American Journal of Clinical Nutrition,* 1979, *32*(5): 1051–1057.

FORD, B. Old conductors. OMNI, August 1979: 37.

FORDHAM, C. C. III. Public policy and health manpower. *Science,* May 4, 1979, *204*(4392). Editorial page.

FOSTER, C., COSTILL, D. L., AND FINK, W. J. Effects of pre-exercise feedings on endurance performance. *Medicine and Science in Sports,* 1979, *11*(1): 1–5.

FOWINKLE, E. W. New directions in preventive medicine. *Journal of the Tennessee Medical Association,* December 1977, *70*(12): 894–896.

FOX, K. M., SELWYN, A. P., AND SHILLING, J. P. Praecordial electro-cardiographic mapping after exercise—improved diagnosis of coronary-artery disease. *American Journal of Cardiology,* 1979, *43*(2): 353.

FOZARD, J. L., AND POPKIN, S. J. Optimizing adult development: Ends and means of an applied psychology of aging. *American Psychologist,* November 1978: 975–989.

FRANCIS, K. T. Effect of water and electrolyte replacement during exercise in the heat on biochemical indexes of stress and performance. *Aviation, Space, and Environmental Medicine,* 1979, *50*(2): 115–119.

FRANK, B. S. *Dr. Frank's No-aging Diet.* New York: Dial Press, 1976.

————. *Nucleic Acid, Nutrition and Therapy.* New York: Rainstone Publishing, 1977.

FRANK, J. A., AND DOUGHERTY, T. F. The assessment of stress in human subjects by means of qualitative changes in blood lymphocytes. *Journal of Laboratory and Clinical Medicine,* 1975, *42,* 538–549.

FRANK, J. D. The faith that heals. *Johns Hopkins Medical Journal,* 1975, *137:* 127–131.

————. Psychotherapy of bodily disease. *Psychotherapy and Psychosomatics,* 1975, *26:* 192–202.

————. The medical power of faith. *Human Nature,* August 1978: 40–49.

FRANKE, H. Criteria for above-average life expectancy. *Medicine Clinica,* June 11, 1971, *66*(24): 896–898.

———. The problem of longevity. *Lebensversicherungs-Medizin,* July 1971, *23*(4): 85–87.

FREDERICK, P. L. Working-life span of physicians. *Journal of the American Medical Association,* November 4, 1968, *202*(6): 1308.

FREEDMAN, A. M., KAPLAN, H. I., AND SADOCK, B. J. *Comprehensive Textbook of Psychiatry II, Vol. II,* pp. 1349–1599. Baltimore: Williams & Wilkins, 1975.

FRENCH, D., FAHRION, S., AND LEEB, C. Self-induced scrotal hyperthermis in man followed by a decrease in sperm output: A preliminary report. *Andrologie,* 1973, *5*(4): 311–316.

FRENCH, J. D. The reticular formation. *Scientific American,* 1957, *196:* 54–73.

Fresh clues for cutting toll of heart disease. *U.S. News & World Report,* January 29, 1979: 59.

FRIDOVICH, I. The biology of oxygen radicals. *Science,* September 8, 1978, *201:* 875–880.

FRIED, M. RNA. *Body Forum,* December 1978: 9–37.

FRIEDMAN, M. Holistic health: Is Washington listening? *Nutritional Journal,* January 1979: 42–46.

FRIEDMAN, M., AND ROSENMAN, R. H. *Type A Behavior and Your Heart.* New York: Alfred A. Knopf, 1974.

FROLKIS, F. On the road to longevity. *Gerontologist,* Autumn 1968, *8*(3): 198–200.

FROLKIS, V. V. Regulation and adaptation processes in aging. In *The Main Problems of Soviet Gerontology,* Kiev, 1972.

———. Functions of cells and biosynthesis of protein in aging. *Gerontologia,* 1973, *19:* 189–202.

——— ET AL. Catecholamines in the metabolism and functions regulation in aging. *Gerontologia,* 1970, *16:* 129–140.

FULLER, M. M. Social challenge of aging. Book review by D. Hobman. *Contemporary Sociology,* 1979, *8*(1): 67.

GACH, M. Short report on longevity of male home inhabitant. Author's translation. *ZFA Dresden,* 1977, *32*(2): 187–189.

GALBO, H., AND CHRISTEN, N. J. Effect of fasting on the response to exercise of catecholamines in plasma. Meeting abstract. *Acta Physiologica Scandinavica,* 1979, *105* (1): A61.

GALLAGHER, E. B. The health enterprise in modern society. *Social Science and Medicine,* October 1972, *6*(5): 619–633.

GARDNER, E. *Fundamentals of Neurology.* Philadelphia: W. B. Saunders, 1968.

GARFIELD, S. R. The delivery of medical care. *Scientific American,* April 1970, *222:* 15–23.

———— ET AL. Evaluation of an ambulatory medical-care delivery system. *New England Journal of Medicine,* February 16, 1976, *294: 426–431.*

GARRISON, F. H. *History of Medicine.* Philadelphia: W. B. Saunders, 1914. P. 242.

GARROS, B. Excess mortality of men in France and causes of death. *Population,* 1978, *33* (6): 1095–1114.

GAYLORD, H. R., AND CLOWES, G. H. A. On spontaneous cure of cancer. *Surgical Gynecology Obstetrics,* 1903, *2:* 633–658.

GEISS, R. Dietary counseling in practice of internal medicine. *Ernahrungsumschau,* 1978, *25* (11): 543–548.

GELLMAN, D. D. The price of progress: Technology and the cost of medical care. *Canadian Medical Association Journal,* March 6, 1971, *104*(5): 401–406.

GERFELDT, E. Environment and life expectancy. *Lebensversicherungs-Medizin,* July 1967, *19*(4): 86–93.

Gerontologist, Very old people in the USSR, Summer 1970, *10*(2): 151–152.

GERSHFELD, N. L. Selective phospolipid adsorption and atherosclerosis. *Science,* May 1979, *204:* 506–508.

GEYMAN, J. P. Geriatrics in family-practice education. Editorial. *Journal of Family Practice,* 1978, *7*(6): 1093–1094.

GILCHRES, G. A., BLOG, F. B., AND SZABO, G. Effects of aging and chronic sun exposure on melanocytes in human skin. *Clinical Research* 1979, *27*(2): A527.

GILLIAM, H. Secrets of the super healthy. *San Francisco Chronicle,* April 5, 1978: 4–6.

GINZBERG, E. Don't swallow all those scare stories about health reforms. *Medical Economics,* April 16, 1979: 93–110.

GLADMAN, A. E., AND ESTRADA, N. Biofeedback in clinical practice. In S. R. Dean, ed., *Psychiatry and mysticism.* New York: Nelson-Hall, 1975.

GLOBUS, G. G. Consciousness and brain. *Archives of General Psychiatry,* 1973, *29:* 153–177.

GLOBUS, G. G. Unexpected symmetries in the "world knot." *Science,* 1973, *180:* 1129–1136.

GLUECK, C. J. ET AL. Longevity syndromes: Familial hypobeta and familial hyperalpha liproteinemia. *Journal of Laboratory and Clinical Medicine,* December 1976, *88*(6): 941–957.

GLUECK, C. J. ET AL. Octogenarian kindred: Hyper-α-lipoproteinemia. *Preventive Medicine,* 1978, *7:* 1–14.

GLUECK, C. J., GARTSIDE, P. S., STEINER, P. M., MILLER, M., TODHUNTER, T., HAFF, J., PUCKE, M., TERRANA, M., FALLAT, R. W., AND KASHYAP, M. L. Hyperalpha- and hypobeta-lipoproteinemia in octogenarian kindred. *Atherosclerosis,* August 1977, *27*(4): 387–406.

GOLD, P. W., AND GOODWIN, F. K. Vasopressin in affective illness. *Lancet,* June 10, 1978: 1233–1235.

GOLDMAN, S. Aging, noise and choice. *Perspectives in Biology and Medicine,* Autumn 1968, *12*(1): 12–30.

GOLDSTEIN, A. L., AND WHITE, A. Thymosin and other thymic hormones: Their nature and roles in the thymic dependency of immunological phenomena. In A. J. S. Davis and R. L. Carter, eds., *Contemporary Topics in Immunology,* Vol. 2. New York: Plenum Publishing Corp., 1973.

GOLDSTEIN, S. The biology of aging, *New England Journal of Medicine,* November 1971, *285*(20): 1120–1129.

GOLDWYN, R. M. Spontaneous regeneration of a lost achilles-tendon. Letter. *Plastic and Reconstructive Surgery,* 1979, *63*(5): 717–718.

GOODMAN, A. Secret of the old ones. *The Berkeley Barb,* September 20–October 3, 1979: 4.

GOODMAN, L. S., AND GILMAN, A. *The Pharmacological Basis of Therapeutics.* New York: Macmillan, 1975.

GOODRICH, C. L. Fasting fosters longevity in rats. *Science News,* December 1, 1979, *116:* 375.

GOODWIN, J. S., GOODWIN, J. M., AND VOGEL, A. V. Knowledge

and use of placebos by house officers and nurses. *Annals of Internal Medicine,* 1979, *91:* 106–110.

GORDON, J. S. *Final Report to the President's Commission on Mental Health of the Special Study on Alternative Mental Health Services.* Washington, D.C.: NIMH, February 15, 1978.

GORNIAK, G. C., GANS, C., AND FAULKNER, J. A. Muscle fiber regeneration after transplantation: Prediction of structure and physiology from electromyograms. *Science,* June 8, 1979, *204:* 1085–1087.

GOSS, R. J. *Principles of Regeneration.* New York: Academic Press, 1969.

————. Aging versus growth. *Perspectives in Biological Medicine,* Summer 1974, *17*(4): 485–494.

GOSS, R. J., AND CARLSON, B. M. Control mechanisms in regeneration—introduction to the symposium. Editorial. *American Zoologist,* 1978, *18*(4): 823–824.

GOULART, F. S. Frightening facts about coffee. *Bike World,* March 1979: 46–47.

GOULD, S. J. Our allotted lifetimes. *Natural History,* August/September 1977: 40–41.

GRAEDON, J. *The People's Pharmacy.* New York: Avon, 1976.

GRAHAM, D. T. Psychosomatic medicine. In N. S. Greenfield and R. A. Sternbach, eds., *Handbook of Psychophysiology,* pp. 839–924. New York: Holt, Rinehart & Winston, 1972.

GRANDE, F., ANDERSON, J. T., CHLOUVERAKIS, C., PROJA, M., AND KEYS, A. Effect of dietary cholesterol on man's serum lipids. *Journal of Nutrition,* 1965, *87:* 52.

GREEN, E. E., FERGUSON, J., GREEN, A., AND WALTER, D. *Voluntary Control of Internal States:* Psychological and physiological. *Journal of Transpersonal Psychology,* 1970, *2*(1): 1–26.

GREEN, E. E., GREEN, A. M., AND WALTERS, E. D. *Biofeedback for Mind-body Regulation: Healing and Creativity.* Paper for symposium, "The Varieties of Healing Experience," De Anza College, Cupertino, California, 1971.

GREEN, J. On how to live 90 to 100 healthy years (the syndrome of longevity . . . its seven great constants). *Executive Health,* 1974, *6*(10).

GREEN, J. A. The public's interest. Paper presented at "Health

Renaissance"—a program for California State health-related agencies. State Capitol, Sacramento, January 29, 1979.

GREEN, R. What makes the Tarahumara run? *HSC Magazine,* Spring 1979, *1*(1): 6–10. Health Sciences Center, University of Oklahoma.

GREENBERG, B. Sanguine/seafarer extremely low frequency electromagnetic fields: Effect of long-term exposure on soil arthropods in nature. University of Illinois at Chicago Circle, NTIS, No. AD A027513, July 1976.

GREENBERG, D. S. Nutrition: A long wait for a little advice. *New England Journal of Medicine,* February 28, 1980, *302*(1): 535–536.

GREENBERG, J. Adulthood comes of age. *Science News,* July 29, 1978, *114*(5): 74–79.

———. Old age: What is normal? *Science News,* April 28, 1979: 284–285.

———. Psyching out pain. *Science News,* May 19, 1979: 332–333.

GREENBERG, L. J., AND YUNIS, E. J. Histocompatibility determinants, immune responsiveness and aging in man. *Federal Proceedings,* April 1978, *37*(5): 1258–1262.

GREENBLATT, R. B. Aging through the ages. *Geriatrics,* June 1977, *32*(6): 101–102.

GREENLEIGH, L. Facing the challenge of change in middle age. *Geriatrics,* 1969, *29*(11): 61–68.

GROBSTEIN, C. The recombinant-DNA debate. *Scientific American,* July 1977, *237*(1): 22–33.

GROSS, S. J. The myth of professional licensing. *American Psychologist,* November 1978, *33*(11): 1009–1016.

GROSS, W., FRANKE, H., GALL, L., MOLL, E., WEISSHARD, G., AND BRACHARZ, H. Risk factors in 100-year-old and older persons. *Verh. Dtsch. Ges. inn Med.,* 1973, *79*: 1286–1287.

GROSSER, P. J., KLEMM, P., AND GORN, A. Health in the world of tomorrow. *Zeitschrift Medical Education (JENA),* May 15, 1968, *62*(10): 517–520.

GRUENBERG, E. M. The failures of success. *Milbank Memorial Fund Quarterly,* Winter 1977, *55*(1): 3–24.

GUBERAN, E. Surprising decline of cardiovascular mortality in Switzerland—1951–1976. *Journal of Epidemiology and Community Health,* 1979, 33(2): 114–120.

GUERRERO-MUNOZ, F., GUERRERO, M. L., AND WAY, E. LEONG. Effect of β-endorphin on calcium uptake in the brain. *Science,* October 5, 1979, *206:* 89–91.

GUILLEMIN, R., AND BURGUS, R. The hormones of the hypothalamus. *Scientific American,* November 1972: 24–33.

GUILLEMIN, R. ET AL. β-endorphin and adrenocorticotropin are secreted concomitantly by the pituitary gland. *Science,* September 30, 1977, *197:* 1367–1369.

GUNDERSON, E. K. E., AND RAHE, R. H. *Life Stress and Illness.* Springfield, Ill.: Charles C. Thomas, 1974.

GUTTMACHER, S. Whole in body, mind and spirit: Holistic health and the limits of medicine. *Hastings Center Report,* April 1979: 15–20.

GWARTNEY, R. H. Biofeedback in psychosomatic medicine. *Psychosomatics,* August 1979, *20*(8): 513–514.

HAGEN, D. Q. The executive under stress. *Psychiatric Annals,* 1978, *8:* 49–51.

HALBERSTAM, M. J. Holistic healing: Limits of "the new medicine." *Psychology Today,* August 1978: 26–27.

———. Stress testing in the office: Playing fair with "false positives." *Modern Medicine,* May 30–June 15, 1979: 15–21.

HALES, D. R. Exercise gaining more respect as deterrent of heart attacks. *Medical Tribune,* September 5, 1979: 30.

HALL, J. H., ROBBINS, L. C., AND GESNER, N. B. Whose health problem? *Postgraduate Medicine,* January 1972, *51*(1): 114–120.

HALSELL, G. *Los Viejos—Secrets of Long Life from the Sacred Valley.* Emmaus, Pa.: Rodale Press, 1976.

HALTER, S. Increase in longevity and its consequences. *Archives of the Belgian Medical Society,* January 1968, *26*(1): 1–21.

HAMMAN, R. F. ET AL. Patterns of mortality in the Old Order Amish. Paper delivered to annual meeting of the American Public Health Association, October 16, 1978.

HAMMOND, E. C. Life expectancy of American medicine in relation to their smoking habits. *Journal of the National Cancer Institute,* October 1969, *43*(4): 951–962.

———, GARFINKEL, L., AND SEIDMAN, H. Longevity of parents and grandparents in relation to coronary heart disease and associated variables. *Circulation,* January 1971, *43*(1): 31–44.

HANDEL, P. J. The relationship between subjective life expectancy, death anxiety and general anxiety. *Journal of Clinical Psychology,* January 1969, *25*(1): 39–42.

HARANGHY, L., AND UREDI, D. Postmortem examination of five persons died above 100 years of age. *Acta Morphologica Academiae Scientarium Hungaricae,* 1970, *18*(1): 91–94.

HARKINS, S. W. Memory loss and response bias in senescence. *Journal of Gerontology,* 1979, *34*(1): 66–72.

HARLEY, C. B., AND GOLDSTEIN, S. Retesting the commitment theory of cellular aging. *Science,* January 11, 1980, *207:* 191–193.

HARMAN, D. Atherosclerosis: Possible ill-effects of the use of highly unsaturated fats to lower serum-cholesterol levels. *Lancet,* November 30, 1957: 116–117.

————. Prolongation of life: Role of free radical reactions in aging. *Journal of the American Geriatrics Society,* August 1969, *17*(8): 721–735.

————. Free radical theory of aging: Effect of the amount and degree of unsaturation of dietary fat on mortality rate. *Journal of Gerontology,* 1971, *26*(4): 451–457.

————. Free radical theory of aging: Dietary implications. *American Journal of Clinical Nutrition,* August 1972, *25*(8): 839–843.

————. Free radical theory of aging. *Triangle,* 1973, *12*(4): 153–158.

————. Free radical theory of aging—nutritional implications. *Age,* 1978, *1*(4): 145–152.

HARRINGTON, R. L. Systems approach to mental health care in an HMO model. A Three-Year Report—March 1977. NIMH Project MH 24109. San Jose: Kaiser-Permanente Medical Group.

HARRIS, M. J. How to make it to 100. *New West,* January 3, 1977: 16–24.

HART, F. X., AND MARINO, A. A. Biophysics of animal response to an electrostatic field. *Journal of Biological Physics,* 1976, *4*(3-4): 124–143.

HART, P. E. Computerized systems cut dietary departments costs. *Hospitals,* 1978, *52*(24): 123f.

HART, R. W. Role of DNA repair in aging. In K. C. Smith, ed., *Aging, Carcinogenesis and Radiation biology,* pp. 537–556, New York: Plenum Publishing Corp., 1976.

HARTLEY, L. H., HERD, J., DAY, W. C., ABUSAMRA, J., AND

HOWES, B. An exercise testing program for large populations. *Journal of the American Medical Association,* January 19, 1979, *241* (3): 269–271.

HARTMAN, W. E., AND FITHIAN, M. *Treatment of Sexual Dysfunction.* Long Beach: Center for Marital and Sexual Studies, 1972.

HARTUNG, G. H. ET AL. Relation of diet to high-density-lipoprotein cholesterol in middle-aged marathon runners, joggers, and inactive men. *New England Journal of Medicine,* February 14, 1980, *302* (7): 357–361.

————. Analgesic-associated nephropathy. *Harvard Medical School Health Letter.* January 1979, *4* (3): 1.

————. Hardening of the arteries—1980. February 1980, *5* (4).

HAUSMAN, P. Effect of dietary cholesterol on serum cholesterol. *American Journal of Clinical Nutrition,* November 1978, *31* (11): 1970.

HAVRON, D. "Threat test" part of plan that cut arrhythmia deaths. *Medical Tribune,* January 17, 1979: 1.

HAYFLICK, L. Aging human cells. *Triangle,* 1973, *12* (4): 141–147. (a)

————. The biology of human aging. *American Journal of Medical Science,* June 1973, *265* (6): 432–445. (b)

————. The longevity of cultured human cells. *Journal of the American Geriatrics Society,* January 1974, *22* (1): 1–12.

————. The strategy of senescence. *Gerontologist,* February 1974: 37–45.

————. Current theories of biological aging. *Federal Proceedings,* January 1975, *34* (1): 9–13.

————. The cell biology of human aging. *New England Journal of Medicine,* December 2, 1976, *295* (23): 1302–1308.

————. The biology of aging. *Natural History,* August/September 1977: 22–26.

————. On the facts of life: How old would you be if you didn't know how old you were? *Executive Health,* June 1978, *14* (9).

————. What we are discovering about your body's amazing immune system. *Executive Health,* November 1978, 15(2).

————. Cell biology of aging. *Federal Proceedings,* 1979, *38* (5): 1851–1856.

————. On getting a good night's sleep. *Executive Health,* May 1979, *15*(8).

HAYFLICK, L., AND MOOREHEAD, P. S. The serial cultivation of human diploid cell strains. *Experimental Cell Research,* 1961, *25:* 585–621.

HAYNES, S. G., MCMICHAEL, A. J., & TYROLIER, H. A. Survival after early and normal retirement. *Journal of Gerontology,* March 1978, *33*(2): 269–278.

HAZUM, E., CHANG, K.-J., AND CUATRECASAS, P. Specific nonopiate receptors for β-endorphin. *Science,* 1979, *205:* 1033–1035.

HEBB, D. O. On watching myself get old. *Psychology Today,* November 1978: 15–23.

HECHINGER, G. Aging: Growing old in America. An interview with Margaret Mead. *New Age,* 1979: 50–52.

HEGSTED, D. M., MCGANDY, R. B., MYERS, M. L., AND STARE, F. J. Quantitative effects of dietary fat on serum cholesterol in man. *American Journal of Clinical Nutrition,* 1965, *17:* 281.

HELLERBRANDT, F. A. Comment: The senile dement in our midst. *Gerontologist,* 1978, *18*(1): 67–70.

————. Exercise for the long-term care aged—benefits, deterrents, and hazards. *Long-term Care and Health Services Administration Quarterly,* Spring 1979: 33–47.

HELMS, J. B. Personal communication, 1981.

HELPS, E. P. Physiological effects of aging. *Proceedings of the Royal Society of Medicine,* August 1973, *66*(8): 815–818.

HENDRICKS, J., AND HENDRICKS, C. D. The age old question of old age: Was it really so much better back when? *International Journal of Aging and Human Development,* 1977–1978, *8*(2): 139–154.

HEPNER, G., FRIED, R., AND JEOR, S. S. Hypercholesterolemic effect of yogurt and milk. *American Journal of Clinical Nutrition,* 1979, *32:* 19–24.

HERSHBERG, P. I. Exercise testing. *Journal of the American Medical Association,* October 18, 1971, *218*(3): 446.

HESS, E. V. Immune system and aging—case of cart before horse. Editorial. *Journal of Chronic Diseases,* 1978, *31*(11): 647–649.

HESSEL, S. J. Perspectives on benefit-cost analysis in medical care. *American Journal of Roentgenology,* October 1977, *129:* 753–757.

HESSLER, R. M. ET AL. Demographic context, social interaction, and perceived health status: Excedrin headache #1. *Journal of Health and Social Behavior,* September 12, 1971, 191–199.

HETZEL, B. S. The implications of health indicators: A comment. *International Journal of Epidemiology,* September 1973, *1*(4): 315–382.

HIGDON, H. *Fitness After Forty.* Mountain View, Calif.: Runner's World, 1977.

HIGHLAND, J. H. ET AL. *Malignant Neglect.* New York: Knopf, 1979.

HILDEMANN, W. H. Phylogenetic and immunogenetic aspects of aging. *Birth Defects: Original Article Series, 14*(1): 97–107.

HILL, C. A., JR. Measures of longevity of American Indians. *Public Health Reports,* March 1970, *85*(3): 233–239.

HIRSCH, J. Nutrition. *Drug Therapy,* February 1980: 119–136.

HIRSCH, M. J., AND WURTMAN, R. J. Lecithin consumption increases acetylcholine concentrations in rat brain and adrenal gland. *Science,* October 13, 1978, *202:* 223–225.

HJERMANN, I., ENGER, S. C., HELGELAN, A., HOLME, I., LEREN, P., AND TRYGG, K. Effect of dietary changes on high-density lipoprotein cholesterol. Oslo Study. *American Journal of Medicine,* 1979, *66*(1): 105–109.

HOCHSCHILD, R. Effect of dimethylaminoethyl p-chlorophenoxyacetate on the life span of male Swiss Webster albino mice. *Experimental Gerontology,* 1973, *8:* 177–183.

HOGAN, M. D., CHI, P. Y., HOEL, D. G., AND MITCHELL, T. J. Association between chloroform levels in finished drinking-water supplies and various site-specific cancer mortality rates. *Journal of Environmental Pathology,* 1978, *2*(3): 873–887.

HOLDEN, C. Cancer and the mind: How are they connected? *Science,* June 23, 1978, *200*(23): 1363–1369.

———. Albert Szent-Györgi, electrons, and cancer. *Science,* February 9, 1979, *203:* 522–524.

———. Pain, dying, and the health care system. *Science,* March 9, 1979, *203:* 984–985.

HOLLANDER, C. F. Functional and cellular aspects of organ ageing. *Experimental Gerontology,* October 1970.

HOLLANDER, I. J. The health of leaders and policy-makers. *Ind Med Surg.,* May 1972, *41*(5): 17–21.

HOLLIDAY, R. Errors in protein synthesis and clonal senescence in fungi. *Nature,* March 29, 1969, *221:* 1224–1228.

HOLLIDAY, R., PORTERFIELD, T. S., AND GIBBS, D. D. Premature ageing and occurrence of altered enzyme in Werner's syndrome fibroblast. *Nature,* April 26, 1974.

HOLMES, T. H. Life situations, emotions, and disease. *Psychosomatics,* December 1978, *19*(12): 747–754.

————, AND MASUDA, M. Life change and illness susceptibility. Paper presented as part of "Symposium on Separation and D Depression: Clinical and Research Aspects," at the annual meeting of the American Association for the Advancement of Science, Chicago, December 1970.

————, AND MASUDA, M. Life change and illness susceptibility. In Scott et al., eds., *Separation and Depression.* American Association for the Advancement of Science, 1973.

————, AND RAHE, R. H. The social readjustment rating scale. *Journal of Psychosomatic Research,* 1967, *11:* 213–218.

————, AND RAHE, R. H. Schedule of recent experience (SRE). University of Washington, School of Medicine, Department of Psychiatry, 1967.

HOLMES, T. S., AND HOLMES, T. H. Short-term intrusions into the life style routine. *Journal of Psychosomatic Research,* 1970, *14:* 121–132.

HOLMYARD, E. J. *Alchemy.* New York: Penguin Books, 1968.

HONZIK, M. Report available from: Institute of Human Development, University of California, Berkeley, California 94720, 1979.

HORROBIN, D. F. Schizophrenia as a prostaglandin deficiency disease. *Lancet,* April 30, 1977: 936–937.

————. Schizophrenia: Reconciliation of the dopamine, prostaglandin, and opoid concepts and the role of the pineal. *Lancet,* March 10, 1979: 529–531.

———— ET AL. Prostaglandins and schizophrenia: Further discussion of the evidence. *Psychological Medicine,* 1978, *8:* 43–48.

HORVATH, S. M. Review of energetics and blood-flow in exercise. *Diabetes,* 1979, *28*(S1): 1–7.

HOSOBUCHI, YOSHIO ET AL. Stimulation of human periaqueductal gray for pain relief increases immunoreactive β-endorphin in ventricular fluid. *Science,* January 19, 1979, *203:* 279–281.

HOSTETLER, J. A. *Amish Society.* Baltimore: Johns Hopkins University Press, 1963.

HOWARD, H. Implications of self-help care. *Medical Care,* May 1977: 22–26.

HOWARD, T., AND RIFKIN, J. *Who Should Play God?* New York: Dell, 1977.

HOWELLS, J. G. Holistic approach to medicine. *American Journal of Psychiatry,* 1974, *131:* 1046.

HUEL, G., DERRIENN, F., DUCIMETI, P., AND LAZAR, P. Water hardness and cardiovascular mortality—discussions of evidence from geographical pathology. *Revue D Epidemiologie et de Santé Publique,* 1978, *26*(4): 349–359.

HUGHES, J. ET AL. Identification of two related pentapeptides from the brain with potent opiate agonist activity. *Nature,* 1975, *258:* 577–579.

HUGHES, R. E. Nonscorbutic effect of Vitamin C: Biochemical aspects. *Proceedings of the Royal Society of Medicine,* February 1977, *70*(2): 107–109.

HUHTI, E., IKKALA, J., AND HAKULINEN, T. Chronic respiratory disease, smoking and prognosis for life: An epidemiological study. *Scandinavian Journal of Respiratory Disease,* June 1977, *58*(3): 170–180.

HULBERT, A. J. The thyroid hormones: A thesis concerning their action. *Journal of Theoretical Biology,* 1978, *73:* 81–99.

HURIEZ, C. Because of its evolution and in spite of its revolutions, medicine must stay deeply human. *Lille Medical,* April 1970, *15* (4): 681–712.

HUXLEY, A. *Island.* New York: Harper, 1962.

ILFELD, F. W., JR. Age, stressors, and psychosomatic disorders. *Psychosomatics,* January 1980, *21*(1): 56–64.

ILLICH, I. Medical nemesis. *Lancet,* May 11, 1974, *1*(863): 918–921.

———. *Medical Nemesis—The Expropriation of Health.* New York: Pantheon, 1976.

INGELFINGER, F. J. Review of "The role of medicine" by McKeown. *New England Journal of Medicine,* February 1974: 119.

————. Health: A matter of statistics or feeling? *New England Journal of Medicine,* February 24, 1977: 448–449.

————. Medicine: Meritorious or meretricious? *Science,* May 26, 1978, *200:* 942–946.

————. Will fiber stay in fashion? *Modern Medicine,* January 30–February 15, 1979: 15–16.

INKELES, G., AND TODRIS, M. *The Art of Sensual Massage.* San Francisco: Straight Arrow Books, 1972.

Instituto Nacional de Estadistica. *Censo de población y vivienda de las cabeceras parroquiales: Vilcabamba y San Pedro de la Bendita.* Quito, 1971.

ISAACS, B. A diet to cure heart disease. *New West,* February 14, 1977: 57–60.

JACKSON, R. L., MAIER, S. F., AND COON, D. J. Long-term analgesic effects of inescapable shock and learned helplessness. *Science,* October 5, 1979, *206:* 91–93.

JARVIK, L. F. Thoughts on the psychobiology of aging. *American Psychologist,* 1975, *30:* 576–583.

JAVITS, J. K. Stethoscope. *Modern Medicine,* January 30–February 15, 1979: 17.

JENKINS, C. D. Psychologic and social precursors of coronary disease. *New England Journal of Medicine,* 1971, *284:* 244–255.

————. Psychosocial modifiers of response to stress. *Journal of Human Stress,* December 1979: 3–16.

————, TUTHILL, R. W., TANNENBAUM, S. I., AND KIRBY, C. R. Zones of excess mortality in Massachusetts. *New England Journal of Medicine,* June 9, 1977, *296* (23): 1345–1346.

———— ET AL. Social stressors and excess mortality from hypertensive disease. *Journal of Human Stress,* September 1979: 29–40.

JERNE, N. K. The immune system. *Scientific American,* July 1973, *229* (1): 52–60.

JEVNING, R. Meditation increased blood flow to brain in UC study. *Brain/Mind Bulletin,* January 15, 1979, *4* (5): 1.

JEWETT, S. P. Longevity and the longevity syndrome. *Gerontologist,* Spring 1973, *13* (1): 91–99.

JOHANNSON, F. F. *Food for Thought.* "Nutrition Survival Kit" series, Maryland Center for Public Broadcasting, Owings Mills, Maryland, 1980.

JOHNSEN, A. M. Lowering of retirement age—lowering of life age. *Tidsskr. nor Laegeforen,* May 10, 1971, *91*(13): 1007.

JOHNSON, A. Recent trends in sex morality differentials in the United States. *Journal of Human Stress,* May 1977, *3*(1): 22–32.

JOHNSON, T. H., ED. *The Letters of Emily Dickinson.* Volume 1, pp. 27–28. Cambridge, Mass.: Harvard University Press, 1958.

JONES, T. Longevity: Ah, to be young while old . . . *Harper's,* June 1973: 3–10.

JOOSENS, K. ET AL. The pattern of food and mortality in Belgium. *Lancet,* May 21, 1977: 1069–1072.

JORGENSEN, G. ABO blood groups in physicians over 75 years. (New Arguments in favor of the "little more fitness" of blood group O.) *Cahiers de Medicine,* June 30, 1974, *15*(7): 385–388.

————. ABO blood groups in physicians of 75 years of age. Further evidence in favor of little more fitness on the part of subjects with blood group O. *Minerva Medica,* July 14, 1974, *65*(54): 2881–2886.

Journal of the American Medical Association. Editorial. How to grow old without aging. May 28, 1973, *224*(9): 1289.

————. Suppose we die young, late in life? March 13, 1978, *239*(11): 1036–1037.

Journal of the Mississippi State Medical Association. The United States Senate: No place to grow old. October 1969, *10*(10): 469–470.

JOY, W. B. *Joy's Way.* Los Angeles: J. P. Tarcher, 1979.

JUNG, C. G. *Psychology and Alchemy.* Vol. 12, Bolingen Series 20. Princeton, N.J.: Princeton University Press, 1977.

KAHN, H., AND WINER, A. *The Year 2000: A Framework for Speculation on the Next Thirty-three Years.* New York: Macmillan, 1967.

KALB, L. C. *Noyes Modern Clinical Psychiatry.* Philadelphia: W. B. Saunders, 1963.

KALIL, K., AND REH, T. Regrowth of severed axons in the neonatal central nervous system: Establishment of normal connections. *Science,* September 14, 1979, *205:* 1158–1161.

KALISH, R. A. Non-medical interventions in life and death. *Social Science and Medicine,* December 1970, *4*(6): 655–665.

KAMAN, R., HEFFNER, K., PATTON, R., AND RAVEN, P. Blood-chemistry changes after anaerobic exercise. Meeting abstract. *Medicine and Science in Sports,* 1979, *11*(1): 89.

KAMAN, R. L., AND WADE, T. Effects of near maximal aerobic exercise on serum enzyme-activity in women. *Journal of the American Osteopathic Association,* 1979, *78*(12): 904.

KAPLAN, B. H., CASSILL, J. C., AND GORE, S. Social support and health. *Medical Care,* 1977, *15:* 47–57.

KAPLAN, H. S. *The New Sex Therapy.* New York: Brunner/Mazel, 1974.

KARASU, T. B. Psychological and behavioral therapies in medicine. *Psychosomatics,* September 1979, *20*(9): 578–583.

KARPF, R. J. How a rise in food costs leads to dietary restrictions and a reduction in hemoglobin levels in the United States. Meeting abstract. *Pediatric Research,* 1979, *13*(4): 401.

———. Some observations on a trend toward geriatrics in clinical psychology. *Professional Psychology,* 1978, *9*(4): 672–676.

KARVONEN, M. J. Sports and longevity. *Advances in Cardiology,* 1976, *18,* 243–248.

———. Endurance sports, longevity and health. *Annals of the New York Academy of Sciences,* 1977, *301:* 671–702.

———, KLEMOLA, H., VIRKAJ, A. J., AND KEKKONEN, A. Longevity of endurance skiers. *Medicine and Science in Sports,* Spring 1974, *6*(1): 49–51.

KASTENBAUM, R., AND COSTA, P. T., JR. Psychological perspectives of death. *Annual Review of Psychology,* 1977, *28:* 225–249.

KATSUHIKO, Y., RHOADS, G. G., AND KAGAN, A. Coffee, alcohol and risk of coronary heart disease among Japanese men living in Hawaii. *New England Journal of Medicine,* August 25, 1977, *297* (8): 405–409.

KEABLE-ELLIOT, R. A. Longevity of women G.P.S. *British Medical Journal,* May 5, 1973, *2*(861): 308.

KELLY, A., PETITCLE, C., DRAPEAU, G., MUNAN, L., NADON, R., AND DESHAIES, P. Effects of short and strenuous exercise of serum constituents in young athletes. *UN Med Can,* 1979, *108*(5): 549f.

KEMPER, D. W. *The Healthwise Workshop.* Boise, Idaho: Healthwise, Inc. 111 South Sixth Street, 83702, 1980.

KEMPER, G. B., AND MATZKE, H. Regeneration of the sciatic nerve in hibernating and non-hibernating 13-lined ground-squirrels. *Anatomical Record,* 1979, *193* (3): 585–586.

KENNEDY, E. M. Measurement of quality in medical care. *New England Journal of Medicine,* December 9, 1971, *185* (24): 1381.

KENT, S. Longer life span hinges on control of aging as well as degenerative diseases. *Geriatrics,* August 1976: 128–131.

———. What nutritional deprivation experiments reveal about aging. *Geriatrics,* October 1976: 141–144.

———. Can nucleic acid therapy reverse the degenerative processes of aging? *Geriatrics,* October 1977, *32* (10): 130–136.

———. Do free radicals and dietary antioxidants wage intracellular war? *Geriatrics,* January 1977, *32* (1): 127–136.

———. Can dietary manipulation prolong life? *Geriatrics,* April 1978, *33* (4): 102, 106.

KERN, M. High blood pressure as one result of constant exposure to noise. *The German Tribune,* August 26, 1979, (904): 8–9.

KERNS, J. M., SMITH, D. R., JANNOTTA, F. S., AND ALPER, M. G. Oculomotor nerve regeneration after aneurysm surgery. *American Journal of Ophthalmology,* 1979, *87* (2): 225–233.

KEYS, A., ANDERSON, J. T., AND GRANDE, F. Serum cholesterol response to changes in the diet. II. The effect of cholesterol in the diet. *Metabolism,* 1965, *14:* 759.

KHADZHIKHRISTEV, A. Fat and protein metabolism of long-lived persons and centenarians in Smolyan District. *Vutr Boles,* 1978, *17* (1): 74–76.

KHOSLA, T. Longevity of athletes. *Lancet,* December 16, 1972, *2* (790): 1318.

KIMBALL, C. P. Conceptual developments in psychosomatic medicine: 1939–1969. *Annals of Internal Medicine,* 1970, *73:* 307–316.

KINDIG, N. B., MARTIN, B., MORGAN, E., AND FILLEY, G. Ventilation variations at constant load exercise. *Federal Proceedings,* 1979, *38* (3): 1050.

KINZER, N. S. *Stress and the American Woman.* New York: Doubleday, 1979.

KISCH, A. I. The health care system and health: Some thoughts on a famous misalliance. Keynote address to the American Public Health Association, San Francisco, November 7, 1973.

KLATSKY, A. L., FRIEDMAN, G. D., AND SIEGELAUB, A. B. Alcohol consumption before myocardial infarction. *Annals of Internal Medicine,* September 3, 1974, *81*(3): 294–301.

————, FRIEDMAN, G. D., AND SIEGELAUB, A. B. Alcohol use, myocardial infarction, sudden cardiac death, and hypertension. *Alcoholism: Clinical and Experimental Research,* January 1979, *3* (1): 33–39.

KLEINMAN, A. The failure of western medicine. *Human Nature,* November 1978: 63–68.

KNIGHT, J. A. Holistic health: No stranger to psychiatry. *Journal of Clinical Psychiatry,* February 1980, *41*(2): 38–39.

KNOWLES, J. H. The hospital. *Scientific American,* September 1973, *229*(3): 128–138.

————. The responsibility of the individual. *Daedalus,* Winter 1977: 57–80. Adapted and reprinted in *Science,* December 16, 1977, *198* (4322).

————, ED. *Doing Better and Feeling Worse.* New York: Norton, 1977.

KOBASA, S. C. Stressful life events, personality, and health: An inquiry into hardiness. *Journal of Personality and Social Psychology,* 1979, *37*(1): 1–11.

KOCHEN, M. Dietary fiber. Letter. *Western Journal of Medicine,* 1979, *130*(4): 375.

KOHN, R. R. *Principles of Mammalian Aging.* Englewood Cliffs, N.J.: Prentice-Hall, 1971.

————. Diseases and aging—introductory remarks. *Federal Proceedings,* 1978, *37*(14): 2831.

KOIVISTO, V., SOMAN, V., CONRAD, R., HENDLER, R., NADEL, E., AND DELIG, P. Insulin binding in athletes—possible mechanism of altered metabolism at rest and during exercise. Meeting abstract. *Clinical Research,* 1979, *27*(2), A487.

KOLATA, G. B. Brain biochemistry: Effects of diet. *Science,* April 2, 1976, *192:* 41–42.

————. Mental disorders: A new approach to treatment. *Science,* January 5, 1979, *203:* 36–38.

————. New treatment for coronary artery disease. *Science,* November 23, 1979, *206:* 917.

————. Treatment reduces deaths from hypertension. *Science,* December 21, 1979, *206:* 1386–1387.

KOLLER, F. Limits of the life-preservation in internal medicine. *Praxis,* October 10, 1972, *61*(41): 1259–1263.

KORENMAN, S. G. Endocrine aspects of aging. Conference of NIA, Endocrine Society and Veterans Administration, Bethesda, Maryland, October 18–20, 1979.

KORMENDY, C. G., AND BENDER, A. D. Chemical interference with aging. *Gerontologia,* 1971, *17:* 52064.

KOROBKOVA, V. P. ET AL. Influence of the electric field in 500 and 750 kV switchyards on maintenance staff and means for its protection. International Conference on Large High Tension and Electrical Systems, Paris, 1972.

KOSEL, K. C., WILKINSON, J. M., JEW, J., ITAYA, S. K., BECKWITH, K., AND WILLIAMS, T. H. Enzyme therapy and spinal-cord regeneration—fluorescence microscopic evaluation. *Experimental Neurology,* 1979, *64*(2): 365–374.

KRETSCHM, H. J., SCHLEICH, A., WINGERT, F., ZILLES, K., AND LOBLICH, H. J. Human-brain growth in the 19th and 20th century. *Journal of the Neurological Sciences,* 1979, *40*(2-3): 169–188.

KRISTEIN, M. M., ARNOLD, C. B., AND WYNDER, E. L. Health economics and preventive care. *Science,* February 4, 1977, *195:* 457–462.

KRITCHEVSKY, D. Dietary fiber—reply. Letter. *Western Journal of Medicine,* 1979, *130*(4): 375–376.

———. Metabolic effects of dietary fiber. *Western Journal of Medicine,* 1979, *130*(2): 123–127.

———. Diet, lipid metabolism, and aging. *Federal Proceedings,* May 1979, *38*(6), 2001–2006.

KRUEGER, A. P. Preliminary consideration of the biological significance of air ions. In R. Ornstein, ed., *The Nature of Human Consciousness.* San Francisco: W. H. Freeman, 1973.

KUDROW, L. Current aspects of migraine headache. *Psychosomatics,* January 1978: 48–57.

KUGLER, H. *Slowing Down the Aging Process.* New York: Pyramid Publications, 1973.

KUHN, T. *The Structure of Scientific Revolutions.* Chicago: University of Chicago Press, 1962.

KURTZMAN, J., AND GORDON, P. *No More Dying: The Conquest of Aging and Extension of Human Life.* New York: Fell, 1977.

LABOUVIE, G. Psychosocial-aspects of aging. *Pharmacology Management,* 1979, *151*(2): 88f.

Lakartidningen. American research: Does science done outdoors prolong life? April 15, 1970, *67*(16): 1822–1823.

LALLO, J. W., AND ROSE, J. C. Patterns of stress, disease and mortality in two prehistoric populations from North America. *Journal of Human Evolution,* 1979, *8*(3): 323–335.

LALONDE, M. *A New Perspective on the Health of Canadians.* Ottawa: Minister of National Health and Welfare Information, 1975.

LAMB, L. E. Diet to prevent heart attack and strokes. *The Health Letter,* February 22, 1980, *15*(4).

LANDFIELD, P. W., WAYMIRE, J. C., AND LYNCH, G. Hippocampal aging and adrenocorticoids: Quantitative correlations. *Science,* December 8, 1978, *202:* 1098–1101.

LANGLEY, A. J. Health: A septuagenarian's viewpoint. *Journal of Gerontology Nursing,* September-October 1976, *2*(5): 40–47.

LANGONE, J. *Long Life.* Boston: Little, Brown & Company, 1978.

LAPORTE, R. E., KULLER, L. H., AND CRESANTA, J. L. Geographic and secular relationships of alcohol intake to ASHD death rates. Department of Epidemiology, University of Pittsburgh, Pittsburgh, Pennsylvania 15261, 1978.

LAPPE, F. M. *Diet for a Small Planet.* New York: Ballantine Books, 1975.

LARGEY, G. Athletic activity and longevity. *Lancet,* August 5, 1972, *2*(771): 286.

LARSEN, T., VIKMO, H., MYHRE, K., AND MJOS, O. C. Post-exercise rise in plasma concentration of free fatty-acids (FFA) and adipose-tissue blood-flow. Meeting abstract. *Acta Physiologica Scandinavica,* 1979, *105*(1): A 38-A 39.

LAST, G. Death of the aged, life-shortening factors of the industrial society. *Therapie der Gegenwart,* August 1971, *110*(8): 1103–1117.

LAVALLEE, Y. J., LAMONTAGNE, Y. L., PINARD, G., ANNABLE, L., AND TETREAULT, L. Effects of EMG feedback, diazepam and their combination on chronic anxiety. *Journal of Psychosomatic Research,* 1977, *21:* 65–71.

LAWRENCE, P. S. Patterns of health and illness in older people.

Bulletin of the New York Academy of Medicine, December 1973, *49* (12): 1100–1109.

LAZARUS, R. S. *Psychological Stress and the Coping Process.* New York: McGraw-Hill, 1966.

———. *Patterns of Adjustment.* New York: McGraw-Hill, 1976.

LEAF, A. Every day is a gift when you are over 100. *National Geographic,* 1973, *143* (1): 93–119. (a)

———. Getting old. *Scientific American,* September 1973: 45–52. (b)

———. Unusual longevity: The common denominators. *Hospital Practice,* October 1973: 75–86. (c)

———. Observations of a peripatetic gerontologist. *Nutrition Today,* September-October 1973: 4–12.

———. *Youth in Old Age.* New York: McGraw-Hill, 1975.

———. On the physical fitness of men who live to a great age. *Executive Health,* August 1977, *13* (11).

———. Personal communication. July 12, 1978; February 22, 1980.

LEE, P. R. Nutrition policy—from neglect and uncertainty to debate and action. *Journal of the American Dietetic Association,* June 1978, *72* (6): 5–12.

———, AND FRANKS, P. E. Primary prevention and the executive branch of the federal government. *Preventive Medicine,* 1977, *6:* 209–226.

LEE, R. V., ED. Wine and medical practice. A pamphlet. San Francisco: Wine Institute, 1979.

LEGER, A. S., COCHRANE, A. L., AND MOORE, F. Factors associated with cardiac mortality in developed countries with particular reference to the consumption of wine. *Lancet,* May 12, 1979: 1017–1020.

LEIPZIG, A. Enclave of "Ancianos"—an Andean Shangri-la. *Hospital Practice,* October 1973: 92–95.

LEMAIRE, A. Aging. 1. Approach to the phenomenon. *Nouvelle Presse Medicale,* February 3, 1973, *2* (5), 301–305.

———. Aging. 2. Consequences of aging. *Nouvelle Presse Medicale,* February 10, 1973, *2* (6): 367–369.

LEON, A. S., AND BLACKBURN, H. The relationship of physical activity to coronary heart disease and life expectancy. *Annals of the New York Academy of Sciences,* 1977, *301:* 561–578.

LERNER, M., AND STUTZ, R. N. Mortality by socioeconomic status,

1959–61 and 1969–71. *Maryland State Medical Journal,* 1978, *27* (12): 35–42.

LEVI, L. *Stress: Sources, Management and Prevention, Medical and Psychological Aspects of the Stress of Everyday Life.* New York: Liveright Co., 1967.

LEVINE, J. D. ET AL. The narcotic antagonist naloxone enhances clinical pain. *Nature,* April 27, 1978, *272*(5656): 826–827. (a)

LEVINE, J. D., GORDON, N. C., AND FIELDS, H. L. The mechanism of placebo analgesia. *Lancet,* September 23, 1978: 654–657. (b)

LEVINE, R. A. High fiber diets: The theories . . . and the facts. *Current Prescribing,* July 1978: 56–61.

LEVINE, R. L. Retinal regeneration in the frog, *Xenopus laevis. Investigative Ophthalmology and Visual Science,* 1979: 43.

LEVINSON, D. *Seasons of a Man's Life.* New York: Ballantine Books, 1978.

LEW, E. A. High blood pressure, other risk factors and longevity: The insurance viewpoint. *American Journal of Medicine,* September 1973, *55*(3): 281–294.

LEWIS, C. E., AND LEWIS, M. A. The potential impact of sexual equality on health. *New England Journal of Medicine,* October 20, 1977, *297*(16): 863–869.

LEWIS, I. J. Science and health care: The political problem. *New England Journal of Medicine,* 1970, *281:* 888.

LEWITTER, M., AND ARBARBANEL, A. Aging and sex. In Ellis and Arbarbanel, eds., *Encyclopedia of Sexual Behavior.* New York: Hawthorne Books, 1973.

LEX, B. W. Voodoo death: New thoughts on an old explanation. *American Anthropologist,* 1974, *76:* 818–823.

LI, C. H., AND CHUNG, D. Isolation and structure of an untriakontapeptide with opiate activity from camel pituitary glands. *Proceedings of the National Academy of Science—USA,* 1976, *73:* 1145–1148.

LI, F. P. Working life-span of physicians. *Journal of the American Medical Association,* November 4, 1968, *206*(6): 1308.

LIBOW, L. S. Interaction of medical, biologic, and behavioral factors on aging, adaptation, and survival: An 11 year longitudinal study. *Geriatrics,* November 1974: 75–88.

LICATA, A. A. Increased dietary-protein can alter the biochemical manifestations of hyper-parathyroidism. *Clinical Research,* 1979, *27*(2): A371.

LIEBER, C. S. The metabolism of alcohol. *Scientific American,* March 1976, *234*(3): 25–33.

LILLY, J. C. *Communication Between Man and Dolphin.* New York: Crown Publishers, 1978.

LINDNER, J. Trends in modern international gerontological research, morphological aspects. *Aktuelle Gerontologie,* January 1978, *8*(1): 7–25.

LINN, G. S., LINN, M. W., AND GUREL, L. Physical resistance and longevity. *Gerontol Clinic* (Basel), 1969, *11*(6): 363–370.

LINN, M. W., LINN, B. S., AND GUREL, L. Patterns of illness in persons who lived to extreme old age. *Geriatrics,* June 1972, *27*(6): 67–70.

LIPMAN, A. G. A review of findings on aspirin's role in preventing emboli. *Modern Medicine,* April 30–May 15, 1979: 77.

LITTLE, J. C. Neurotic illness in fitness fanatics. *Psychiatric Annals,* March 1979, *9*(3): 49–56.

LIU, R. K., AND WALFORD, R. L. The effect of lowered body temperatures on lifespan and immune and non-immune processes. *Gerontologia,* 1972, *18:* 363–388.

LOFTUS, E. F., AND FRIES, J. F. Informed consent may be hazardous to health. *Science,* April 6, 1979, *204* (4388): 11.

LOHMANN, R. Indication and methods of psychotherapeutic rehabilitation of chronic physically ill patients. *Psychotherapy and Psychosomatics,* 1967, *15* (1): 41.

LOOFBOURROW, G. N. Grow old along with me. Physiological aspects of aging. *Journal of the Kansas Medical Society,* March 1969, *70*(3): 109–116.

LORENZ, N. G., DAVIS, N. Y., DEVRA, L., AND MANDERSCHEID, R. W. The health promotion organization: A practical intervention designed to promote healthy living. *Public Health Reports,* September-October 1978, *93* (5): 446–455.

LOSSE, H. Is long term treatment with anti-hypertensive agents hazardous? *Krankenpflege,* April 1978, *32* (4): 120–121.

LOUP, P., GHAVAMI, B., BAMBULE, J., AND MOSIMANN, R. Regeneration of vagus nerve—possible explanation of recurrent ulcers after vagotomies. *Schweizerische Medizinische Wochenschrift,* 1979, *109*(16): 627.

LUBLIN, J. S. Companies fight back against soaring cost of medical coverage. *The Wall Street Journal,* May 10, 1978: 1.

LUCE, G. G. *Biological Rhythm in Human and Animal Physiology.* New York: Dover Books, 1971.

———. *Your Second Life.* New York: Delacorte Press/Seymour Lawrence, 1979.

LURIA, S. M. Average age at death of scientists in various specialties. *Public Health Reports,* July 1969, *84*(7): 661–664.

LUTHE, W. Autogenic training: Method, research and application in medicine. *American Journal of Psychotherapy,* 1963, *17:* 174–195.

LYNCH, J. L., AND CONVEY, W. H. Loneliness, disease, and death: Alternative approaches. *Psychosomatics,* October 1979, *20*(10): 702–708.

LYTLE, L. D., AND ALTAR, A. Diet, central nervous system, and aging. *Federal Proceedings,* May 1979, *38*(6): 2017–2022.

MCCANDLISH, J. Village where people live to 100, 120, even 140. *Enquirer,* April 15, 1973, *47*(33).

MCCANN, J. What the experts do—unofficially—to dodge cancer. *Medical Tribune,* November 22, 1978, *19*(38): 1–22.

———. Rx may prevent stress-caused fibrillation deaths. *Medical Tribune,* May 2, 1979, *20*(17): 1.

MCCAY, C. M. ET AL. Retarded growth, life span, ultimate body size, and age changes in the albino rat after feeding diets restricted in calories. *Journal of Nutrition,* 1939, *18:* 1–13.

MCDERMOTT, S. *Female Sexuality.* New York: Simon & Schuster, 1971.

MACDONALD, I. Nutritional consequences of affluence. *Guy's Hospital Report,* 1972, *121*(2): 193–198.

MCDONALD, J. T., AND MARGEN, S. Wine versus ethanol in human nutrition. *American Journal of Clinical Nutrition,* April 1979, *32:* 823–833.

MCDONALD, W. *An Old Guy Who Feels Good.* Berkeley, Calif.: Thorp Springs Press, 1978.

———. Aging: Still growing. *New Age,* 1979: 43–47.

MCDUGAL, H. D., AND ADAMSON, J. E. Preliminary report on a

comparative analysis of peripheral nerve regeneration rates in transected and repaired rat sciatic nerve—microsurgical versus macrosurgical methods. *Anatomical Record,* 1979, *193* (3): 619.

McGOVERN, G. Dietary goals for the United States. Report of the Select Committee on Nutrition and Human Needs, U.S. Senate, February 1977. Washington, D.C.: Superintendent of Documents, U.S. Government Printing Office, Stock #052-070-04376-8.

———. Dietary goals for the United States. 2d edition. Report of the Select Committee on Nutrition and Human Needs, U.S. Senate, December 1977. Washington, D.C.: U.S. Government Printing Office, Stock #052-070-04376-8.

McKAIN, W. C. Are they really that old? *Gerontologist,* 1967, *7:* 70–80.

McKEOWN, T. A historical appraisal of the medical task. In G. McLachlan and T. McKeown, eds., *Medical History and Medical Care.* London: Oxford University Press, 1971.

———. *Modern Rise of the Population.* London: Blackwell Scientific Publications, 1976.

———. *The Role of Medicine: Dream, Mirage, or Nemesis.* London: Nuffield Provincial Hospital Trust, 1976. Revised edition: Princeton, N. J.: Princeton University Press, 1979.

———. Determinants of health. *Human Nature,* April 1978: 60–67.

———. Man's health: The past and the future. *Western Journal of Medicine,* January 1980, *132:* 49–57.

McKINNELL, R. G. *Cloning.* Minneapolis: University of Minnesota Press, 1978.

McKINNEY, R. V., SINGH, B. B., BREWER, P. D., AND ALLEN, E. Wound-healing—epithelial-cell regeneration and keratinization. Meeting abstract. *Journal of Dental Research,* 1979, *58*(NSIA): 418.

McLEAN, A. E. M. Cancer and nutrition. *Die Nahrung,* 1976, *4* (20): 339–342.

McNAIR, D. M., GARDOS, G., HASKELL, D. S., AND FISHER, S. Placebo response, placebo effect and two attributes. *Psychopharmacology,* 1979, *63:* 245–250.

McNEER, J. F., MARGOLIS, J. R., LEE, K. L., KISSLO, J. A., PETER, R. H., KONG, Y., BEHAR, V. S., WALLACE, A. G., McCANTS, C. B., AND ROSATI, R. A. The role of the exercise test in the evaluation of patients for ischemic heart disease. *Circulation,* January 1978, *57*(1): 64–70.

McWHIRTER, N., ed. *Guinness Book of World Records.* New York: Bantam, 1978.

MADDOX, G. L. Self-assessment of health status: A longitudinal study of selected elderly subjects. *Journal of Chronic Disease,* 1964, *17:* 449–460.

————, AND DOUGLASS, E. B. Aging and individual differences: A longitudinal analysis of social, psychological, and physiological indicators. *Journal of Gerontology,* 1974, *29*(5): 555–563.

MADERNA, A. M. Psychology and geriatrics: General formulations of problem. *Giornale Di Gerontologia,* 1978, *26:* 425–432.

MAJNO, G. *The Healing Hand: Man and Wound in the Ancient World.* Boston: Harvard University Press, 1975.

MAKINODAN, T. Mechanism, prevention, and restoration of immunologic aging. *Birth Defects,* 1978, *14*(1): 197–212.

MALIN, S. R. C., AND SRIVASTAVA, B. J. Correlation between heart attacks and magnetic activity. *Nature,* 1979, *277:* 5691–5698.

MANCUSE, T. F., AND MORDELL, J. S. Proposed initial studies of the relationship of community air pollution to health. *Environmental Research,* February 1969, *2*(2): 102–133.

MANDELL, DR. M. *Dr. Mandell's 5-Day Allergy Relief System.* New York: Crowell Publishers, 1979.

MANGIAPAN, P. D. Personal communication, January 17, 1979.

MANGIAPAN, T. Case histories: John Traynor, Serge Perrin, Vittoria Micheli, Evasio Ganora, Edeltrout Fulda, Alice Couteault, and Elisa Aloi. *Bulletin of the International Medical Association of Lourdes,* 1980. Bureau Medical Constantions, F-65100, Lourdes, France.

————. Cures and miracles in Lourdes. *Bulletin of the International Medical Association of Lourdes,* 1981.

————. Cures of Lourdes recognized as miraculous by the church. *Bulletin of the International Medical Association of Lourdes,* 1981.

MANN, D. M. A., AND YATES, P. O. Lipoprotein pigments—their relationship to ageing in the human nervous system. *Brain,* 1974, *97:* 489–498.

MANN, G. V. Diet—heart: End of an era. *New England Journal of Medicine,* 1977, *297:* 644, 650.

————, SPOERRY, A., GRAY, M., AND JARASHOW, D. Atherosclerosis in the Masai. *American Journal of Epidemiology*, 1972, *95:* 26–37.

MANUSO, J. S. J. Coping with job abolishment. *Journal of Occupational Medicine*, September 1977, *19*(9): 598–602.

MARIN, P. Spiritual obedience. *Harper's*, February 1979: 43–58.

MARINO, A. A., AND BECKER, R. O. Hazard at a distance: Effects of exposure to the electric and magnetic fields of high voltage transmission lines. *Medical Research Engineering*, 1978, *12:* 6–9.

————, BECKER, R. O., AND ULLRICH, B. The effect of continuous exposure to low frequency electric fields on three generations of mice: A pilot study. *Experientia*, 1976, *32:* 565.

————, BERGER, T. J., AUSTIN, B. P., BECKER, R. O., AND HART, F. X. *In vivo* bioelectrochemical changes associated with exposure to ELF electric fields. *Physiological Chemistry and Physics*, 1977, *9:* 433–441.

————, BERGER, T. J., MITCHELL, J. T., DUHACEK, B. A., AND BECKER, R. O. Electric field effects in selected biologic systems. *Annals of New York Academy of Sciences*, 1974, *238*, 436–444.

MARS, M. B., GARRITY, T. F., AND SOMES, G. W. The effect of imbalance in life satisfactions and frustrations on illness behavior in college students. *Journal of Psychosomatic Research*, 1977, *21:* 423–427.

MARSHALL, J. F., AND BERRIOS, N. Movement disorders of aged rats: Reversal by dopamine receptor stimulation. *Science*, October 26, 1979, *206:* 477–479.

MARTIN, G. M. Genetic and evolutionary aspects of aging. *Federal Proceedings*, May 1979, *38*(6): 1962–1967.

MARTIN, M. J. Psychosomatic medicine: A brief history. *Psychosomatics*, November 1978, *19*(11): 697–700.

MARWICK, C. S. Religion and medicine draw closer. *Medical World News*, December 25, 1978: 26–33.

MARX, H. Understanding old age. *America's Health*, Spring 1979: 2.

MARX, J. L. Aging research (I): Cellular theories of aging. *Science*, December 20, 1974, *186*(4169): 1105–1107. (a)

————. Aging research (II): Pacemakers for aging. *Science*, December 22, 1974, *186* (4170): 1196–1197. (b)

————. Suppressor T cells: Role in immune regulation. *Science*, April 18, 1975, *188*(4185): 245–247. (a)

————. Thymic hormones: Inducers of T cell maturation. *Science,* March 28, 1975, *187*(4184): 1183–1185. (b)

————. Analgesia: How the body inhibits pain perception. *Science,* February 4, 1977, *195:* 471–473.

————. New information about the development of the autonomic nervous system. *Science,* October 26, 1979, *206:* 434–437. (a)

————. Interferon (II): Learning about how it works. *Science,* June 22, 1979, *204:* 1293–1295. (b)

————. Brain peptides: Is substance P a transmitter of pain signals? *Science,* August 31, 1979, *205:* 886–889. (c)

————. Hormones and their effects in the aging body. *Science,* November 16, 1979, *205:* 805–806. (d)

————. The HDL: The good cholesterol carrier? *Science,* August 17, 1979, *205:* 677–679. (e)

————. Osteoporosis: New help for thinning bones. *Science,* February 8, 1980, *207:* 628–630.

MASTERS, W. J., AND JOHNSON, V. E. *Human Sexual Response.* Boston: Little, Brown & Company, 1966.

————, AND JOHNSON, V. E. *Human Sexual Inadequacy.* Boston: Little, Brown & Company, 1970.

————, AND JOHNSON, V. E.,/EDS. Sexual inadequacy in the aging male and female. In *Human Sexual Inadequacy,* pp. 316–335. Boston: Little, Brown & Company, 1970.

MATTSON, F. H., ERICKSON, B. A., AND KLIGMAN, A. M. Effect of dietary cholesterol on serum cholesterol in man. *American Journal of Clinical Nutrition,* 1972, *25:* 589.

MAYER, J. *Nutrition and the Aged.* Hearing before the Select Committee on Nutrition and Human Needs. Washington, D.C., U.S. Government Printing House, 1969.

————. Aging and nutrition. *Geriatrics,* 1974, *29:* 57–59.

————. Fats, diet, and your heart. New York *Daily News,* 1976: 3–4.

MAZESS, R. B. Bone mineral in Vilcabamba, Ecuador. *American Journal of Roentgenology,* April 1978, *130:* 671–674.

————, AND FORMAN, S. H. Longevity and age exaggeration in Vilcabamba, Ecuador. *Journal of Gerontology,* 1979, *34*(1): 94–98.

MAZZONI, L. Anatomo-clinical contribution to the study of longevity. IV. Clinical evaluation of endogenous factors in aging. *Gerontology,* July 1967, *15*(7): 801–812.

MD. Medicine and the law: Cover story. January 1979, 71–83. (a)

MD. Running. April 1979: 96–107. (b)

MECHANIC, D. Effects of psychological distress in perceptions of physical health and use of medical and psychiatric facilities. *Journal of Human Stress,* December 1978: 26–32.

Medical Tribune. Obesity and endorphin. January 10, 1979, *20*(2): 7.

―――. Low-calorie diets immunologic aid to a longer life? February 27, 1980: 8.

―――. Retirement found raising coronary death risk by 80%. March 5, 1980: 8.

Medical World News. Roughage in the diet. September 6, 1974: 35–42.

―――. Companies urged to get more involved in health care. November 13, 1978: 85. (a)

―――. Keeping fit holds medical bills down, says Purdue study. December 25, 1978: 16. (b)

―――. Califano fears US is headed for doctor surplus. November 13, 1978: 18–20. (c)

―――. Placebos may kill pain by triggering endorphin release. September 18, 1978: 16–17. (d)

―――. Spared affluence, they've lived past 90. January 23, 1978: 42. (e)

―――. FTC gaining allies in attack on MDs. January 8, 1979: 13–14. (a)

―――. Endorphin link to pain relief is confirmed. February 19, 1979: 88–93. (b)

―――. Even moderate jogging lowers cholesterol. February 19, 1979: 96. (b)

―――. Poll shows doctor's orders could boost US fitness. March 5, 1979: 56. (c)

―――. Old runners overtake the aging process. April 30, 1979: 50. (d)

―――. HMO's and NHI rate high on index of public ignorance. June 25, 1979: 52. (e)

―――. "Retired" physiologist breaks own record. August 20, 1979: 17. (f)

―――. Diazepam hearings draw scorn, acclaim. October 1, 1979: 20–21. (g)

————. AAFP joins a labor union in preventive-care effort. October 29, 1979: 11–12. (h)

————. Neglected benefit of sex: Relief from arthritis pain. October 29, 1979: 44–45. (h)

————. Less fat, less cancer risk, says NCI. October 29, 1979: 37–38. (h)

MEDVEDEV, Z. A. *Protein Biosynthesis and Problems of Heredity, Development, and Ageing.* Edinburgh: Oliver & Boyd, 1966.

————. Possible role of repeated nucleotide sequences in DNA in the evolution of life spans of differentiated cells. *Nature,* June 23, 1973.

————. Caucasus and Altay longevity: A biological or social problem. *Gerontologist,* 1974, *14*(5): 381–387.

————. Repetition of genetic information as a possible factor in evolutionary changes in individual life span. *Zhurnal Evol. Biokhu, Fiziol,* March-April 1973, *9*(2): 113–122.

MEHNERT, H. Normal weight—ideal weight. Letter. *Medicine Clinica,* April 5, 1974, *69*(14): 615–616.

MEITES, J. ET AL. Relation of endogenous opioid peptides and morphine to neuroendocrine functions. *Life Sciences,* 1979, *24*(15): 1325–1336.

MEKHJIAN, H. S. Alcohol: The starvation diet. *Science News,* March 10, 1979, *115:* 152.

MENDELSOHN, R. Medicine without idolatry. *East West Journal,* January 1979: 62–65.

————. An interview. *PSA Magazine,* January 1980: 79–148.

Metropolitan Life Insurance Co. Presidents and their survival. *Statistical Bulletin,* June 1964, *50:* 3–4.

————. Longevity dips in 1968. *Statistical Bulletin,* March 1969, *50:* 7–9.

————. Longevity of United States Senators. *Statistical Bulletin,* May 1969, *50:* 2–11.

————. More about longevity of United States Senators. *Statistical Bulletin,* July 1969, *50:* 9.

————. Longevity at 65—international trends. *Statistical Bulletin,* July 1970, *51:* 4–6.

————. American longevity in 1968. *Statistical Bulletin,* August 1970, *51:* 9–11.

————. Generation life tables. *Statistical Bulletin,* October 1970, *51:* 8–11.

————. Longevity of state governors. *Statistical Bulletin,* April 1971, *52:* 2–5.

————. The age of grandparents. *Statistical Bulletin,* September 1972, *53:* 8–10.

————. Current patterns of regional longevity. *Statistical Bulletin,* May 1973, *54:* 3–4.

————. Regional variations in longevity at ages 65 and older. *Statistical Bulletin,* September 1973, *54:* 10–11.

————. Longevity of corporate executives. *Statistical Bulletin,* February 1974: *55,* 2–4.

————. Longevity of presidents of the United States. *Statistical Bulletin,* March 1976, *57:* 3–4.

————. Longevity of signers of the declaration of independence. *Statistical Bulletin,* April 1976, *57:* 3–4.

————. Longevity at 65—international trends. *Statistical Bulletin,* July 1976, *57:* 2–4.

————. Longevity of first ladies of the U.S. *Statistical Bulletin,* January 1977, *58:* 2–4.

————. Expectation of life among nonwhites. *Statistical Bulletin,* March 1977, *58:* 5–7.

————. Longevity in the United States at new high. *Statistical Bulletin,* May 1977, *58:* 9–11.

————. Survival after midlife. *Statistical Bulletin,* July-August 1977.

————. Geographic differences in survival after age 65 among nonwhites. *Statistical Bulletin,* December 1977, *58:* 6–7.

————. Number of elders growing nationwide. *Statistical Bulletin,* January 1978, *54:* 4–8.

MEYERS, M. A., GUIMARAE, J. R., AND AVILLEZ, R. R. Stress-relaxation experiments and their significance under strain-aging conditions. *Metallurgical Transactions A: Physical Metallurgy and Materials Science,* 1979, *10*(1): 33–40.

MICHEL, D., ZIMMERMANN, W., SERAPHIM, P. H., ALBER, G., EIGER, E., AND TEUBNER, W. Reanimation procedures in a general medical hospital. *Klinische Wockenschrift,* March 15, 1971, *49* (6): 335–340.

MICKELSEN, O., MAKDANI, D. D., AND COTTON, R. H. Effects of

a high fiber bread diet on weight loss in college males. *American Journal of Clinical Nutrition,* August 1979, *32:* 1703–1709.

MILL, T., HENDRY, D. G., AND RICHARDSON, H. Free-radical oxidants in natural waters. *Science,* February 22, 1980, *207:* 886–887.

MILLER, J. A. Artificial organs and beyond. *Science News,* September 3, 1977, *112:* 154–156.

———. DNA: On to the loose ends. *Science News,* July 8, 1978, 114(2), 25–30.

———. The cloning of an antibody. *Science News,* December 23 and December 30, 1978, *112:* 444–447.

MILLER, L. Toward a classification of aging behaviors. *Gerontology,* 1979, *19*(3): 283–290.

MILLER, P., AND INGHAM, J. G. Friends, confidants, and symptoms. *Social Psychiatry,* 1976, *11:* 51–58.

MIRKIN, G. Exercise: How much do you need? *U.S. News & World Report,* December 4, 1978: 58–62.

MISHARA, B. L., AND KASTENBAUM, R. Wine in the treatment of long-term geriatric patients in mental institutions. *Journal of the American Geriatrics Society,* 1974, *22*(2): 88–94.

Modern Medicine. Blue Cross halts pay for routine tests. June 15–June 30, 1979: 18.

———. Placebos misunderstood, sometimes misused. October 30–November 15, 1979: 14.

MOLDAVE, K., HARRIS, J., SABO, W., AND SADNIK, I. Protein synthesis and aging: Studies with cell-free mammalian systems. *Federation Proceedings,* May 1979, *38*(6): 1979–1983.

MONAT, A., AND LAZARUS, R. *Stress and Coping.* New York: Columbia University Press, 1977.

MONTAGUE, A. Voluntary simplicity. *Somatics,* 1977, *1*(3): 3–8.

MONTE, T. The US finally takes a stand on diet. *Nutrition Action,* September 1979, 3–6.

MONTGOME, J. E. Human development—adult years and aging. Book review by C. E. Kennedy. *Family Coordination,* 1979, *28*(1): 136.

MOORE, J. T. Functional disability of geriatric patients in a family medicine program—implications for patient care, education, and research. *Journal of Family Practice,* 1978, *7*(6): 1159–1166.

MORGAN, W. P. Anxiety reduction following acute physical activity. *Psychiatric Annals,* March 1979, *9*(3): 141–147.

MORISIO-GUIDETTI, L. Comparative study of longevity in groups of nuns with different nutrition and living habits. *Gerontologist,* August 1968, *16*(8): 827–830.

MOUSTAFA, A. T., AND SEARS, D. W. Feasibility of simulation of health maintenance organizations. *Inquiry,* June 1974, *11*(2): 143–150.

MUNOZ, J. M., SENDSTEA, H. H., JACOB, R. A., JOHNSON, L., AND MAKO, M. E. Effects of dietary fiber on glucose tolerance of normal men. *Diabetes,* 1979, *28*(5): 496–502.

MURPHY, M. Transformation project gathers data. *Brain/Mind Bulletin,* September 3, 1979, *4*(20): 1.

MURRAY, J., AND MURRAY, A. Suppression of infection by famine and its activation by refeeding—a paradox? *Perspectives in Biology and Medicine,* Summer 1977, *20*(4): 471–483.

MURRAY, M. J. ET AL. Diet and cerebral malaria: The effect of famine and refeeding. *American Journal of Clinical Nutrition,* January 1978, *31:* 57–61.

MYERS, G. C. Cross-national trends in mortality rates among the elderly. *Gerontologist,* 1978, *18*(5): 441–448.

MYERS, R. J. Overstatement of census age. *Demography,* 1966, *3*(2). (a)

———. Analysis of mortality in the Soviet Union according to 1958–59 life tables. *Transaction of Society of Actuaries,* 1965, *16:* 309–317. (b)

———. Validity of centenarian data in the 1960 census. *Demography,* 1966, *3:* 470–476. (b)

NAMEKATA, T., CARNOW, B., AND REDA, D. Effects of air-pollution on mortality in human population. Meeting abstract. *Biometrics,* 1978, *34*(4): 743.

National Academy of Sciences. *Human Factors in Long-duration Spaceflight.* Washington, D.C., NAS, 1972.

Nature. Asilomar conference on DNA recombinant molecules. June 5, 1975, *255:* 442–444.

NAVARRO, V. Justice social policy and the public's health. *Medical Care,* May 1977, *4*(5).

NEEDLEMAN, J. The two sciences of medicine. *Parabola,* August 1978, *3* (3): 34–55.

NEEL, J. V. Health and disease in unacculturated American Indian populations. *Ciba Foundation Symposium,* 1977, *49:* 155–168.

NELSON, N. M. ET AL. A randomized clinical trial of the Leboyer approach to childbirth. *New England Journal of Medicine,* March 20, 1980, *302* (12): 655–660.

NELSON, R. Beneficial effects of dietary vitamin E and carbohydrate supplementation upon the adaptive ability in swim test stress. Meeting abstract. *Clinical Research,* 1979, *27* (1): A33.

Newsweek. The battle over health care. May 28, 1979: 26–38.

NG, L. K. Y., DAVIS, D. L., AND MANDERSCHEID, R. W. The health promotion organization: A practical intervention designed to promote healthy living. *Public Health Reports,* September-October 1978, *93* (5): 446–455.

———, DAVIS, D. L., AND MANDERSCHEID, R. W. Toward a conceptual formulation of health and well being. Paper presented to AAAS, Houston, Texas, January 14, 1979.

NIAGEM, E. T., AND HARWELL, D. J. Who benefits in marriage with respect to longevity, the male or the female? Meeting abstract. *Ohio Journal of Science,* 1979, *79* (NSI): 61.

NIAZI, I. A., JANGIR, A. P., AND SHARMA, K. K. Forelimb regeneration at wrist level in adults of skipper frog *Rana cyanophlyctia* (Schneider) and its improvement by vitamin A treatment. *International Journal of Experimental Biology,* 1979, *17* (4): 435–437.

NICHOLS, J. R., AND SHAFIQ, S. A. Muscle regeneration in the muscular dystrophies. *Annals of the New York Academy of Sciences,* 1979, *31* (7): 478–493.

Ninth International Congress of Gerontology, Summary of the proceedings, March 3, 1973, 458–459.

Novosti Press Agency. Very old people in the USSR. *Gerontologist,* Summer 1970: 151–152.

NUCKOLLS, K., CASSEL, J., AND KAPLAN, B. Psychosocial assets, life crisis, and the prognosis of pregnancy. *American Journal of Epidemiology,* 1972, *95:* 431–441.

NULL, G., AND HOUSTON, R. The great cancer fraud. *Penthouse,* August 1979.

Nutrition Action. Added sugar in processed foods. August 1979: 10–11.

Nutrition Today. Paradise lost. May-June 1978: 6–9.

OCHSNER, A. How to live a full life. *Executive Health,* September 1979, *15* (12).

OFFIT, A. K. *The Sexual Self.* Philadelphia: J. B. Lippincott, 1977.

OLSON, H. W., TEITELBAUM, H., VAN HUSS, W. D., AND MONTOYE, H. J. Years of sports participation and mortality in college athletes. *Journal of Sports Medicine and Physical Fitness,* September 1977, *17* (3): 321–326.

OMRAN, A. R. A century of epidemiologic transition in the United States, *Preventive Medicine,* March 1977, *6* (1): 30–51.

OOKA, H., SEGALL, P. E., AND TIMIRAS, P. S. Neural and endocrine development after chronic tryptophan deficiency in rats: II. Pituitary-thyroid axis. *Mechanisms of Ageing and Development,* 1978, *7:* 19–24.

ORBACH, H. L. Aging and mental health—Positive psychosocial approaches. *Contemporary Sociology,* 1979, *8* (1): 65–66.

ORGEL, L. E. Ageing of clones of mammalian cells. *Nature,* June 22, 1973, *243:* 441–445.

OSTER, K. A. The decline of common sense and the ascent of computerized non-sense in medicine. *Journal of Applied Nutrition,* Winter 1975, *27* (4): 10–15.

———. Dietary goals—dreams and reality. *Connecticut Medicine,* November 1978, *42* (11): 705–708.

OSTERGARD, D. R., BROEN, E. M., AND MARSHALL, J. R. A training program for allied health personnel in family planning and cancer screening. *Journal of Rehabilitation,* July 1971, *7:* 26–27.

OTTO, A. S. Panaceas a-plenty, but opinions differ. *Life Lines,* April 1979. (a)

———. That matter of location. *Life Lines,* August 1979 (4). (b)

———. Don't wait—start applying now. *Life Lines,* December 1979. (c)

PACKER, L. Protection of environmentally stressed human cells in culture with the free radical scavenger, dl-α-tocopherol. In K. C. Smith, ed., *Aging, Carcinogenesis, and Radiation Biology,* pp. 519–535. New York: Plenum Publishing Corp., 1976.

————, AND SMITH, J. R. Extension of the lifespan of cultured normal human diploid cells by vitamin E: A reevaluation. *Proceedings of the National Academy of Sciences,* April 1977, *74*(4): 1640–1641.

————, AND WALTON, J. Antioxidants vs. aging. *Chemtech.,* May 1977, *7*(5): 276–281.

PAILLAT, P. Superannuation: A problem of the future. *Krankenpflege,* December 1977, *31*(12): 398.

PALMER, W. K., AND GOLDBERG, D. I. Sexual differences in cardiac response to exhaustive exercise. *Federal Proceedings,* 1979, *38*(3): 447.

PALMORE, E. B. Physical, mental and social factors in predicting longevity. *Gerontologist,* Summer 1969, *9*(2): 103–108. (a)

————. Predicting longevity: A follow-up controlling for age. *Gerontologist,* Winter 1969, *9*(4): 247–250. (b)

————. Longevity predictors—implications for practice. *Postgraduate Medical Journal,* July 1971, *50*(1): 160–164.

————, AND CLEVELAND, W. Aging, terminal decline, and terminal drop. *Journal of Gerontology,* 1976, *31*(1): 76–81.

PARSONS, P. A. The genetics of aging in optimal and stressful environments. *Experimental Gerontology,* 1978, *13:* 357–363.

PASTERNAK, B. *Doctor Zhivago.* New York: Pantheon, 1958.

PAUL, H. A. Trends in modern international gerontological research: Epidemiological aspects. *Aktuel Gerontological,* January 1978, *8*(1): 27–36.

PAULING, L. Orthomolecular psychiatry. *Science,* April 16, 1968, *160:* 265–271.

————. Good nutrition for the good life. *Engineering Science,* June 1974.

————. Chemotherapy and vitamin C. *Science News,* January 5, 1980, *117,* 3.

PAYNE, B., AND WHITTINGTON, F. Older women: An examination of popular stereotypes and research evidence. *Social Problems,* April 1976, *23*(4): 488–504.

PEARL, R., AND PEARL, R. DE W. *The Ancestry of the Long Lived.* Baltimore: Johns Hopkins University Press, 1934.

PELLETIER, K. R. Neurological, psychophysiological, and clinical differentiation of the alpha and theta altered states of consciousness. *Dissertation Abstracts International,* 1974, *35/1:* 520–28.

————. Neurological substrates of consciousness: Implications for psychosomatic medicine. *Journal of Altered States of Consciousness,* 1974, 2(1): 75–85.

————. Psychophysiological parameters of the voluntary control of blood flow and pain. In D. Kanellakos and J. Lukas, eds., *The Psychobiology of Transcendental Meditation.* Reading, Mass.: W. A. Benjamin, 1974.

————. Theory and applications of clinical biofeedback. *Journal of Contemporary Psychotherapy,* 1975, 7(1): 29–34.

————. Diagnostic and treatment protocols for clinical biofeedback. *Journal of Biofeedback,* Fall/Winter 1975, 2(4): 4–10.

————. Holistic applications of clinical biofeedback and meditation. *Journal of Holistic Health,* 1976, 1: 31–36.

————. Adjunctive biofeedback with cancer patients: A case presentation. *Proceedings of the Biofeedback Society of America,* Denver, Colorado, 1977. Reprinted in *Biofeedback and Self-Regulation,* September 1977, 2(3): 317. Reprinted in C. Garfield, ed., *Stress and Survival: The Emotional Realities of Life-threatening Illness,* pp. 86–93. St. Louis: C. V. Mosby Company, 1979.

————. Biofeedback. In *Collier's Encyclopedia,* pp. 164–165. New York: Macmillan, 1977.

————. Influence of transcendental meditation upon autokinetic perception. *Journal of Perceptual and Motor Skills,* 1974, 39: 1031–1034. Reprinted in D. Orme-Johnson, ed., *Scientific Research on the Transcendental Meditation Program.* Vol. I. Lake Lucerne, Switzerland: MIU Press, 1977.

————. Mind as healer, mind as slayer. *Psychology Today,* February 1977: 35–42. Reprinted in C. F. Wilson and D. L. Hall, eds., *Stress Management for Educators.* San Diego: Department of Education, 1980.

————. *Mind as Healer, Mind as Slayer: A Holistic Approach to Preventing Stress Disorders.* New York: Delacorte and Delta, 1977.

————. *Toward a Science of Consciousness.* New York: Delacorte and Delta, 1978.

————. Stress: Managing and overcoming it. In the "Tools for transformation" section of *New Realities,* August 1978: 43–45.

————. Uncertainty principle factors in holographic models of neurophysiology. *Revision Journal,* Summer/Fall 1978.

————. Holistic medicine: From pathology to prevention. *Western Journal of Medicine,* December 1979, *13* (6): 481–483.

————. *Holistic Medicine: From Stress to Optimum Health.* New York: Delacorte and Delta, 1979.

————. Introduction to D. Saltoon, *The Common Book of Consciousness.* San Francisco: Chronicle Books, 1979.

————. Stress/unstress: A conversation with Kenneth R. Pelletier. *Medical Self-Care, Number Five,* 1979: 3–9.

————. Holistic approaches to healing. In G. G. Meyer, K. Blum, and J. Cull, eds., *Folk Healing and Herbal Medicine.* Springfield, Ill.: Charles C. Thomas, 1980.

————. The mind in health and disease. In A. Hastings, J. Fadiman, and J. S. Gordon, eds., *Holistic Medicine: An Annotated Bibliography.* Rockville, Md.: National Institute of Mental Health, 1980. Reprinted as *Health Care for the Whole Person: A Comprehensive Guide to Holistic Medicine.* Boulder, Colo.: Westview Press, 1980.

————. A preventive approach to psychosomatic medicine. In D. Bresler, J. Gordon, and D. Jaffe, eds., *Body, Mind and Health: Toward an Integral Medicine.* Washington, D.C.: National Institute of Mental Health, 1980.

————, AND GARFIELD, C. *Consciousness: East and West.* New York: Harper & Row, 1976.

————, AND GARFIELD, C. Meditative states of consciousness. In P. Zimbardo and C. Maslach, eds., *Psychology for Our Times: Readings.* 2d edition. Glenview, Ill.: Scott, Foresman & Company, 1977.

————, GLADMAN, A. E., AND MIKURIYA, T. H. Clinical protocols —professional group socializing in psychosomatic medicine. *Handbook of Physiological Feedback.* Berkeley: Autogenic Systems, 1976.

————, AND PEPER, E. The chutzpah factor in altered states of consciousness. *Journal of Humanistic Psychology,* 1977, *17* (1): 63–73. Reprinted in G. Henricks and J. Fadiman, eds., *Transpersonal Education,* pp. 86–95. Englewood Cliffs, N.J.: Prentice-Hall, 1976.

————, AND PEPER, E. Alpha EEF feedback as a means for pain control. *Journal of Clinical and Experimental Hypnosis,* 1977, *25* (4): 361–371.

————,AND SHEALY, C. N. Biofeedback training: Office management of stress disorders, *American Journal of Clinical Biofeedback,* 1979, *2*(2): 2–6.

PENFIELD, W. *The Mystery of the Mind.* Princeton, N.J.: Princeton University Press, 1976.

PENNINGTON, C. W. *The Tarahumara of Mexico.* Salt Lake: University of Utah Press, 1963.

PEPER, E., ANCOLI, S., AND QUINN, M., eds., *Mind/Body Integration: Essential Readings in Biofeedback.* New York: Plenum Publishing Corp., 1979.

PEPER, E., PELLETIER, K. R., AND TANDY, B. Biofeedback training: Holistic and transpersonal frontiers. In E. Peper, S. Ancoli, and M. Quinn, eds., *Mind/Body Integrations: Essential Readings in Biofeedback.* New York: Plenum Publishing Corp., 1979.

PEPPER, C. (Congressman) *Life Extension and Tomorrow's Elderly.* U.S. House of Representatives. Washington, D.C.: Government Printing Office. Committee Pub. #95-127, February 8, 1978.

————. *Americans over 100.* U.S. House of Representatives. Washington, D.C.: Government Printing Office. Committee Pub. #96-203, November 14, 1979.

————. (Congressman). U.S. Congressional Committee testimony: "The centenarian explosion." Washington, D.C.: U.S. House of Representatives, 1979.

PEREIRA, O. M., SMITH, J. R., AND PACKER, L. Photosensitization of human diploid cell cultures by intracellular flavins and protection by antioxidants. *Photochemistry and Photobiology,* 1976, *24:* 237–242.

PERKINS, D. *English Romantic Writers.* New York: Harcourt, Brace & World, 1967.

PERLMAN, D. New prescription drug findings puzzle scientists. *San Francisco Chronicle,* March 21, 1980: 24.

PERRY, J. W. Reconstitutive process in the psychopathology of the self. *Annals of the New York Academy of Sciences,* 1962, *96*(2-4): 853–876.

PERTOS'IANTS, V. S., AND BURMIN, L. S. Longevity and prolongation of life among the population of Kirghizia SSR in the modern era. *Soviet Zdravookhr. Kirg,* January-February 1972, *1:* 3–7.

PESZNECKER, B. L., AND MCNEIL, J. Relationship among health habits, social assets, psychologic well-being, life change, and alterations in health status. *Nursing Research,* November-December 1975, *24*(6): 442–447.

PETERKIN, B. B., SHORE, L. J., KERR, R. L. Some diets that meet the dietary goals for the United States. *Journal of the American Dietetic Association,* 1979, *74*(4): 423–430.

PETERSON, B. H. The age of aging. *Australian and New Zealand Journal of Psychiatry,* March 1973, *7*(1): 9–15.

PETROVSKY, C. C., AND MAXWELL, V. K. Proceedings: Ninth International Congress of Gerontology. *The Medical Journal of Australia,* March 3, 1973: 458–464.

PFEIFFER, C. C. On the 5 trace elements that can help, heal, or harm us. *Executive Health,* October 1979, *16*(1).

PFEIFFER, E. Survival in old age: Physical, psychological and social correlates of longevity. *Journal of the American Geriatrics Society,* April 1970, *18*(4): 273–285.

PFEIFFER, G. Xerox launches an employee health management program. News from Xerox Corporation, Stamford, Connecticut, 1980.

PHILLIPPE, P., AND YELLE, L. Effect of family size on mother's longevity. *Annals of Human Biology,* 1976, *3*(5): 431–439.

PHILLIPS, D. P. Airplane accident fatalities increase just after newspaper stories about murder and suicide. *Science,* August 25, 1978, *201:* 748–750.

Physician's Desk Reference. Oradell, N.J.: Medical Economics Co., 1980.

PINCHERLE, B. Mortality of members of parliament. *British Journal of Preventive Social Medicine.*

PITOT, H. C. Interactions in natural-history of aging and carcinogenesis. *Federal Proceedings,* 1978, *37*(14): 2841–2847.

PITSKHELAURT, G. Z. Several social hygienic factors in the longevity of persons 100 years old and older. *Gigenia I Sanitariia,* July 1968, *33*(7): 67–70.

POLEDNAK, A. P. Longevity and cardiovascular mortality among former college athletes. *Circulation,* October 1972, *46*(4): 649–654.

———. Previous health and longevity of male athletes. *Lancet,* September 30, 1972, *2*(779): 711.

————. Longevity and cause of death among Harvard College athletes and their classmates. *Geriatrics,* October 1972, *27*(10), 53–64.

————. College athletics, body size and cancer mortality. *Cancer,* 1976, *38:* 382–387.

————, AND DAMON, A. College athletics, longevity, and cause of death. *Human Biology,* February 1970, *42*(1): 28–46.

POMA, P. A. Letter. *New England Journal of Medicine,* August 25, 1977.

POMERANZ, B. Brain's opiates at work in acupuncture. *New Scientist,* January 1977, *6:* 12–13.

POMERLEAU, O. V. Behavioral medicine: The contribution of the experimental analysis of behavior to medical care. *American Psychologist,* August 1979, *34*(8): 654–663.

POPKIN, R. J. Implications of increasing disparity between the mortality of the sexes. *Journal of the American Medical Association,* August 27, 1973, *225*(9): 1123–1124.

POPOV, I. M., PANJWANI, H. K., AND GOLDWAG, E. M. The multitherapeutic approach to premature aging. *Journal of the American Society Psychosomatic Dental Medicine,* 1976, *23*(3): 99–107.

Population Reference Bureau, Inc. Our population predicament: A new look. Washington, D.C., 1980.

PORTA, E. A., NITTA, R., AND KIA, L. Cerebral lipofuscin accumulation in relation to age, dietary factors and lipo-peroxidation in rats. *Federal Proceedings,* 1979, *38*(3): 1370.

PORTER, A. L., PEARMAN, H. E., AND MCCARTHY, C. D. Effect of stressful physical illness on future time perspective. *Journal of Clinical Psychology,* October 1971, *27*(4): 447–448.

POST, J. Open letter of the Xerox Recreation Association, Inc. Rochester, N.Y., 1980.

PRAUL, D. Ailing boy who preferred to die. *San Francisco Chronicle,* February 1978: 1.

President's Council on Physical Fitness and Sports. *Physical Fitness Research Digest.* Washington, D.C.: Quarterly publication of Government Printing Office, Series 9, No. 4, October 1979.

President's Council on Physical Fitness. *One Step at a Time.* Washington, D.C.: Government Printing Office, 1981.

PRESMAN, A. S. *Electromagnetic Fields and Life.* New York: Plenum Publishing Corp., 1970.

PREUSS, K. *Life Time.* Santa Cruz, Calif.: Unity Press, 1978.

PRIBRAM, K. H. *Languages of the Brain: Experimental Paradoxes and Principles of Neuropsychology.* Englewood Cliffs, N.J.: Prentice-Hall, 1971.

PRITIKIN, N. The longevity center. Santa Monica, Calif., 1981.

———, AND MCGRADY, P. M. *The Pritikin Program for Diet and Exercise.* New York: Grosset & Dunlap, 1979.

PROUT, C. Life expectancy of college oarsmen. *Journal of the American Medical Association,* June 26, 1972, *220*(13): 1709–1711.

Quality of life and longevity. Editorial. *Sykepleien,* September 20, 1976, *63*(16): 830–849.

A Quantitative approach to the world organizational definition of health: Physical, mental and social well-being. *International Journal of Epidemiology,* 1972, *1:* 347–355.

QUINT, J. V., AND CODY, B. R. Preeminence and mortality: Longevity of prominent men. *American Journal of Public Health,* June 1970, *60*(6): 1118–1124.

RAAB, W. Cardiotoxic biochemical effects of emotional-environmental stressors: Fundamentals of Psychocardiology. *Society Stress and Disease,* 1971, *1:* 331–336.

RABKIN, J. G., AND STRUENING, E. Life events, stress and illness. *Science,* 1976, *194:* 1013–1020.

RAE-GRANT, N. I. Longevity, mobility, and spare parts: The future imperfect and human service delivery. *American Journal of Orthopsychiatry,* October 1972, *42*(5): 835–846.

RAHE, R. H. Life crisis and health change. In *Psychotropic Drug Response: Advance in Prediction.* Springfield, Ill.: Charles C. Thomas, 1969.

———. Life-change measurement as a predictor of illness. *Proceedings of the Royal Society of Medicine,* 1973, *61:* 1124–1126.

———. Life change events and mental illness: An overview. *Journal of Human Stress,* September 1979: 2–9.

———, AND ARTHUR, R. J. Life change and illness studies: Past history and future directions. *Journal of Human Stress,* March 1978: 3–15.

————, MEYER, M., SMITH, M., KJAER, G., AND HOLMES, T. H. Social stress and illness onset. *Journal of Psychosomatic Research,* 1964, *8:* 35–44.

RAKSTIS, T. J. Helping cancer victims come back. *Today's Health,* 1968, *46:* 40–41.

RANDOLPH, T. G. The ecologic unit. *Hospital Management,* March 1964: 45–48.

————. Ecologic orientation in medicine: Comprehensive environmental control in diagnosis and therapy. *Annals of Allergy,* January 1965, *23:* 7–22.

————. The realities of food addiction: I. Description and recognition. *Health News and Views,* Spring 1971, No. 10.

————. The realities of food addiction: II. Treatment and prophylaxis. *Health News and Views,* Summer 1971, No. 11.

————. *Human Ecology and Susceptibility to the Chemical Environment.* Springfield, Ill.: Charles C. Thomas, 1972.

————. Specific adaptation. *Annals of Allergy,* May 1978, *40*(5): 333–345.

RASHKIS, H. A. Systemic stress as an inhibitor of experimental tumors in Swiss mice. *Science,* 1952, *116:* 169–171.

RASPER, V. F. Chemical and physical properties of dietary cereal fiber. *Food Technology,* 1979, *33*(1): 40–44.

RATHJUE, W., AND McCARTHY, M. Regularity and variability in contemporary garbage. In S. Smith, ed., *Research Strategies in Historical Archeology,* pp. 261–286. New York: Academic Press, 1977.

RAUSCHER, R. J., JR. The outlook for cancer prevention. *Preventive Medicine,* August 1972, *1*(3): 293–299.

RAVINA, A. Current problems of nutrition: The struggle against diseases of civilization. *Presse Med,* October 26, 1968, *76*(41): 1979–1980.

REED, L. S. *The Healing Cults,* pp. 133–134. Chicago: University of Chicago Press, 1932.

REICHMANIS, M., AND BECKER, R. O. Relief of experimentally-induced pain by stimulation at acupuncture loci: A review. *Comparative Medicine East and West,* 1977, *3-4:* 281–288.

————, MARINO, A. A., AND BECKER, R. O. Electrical correlates of acupuncture points. *Biomedical Engineering (IEEE Transactions),* 1975, *BME22:* 533–535.

REID, D. D., AND EVANS, J. G. New drugs and changing mortality from non-infectious disease in England and Wales. *British Medical Bulletin,* September 1970, *26*(3): 191–196.

RELMAN, A. S. Holistic medicine. Editorial section. *New England Journal of Medicine,* February 8, 1979: 312–313.

REMEN, N. What is health? *New Physician,* February 1977: 41.

RENFROW, N. E., AND BOLTON, B. Personality characteristics associated with aerobic exercise in adult males. *Journal of Personality Assessment,* 1979, *43*(3): 261–266.

RESNICK, J. L. Women and aging. *Counseling Psychologist,* 1979, *8* (1): 29–30.

Revue Med. Suisse Romande. Life expectancy in the year 2000. March 1977, *97*(3): 151–152.

REYNOLDS, D. K., AND KALISH, R. A. Anticipation of futurity as a function of ethnicity and age. *Journal of Gerontology,* March 1974, *29*(2): 224–231.

RHODES, J. N., BISHOP, M., AND BENFIELD, J. Tumor surveillance: How tumors may resist macrophage mediated host defense. *Science,* January 12, 1979, *203:* 179–181.

RHODES, R. Intimations of immortality. *Playboy,* June 1979: 134–228.

RICHARDSON, A. H. Social and medical correlates of survival among octogenarians: United Auto Workers retirees and Spanish-American War veterans. *Journal of Gerontology,* April 1973, *28*(2): 207–215.

RICHTER, C. P. On the phenomenon of sudden death in animals and man. *Psychosomatic Medicine,* 1957, *19:* 191–198.

RILEY, J. N., AND WALKER, D. W. Morphological alterations in hippocampus after long-term alcohol consumption by mice. *Science,* August 18, 1978, *201:* 646–648.

RILEY, M. W. Aging, social change, and the power of ideas. *Daedalus,* Fall 1978, *107*(4): 39–53.

RINGSDORF, W. M., AND CHERASIN, E. *Predictive Medicine.* Mountain View: California Pacific Press, 1973.

RINKEL, H. J., RANDOLPH, T. G., AND ZELLER, M. *Food Allergy.* Springfield, Ill.: Charles C. Thomas, 1951.

ROBBINS, L. C., AND HALL, J. H. *How to Practice Prospective Medicine.* Indianapolis: Slaymaker Enterprises, 1970.

ROBBINS, P. I. Successful midlife career change. AMACON of the American Management Association, 1978.

ROBERTS-THOMPSON, I. C. ET AL. Ageing, immune response, and mortality. *Lancet,* August 17, 1974: 368–370.

RODAN, G. A., BOURRET, L. A., AND NORTON, L. A. DNA synthesis in cartilage cells is stimulated by oscillating electric fields. *Science,* February 10, 1978, *199:* 690–692.

RODIN, J., AND LANGER, E. J. Effects of a control-relevant intervention with the institutionalized aged. *Journal of Personality and Social Psychology,* 1977, *35* (12): 903–911.

ROGERS, M., DUBEY, D., AND REICH, P. The influence of the psyche and the brain on immunity and disease susceptibility: A critical review. *Psychosomatic Medicine,* 1979, *41:* 147–164.

RORVIK, D. *In His Image: The Cloning of a Man.* New York: J. B. Lippincott, 1978.

ROSE, C. L., AND COHEN, M. L. Relative importance of physical activity for longevity. *Annals of the New York Academy of Sciences,* 1977, *301,* 671–702.

———, ENSLEIN, K., AND NUTTALL, R. L. Univariate and multivariate findings from a longevity study. *Proceedings of the 20th Annual Meeting of the Gerontological Society,* 1967: 42.

ROSE, K. D. Exercise for seniors. Letter. *Journal of the American Medical Association,* 1979, *241* (22): 2435.

ROSEMAN, R. H., AND FRIEDMAN, M. Neurogenic factors in pathogenesis of coronary heart disease. *Medical Clinics of North America,* 1974, *59:* 269–279.

ROSEN, D. H. Suicide survivors: A follow-up study of persons who survived jumping from the Golden Gate and San Francisco–Oakland Bay Bridges. *Western Journal of Medicine,* 1975, *7:* 289–294.

ROSEN, J. C., AND WIENS, A. N. Changes in medical problems and use of medical services following psychological intervention. *American Psychologist,* *34* (5): 420–431.

ROSENBERG, B. ET AL. Quantitative evidence for protein denaturation as the cause of thermal death. *Nature,* August 13, 1971, *232:* 471–473.

———. ET AL. The kinetics and thermodynamics of death in multicellular organisms. *Mechanisms of Ageing and Development,* 1973, *2:* 275–293.

ROSENFELD, A. *Pro-longevity.* New York: Discus/Avon, 1977.

ROSENWAIKE, I. On measuring the extreme aged in the population. *Journal of the Statistical Association,* 1968, *63:* 29–40.

ROSS, M. H. Length of life and caloric intake. *American Journal of Clinical Nutrition,* 1972, *25:* 834–838.

————. Nutrition and longevity in experimental animals. In M. Winick, ed., *Nutrition and Aging.* New York: John Wiley & Sons, 1976.

————. Dietary behavior and longevity. *Nutritional Review,* October 1977, *35*(10): 257–265.

————, LUSTBADER, E., AND BRAS, G. Dietary practices and growth responses as predictors of longevity. *Nature,* 1976, *262:* 548–553.

ROSSI, A. S. Family development in a changing world. *American Journal of Psychiatry,* March 1972, *128*(9): 1057–1066.

ROSSIER, J., BLOOM, F. E., AND GUILLEMIN, R. Stimulation of human periaqueductal gray for pain relief increases immunoreactive β-endorphin in ventricular fluid. *Science,* January 19, 1979, *203:* 279–281.

ROTH, G. S. Hormone receptor changes during adulthood and senescence: Significance for aging research. *Federal Proceedings,* April 1979, *38*(5): 1910–1914.

————. Hormone action and receptors during aging. Conference of NIA, Endocrine Society and Veterans Administration, Bethesda, Maryland, October 18–20, 1979.

ROWE, A. *Food Allergy.* Springfield, Ill.: Charles C. Thomas, 1972.

ROWE, J. W. Clinical research on aging: Strategies and directions. *New England Journal of Medicine,* December 15, 1977: 1332–1336.

RUBIN, I. *Sexual Life After Sixty.* New York: Basic Books, 1965.

————. *Sexual Life in the Later Years.* Study guide 12, New York Sex Information and Education Council of the United States, 1970.

RYAN, A. J. Sports medicine today. *Science,* 1978, *200:* 919–924.

SACHER, G. A. Longevity, aging and death: Evolutionary perspective. 1976 Robert W. Kleemeir Award lecture. *Gerontologist,* April 1978, *18*(2): 112–119.

SACHUK, N. N. Population longevity study: Sources and indices. *Journal of Gerontology,* July 1970, *25*(3): 262–264.

SAFLOFF, L. A. Sexual activity in the heart patient. *Psychosomatics,* 1977, *18:* 23–28.

SALK, J. In R. N. Anshen, ed., *Man Unfolding.* New York: Harper & Row, 1972.

————. *Survival of the Wisest.* New York: Harper & Row, 1973.

SALMON, M-M. The cure of Mr. Vittorio Micheli: Sarcoma of pelvis. Report of the Medical Bureau of Lourdes, 1972.

SALVADOR, M. *Vilcabamba: Tierra de longevos.* Quito, Ecuador: Casa de la Cultura, 1972.

SAMUELS, M., AND BENNETT, H. *The Well Body Book.* New York: Random House, 1973.

SAMUELS, M., AND SAMUELS, N. *Seeing with the Mind's Eye.* New York: Random House/Bookworks, 1975.

San Francisco Chronicle. 146 year old woman with baby teeth. November 23, 1978: 12.

————. 800 years of advice. November 15, 1979: 12.

SARASON, S. B., SARASON, E. K., AND CODEN, P. Aging and the nature of work. *American Psychologist,* 1975, *30:* 584–592.

SATO, K. Death of Zen masters. *Psychologia,* 1964, *7:* 143–147.

SAUER, W. J. Empirical studies in the psychology and sociology of aging. Book review. *Contemporary Sociology,* 1979, *8*(3): 397.

SAUVY, A. Quantitative and qualitative changes in the human population under the influence of biomedical or biomedico-social progress. *Experientia,* 1972, *17*(Supp.): 266–285.

SAWARD, E. W. The organization of medical care. *Scientific American,* September 1973, 160–175.

————. The effect on future physician requirements of an HMO policy. *Journal of Community Health,* 1975, *1*(1): 53–71.

————. Medicare, medical practice and the medical profession. *Public Health Reports,* 1976, *91*(4): 317–321.

————, BLANK, J., AND LAMB, H. *Some Information Descriptive of a Successfully Operating HMO.* Washington, D.C.: Department of Health, Education, and Welfare, 1972.

————, AND SORENSEN, A. The current emphasis on preventive medicine. *Science,* May 26, 1978, *200:* 889–894.

SCHAEFER, H. The environment of man in the light of a theory of medicine. *Klinische Wochenschrift,* December 1977, *55*(24): 1197–1207.

SCHEIDEGGER, S. Maximal human life span. A pathological study. *Praxis,* September 6, 1977, *66*(36): 1138–1140.

SCHEINFELD, A. Longevity. *Journal of the American Medical Association.* August 30, 1973, *225*(5): 526.

SCHETTLER, G. Man and his lifetime. *Deutsche Medical Journal,* May 20, 1971, *22*(10): 297–308.

SCHIEFELBEIN, S. The miracle of regeneration: Can human limbs grow back? *Saturday Review,* July 8, 1978: 8–11.

———. The invisible threat. *Saturday Review,* September 15, 1979: 16–20.

SCHLENKER, E. D., FEURIG, J. S., STONE, L. H., OHLSON, M. A., AND MICHELSEN, O. Nutrition and health of older people. *American Journal of Clinical Nutrition,* October 1973, *26*(10): 1111–1119.

SCHMALE, A. H., AND AMKRAUT, A. A. Emotions, stress and immunity. *Frontiers of Radiation Therapy and Oncology,* 1972, *7:* 84–96.

SCHMECK, H. M. Is the US facing an epidemic of insanity? *San Francisco Chronicle,* December 10, 1979: 6.

SCHMITT, H. A scientist-senator on recombinant DNA research. *Science,* July 14, 1978, *201:* 106–108.

SCHNOHR, P. Longevity and causes of death in male athletic champions. *Lancet,* December 18, 1971, *2*(738): 1364–1366.

———. Athletic activity and longevity. *Lancet,* September 16, 1972, *2*(777): 605.

SCHUCKIT, M. A., AND RAYSES, V. Ethanol ingestion: Differences in blood acetaldehyde concentrations in relatives of alcoholics and controls. *Science,* January 5, 1979, *203:* 54–55.

SCHUMAN, L. M. The benefits of cessation of smoking. *Chest,* April 1971, *59*(4): 421–427.

SCHUTZ, Y., MARGEN, S., AND BRAY, G. A. Exercise and dietary induced thermogenesis in elderly men. *American Journal of Clinical Nutrition,* 1979, *32*(4): 804–808.

SCHWAB, J. J. Comprehensive medicine and the concurrence of physical and mental illness. *Psychosomatics,* November/December 1970, *11*(6): 591–595.

Science. Surgeon General seeks physicians' help in DES alert. January 12, 1979, *203:* 159.

Science News. Switching cancer cells back to normal. April 16, 1977, *111:* 246.

————. Psychochemical treatment counteracts senility. May 7, 1977, *111:* 292.

————. Pain: Placebo effect linked to endorphins. September 2, 1978: 164.

————. Preventive medicine: The need for trust. September 23, 1978, *114* (13): 216.

————. Heart attacks from stress, via brain. November 18, 1978, *114* (21): 342.

————. Elective surgery: Cut it out. January 6, 1979, *115:* 9.

————. Cancer statistics and views of causes. January 13, 1979, *115:* 23.

————. Rx for the sick doctor: Seek help. January 13, 1979, *115:* 25.

————. Shock treatment and diet. January 13, 1979, *115:* 24.

————. Alcohol level and offspring. January 20, 1979, *115:* 41.

————. Americans hanker after cancer cure. January 20, 1979, *115:* 41.

————. Dietary cholesterol and colon cancer. January 20, 1979, *115:* 37.

————. New species of man: Ancestors from "afar." January 20, 1979, *115:* 36.

————. Updates report blasts cigarettes. January 20, 1979, *115:* 39.

————. How diet can prolong life. January 27, 1979, *115:* 54–55.

————. The pill and heart attacks: Exaggerated. April 14, 1979, *115:* 247.

————. Health in women and women in health. August 11, 1979, *116:* 101–102.

————. Heart death decline examined. October 6, 1979, *116,* 230–231.

————. Conquering the chronic disease. October 27, 1979, *116:* 277–278.

————. Unhappiness: Closing the generation gap. November 3, 1979, *116:* 313.

————. Reversing atherosclerosis. January 12, 1980: 25.

————. Smoking alarm: Women in danger. January 19, 1980, *117:* 37.

————. Working women and heart disease. February 9, 1980, *117:* 86.

————. The female edge against disease. February 23, 1980, *117:* 118.

Scientific American. The brain. September 1979.

Scott Medical Journal. Longevity. September 1968, *13* (9): 317–319.

SEGAL, J. Biofeedback as medical treatment. *Journal of the American Medical Association,* April 14, 1975, *232* (2): 179–180.

SEGALL, P. E. Long term tryptophan restriction and aging in the rat. *Aktuelle Gerontologie,* October 1977, *7* (10): 535–538.

————. Interrelations of dietary and hormonal effects in aging. *Mechanisms of Ageing and Development,* 1979, 9(5-6), 515–525.

————, OOKA, H., ROSE, K., AND TIMIRAS, P. S. Neural and endocrine development after chronic tryptophan deficiency in rats: Brain monoamine and pituitary responses. *Mechanisms of Ageing and Development,* 1978, *7:* 1–17.

————, AND TIMIRAS, P. S. Age-related changes in thermoregulatory capacity of tryptophan-deficient rats. *Federal Proceedings,* January 1975, *34* (1): 83–85.

————, AND TIMIRAS, P. S. Patho-physiologic findings after chronic tryptophan deficiency in rats: A model for delayed growth and aging. *Mechanisms of Ageing and Development,* 1976, *5:* 109–124.

SELIGMAN, J. Temperamental ills. *Newsweek,* August 13, 1979: 40.

SELIGMAN, M. E. P. *Helplessness: On Depression, Development, and Death.* San Francisco: W. H. Freeman & Company, 1975.

SELYE, H. The physiology and pathology of exposure to stress. *Acta,* Montreal, 1950.

————. *The Stress of Life.* New York: McGraw-Hill, 1956.

————. *Stress in Health and Disease.* Boston: Butterworth Press, 1974.

————. *Stress Without Distress.* Philadelphia: J. B., Lippincott, 1974.

————. *Creative Psychiatry.* Booklet. Ardsley, N.Y.: Geigy Pharmaceuticals, 1977.

————. They all looked sick to me. *Executive Health,* October 1979, *16* (1): 1–4.

SELZER, R. *Mortal Lessons: Notes on the Art of Surgery.* New York: Simon & Schuster, 1979.

SETTLES, H. E. Limb regeneration from partial amputation surfaces in the adult newt, *Notophthalmus viridescens. Anatomical Record,* 1979, *193* (3): 680.

SHAKOCIUS, S., AND PEARSON, D. Mind food. *OMNI,* May 1979: 55–127.

SHANAS, E. Aging and life space in Poland and the United States. *Journal of Health and Social Behavior,* September 1970, *11*(3): 183–190.

SHAPIRO, A. K. The placebo effect in the history of medical treatment: Implications for psychiatry. *American Journal of Psychiatry,* 1959, *116:* 198–304.

SHAPIRO, A. P. Behavioral and environmental aspects of hypertension. *Journal of Human Stress,* December 1978: 9–17.

SHARFSTEIN, L. 20 year California study of 1 million finds exercise prolongs life. *Medical Tribune,* December 12, 1979: 20.

SHEDRAIN, V. S., MATTOCK, M. B., AND SUBRAMA, D. Sex-dependence in triglyceride-metabolism in response to dietary carbohydrates. *Experientia,* 1979, *35*(2): 162–163.

SHEEHAN, G. A. Athletic activity and longevity. *Lancet,* November 4, 1972, *2*(784): 974.

———. Longevity of athletes. *American Heart Journal,* September 1973, *86*(3), 425–426.

———. *Running and Being: The Total Experience.* New York: Simon & Schuster, 1978.

SHELDRAKE, A. R. The ageing, growth and death of cells. *Nature,* August 2, 1974, *250:* 381–385.

SHERMAN, B., AND WALLACE, R. Pathogenic implications of perimenopausal menstrual and hormonal patterns. Conference of NIA, Endocrine Society and Veterans Administration, Bethesda, Maryland, October 18–20, 1979.

SHIH, J. C., AND YOUNG, H. The alteration of serotonin binding sites in aged human brain. *Life Sciences,* 1978, *23:* 1441–1448.

SHNEIDMAN, E. S. *Deaths of Man.* New York: Quadrangle, New York Times Book Co., 1973.

SHOCK, N. W. The physiology of aging. *Scientific American,* January 1962: 100–110.

———. Age with a future. *Gerontologist,* Autumn 1968, *8*(3): 147–152.

———. Current publications in gerontology and geriatrics. *Journal of Gerontology,* 1979, *34*(2): 286–319.

————, ED. Perspectives in experimental gerontology. Springfield, Ill.: Charles C. Thomas, 1966.

SIEGEL, J. S., AND O'LEARY, W. E. Some demographic aspects of aging in the United States. *Current Population Reports.* Washington, D.C.: Government Printing Office, 1973.

SIITERI, P. Interaction of androgens, estrogens and the sex hormone binding globulin. Conference of NIA, Endocrine Society and Veterans Administration, Bethesda, Maryland, October 18–20, 1979.

SILBERNER, J. Is stress hormone CAD co-conspirator? *Medical Tribune,* December 5, 1979: 1, 4.

SILVERSTEIN, A. *Conquest of Death.* New York: Macmillan, 1979.

SIMKO, V., AND KELLEY, R. E. Effect of physical exercise on bile and red blood-cell lipids in humans. *Atherosclerosis,* 1979, *32*(4): 423–434.

————, AND KELLEY, R. E. Physical exercise modifies the effect of high cholesterol-sucrose feeding in the rat. *European Journal of Applied Physiology,* 1979, *40*(3): 145–153.

SIMONTON, O. C., MATTHEWS-SIMONTON, S., AND CREIGHTON, J. *Getting Well Again.* Los Angeles: J. P. Tarcher, 1978.

————, AND SIMONTON, S. Belief systems and management of the emotional aspects of malignancy. *Journal of Transpersonal Psychology,* 1975, *7*(1): 29–48.

SINEX, F. M. Cross-linkage and aging. *Advanced Gerontological Research,* 1964, *1:* 173.

SINGEWALD, H., LANGWORTHY, O., AND KOUWENHOVEN, W. Medical follow-up study of high voltage linemen working in AC electric fields. *IEEE Transmission Power Applied Systems,* 1967, PAS-86: 506.

SMITH, J. M. A theory of ageing. *Nature,* September 26, 1958, *84:* 956–957.

SMITH, K. J., AND LIPMAN, A. Constraint and life satisfaction. *Journal of Gerontology,* January 1972, *27*(1): 77–82.

SMITH, R. J. Study finds sleeping pills overprescribed. *Science,* April 20, 1979, *204:* 287–288.

SMITH-SONNEBORN, J. DNA repair and longevity assurance in paramecium tetraurelia. *Science,* March 16, 1979, *203:* 1115–1117.

SMYTHIES, J. R. Recent progress in schizophrenia research. *Lancet,* July 17, 1976, 136–137.

SNYDER, S. H. *Madness and the Brain.* New York: McGraw-Hill, 1974.

——. Opiate receptors in the brain. *New England Journal of Medicine,* February 3, 1977: 266–271.

——. Opiate receptors and internal opiates. *Scientific American,* May 1977, *236*(3): 44–56.

SOBEL, D. Proof of age. OMNI, October 1979: 53.

SOBEL, H. Ageing and age-associated disease. *Lancet,* December 1970, *2*(684): 1191–1192.

SOLOMON, G. F. Emotions, stress, the central nervous system and immunity. *Annals of the New York Academy of Sciences,* 1969, *164* (2): 335–343.

SONTAG, S. *Illness as Metaphor.* New York: Farrar, Straus & Giroux, 1978.

SOUTHERN, W. Orientation of gull chicks exposed to Project Sanguine's electromagnetic field. *Science,* 1975, *189:* 143–145.

SPADARO, J. A. Electrically stimulated bone growth in animals and man. *Clinical Orthopaedics and Related Research,* 1977, *122:* 325–332.

SPARACIN, J. Type-A (coronary-prone) behavior pattern, aging, and mortality. *Journal of the American Gerontology Society,* 1979, *27* (6): 251–257.

SPECTOR, I. M. Animal longevity and protein turnover rate. *Nature,* May 3, 1974, *249*(452): 66.

SPEER, F., ed. *Allergy of the Nervous System.* Springfield, Ill.: Charles C. Thomas, 1970.

SPILLER, G. A., SHIPLEY, E. A., AND BLAKE, J. A. Recent progress in dietary fiber (plantix) in human nutrition. *CRC Critical Reviews in Food Technology,* September 1978, *10*(1): 31–90.

SPITZER, W. O., FEINSTEIN, A. R., AND SACKETT, D. L. What is a health care trial? *Journal of the American Medical Association,* 1975, *233:* 161–163.

SQUIRES, W. G., HARTUNG, G. H., WELTON, D., YOUNG, J., JESSUP, G., AND ZINKGRAF, S. Effect of exercise and diet modification on blood-lipids in middle-aged men. *Medicine and Science in Sports,* 1979, *11*(1): 109.

STANTON, R. On the syndrome of longevity. *Executive Health,* August 1978, *14*(11).

STANYAN, M. Secrets of long life from the Andes. *San Francisco Examiner and Chronicle,* September 26, 1976: 3.

STAPLETON, R. *The Experience of Inner Healing.* New York: Bantam, 1979.

STARKIE, C. Must Adam die before Eve? *R. Soc. Health Journal,* November-December 1969, *89*(6): 286–288.

STAUTH, C. Aging: Health and longevity. *New Age,* April 1979: 39042.

STAVER, S. Longevity for sale. *American Medical News,* January 16, 1978: 10–17.

STEAD, E. A., JR. Training and use of paramedical personnel. *New England Journal of Medicine,* October 12, 1967, *277:* 800–801.

STEIN, G. S., STEIN, J. S., AND KLEINSMITH, L. J. Chromosomal proteins and gene regulation. *Scientific American,* February 1975: 47–57.

STEIN, K. Some of us may never die. OMNI, October 1978, 52–173.

STEIN, M., SCHIAVI, R. C., AND CAMERINO, M. Influence of brain and behavior on the immune system. *Science,* February 6, 1976, *191:* 435–440.

STENT, G. S. Prematurity and uniqueness in scientific discovery. *Scientific American,* December 1972, *227*(6).

————. Limits to the scientific understanding of man. *Science,* May 21, 1975, *187:* 1052–1057.

STERN, M. P. The recent decline in ischemic heart disease mortality. *Annals of Internal Medicine,* 1979, *91:* 630–640.

STEWART, H. L., SNELL, K. C., DURHAM, L. J., AND SCHLYEN, S. M. *Transplantible and Transmissible Tumors of Animals.* Washington, D.C.: Armed Forces Institute of Pathology, 1959.

STILL, J. W. Medical, social and economic aspects of preventive geriatrics. *Medical Annals of the District of Columbia,* February 1959, *28*(2): 71–76.

————. Personal preventive medicine: The fourth phase in the evolution of medicine. *Journal of the American Geriatrics Society,* 1968, *16*(1): 395–406.

————. The cybernetic theory of aging. *Journal of the American Geriatrics Society,* July 1969, *17*(7): 625–637.

STINE, G. H. The bionic brain. OMNI, July 1979: 84–122.

STOKES, B. Self-care: A nation's best health insurance. Editorial page. *Science,* August 10, 1979, *205* (4406).

STONE, A. Crosscurrents of law and medicine. *MD,* January 1979: 11.

STONE, H. L. Myocardial oxygen consumption and exercise. *Federal Proceedings,* 1979, *38*(3): 1050.

STOUT, C. ET AL. Unusually low incidence of death from myocardial infarction. *Journal of the American Medical Association,* 1964, *188:* 845.

STRAUSS, S. Abkhazia. *Harper's Magazine,* 1973, *246:* 6.

STREHLER, B. L. Environmental factors in aging and mortality. *Environmental Research,* 1967, *1:* 46–88.

―――. The Prometheus experiment. *Perspectives in Biology and Medicine,* Winter 1968: 293–324.

―――. A new age for aging. *Natural History,* 1973, *82:* 8–85.

―――. *Time, Cells, and Aging.* Second edition. New York: Academic Press, 1977.

―――. The mechanisms of aging. *Body Forum,* March 1979: 34–45.

―――, AND MILDVAN, A. A. General theory of mortality and aging. *Science,* July 1, 1960, *132:* 14–21.

STRONG, D. J., AND WENZ, B. T. A fine tuning model with athletes. Unpublished paper, California State University, Hayward, 1980.

STRUMZA, M. Influence sur la santé humaine de la proximité des conduits d'électricité à haute tension. *Archives Mal. Prof., 31* 1970, *31:* 269.

STUB, H. R. Education, the professions, and long life. *British Journal of Sociology,* June 1969, *20*(2): 177–189.

STUNKARD, A. J. Nutrition, aging and obesity. In M. Rockstein and M. L. Sussman, eds., *Nutrition, Longevity and Aging,* pp. 240–247. New York: Academic Press, 1976.

SUAREZ, R. M. Aging: Introductory remarks. *Bulletin of the New York Academy of Medicine,* November 1971, *47*(11): 1300–1303.

SUDA, M. Life and death—Life expectancy. 1. *Japanese Journal of Clinical Medicine,* July 1967, *26*(7): 1713–1717.

―――. Life and death—Definition of life, 2. *Japanese Journal of Clinical Medicine,* August 1968, *26*(8): 1948–1956.

―――. Life and death. 5. What is longevity? *Japanese Journal of Clinical Medicine,* November 1968, *26*(11): 3222–3230.

SUINN, R. M. Body thinking: Psychology for Olympic champs. *Psychology Today,* July 1976: 38–43.

SUN, A. S., AGGARWAL, B. B., AND PACKER, L. Enzyme levels of normal human cells: Aging in culture. *Archives of Biochemistry and Biophysics,* 1975, *170:* I–II.

Sunday Star-Bulletin and Advertiser, Honolulu, Hawaii. Prescription for Americans: A "public health revolution." July 29, 1979: I.

SUTTON, H. Check in, pep up, pass out. *Saturday Review,* September 29, 1979: 52.

SWAMI RAMA. *A Practical Guide to Holistic Health.* Honesdale, Pa.: The Himalayan Institute, 1978.

SWEENY, K. C., MALLOY, R. B., YUKNA, R. A. Effect of zinc supplementation on bone regeneration following decalcified freeze-dried bone allografts. *Journal of Dental Research,* 1979, *58* (NSIZ): 431.

SYME, L. S. Social and psychological risk factors in coronary disease. *Modern Concepts of Cardiovascular Disease,* 1975, *44* (17).

SZAMEITAT, K. What is the cost of health? Numbers and critical aspects. *Offentliche Gesundheitswesen,* December 1970, *32* (12): 672–690.

SZENT-GYÖRGYI, A. *Introduction to a Submolecular Biology.* New York: Academic Press, 1960.

———. *Electronic Biology and Cancer: A New Theory of Cancer.* New York: Marcel Dekker, 1976.

———. On a substance that can make us sick (if we do not eat it!). *Executive Health,* June 1977, *13* (9): 1–6.

———. How new understandings about the biological functions of ascorbic acid may profoundly affect our lives. *Executive Health,* May 1978, *14* (8).

SZILARD, L. Editorial letter. *Nature,* September 26, 1959, *184* (4691): 957–958.

TAPPEL, A. L. Will antioxidant nutrients slow aging processes? *Geriatrics,* October 1968: 97–105.

———. On antioxidant nutrients. *Executive Health,* March 1980, *26* (6).

———, FLETCHER, B., AND DEAMER, D. W. Effect of antioxidants

and nutrients on lipid peroxidation fluorescent products and ageing parameters in the mouse. *Journal of Gerontology,* 1973, *28:* 415–424.

TERESI, D. The real bionic man. *OMNI,* May 1979: 44–140.

TERRY, R. D. Senile dementia. *Federal Proceedings,* December 1978, *37*(14): 2837–2840.

THOMAS, C. B., AND DUSZYNSKI, K. R. Closeness to parents and the family constellation in a prospective study of five disease states: Suicide, mental illness, malignant tumor, hypertension and coronary heart disease. *Johns Hopkins Medical Journal,* May 1974, *134* (5): 251–270.

THOMAS, L. *The Medusa and the Snail.* New York: Viking, 1979.

THOMPSON, P. D., STERN, M. P., AND WILLIAMS, P. Death during jogging or running: A study of 18 cases. *Journal of the American Medical* Association, September 1979, *242:* 1265–1267. Reprinted as Physical fitness: A guarantee against exercise related death? in *Modern Medicine,* January 15–30, 1980: 89.

THOMPSON, R. G., MAYFORD, J. T., AND HENDRIX, J. A. Triglyceride concentrations: The disaccharide effect. *Science,* November 16, 1979, *206:* 838–839.

THOMPSON, W. A., JR. On the treatment of grouped observations in life studies. *Biometrics,* September 1977, *33* (3): 463–470.

TIBBITTS, C. Can we invalidate negative stereotypes of aging? *Gerontology,* 1979, *19* (1): 10–20.

Time. No telling how old is old. October 10, 1977: 28.

———. The first test-tube baby. July 31, 1978: 58–70.

———. Psychiatry's depression. Cover story. April 2, 1979: 74–82.

———. Medical costs: Seeking the cure. May 28, 1979: 60–68.

———. Valium abuse: The yellow peril. September 24, 1979: 66.

TIMIRAS, P. Neuroendocrine strategies to modify aging. Conference of NIA, Endocrine Society and Veterans Administration, Bethesda, Maryland, October 18–20, 1979.

TINBERGEN, N. Etiology and stress diseases. *Science,* July 1974, *185,* 24: 26.

TODD, G. F., HUNT, B. M., AND LAMBERT, P. M. Four cardiorespiratory symptoms as predictors of mortality. *Journal of Epidemiology and Community Health,* 1978, *32:* 267–274.

TODD, H. J. A look at the basic correlates of longevity: Is longevity a superficial trait? _Mechanisms of Ageing and Development,_ January 1978, _7_(1): 33–52.

TOMASSON, R. F. The mortality of Swedish and US white males: A comparison of experience, 1969–1971. _American Journal of Public Health,_ October 1976, _66_(10): 968–974.

TOOLE, J. F. Can an aspirin a day keep a stroke away? _Executive Health,_ January 1979, _15_(4).

TOWNES, C. The convergence of science and religion. _California Monthly,_ February 1976: 10–19.

TRAFFORD, A. Is your job dangerous to your health? _U.S. News & World Report,_ February 5, 1979: 39–42.

TRAUTWEIN, H. Life expectancy of arterioscloerotics. _Lebensversicherungs-Medizin,_ May 1968, _20_(3): 62–67.

TROSKO, J. E., AND CHANG, C.-C. Genes, pollutants, and human diseases. _Quarterly Review of Biophysics,_ 1979, _3:_ 1–25.

———, AND CHU, E. H. Y. Effects of caffeine on the UV-induction of mutations in Chinese hamster cells. _Mutation Research,_ 1971, _12:_ 337–340.

TROWELL, H. C. A new dietary explanation for the cause of essential hypertension. _Executive Health,_ November 1979, _16_(2).

TURPEINE, O. Effect of cholesterol-lowering diet on mortality from coronary heart disease and other causes. Editorial. _Circulation,_ 1979, _59_(1): 1–7.

TYSON, R. Procaine: The European secret of youth. _Body Forum,_ June 1979, _4_(6).

U.S. News & World Report. How to deal with stress on the job. March 13, 1978: 80–81.

VALLIANT, G. E. _Adaptation to Life: How the Best and Brightest Came of Age._ Boston: Little, Brown & Company, 1977.

———. Natural history of male psychologic health: Effects of mental health on physical health. _New England Journal of Medicine,_ 1979, _301:_ 1249–1254.

VAKIL, R. J. Diseases of the heart and their prevention. _Indian Journal of Chest Diseases and Allied Sciences,_ April 1972, _14_(2): 112–118.

VAUX, K. Religion and health. *Preventive Medicine,* December 1976, *5*(4): 522–536.

VAYDA, E. Keeping people well: A new approach to medicine. *Human Nature,* July 1978: 64–71.

VEREBY, K., VOLAVKA, J., AND CLOVET, D. Endorphins in psychiatry: An overview and a hypothesis. *Archives of General Psychiatry,* July 1978, *35:* 877–888.

VERMEULEN, A. Clinical reproductive physiology in the aging male. Conference of NIA, Endocrine Society and Veterans Administration, Bethesda, Maryland, October 18–20, 1979.

VEYLON, R. Aging, considerations on its demographic consequences. *Nouvelle Presse Medicale,* April 30, 1977, *6*(18): 1538–1573.

VOLK, H. Europe—continent of the aged? *Schwest Review,* November 15, 1976, *14*(11): 14.

VON HAHN, H. P. The regulation of protein synthesis in the aging cell. *Experimental Gerontology,* October 1979, *5:* 323.

WALDRON, I. Why do women live longer than men? *Journal of Human Stress,* March 1976, *2*(1): 2–13.

———. Why do women live longer than men? *Social Science & Medicine,* July-August, 1976, *10*(7-8): 349–362.

———. Why do women live longer than men? *New England Journal of Medicine,* January 5, 1978, *298*(1): 57–58.

———, AND JOHNSTON, S. Why do women live longer than men? *Journal of Human Stress,* June 1976, *2*(2): 19–30.

WALKER, A. R. Can expectation of life in western populations be increased by changes in diet and manner of life? *South African Medical Journal,* September 21, 1968, *42*(36): 944–950.

———. Can expectation of life in western populations be increased by changes in diet and manner of life? II. *South African Medical Journal,* June 21, 1969, *43*(25): 767–775.

———. Decline and fall? *American Heart Journal,* September 1972, *84*(3), 420–422.

WALKER, W. J. Coronary mortality: What is going on? *Journal of the American Medical Association,* March 1974, *227*(9): 1045–1046.

WALLACE, D. J. The biology of aging. 1976. An overview. *Journal of the American Geriatrics Society,* March 1977, *25*(3): 104–111.

WALLACE, M., SAFER, M., AND RATHER, D. Our three patients. *60 Minutes,* CBS Television, October 22, 1978.

WALLACE, V. H. Human longevity. *Medical Journal of Australia,* February 1970, *1*(9), 442–446.

WALTER, W. G. *The Living Brain.* New York: Norton, 1963.

WALTON, S. Holistic medicine. *Science News,* December 15, 1979, *116,* 410–412.

WARD, B., AND DUBOS, H. *Only One Earth.* New York: Penguin Books, 1972.

WARR, G. W., AND MARCHALONIS, B. "Specific immune recognition by lymphocytes: An evolutionary perspective." *Quarterly Review of Biology,* September 1978, *53* (3): 225–241.

WATANABE, T., YUKAWA, K., AND SAKAMOTO, A. Nutritional intake and longevity. International Comparative Study. *Acta Medica of Nagasaki,* October 1968, *13* (1): 44–66.

WATERLOW, J. C. Uses of recommended intakes—purpose of dietary recommendations. *Food Policy,* 1979, *4* (2): 107–114.

WATKIN, D. M. Nutrition and aging. *American Journal of Clinical Nutrition,* 1972, *25:* 807.

———. The aged. In J. Mayer, ed., *U.S. Nutrition Policies in the Seventies,* pp. 53–66. San Francisco: W. H. Freeman & Company, 1973.

———. Nutritional needs of elderly are intertwined with other factors and attitudes affecting health. *Geriatrics,* 1974, *29:* 40–42.

———. Logical bases for action in nutrition and aging. *Journal of American Geriatrics Society Journal,* May 1978, *26*(5): 193–202.

WATSON, A. W. S. 3-year study of the effects of exercise on active young men. *European Journal of Applied Physiology and Occupational Physiology,* 1979, *40*(2): 95–106.

WATSON, J. D., AND CRICK, F. H. C. Molecular structure of nucleic acids. *Nature,* April 25, 1953, *171*(4356): 737–738.

WATSON, S. J., AKIL, J., BEGER, P. A., AND BARCHAS, J. D. Some observations on the opiate peptides and schizophrenia. *Archives of General Psychiatry,* 1979, *36:* 35–41.

WEICHERT, R. F., III, PEARCE, C. W., AND GIBSON, W. E., III Relief of angina pectoris and improved life expectancy following coronary bypass surgery. *Journal of the Louisiana State Medical Society,* February 1978, *130*(2): 39–44.

WEIL, W. B. National dietary goals. Editorial. *American Journal of Diseases of Children,* 1979, *133* (4): 368–370.

WEINDRUCH, R. H., KRISTIE, J. A., CHENEY, K. E., AND WALFORD, R. L. Influence of controlled dietary restriction on immunological function and aging. *Federal Proceedings,* 1979, *38* (6): 2007–2016.

WEISMAN, A. D. Coping with untimely death. *Psychiatry,* November 1973, *36* (4): 366–378.

WEITZMAN, E. D. How to get a night's sleep. *U.S. News & World Report,* August 8, 1977: 62–64.

WELLBORN, S. N. Are you eating right? *U.S. News & World Report,* November 28, 1977: 39–43.

WERK, O. L. Preventive cardiology—and what then? *Lakartidningen,* September 1970, *67* (37), 4136–4137 passim.

WHITE, A., AND GOLDSTEIN, A. L. Is the thymus an endocrine gland? Old problem, new data. *Perspectives in Biology and Medicine,* Spring 1968: 475–489.

WILDAVSKY, A. Doing better and feeling worse: The political pathology of health policy. *Daedalus,* 1977, *106:* 105–124.

WILKERSON, J. E., KILKA, M. A., AND STEPHENS, L. A. Exercise induces leukocytosis during a competitive marathon. Meeting abstract. *Medicine and Science in Sports,* 1979, *11* (1): 99.

WILLIAMS, E. W. Longevity therapy with chronic patients in a state hospital. *Hospital Community Psychiatry,* January 1974, *25* (1): 14.

WILLIAMS, G. Z. Individuality of clinical biochemical patterns in preventive health maintenance. *Journal of Occupational Medicine,* 1967, *9* (11): 567–570.

———. Advancing technology of clinical laboratory practice. *Medical College of Virginia Quarterly,* 1973, *9* (4): 293–297.

———. *Health Watch: Your Personal DEW Line in the Prevention of Health Problems and Future Disability.* San Francisco: Institute of Health Research, 1980.

———, WIDDOWSON, G. M., AND PENTON, J. Individual character of variation in time-series studies of healthy people. Differences in values for clinical chemical analyses in serum among demographic groups, by age and sex. *Clinical Chemistry,* 1978, *24* (2): 313–320.

WILLIAMS, R. J. *Biochemical Individuality.* New York: John Wiley & Sons, 1956.

————. *Nutrition in a Nutshell.* New York: William Collins/Dolphin Books, 1962.

————. *Nutrition Against Disease.* New York: Bantam Books, 1973.

————. On the wonderful world within you. *Executive Health,* December 1977: *14* (3).

————. *The Wonderful World Within You.* New York: Bantam Books, 1977.

————. Nutritional individuality. *Human Nature,* June 1978: 46–53.

WILLIAMS, S. V., MUNFORD, R. S., COLTON, T., MURPHY, D. A., AND PSKANZER, D. C. Mortality among physicians: A cohort study. *Journal of Chronic Diseases,* August 1971, *24* (6), 393–401.

WILSON, M. E., AND MATHER, L. E. Life expectancy. Letter. *Journal of the American Medical Association,* September 9, 1974, 229(11): 1421–1422.

WINICK, M. Slow the process of aging and quash its problems—with diet. *Modern Medicine,* February 15, 1978: 68–74.

WINTROBE, M. M. ET AL. *Harrison's Principles of Internal Medicine.* New York: McGraw-Hill, 1974.

WITTE, N. K., KRYSHANOWSKAJA, W. W., AND STESHENSKAYA, E. I. The process of aging in the light of work physiology. *Zeitschrift für Alternsforschung,* 1967, *20* (2): 91–98.

WOLF, S. Disease as a way of life: Neural integration in systemic pathology. *Perspectives of Biology and Medicine,* Spring 1961, *4:* 288–303.

————. Presidential address: Social anthropology in medicine. The climate you and I create. *Trans-American Clinical and Climatological Association,* 1977, *88:* 1–17.

————. Can stress cause fatal arrhythmias if cardiac lesion is absent? *Clinical Psychiatry News,* May 1979, *7* (5): 17.

————, AND GOODELL, H. Causes and mechanisms in psychosomatic phenomena. *Journal of Human Stress,* March 1979: 9–18.

WOLFF, H. G. Changes in the vulnerability of tissue: An aspect of man's response to threat. *The National Institute of Health Annual Lectures,* pp. 38–71. Washington, D.C.: Department of Health, Education, and Welfare, 1953.

————. *Stress and Disease.* 2d ed. revised and edited by Stewart

Wolf and Helen Goodell. Springfield, Ill.: Charles C. Thomas, 1968.

WOLFGANG, O. Is immortality real? *Modern Maturity,* April-May 1978: 25–26.

WOLMAN, M. Life span and life quality. Editorial. *Harefuah,* May 15, 1974, *86*(10): 522–523.

WOLSKY, A. Regeneration and cancer. *Growth,* 1978, *42*(4): 425–426.

WOOD, M. R., AND COHEN, M. J. Synaptic regeneration in identified neurons of the lamprey spinal cord. *Science,* October 19, 1979, *206:* 344–347.

WOODFIN, M. Want to see 140? Don't boil the tea. *The Denver Post,* December 3, 1978.

WOODRUFF, C. W. Dietary goals for the United States. *American Journal of Diseases of Children,* 1979, *133*(4): 371–372.

WOOLFOLK, R. L. Psychophysiological correlates of meditation. *Archives of General Psychiatry,* October 1975, *32:* 1326–1333.

WRIGHT, I. S. Can your family history tell you anything about your chances for a long life? *Executive Health,* February 1978, *14*(5).

———. Fulfillment of hereditary longevity potential. *Bulletin of the New York Academy of Medicine,* 1979, *55*(5): 516–526.

WURTMAN, J. J., AND WURTMAN, R. J. Sucrose consumption early in life fails to modify the appetite of adult rats for sweet foods. *Science,* July 20, 1979, *205:* 321–322.

WUNDER, E. L. Disease prevention: Asking the right questions. Editorial page. *Science,* October 20, 1978, *202*(4365).

WYNDER, E. L., LEMON, F., AND BROSS, I. J. Cancer and coronary artery disease among Seventh-Day Adventists. *Cancer,* 1959, *12:* 1016–1028.

Xerox Corporation. Take charge of your life. Stamford, Conn.: 1980.

———. The road to better health and happier lifestyles. Stamford, Conn.: 1980.

———. Fitbook. Stamford, Conn.: 1980.

———. Executive fitness program. Stamford, Conn.: 1980.

YALLER, R., AND R. *The Health Spas.* Santa Barbara: Woodbridge Press, 1974.

YAMAJI, K., AND SHEPHARD, R. J. Longevity and causes of death of athletes. *Journal of Human Ergolt. (Tokyo),* September 1977, *6*(1): 15–27.

YEN, F. S., MATSUYAMA, S. S., AND JARVIK, L. F. Survival of octogenarians: Six years after initial chromosome examination. *Experimental Aging Research,* January 1976, *2*(1): 17–26.

YOUNG, V. R. Nutrition and aging. *Advances in Experimental Medical Biology,* 1978, *97:* 85–110.

———. Diet as a modulator of aging and longevity. *Federal Proceedings,* May 1979, *38*(6): 1994–2000.

YUNIS, E. J., AND GREENBERG, L. J. Immunopathology of aging. *Human Pathology,* March 1974, *5*(2): 122–125.

ZARET, M. M. Physician worries about "electronic smog." *American Medical News,* September 7, 1979: 14.

ZDICHYNEC, B., STRANCKY, P., HARTMANN, M., HOLAS, V., KONR, A. D. J., HOGEN, J., SVATO, S. Z., AND SABLE, J. Determination of the quantitative significance of various risk factors in physiological aging. *Bratisl. Lek. Listy.,* 1976, *66*(4): 436–443.

ZENKER, R. Development, possibilities and limitations of heart surgery. *Lebensversicherungs-Medizin,* November 1976, *28*(6): 137–140.

ZILBERGELD, B., AND ULLMAN, J. *Male Sexuality.* Boston: Little, Brown & Company, 1978.

ZIMRING, J. G. High-fiber diet versus laxatives in geriatric patient. *New York State Journal of Medicine,* December 1978, *78*(14): 2223–2224.

———. Sexual problems of geriatric patients. *New York State Journal of Medicine,* 1979, *79*(5): 752–753.

ZOPPE, G., ZAMBONI, G., SIVIERO, M., BELLINI, P., AND CANCELLI, M. L. Gamma globulin level and dietary protein intake during the 1st year of life. *Pediatrics,* 1978, *62*(6): 1010–1018.

ZOTINA, I., ZOTINA, R. S., PROKOFIEV, E. A., AND KONOPLEV, V. A. Use of growth equations for determining the maximal life span of mammals and man. *Izv. Akad. Nauk. SSSR. Biol.,* January-February 1978, (1), 87–96.

INDEX

THE AUTHOR

KENNETH R. PELLETIER, Ph.D., is Assistant Clinical Professor at the Langley Porter Neuropsychiatric Institute and in the Department of Psychiatry, University of California School of Medicine, San Francisco; also Assistant Professor, Department of Public Health, University of California, Berkeley; and Director of the California Health and Medical Foundation, Berkeley, California. Dr. Pelletier was a Woodrow Wilson Fellow and studied at the C. G. Jung Institute in Zurich. He has published over one hundred professional journal articles on psychosomatic medicine, clinical biofeedback, and neurophysiology. Dr. Pelletier is currently an advisor to the Department of Health and Human Services, the National Institute of Mental Health, the American Psychological Association, and to the Government of Canada. He was appointed by Governor Edmund G. Brown, Jr., to the California Governor's Council on Wellness and Physical Fitness and serves on the boards of the *Journal of the American Holistic Medical Association*, the journal *Medical Self Care*, and the American Institute of Stress. Dr. Pelletier is also co-author of *Consciousness: East and West*; and author of the international best seller *Mind as Healer, Mind as Slayer: A Holistic Approach to Preventing Stress Disorders; Toward a Science of Consciousness; and Holistic Medicine: From Stress to Optimum Health.*